Shojo Beat

Demon Love Spell

4

STORY AND
ART BY
**MAYU
SHINJO**

Contents

Story Thus Far

Miko Tsubaki is the daughter of the head priest of the Otsubaki Shrine, and she is destined to follow in his footsteps. She works hard day and night to become a great priestess, but it seems she inherited none of her father's powers...

One day Miko seals the powers of the incubus Kagura—the strongest demon—by accident, and the two start living together. After defeating various demons they fall in love, though Miko is having trouble accepting her feelings for a demon.

Kagura spreads flyers around the demon realm to bring demons to the shrine, but his actions put Miko in danger. She narrowly escapes death and is saved by Miyuki, a snow demon. However, now Miko's father is amenable to Kagura's request to take Miko on an overnight trip?!

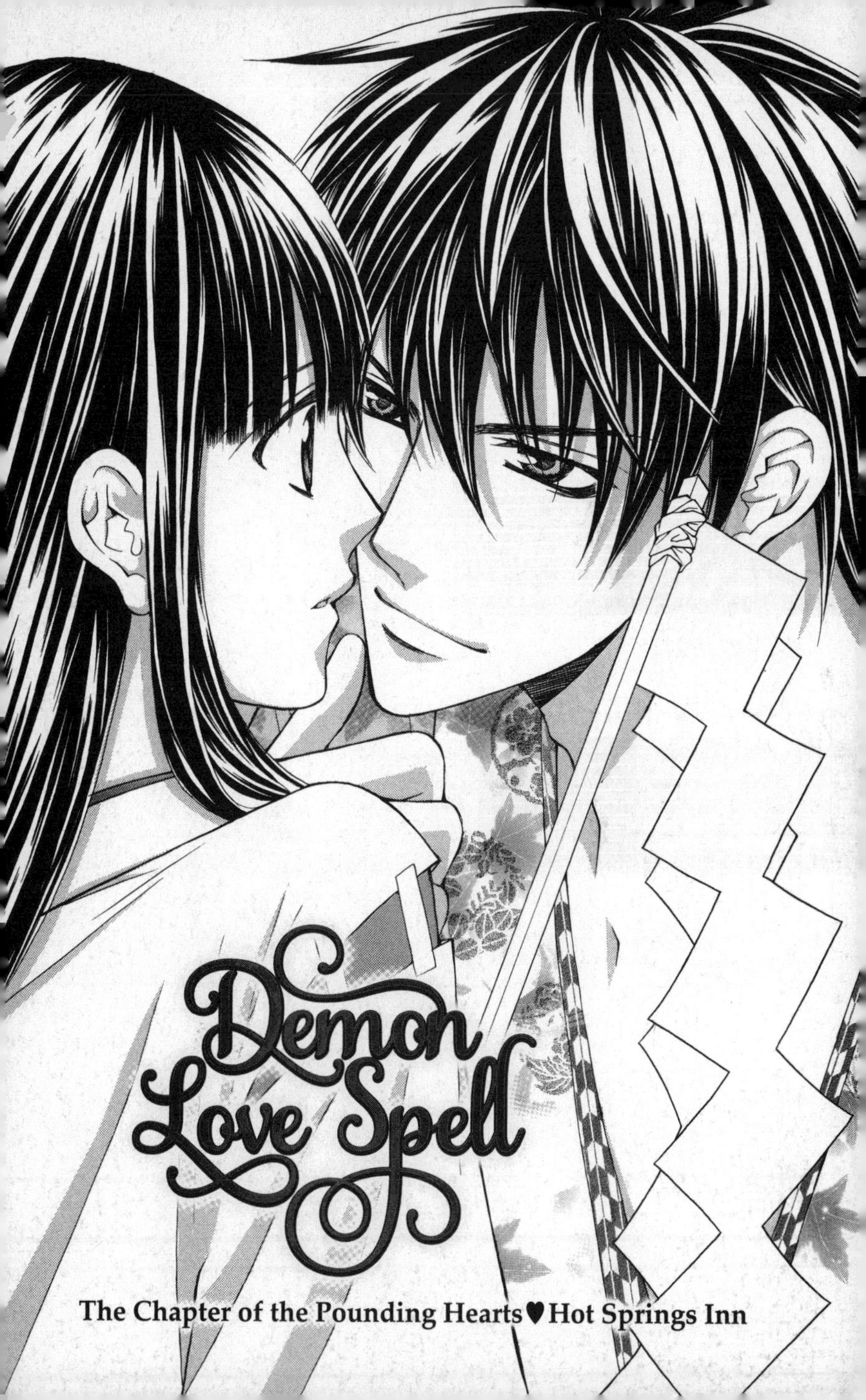
Demon Love Spell
The Chapter of the Pounding Hearts♥Hot Springs Inn

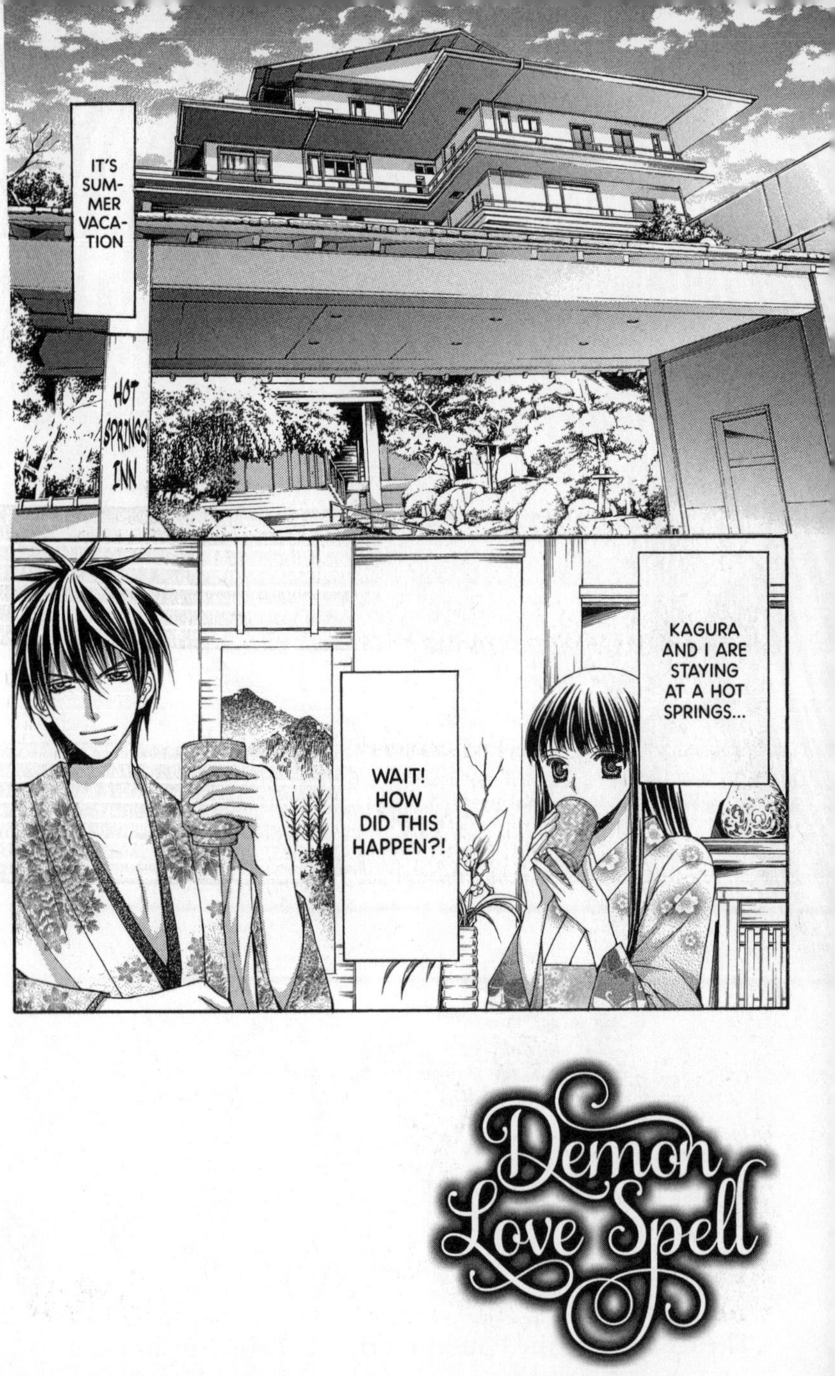
IT'S SUMMER VACATION
HOT SPRINGS INN
KAGURA AND I ARE STAYING AT A HOT SPRINGS...
WAIT! HOW DID THIS HAPPEN?!

Demon Love Spell

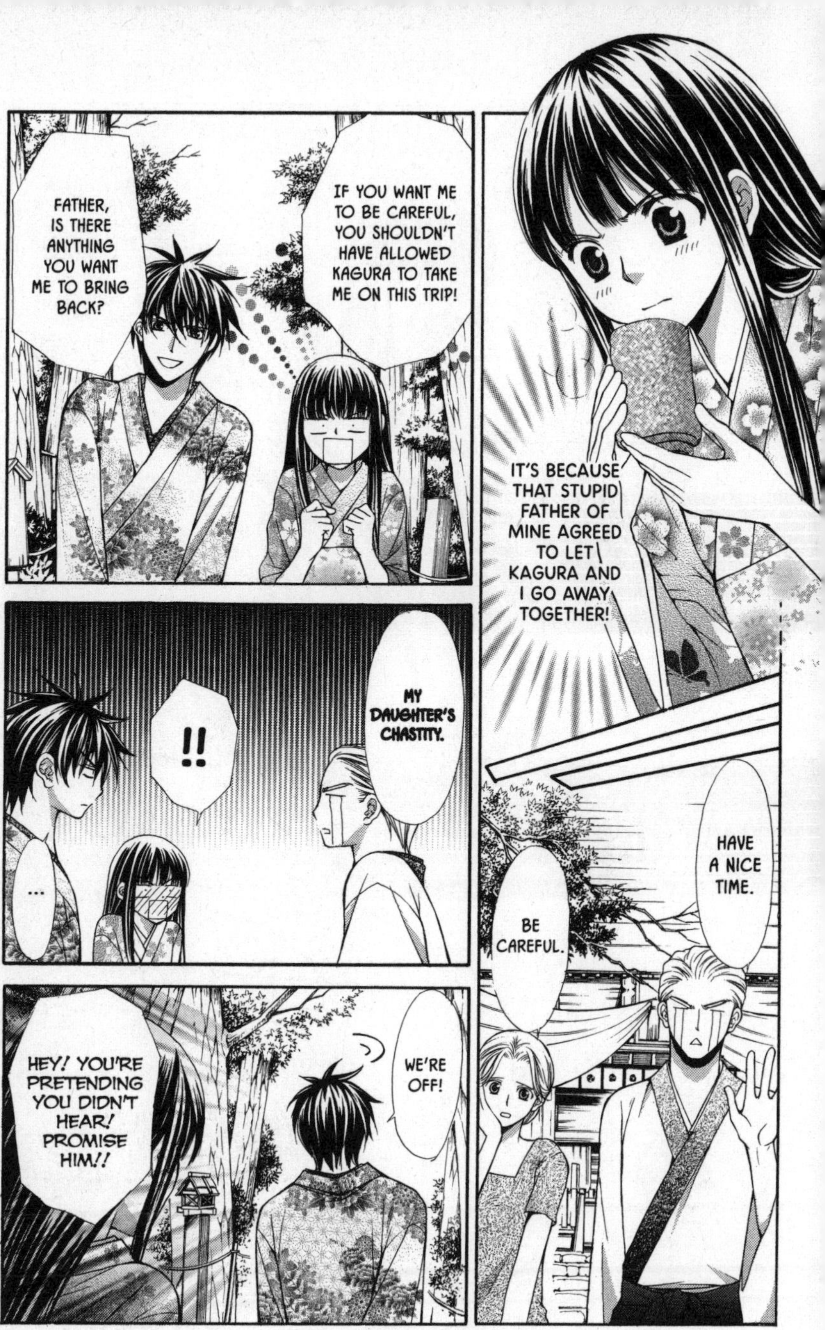
IT'S BECAUSE THAT STUPID FATHER OF MINE AGREED TO LET KAGURA AND I GO AWAY TOGETHER!
HAVE A NICE TIME.
BE CAREFUL.
IF YOU WANT ME TO BE CAREFUL, YOU SHOULDN'T HAVE ALLOWED KAGURA TO TAKE ME ON THIS TRIP!
FATHER, IS THERE ANYTHING YOU WANT ME TO BRING BACK?
MY DAUGHTER'S CHASTITY.
!!
...
WE'RE OFF!
HEY! YOU'RE PRETENDING YOU DIDN'T HEAR! PROMISE HIM!!

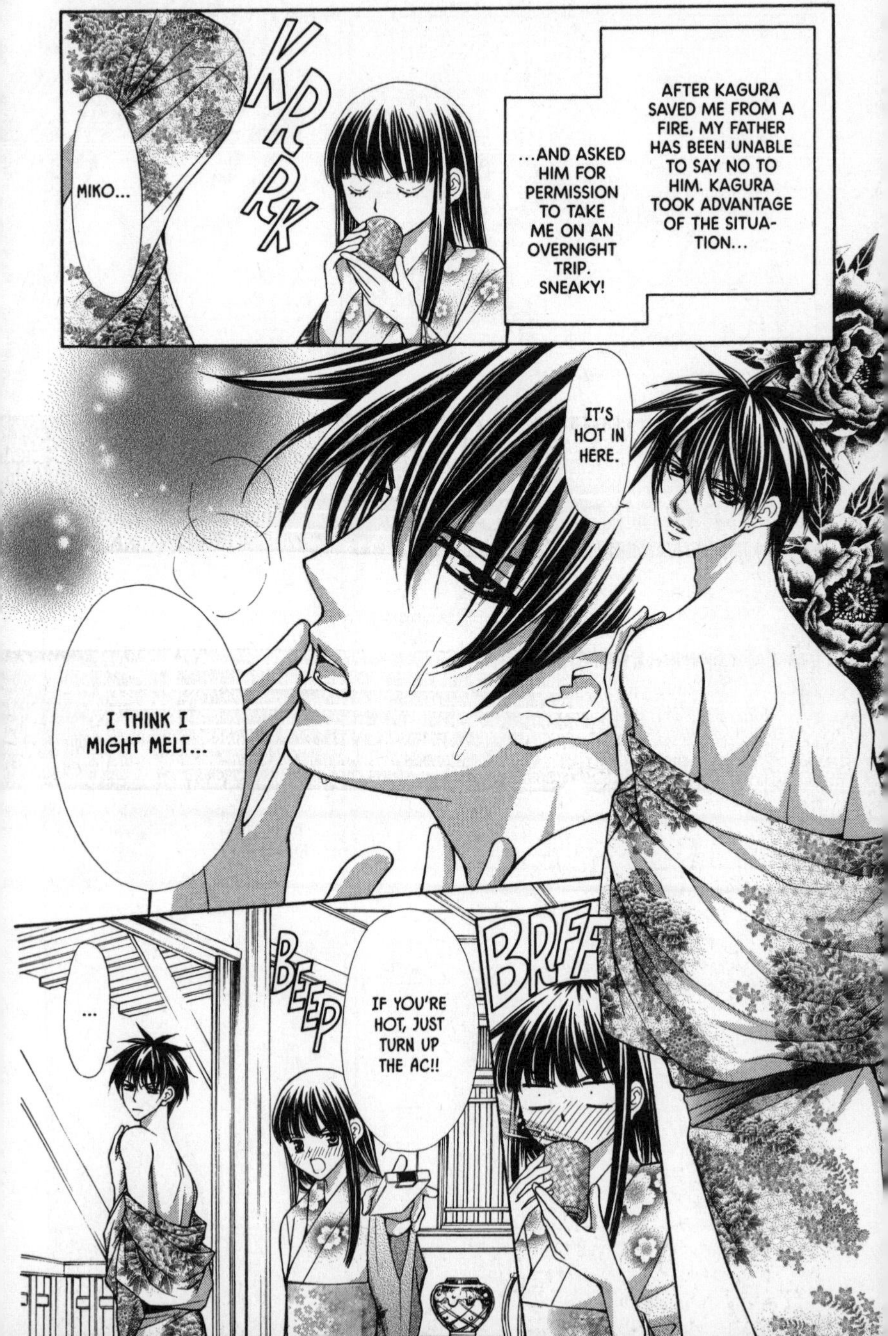
AFTER KAGURA SAVED ME FROM A FIRE, MY FATHER HAS BEEN UNABLE TO SAY NO TO HIM. KAGURA TOOK ADVANTAGE OF THE SITUATION...
...AND ASKED HIM FOR PERMISSION TO TAKE ME ON AN OVERNIGHT TRIP. SNEAKY!
KRRK
MIKO...
IT'S HOT IN HERE.
I THINK I MIGHT MELT...
BRFF
IF YOU'RE HOT, JUST TURN UP THE AC!!
BEEP
...

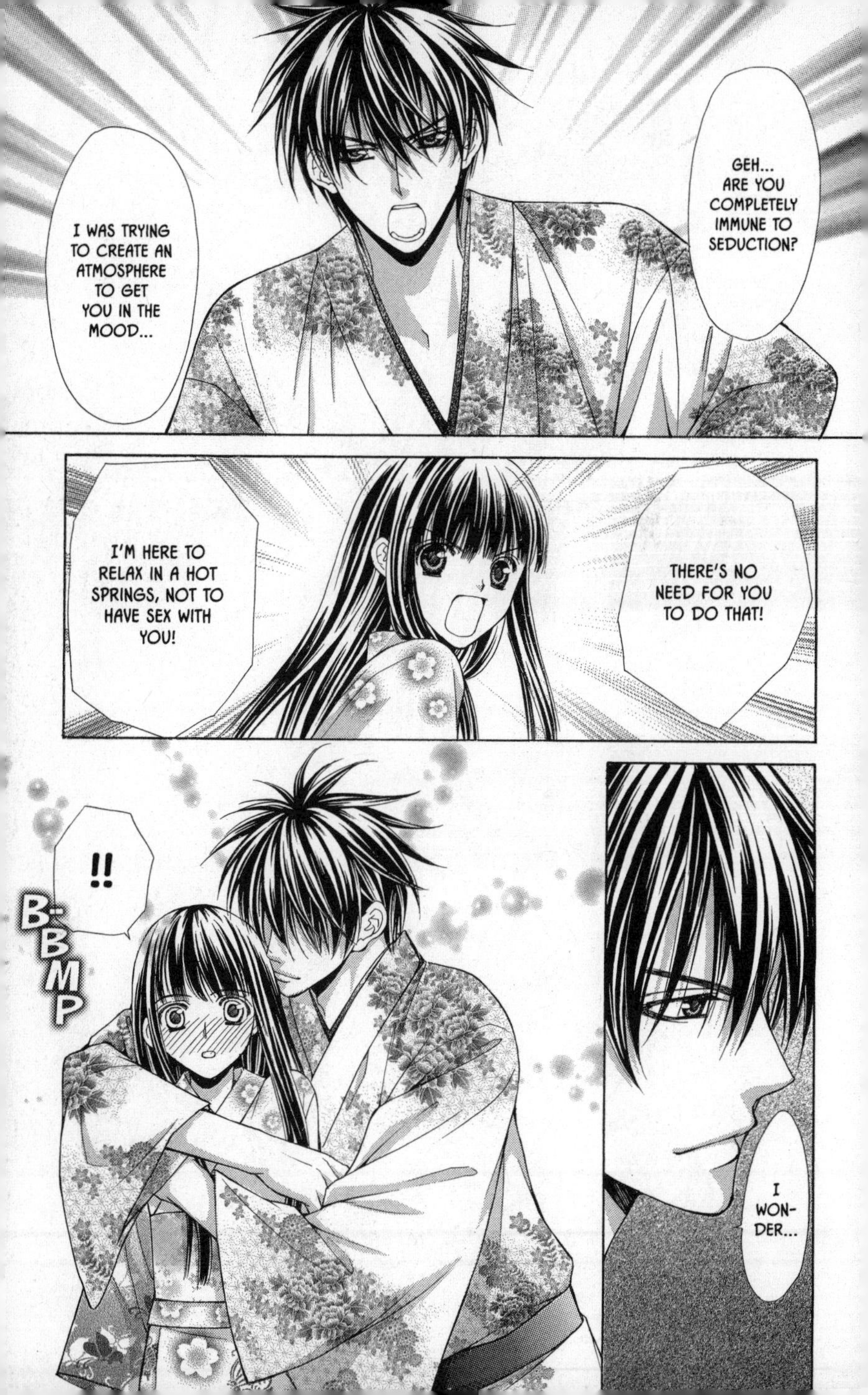
GEH... ARE YOU COMPLETELY IMMUNE TO SEDUCTION?
I WAS TRYING TO CREATE AN ATMOSPHERE TO GET YOU IN THE MOOD...
THERE'S NO NEED FOR YOU TO DO THAT!
I'M HERE TO RELAX IN A HOT SPRINGS, NOT TO HAVE SEX WITH YOU!
I WON-DER...
!!
B-BMP

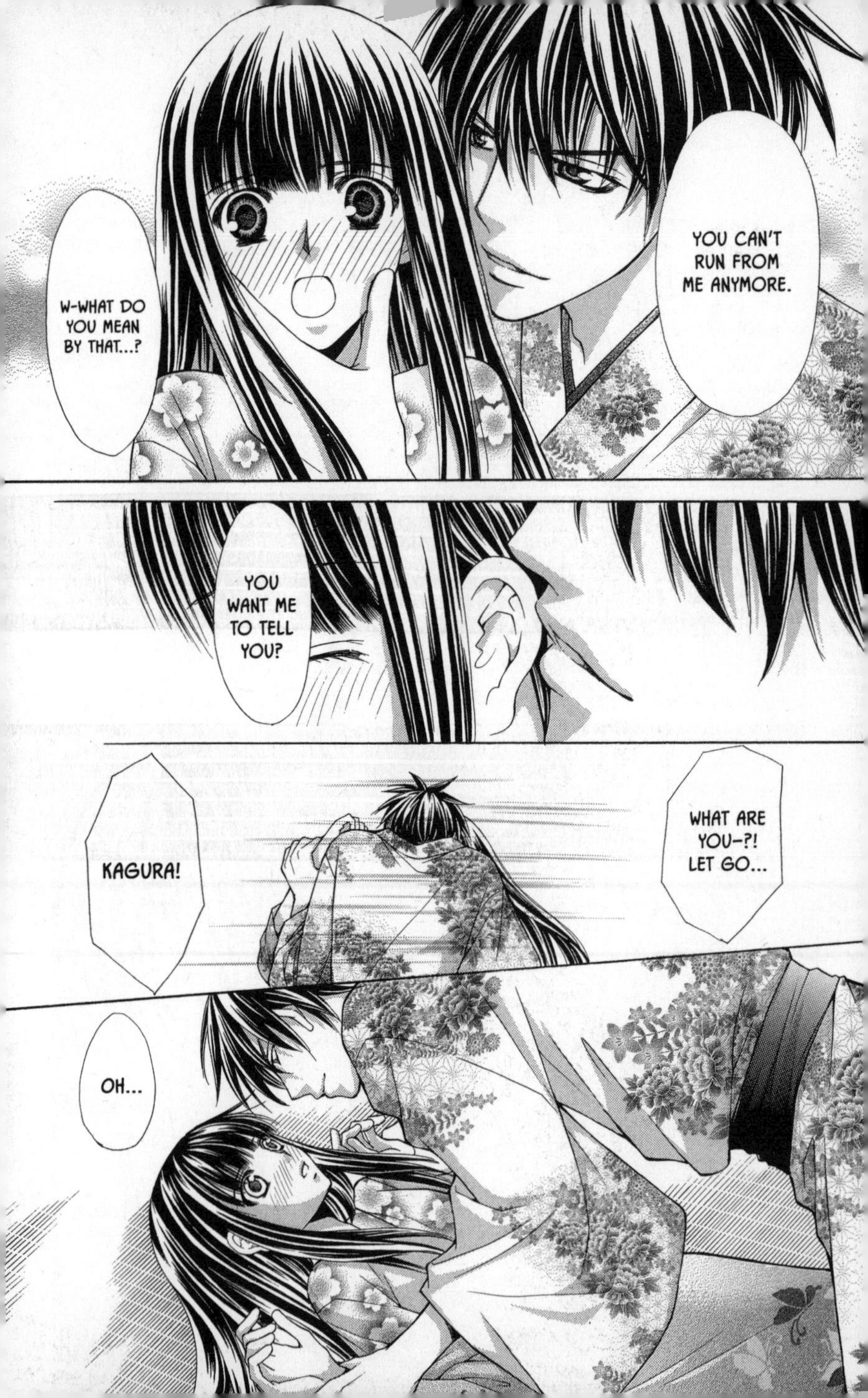
YOU CAN'T RUN FROM ME ANYMORE.
W-WHAT DO YOU MEAN BY THAT...?
YOU WANT ME TO TELL YOU?
WHAT ARE YOU–?! LET GO...
KAGURA!
OH...

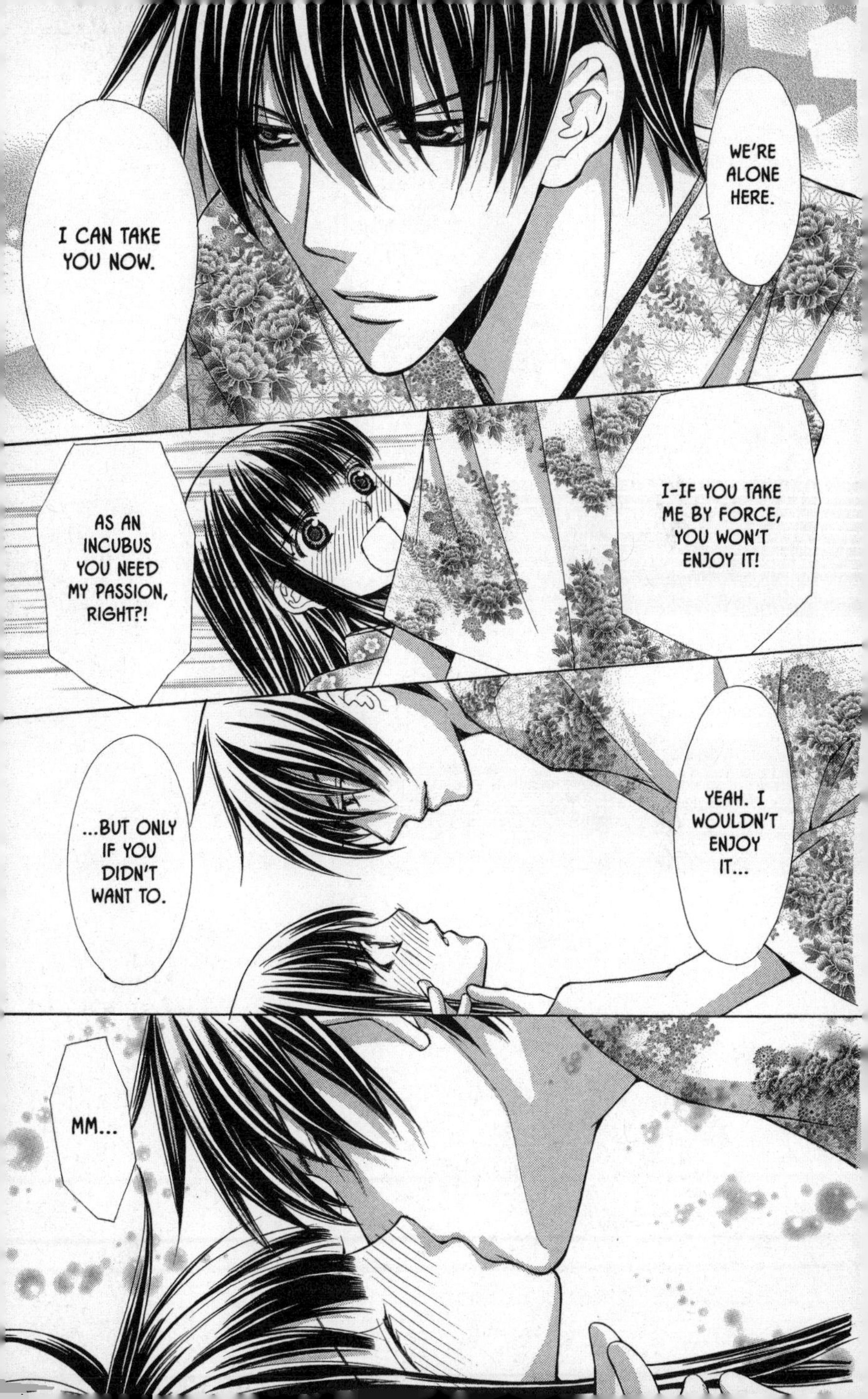
WE'RE ALONE HERE.
I CAN TAKE YOU NOW.
I-IF YOU TAKE ME BY FORCE, YOU WON'T ENJOY IT!
AS AN INCUBUS YOU NEED MY PASSION, RIGHT?!
YEAH. I WOULDN'T ENJOY IT...
...BUT ONLY IF YOU DIDN'T WANT TO.
MM...

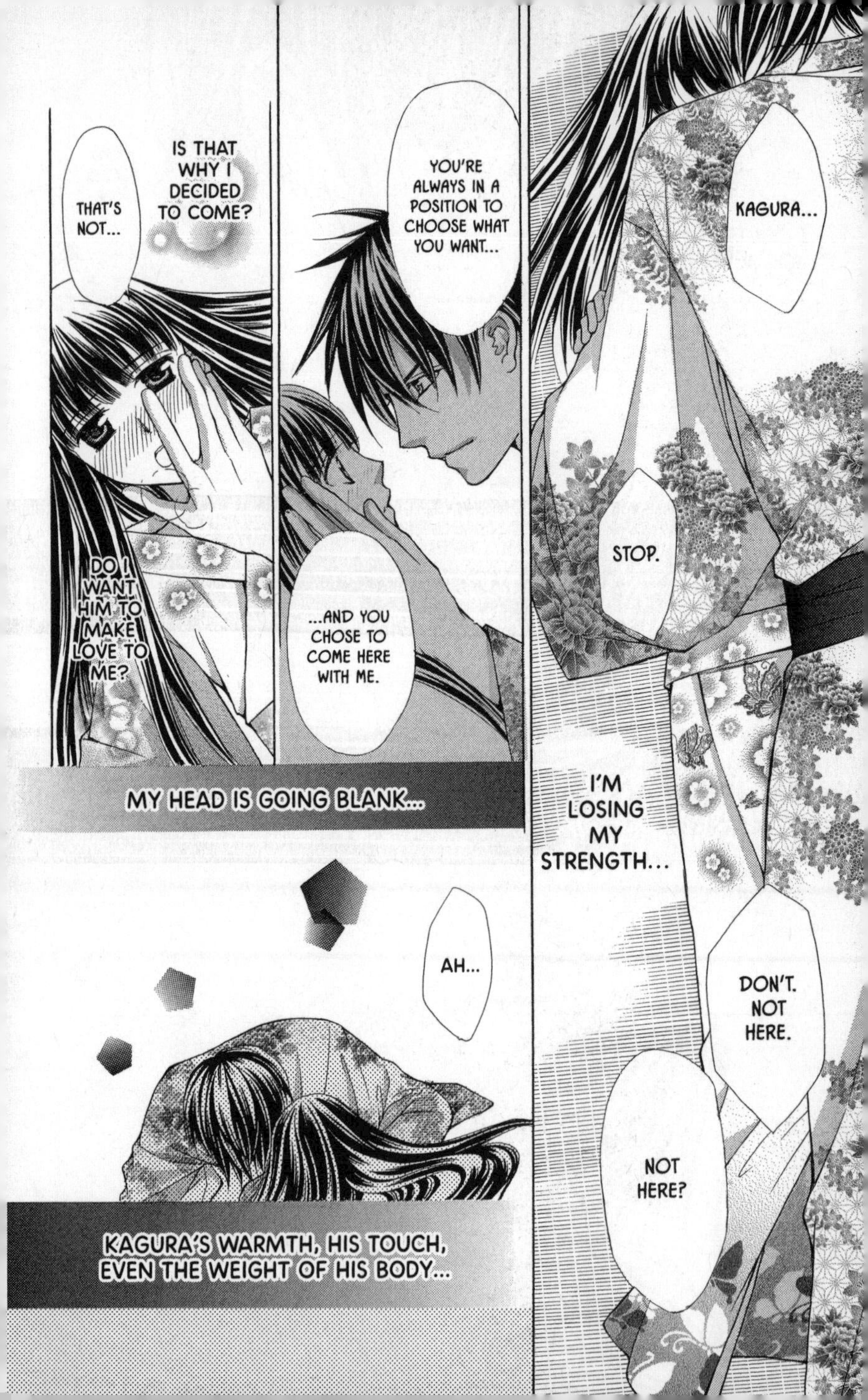
KAGURA...
STOP.
I'M LOSING MY STRENGTH...
DON'T. NOT HERE.
NOT HERE?
YOU'RE ALWAYS IN A POSITION TO CHOOSE WHAT YOU WANT...
...AND YOU CHOSE TO COME HERE WITH ME.
IS THAT WHY I DECIDED TO COME?
THAT'S NOT...
DO I WANT HIM TO MAKE LOVE TO ME?
MY HEAD IS GOING BLANK...
AH...
KAGURA'S WARMTH, HIS TOUCH, EVEN THE WEIGHT OF HIS BODY...

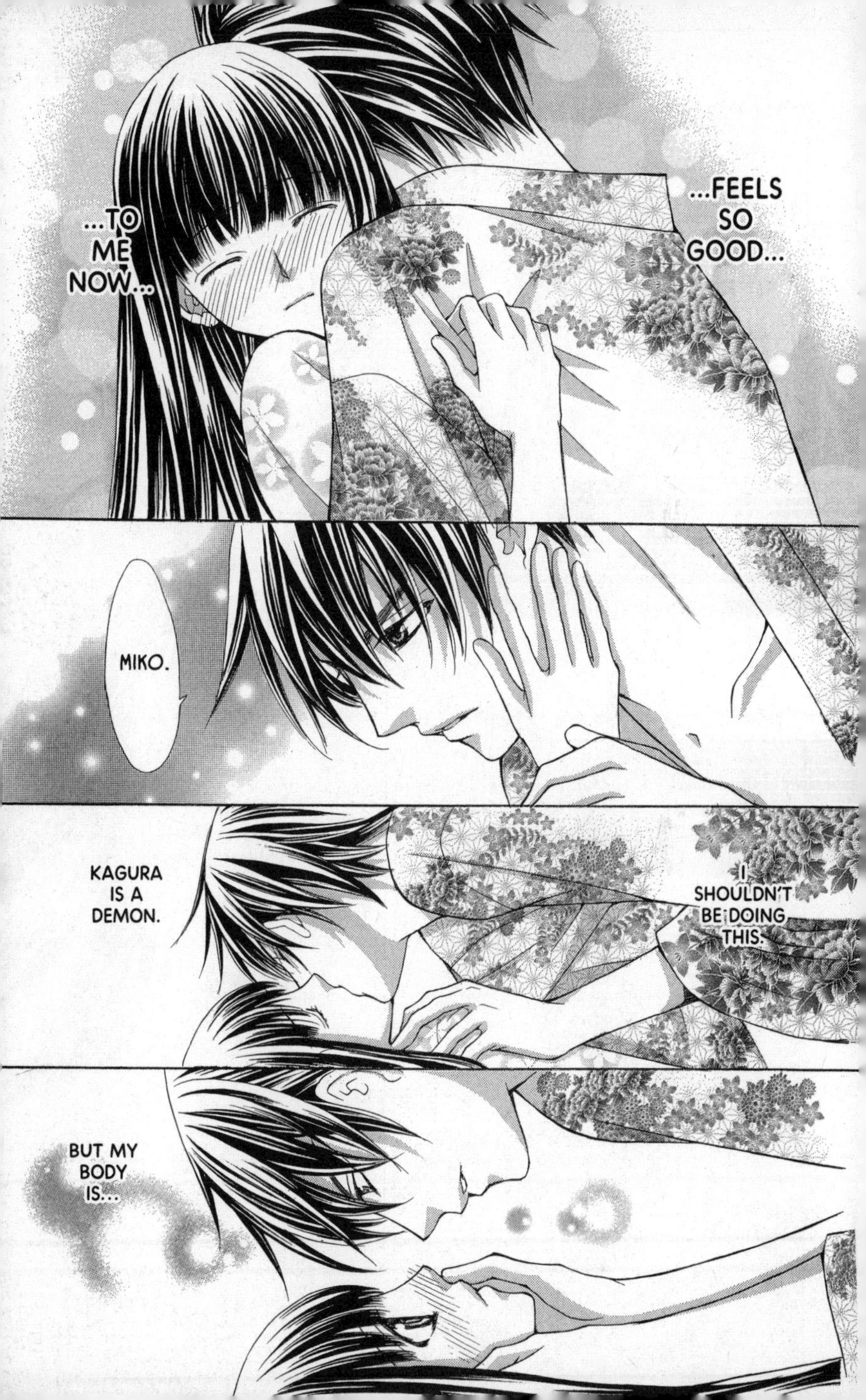
...FEELS SO GOOD...
...TO ME NOW...
MIKO.
I SHOULDN'T BE DOING THIS.
KAGURA IS A DEMON.
BUT MY BODY IS...

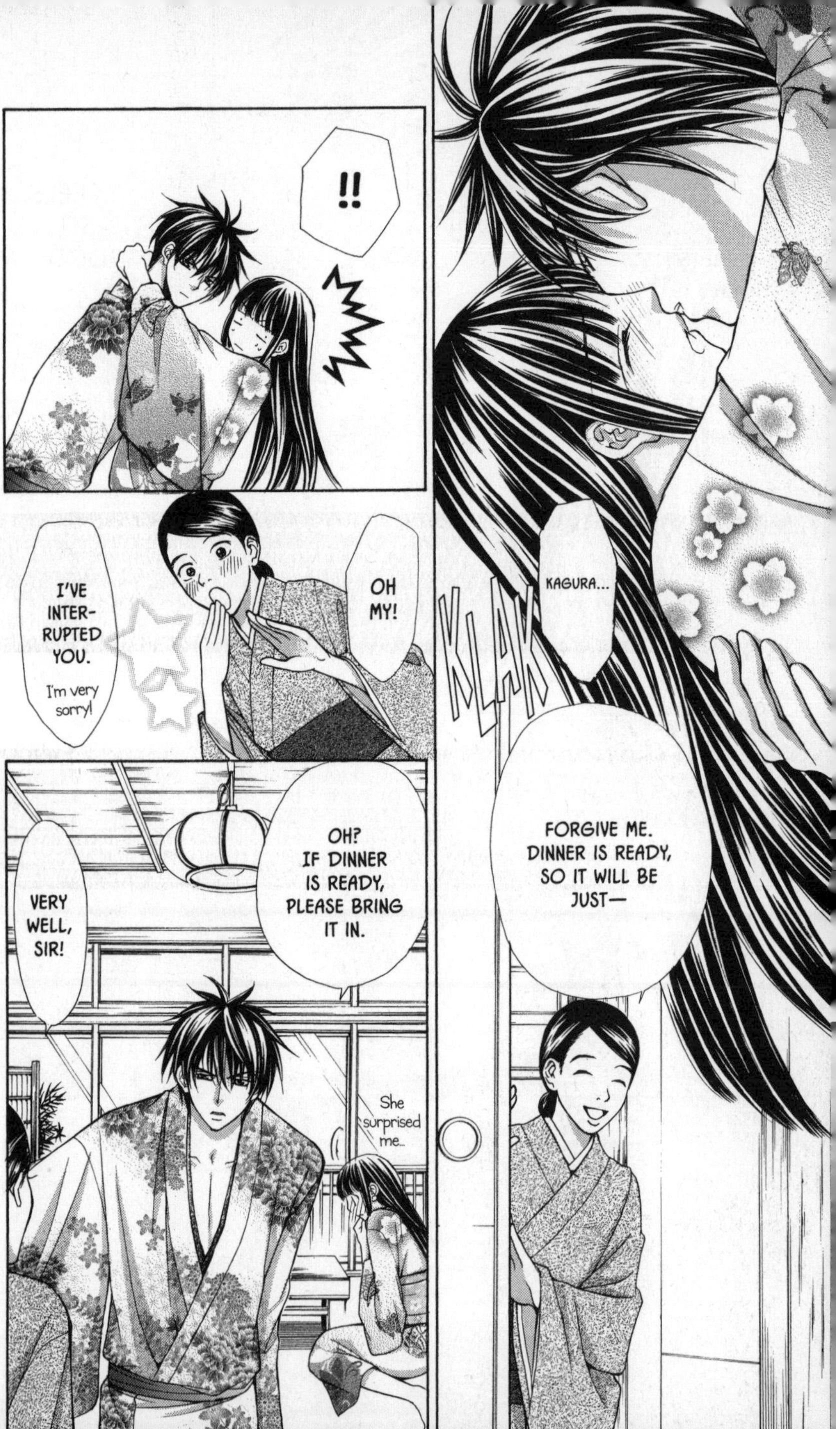
KAGURA...
KLAK
FORGIVE ME. DINNER IS READY, SO IT WILL BE JUST—
!!
OH MY!
I'VE INTER-RUPTED YOU.
I'm very sorry!
OH? IF DINNER IS READY, PLEASE BRING IT IN.
VERY WELL, SIR!
She surprised me...

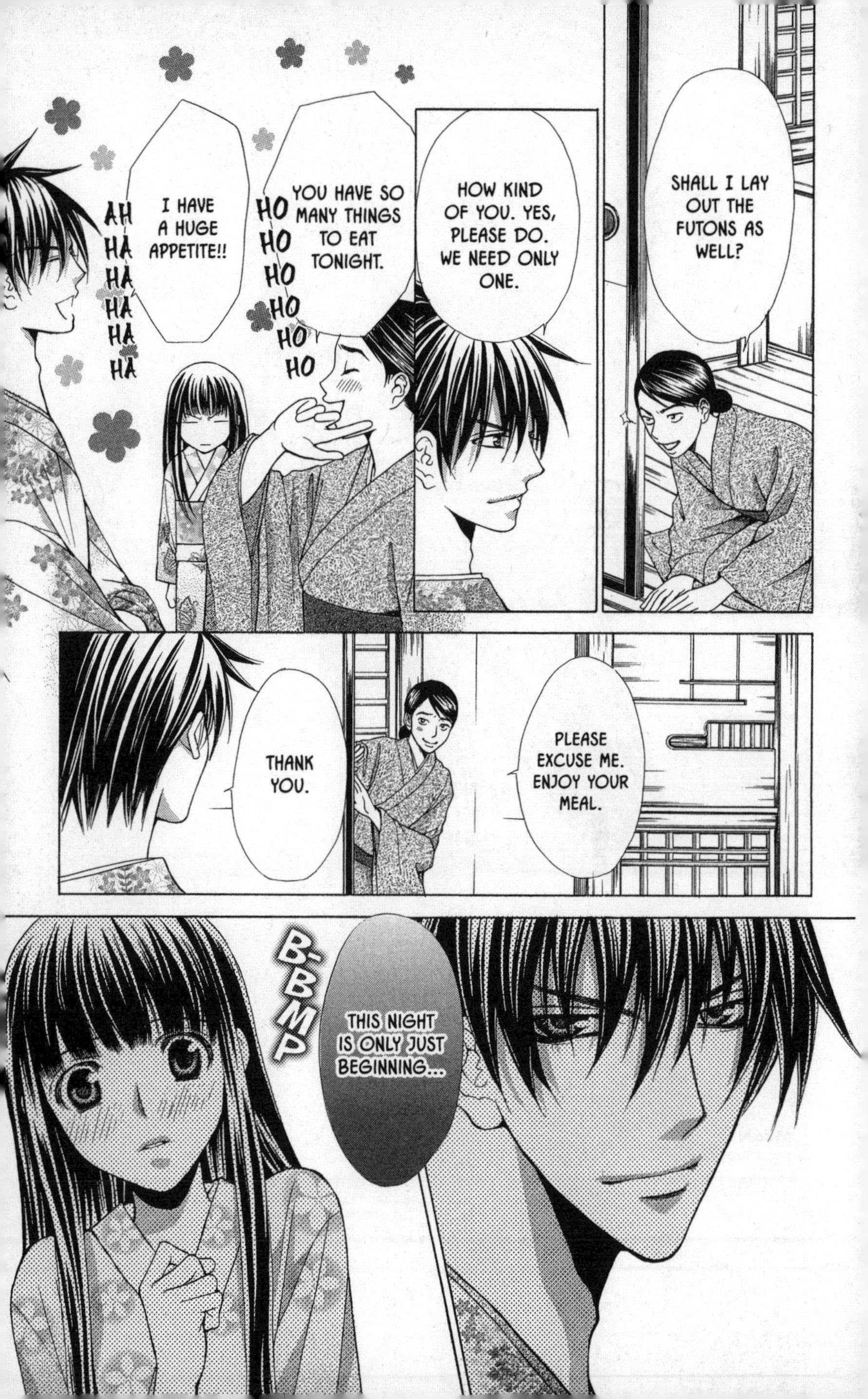
SHALL I LAY OUT THE FUTONS AS WELL?
HOW KIND OF YOU. YES, PLEASE DO. WE NEED ONLY ONE.
YOU HAVE SO MANY THINGS TO EAT TONIGHT.
HO HO HO HO HO HO
I HAVE A HUGE APPETITE!!
AH HA HA HA HA HA
PLEASE EXCUSE ME. ENJOY YOUR MEAL.
THANK YOU.
THIS NIGHT IS ONLY JUST BEGINNING...
B-BMP

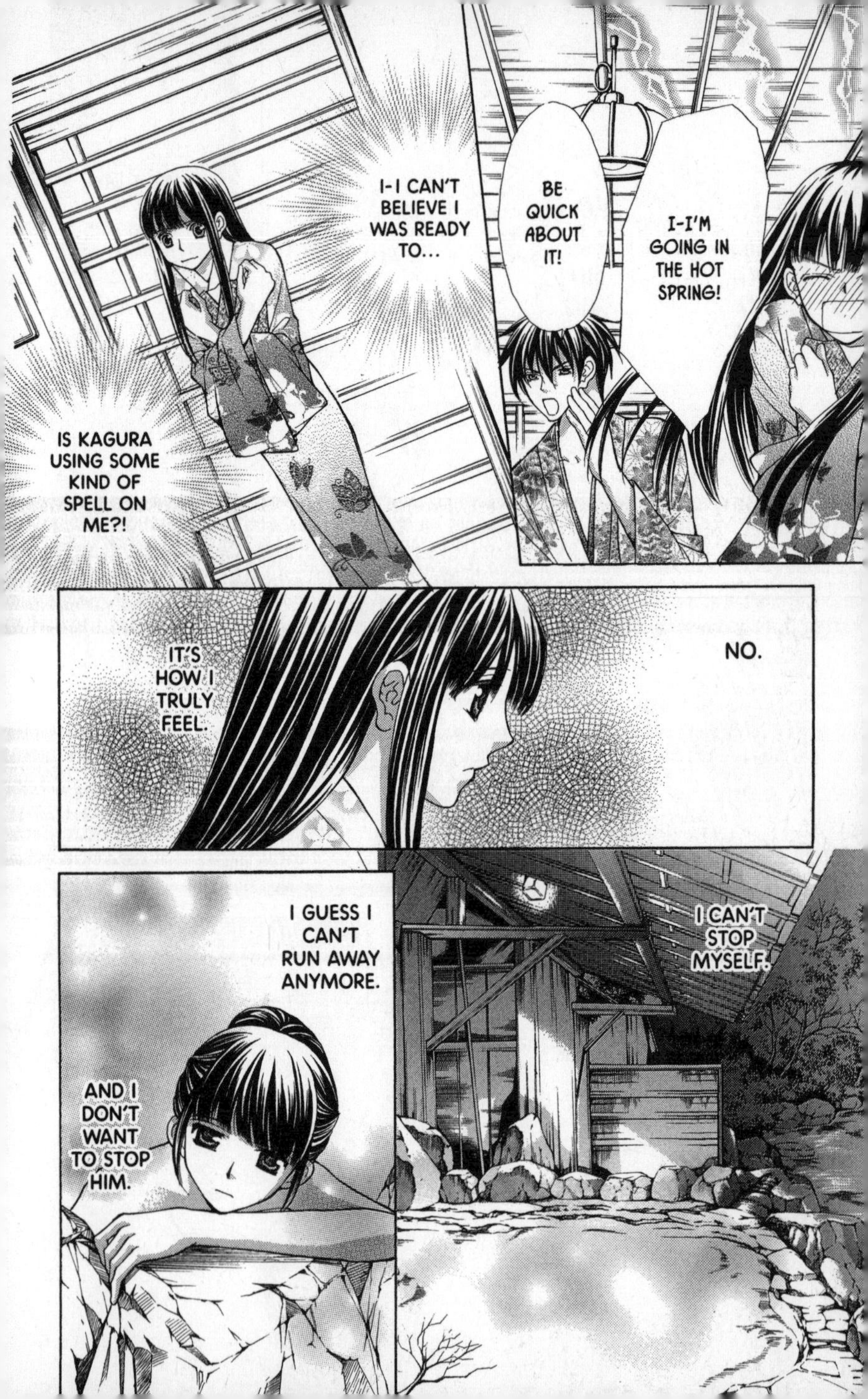
I-I'M GOING IN THE HOT SPRING!
BE QUICK ABOUT IT!
I-I CAN'T BELIEVE I WAS READY TO...
IS KAGURA USING SOME KIND OF SPELL ON ME?!
NO.
IT'S HOW I TRULY FEEL.
I CAN'T STOP MYSELF.
I GUESS I CAN'T RUN AWAY ANYMORE.
AND I DON'T WANT TO STOP HIM.

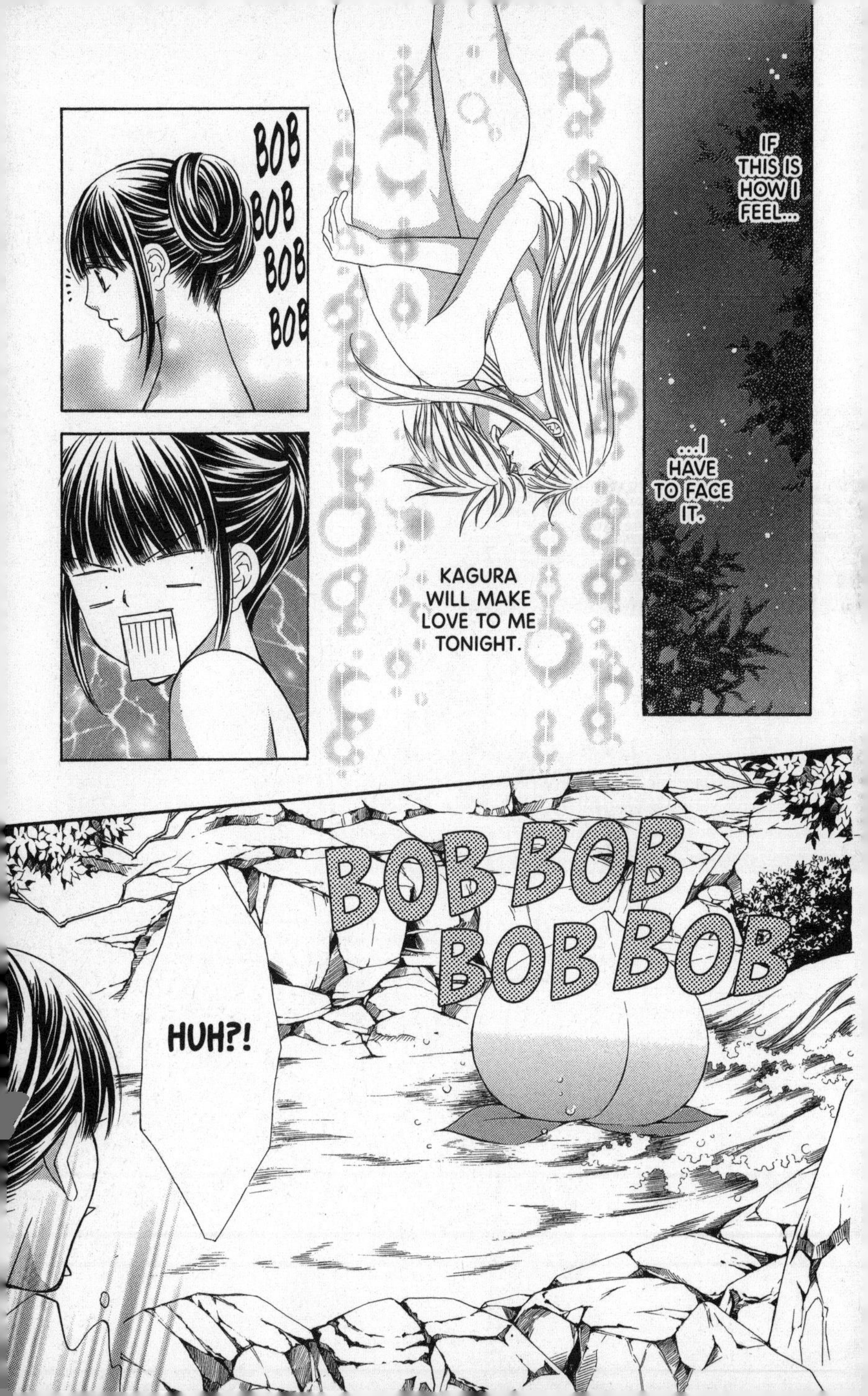
IF THIS IS HOW I FEEL...
...I HAVE TO FACE IT.
KAGURA WILL MAKE LOVE TO ME TONIGHT.
BOB BOB BOB BOB
BOB BOB BOB BOB
HUH?!

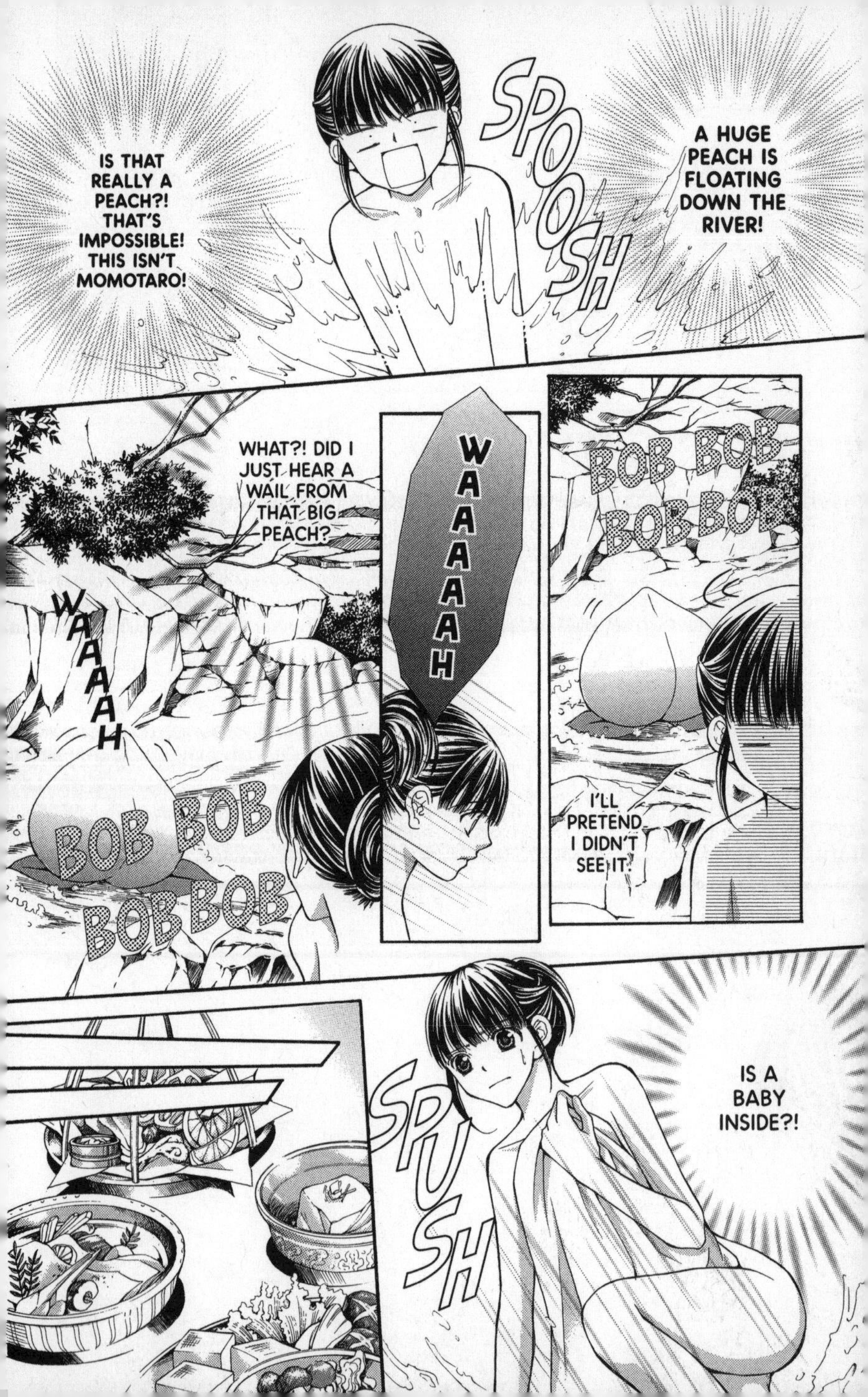
A HUGE PEACH IS FLOATING DOWN THE RIVER!
SPOOSH
IS THAT REALLY A PEACH?! THAT'S IMPOSSIBLE! THIS ISN'T MOMOTARO!
BOB BOB BOB BOB
I'LL PRETEND I DIDN'T SEE IT.
WAAAAAAH
WHAT?! DID I JUST HEAR A WAIL FROM THAT BIG PEACH?
WAAAAH
BOB BOB BOB BOB
IS A BABY INSIDE?!
SPUSH

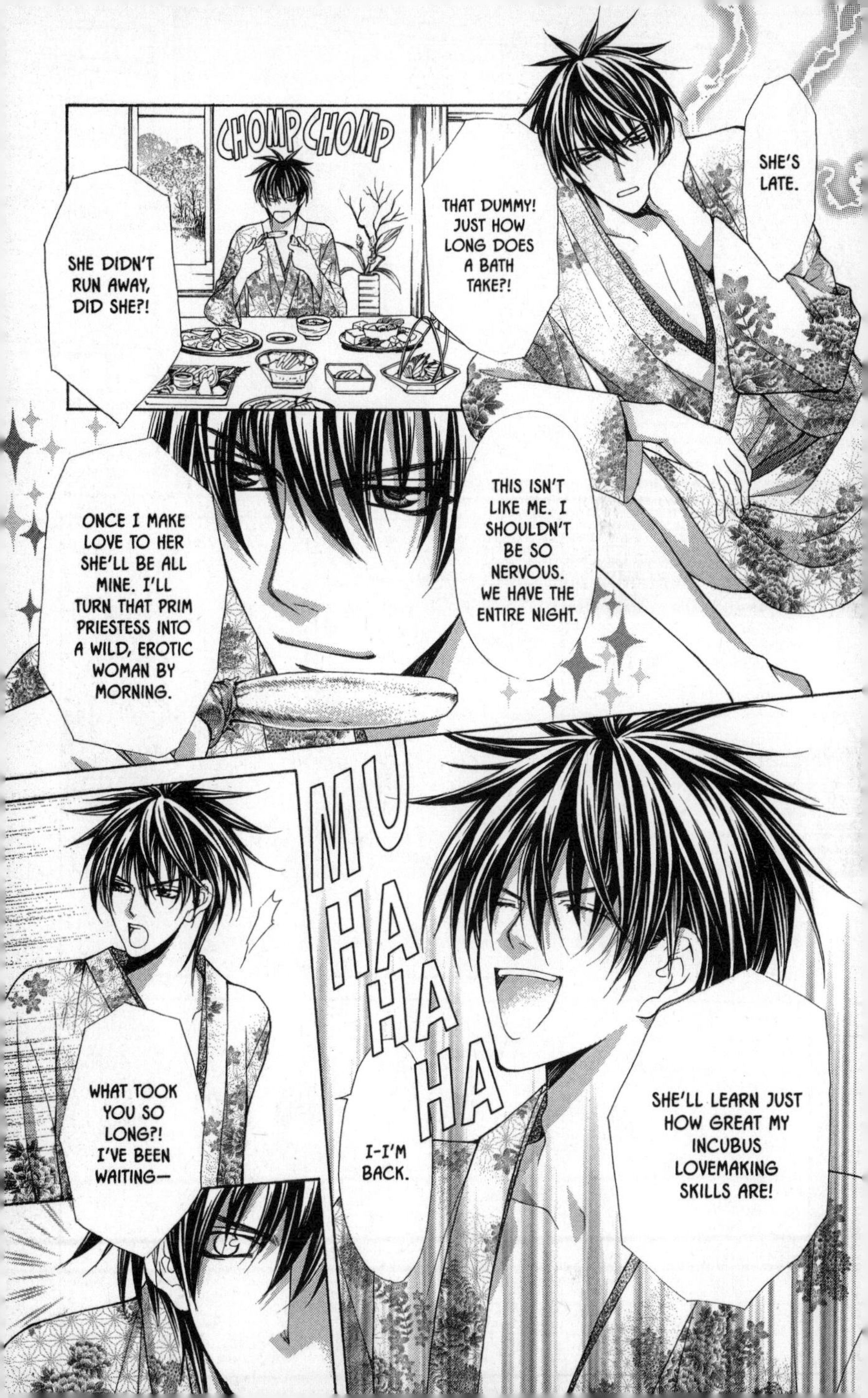
SHE'S LATE.
THAT DUMMY! JUST HOW LONG DOES A BATH TAKE?!
CHOMP CHOMP
SHE DIDN'T RUN AWAY, DID SHE?!
THIS ISN'T LIKE ME. I SHOULDN'T BE SO NERVOUS. WE HAVE THE ENTIRE NIGHT.
ONCE I MAKE LOVE TO HER SHE'LL BE ALL MINE. I'LL TURN THAT PRIM PRIESTESS INTO A WILD, EROTIC WOMAN BY MORNING.
MUHAHAHAHA
SHE'LL LEARN JUST HOW GREAT MY INCUBUS LOVEMAKING SKILLS ARE!
I-I'M BACK.
WHAT TOOK YOU SO LONG?! I'VE BEEN WAITING—

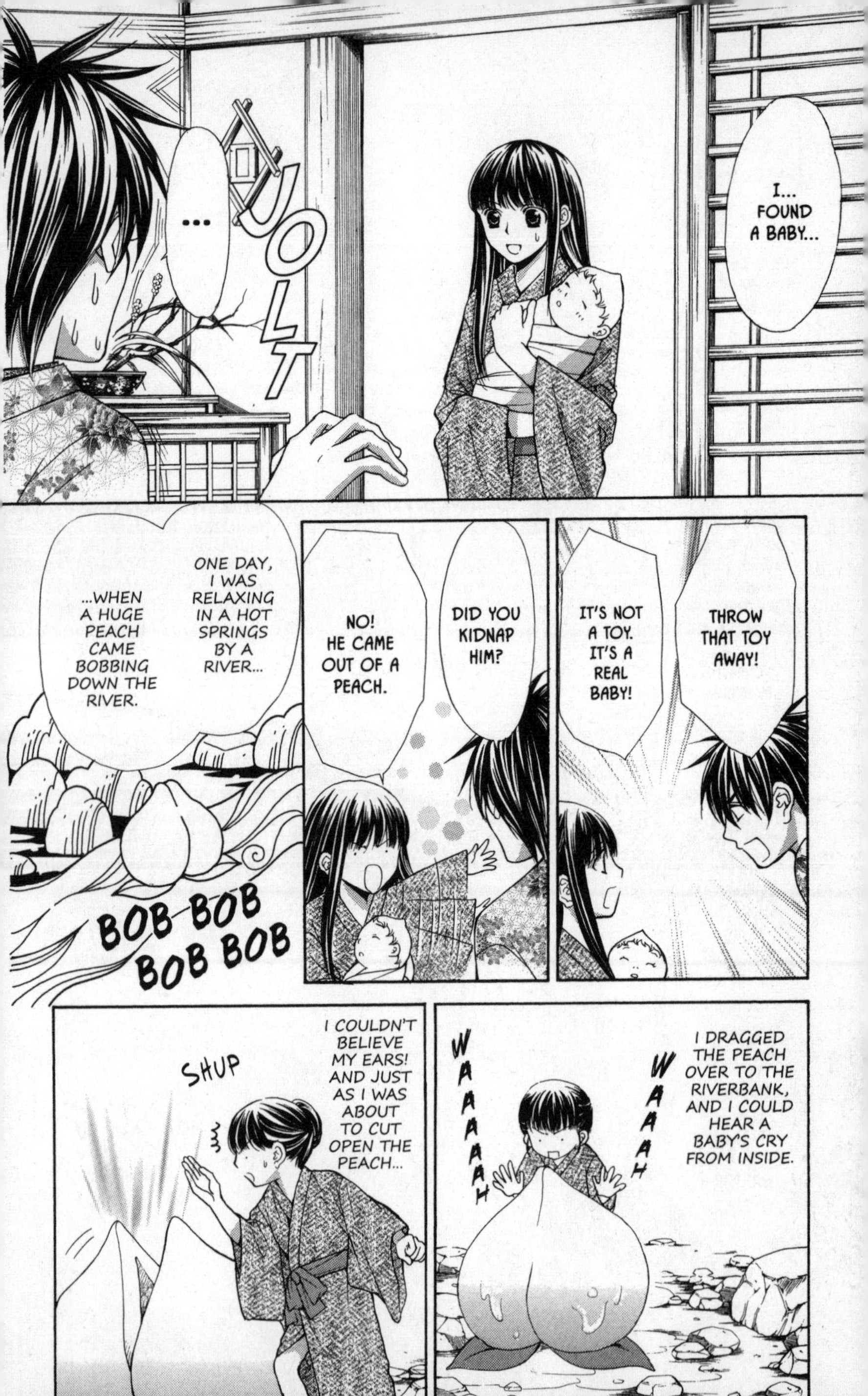
I... FOUND A BABY...
JOLT
...
THROW THAT TOY AWAY!
IT'S NOT A TOY. IT'S A REAL BABY!
DID YOU KIDNAP HIM?
NO! HE CAME OUT OF A PEACH.
ONE DAY, I WAS RELAXING IN A HOT SPRINGS BY A RIVER...
...WHEN A HUGE PEACH CAME BOBBING DOWN THE RIVER.
BOB BOB BOB BOB
I DRAGGED THE PEACH OVER TO THE RIVERBANK, AND I COULD HEAR A BABY'S CRY FROM INSIDE.
WAAAAH
WAAAAH
I COULDN'T BELIEVE MY EARS! AND JUST AS I WAS ABOUT TO CUT OPEN THE PEACH...
SHUP

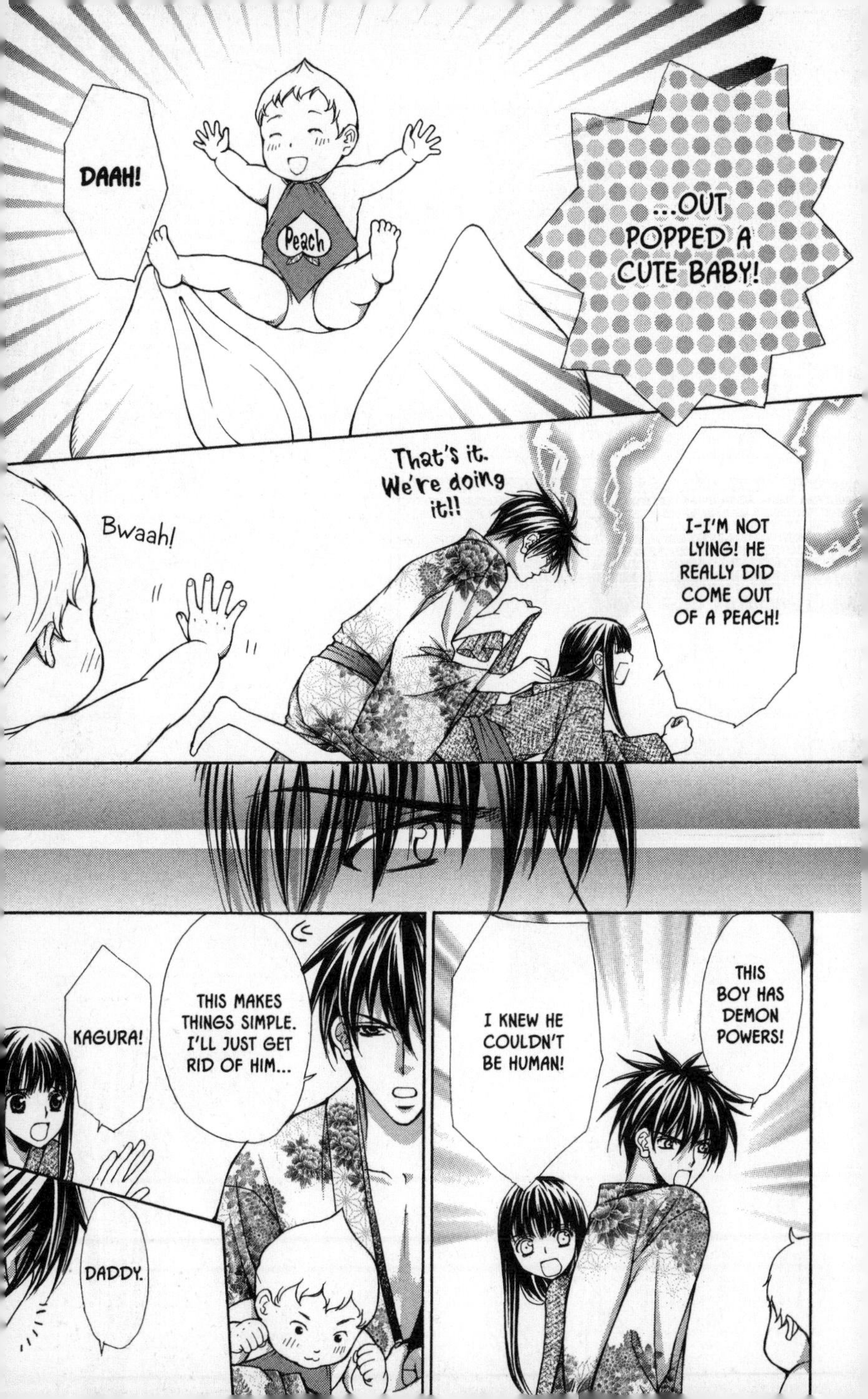
...OUT POPPED A CUTE BABY!
Peach
DAAH!
I-I'M NOT LYING! HE REALLY DID COME OUT OF A PEACH!
That's it. We're doing it!!
Bwaah!
THIS BOY HAS DEMON POWERS!
I KNEW HE COULDN'T BE HUMAN!
THIS MAKES THINGS SIMPLE. I'LL JUST GET RID OF HIM...
KAGURA!
DADDY.

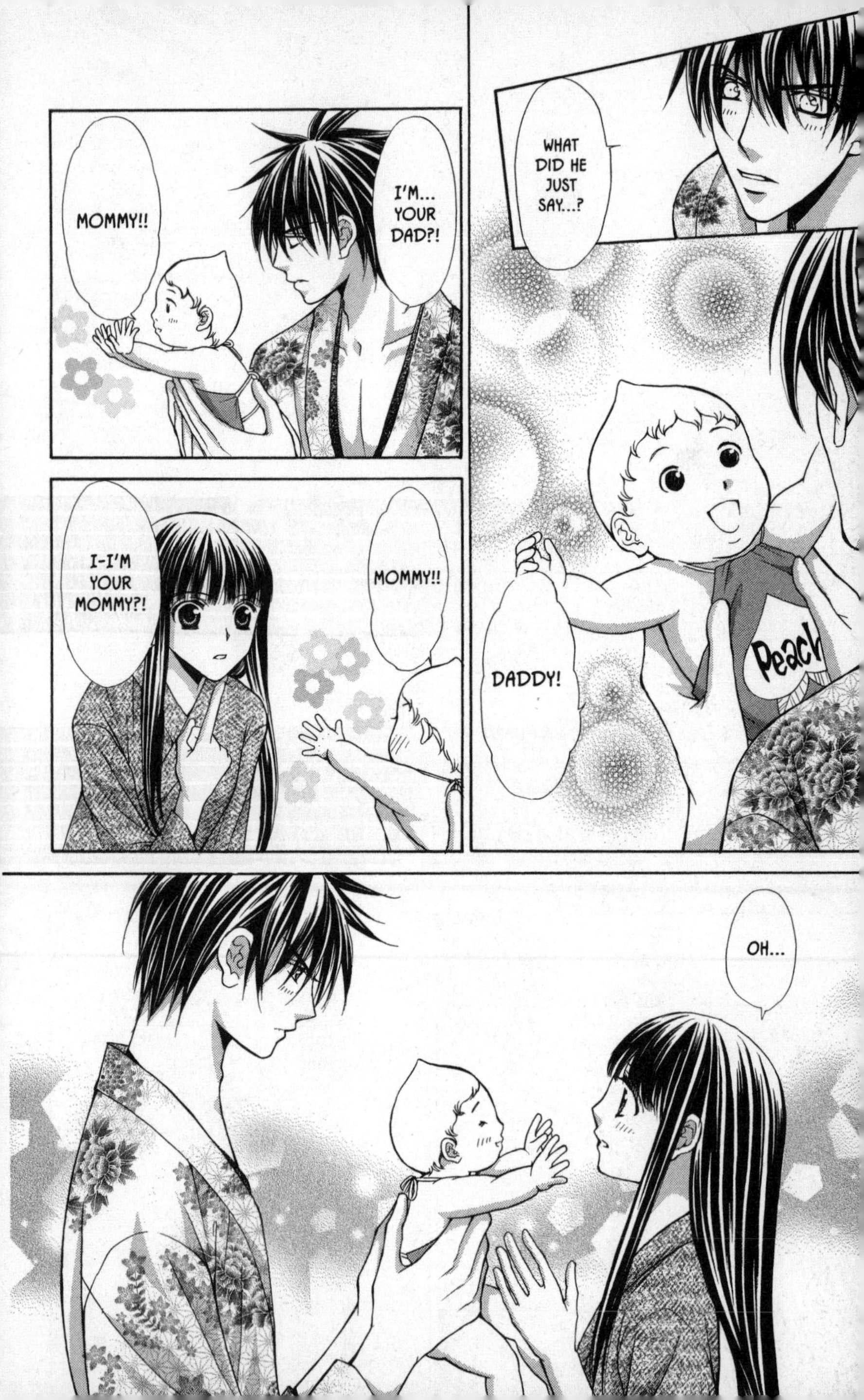
WHAT DID HE JUST SAY...?
DADDY!
I'M... YOUR DAD?!
MOMMY!!
MOMMY!!
I-I'M YOUR MOMMY?!
Peach
OH...

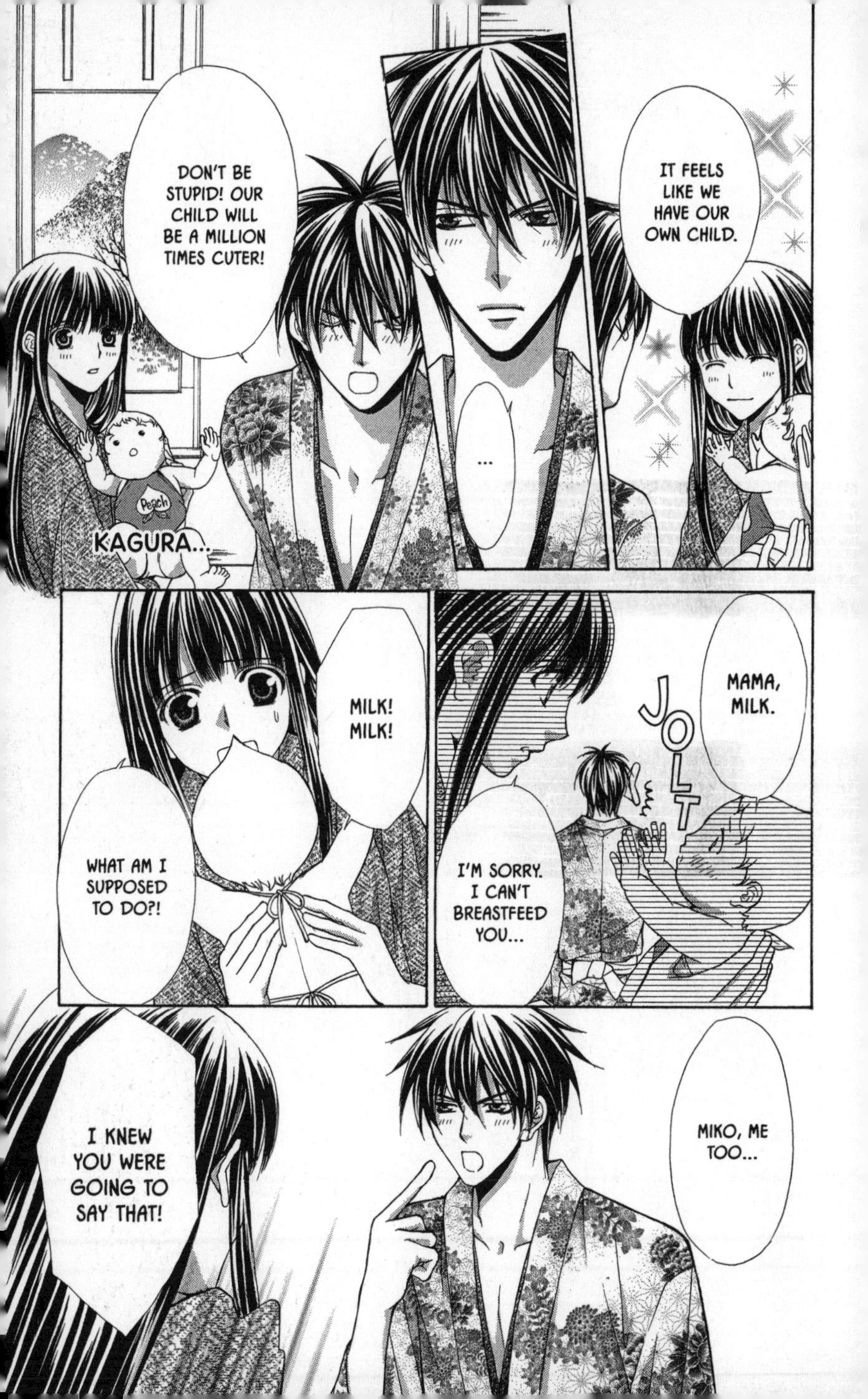
IT FEELS LIKE WE HAVE OUR OWN CHILD.
...
DON'T BE STUPID! OUR CHILD WILL BE A MILLION TIMES CUTER!
KAGURA...
Peach
MAMA, MILK.
JOLT
I'M SORRY. I CAN'T BREASTFEED YOU...
MILK! MILK!
WHAT AM I SUPPOSED TO DO?!
MIKO, ME TOO...
I KNEW YOU WERE GOING TO SAY THAT!

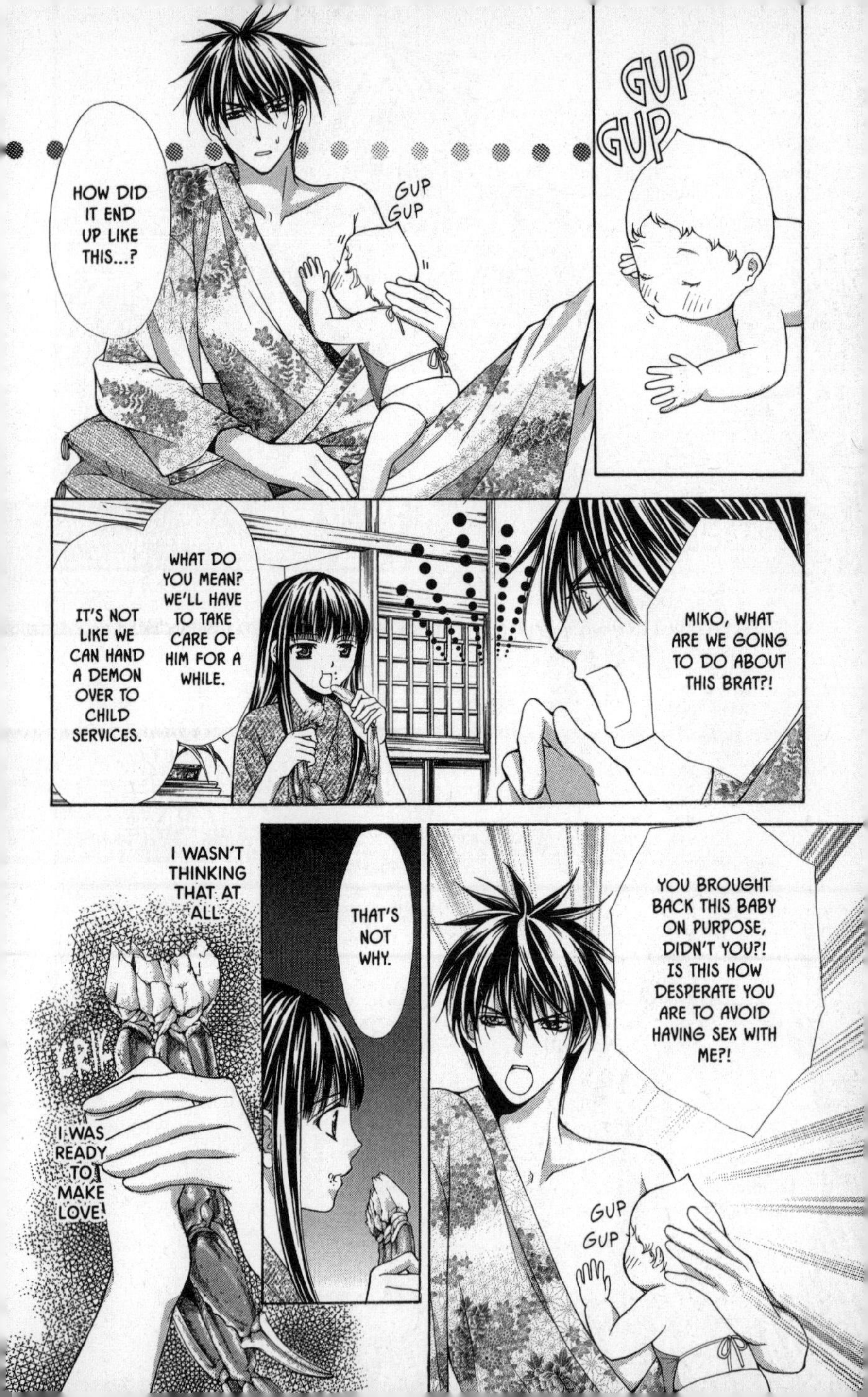
GUP
GUP
HOW DID IT END UP LIKE THIS...?
GUP GUP
MIKO, WHAT ARE WE GOING TO DO ABOUT THIS BRAT?!
WHAT DO YOU MEAN? WE'LL HAVE TO TAKE CARE OF HIM FOR A WHILE.
IT'S NOT LIKE WE CAN HAND A DEMON OVER TO CHILD SERVICES.
YOU BROUGHT BACK THIS BABY ON PURPOSE, DIDN'T YOU?! IS THIS HOW DESPERATE YOU ARE TO AVOID HAVING SEX WITH ME?!
GUP GUP
THAT'S NOT WHY.
I WASN'T THINKING THAT AT ALL.
I WAS READY TO MAKE LOVE.

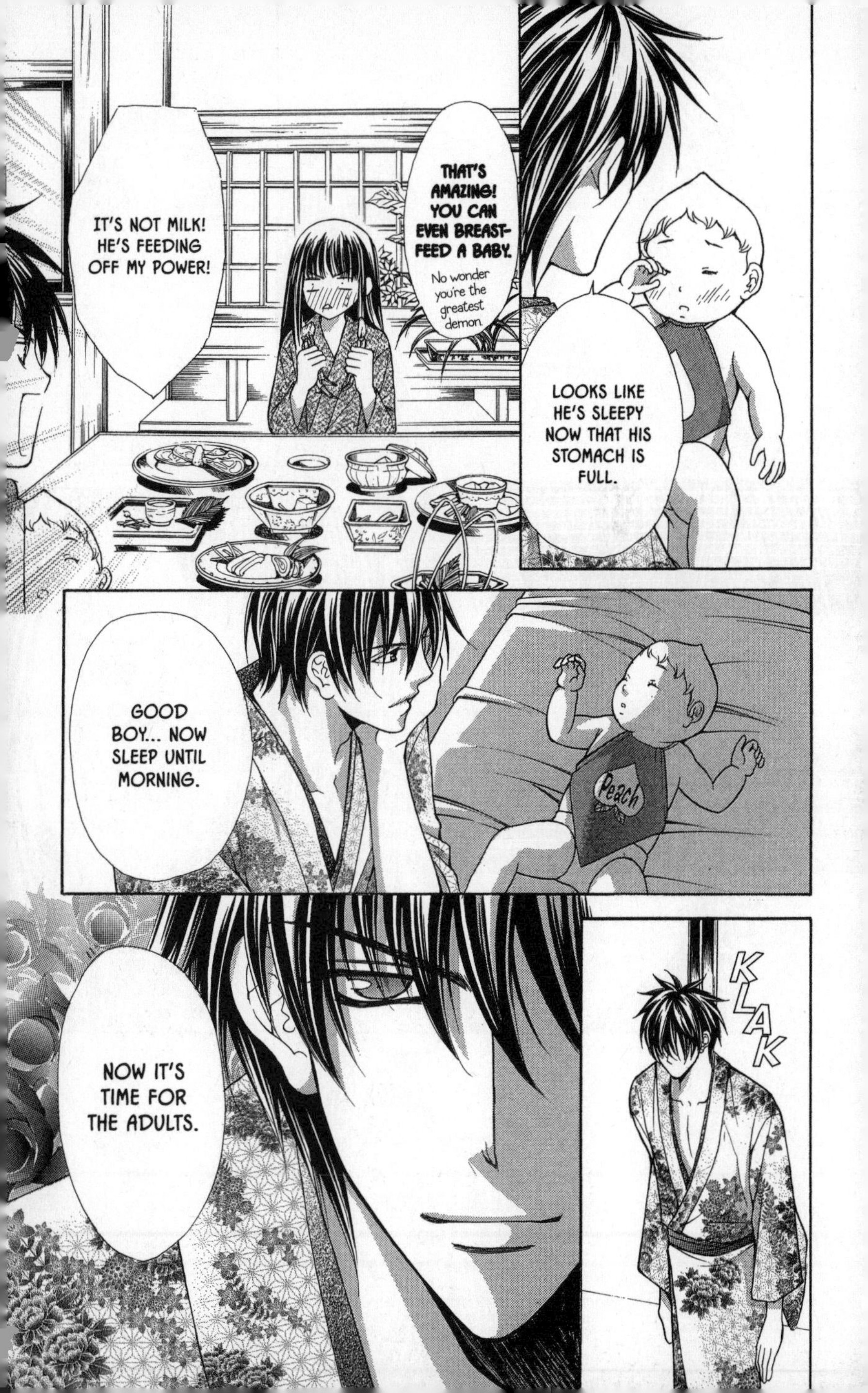
LOOKS LIKE HE'S SLEEPY NOW THAT HIS STOMACH IS FULL.
THAT'S AMAZING! YOU CAN EVEN BREAST-FEED A BABY.
No wonder you're the greatest demon.
IT'S NOT MILK! HE'S FEEDING OFF MY POWER!
GOOD BOY... NOW SLEEP UNTIL MORNING.
KLAK
NOW IT'S TIME FOR THE ADULTS.

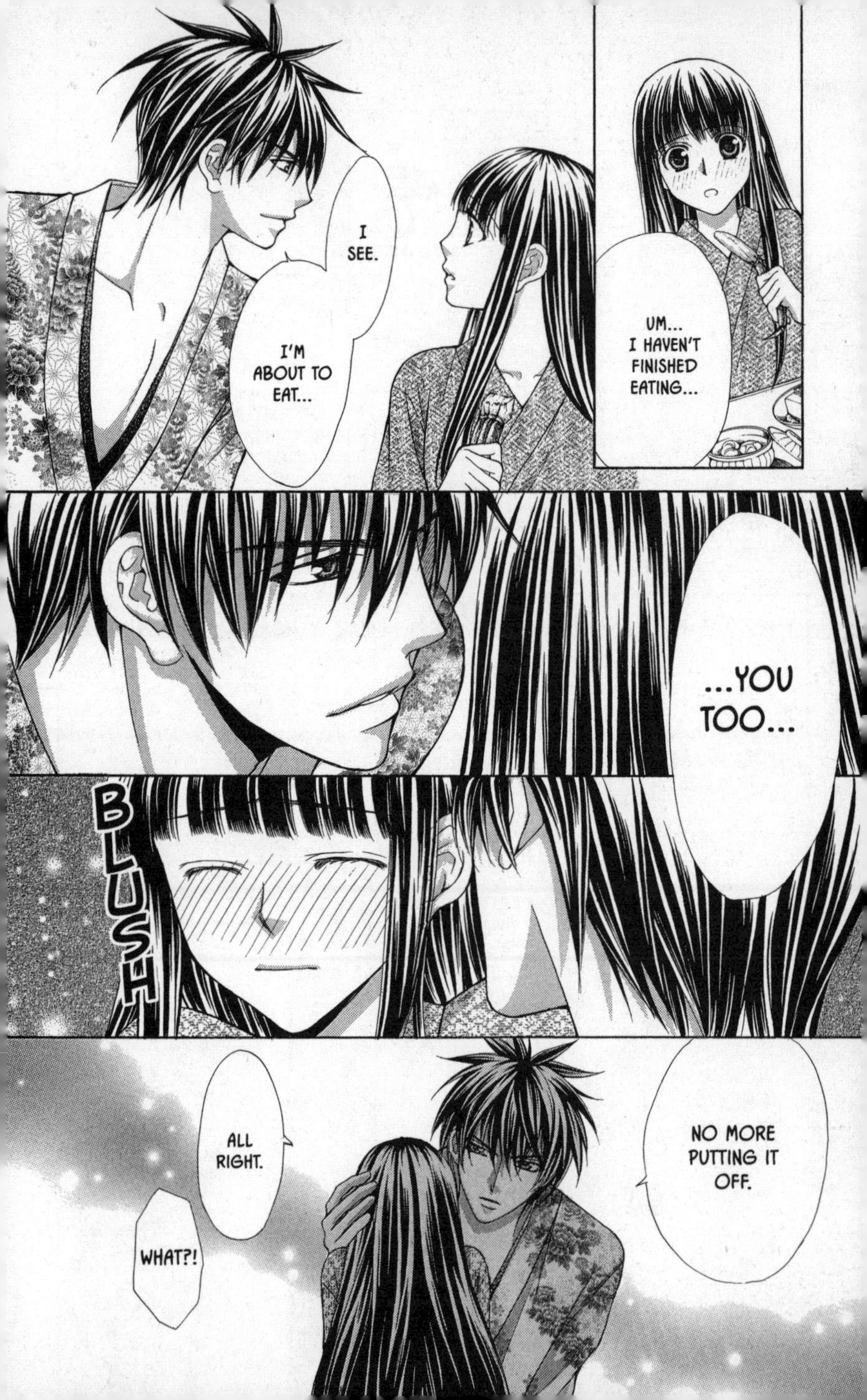
UM... I HAVEN'T FINISHED EATING...
I SEE.
I'M ABOUT TO EAT...
...YOU TOO...
BLUSH
NO MORE PUTTING IT OFF.
ALL RIGHT.
WHAT?!

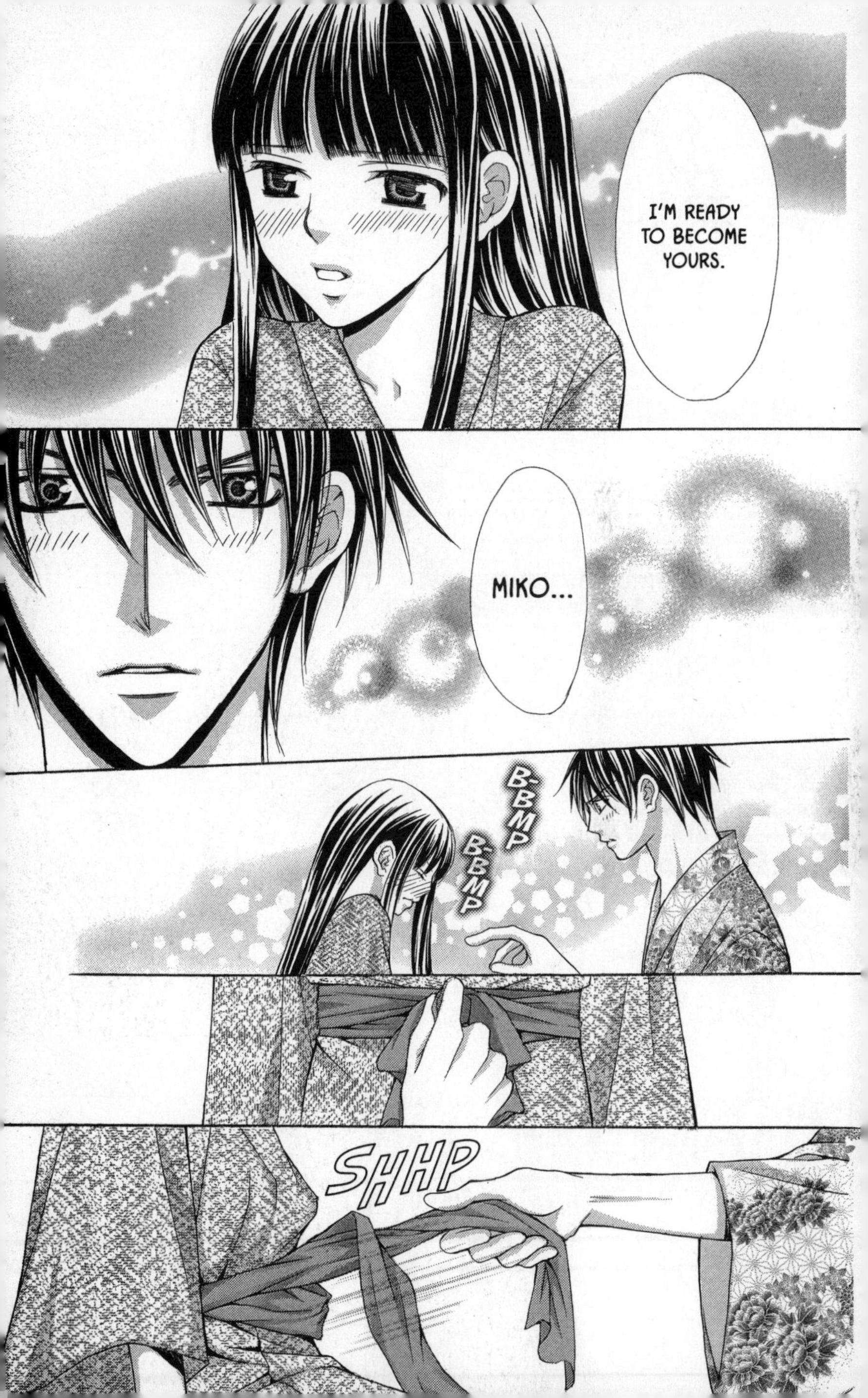
I'M READY TO BECOME YOURS.
MIKO...
B-BMP B-BMP
SHHP

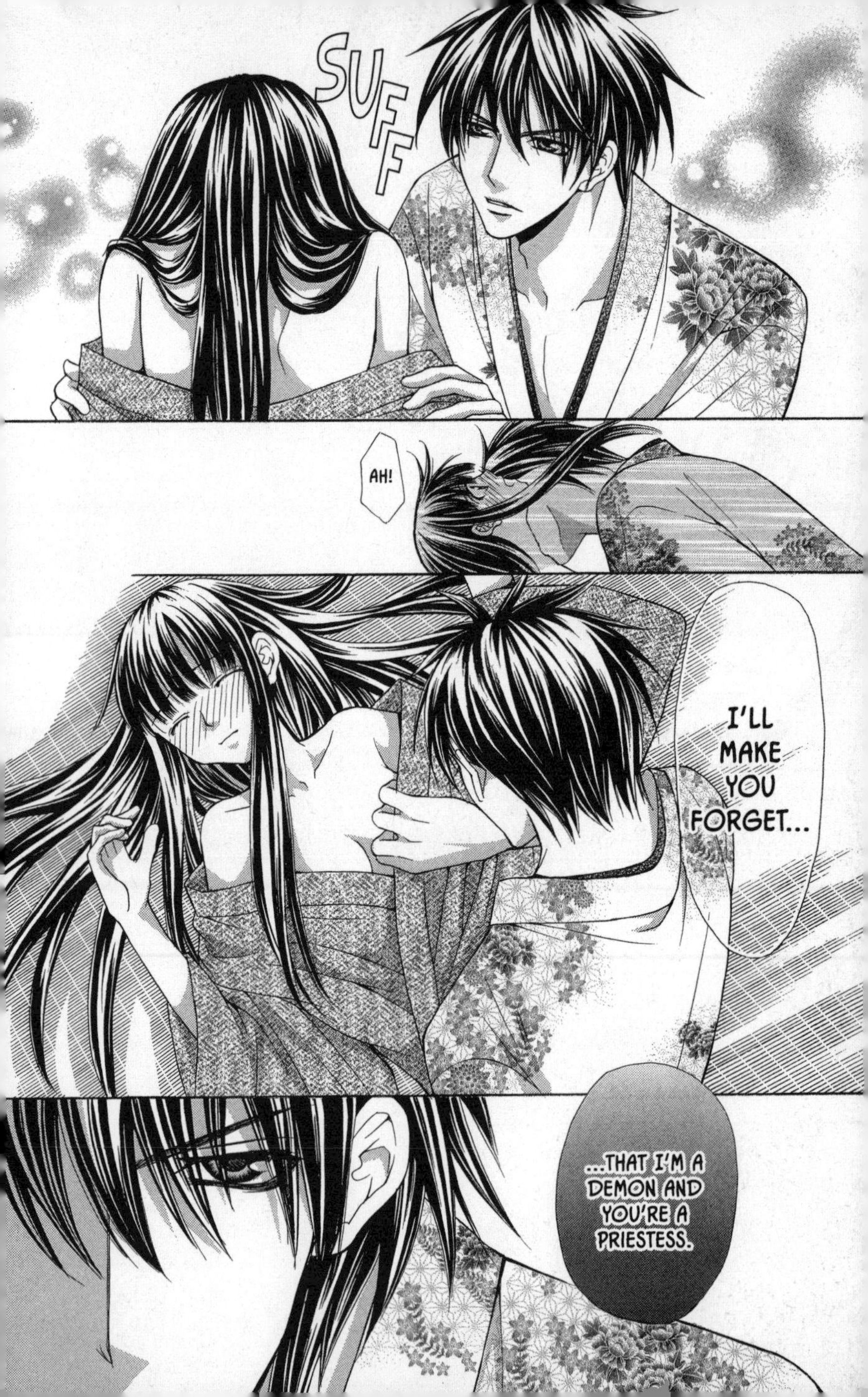
SUFF
AH!
I'LL MAKE YOU FORGET...
...THAT I'M A DEMON AND YOU'RE A PRIESTESS.

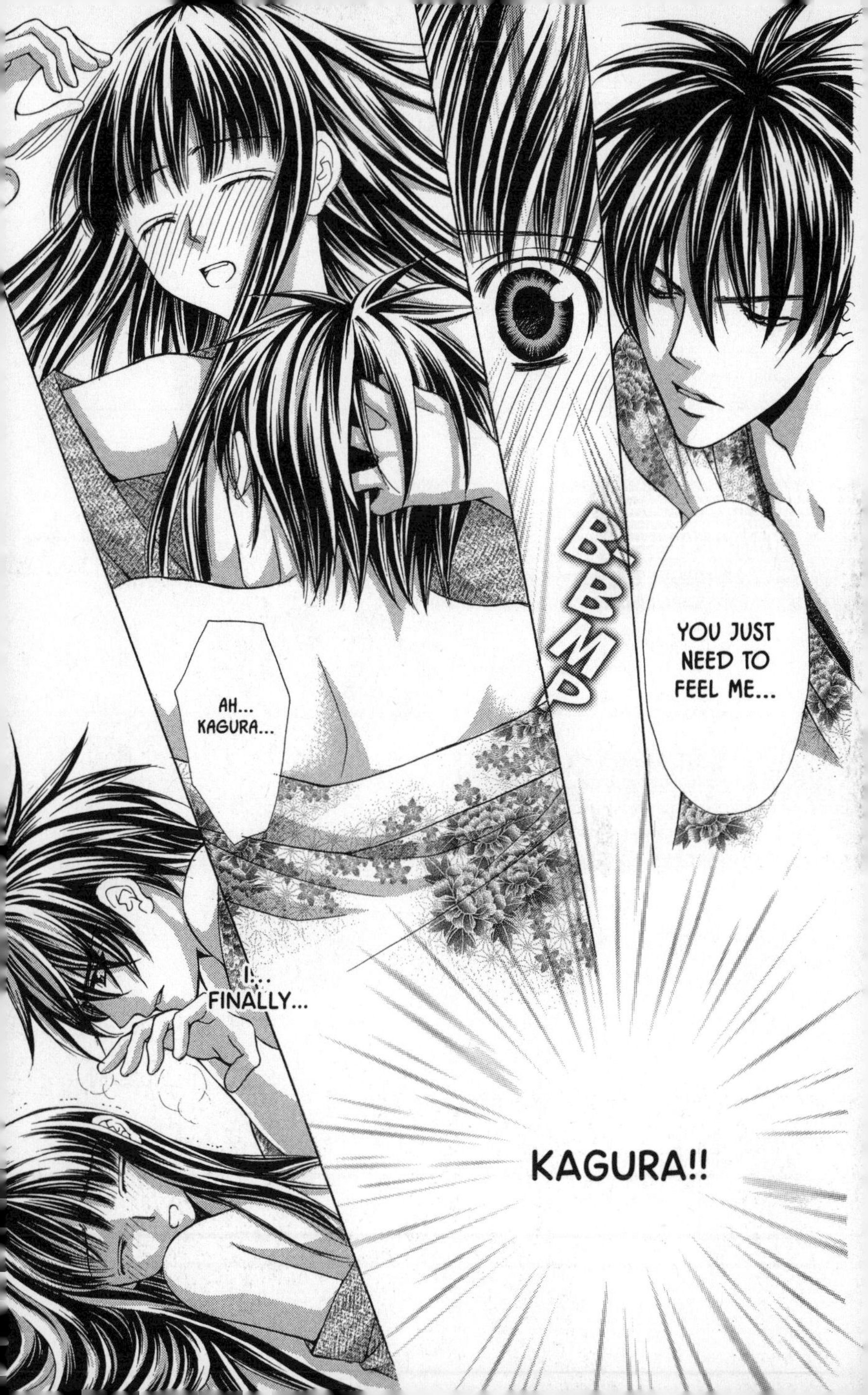
YOU JUST NEED TO FEEL ME...
B-BMP
AH... KAGURA...
I... FINALLY...
KAGURA!!

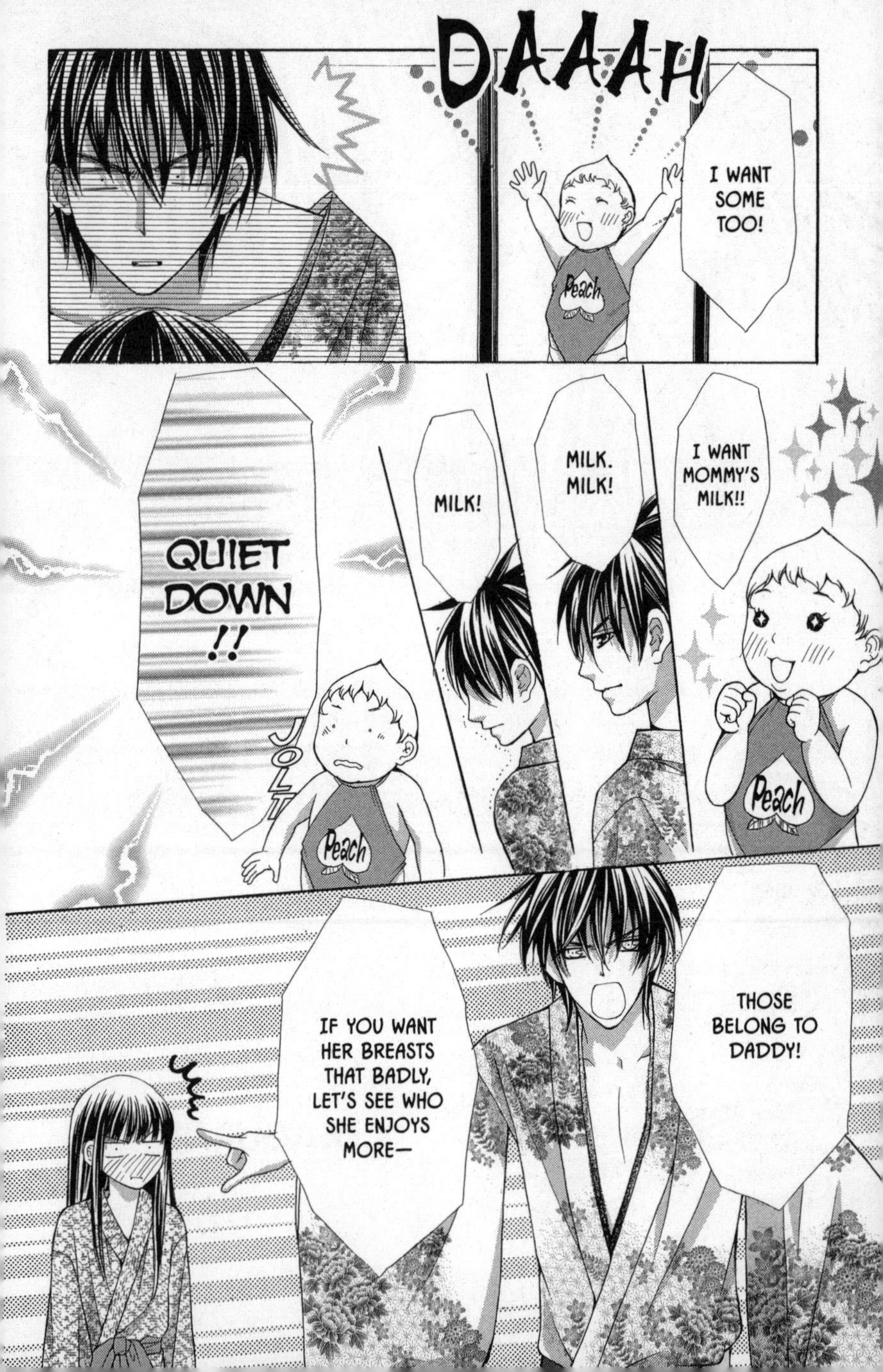
DAAAH
I WANT SOME TOO!
I WANT MOMMY'S MILK!!
MILK. MILK!
MILK!
QUIET DOWN!!
JOLT
THOSE BELONG TO DADDY!
IF YOU WANT HER BREASTS THAT BADLY, LET'S SEE WHO SHE ENJOYS MORE—

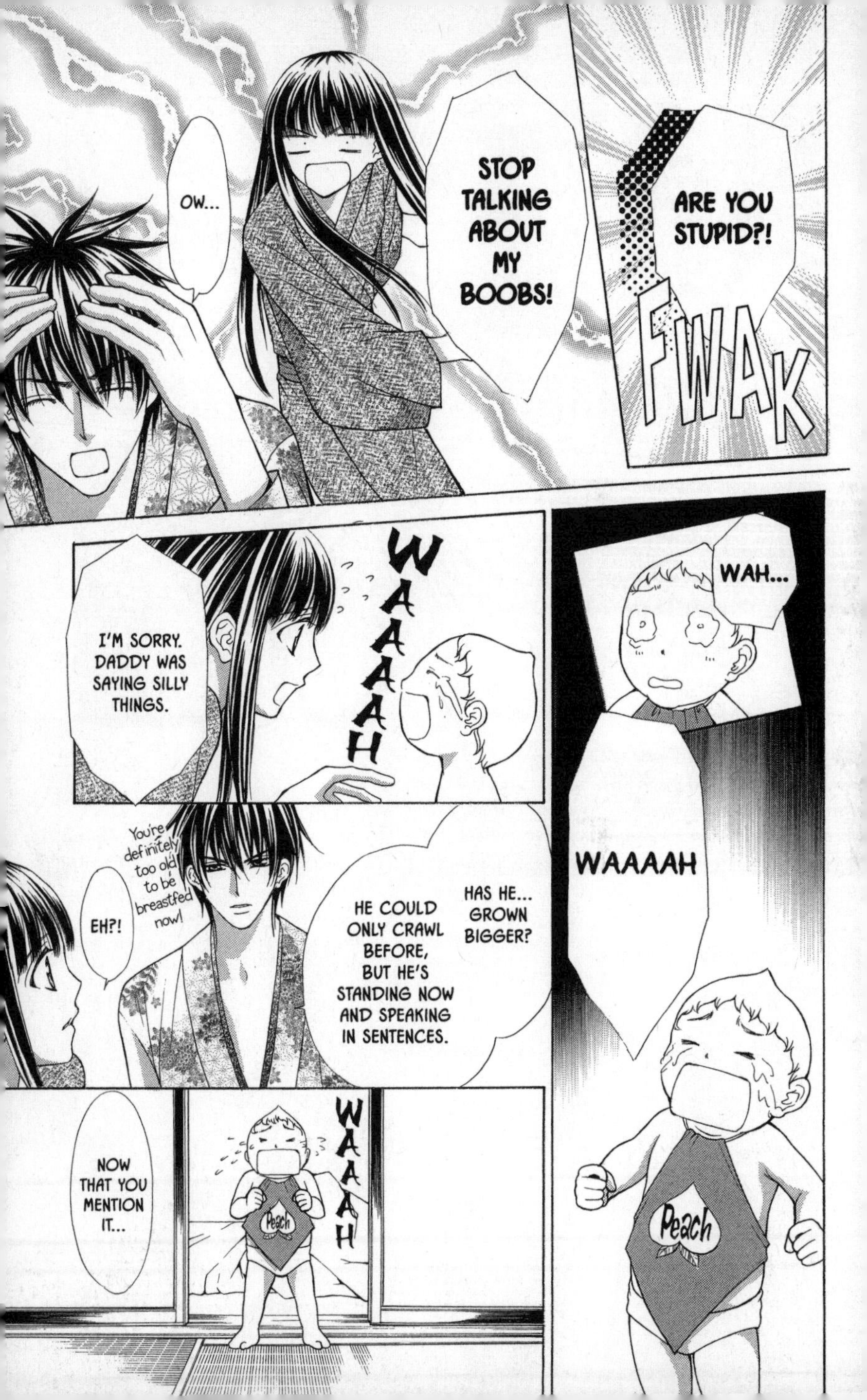
ARE YOU STUPID?!
FWAK
STOP TALKING ABOUT MY BOOBS!
OW...
WAH...
WAAAAH
WAAAAH
I'M SORRY. DADDY WAS SAYING SILLY THINGS.
HAS HE... GROWN BIGGER?
HE COULD ONLY CRAWL BEFORE, BUT HE'S STANDING NOW AND SPEAKING IN SENTENCES.
You're definitely too old to be breastfed now!
EH?!
WAAAH
NOW THAT YOU MENTION IT...

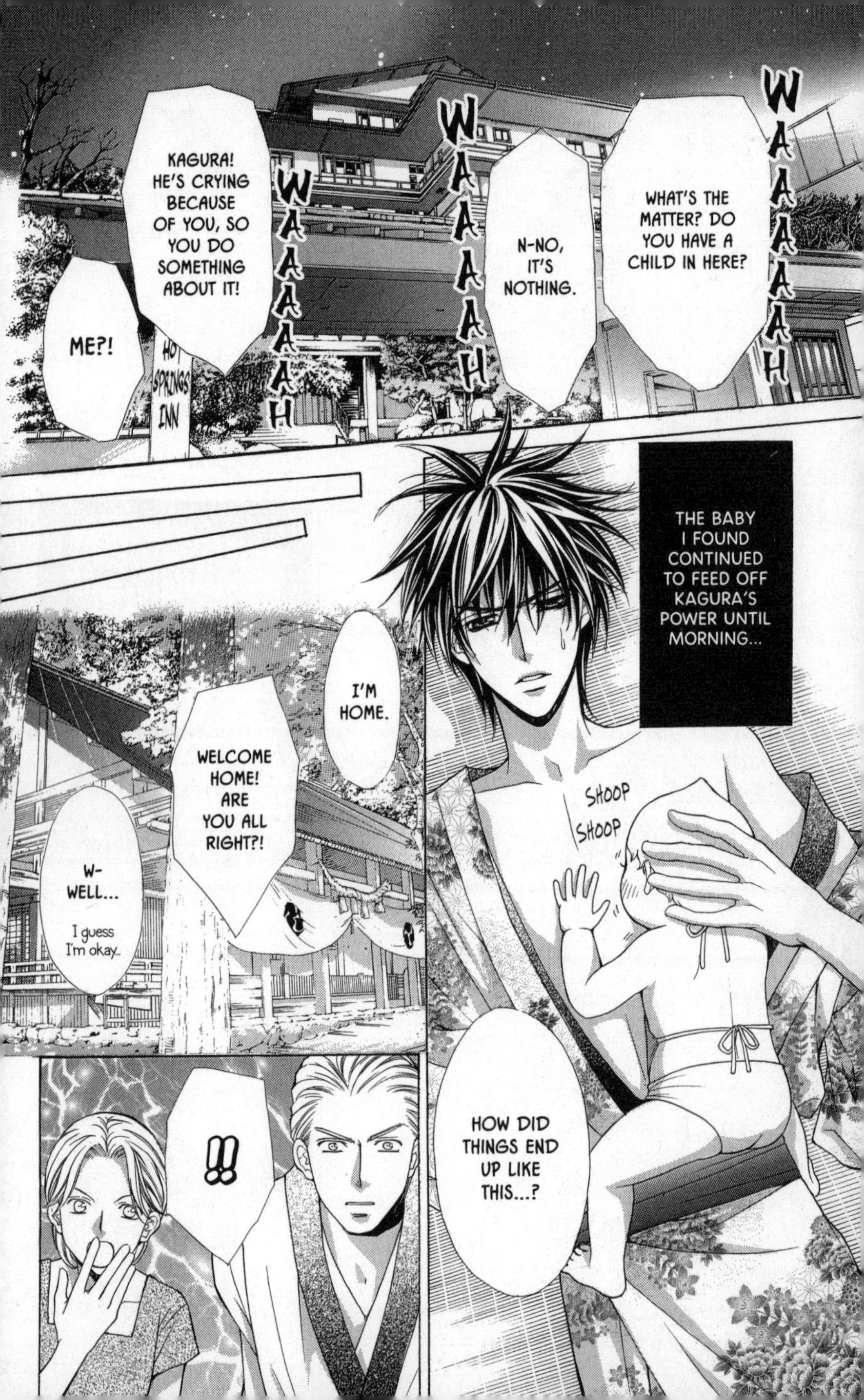
WAAAAAH
WHAT'S THE MATTER? DO YOU HAVE A CHILD IN HERE?
WAAAAAH
N-NO, IT'S NOTHING.
WAAAAAH
KAGURA! HE'S CRYING BECAUSE OF YOU, SO YOU DO SOMETHING ABOUT IT!
ME?!
HOT SPRINGS INN
THE BABY I FOUND CONTINUED TO FEED OFF KAGURA'S POWER UNTIL MORNING...
SHOOP
SHOOP
HOW DID THINGS END UP LIKE THIS...?
I'M HOME.
WELCOME HOME! ARE YOU ALL RIGHT?!
W-WELL...
I guess I'm okay...
!!

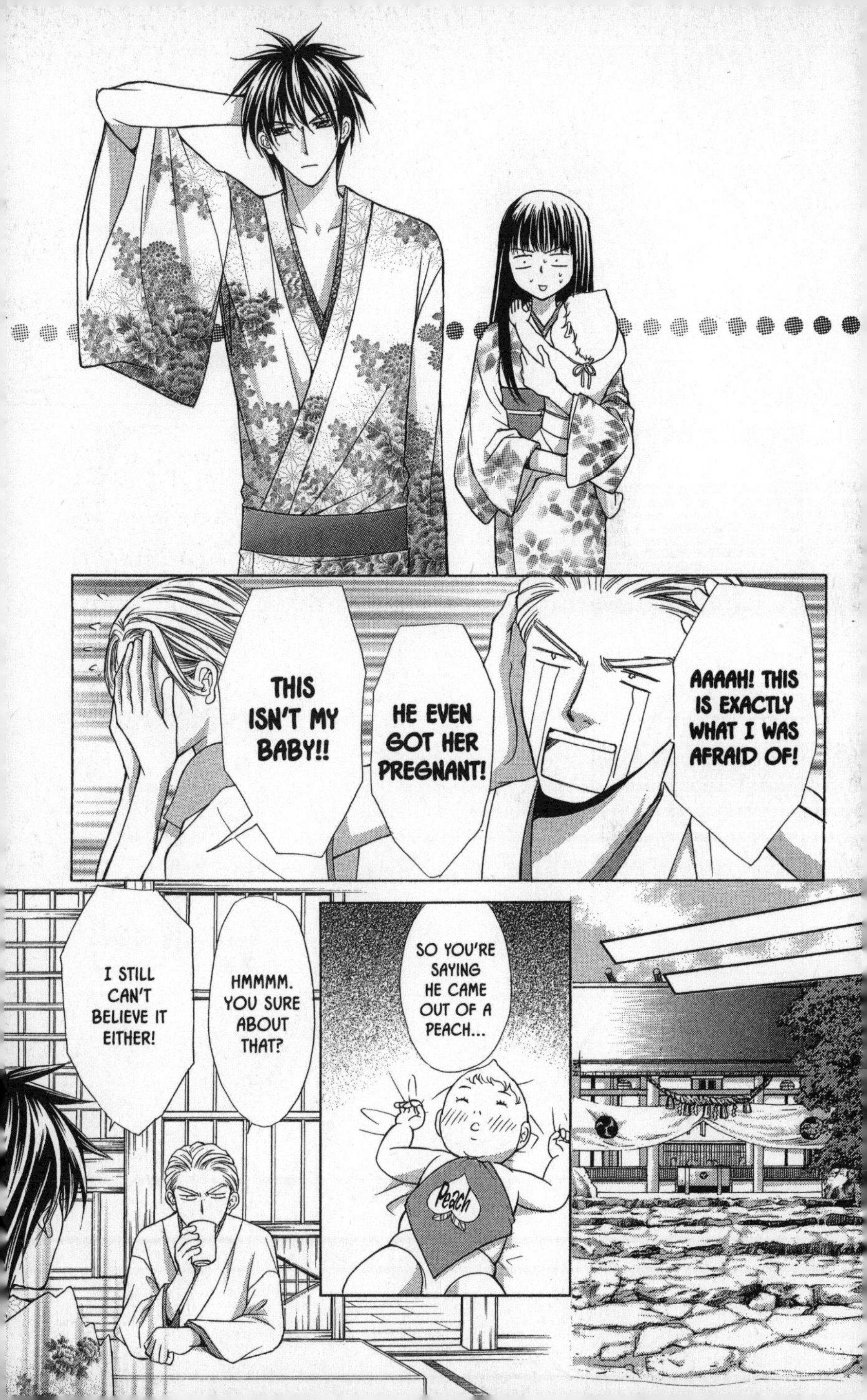
AAAAH! THIS IS EXACTLY WHAT I WAS AFRAID OF!
HE EVEN GOT HER PREGNANT!
THIS ISN'T MY BABY!!
SO YOU'RE SAYING HE CAME OUT OF A PEACH...
Peach
HMMMM. YOU SURE ABOUT THAT?
I STILL CAN'T BELIEVE IT EITHER!

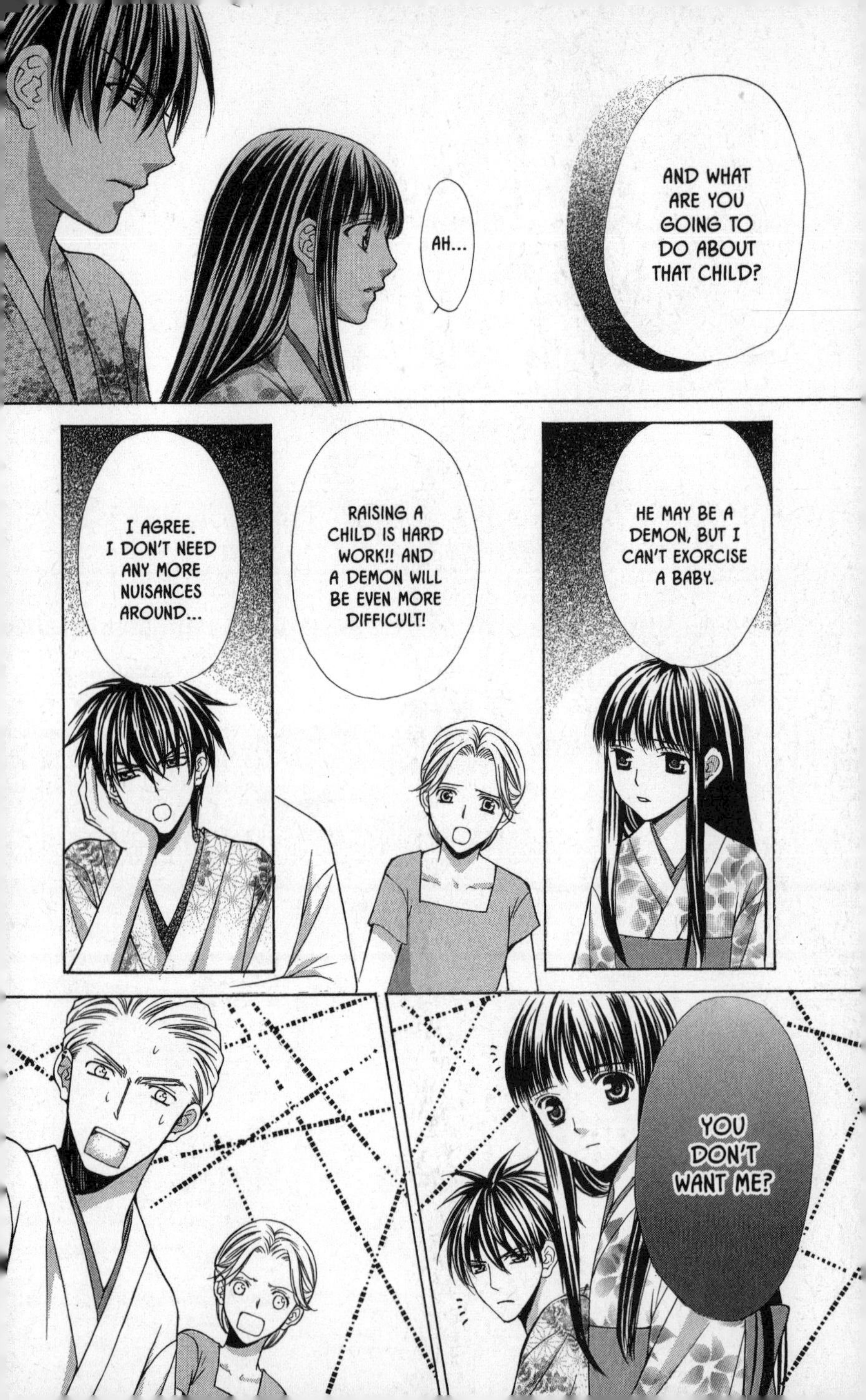
AND WHAT ARE YOU GOING TO DO ABOUT THAT CHILD?
AH...
HE MAY BE A DEMON, BUT I CAN'T EXORCISE A BABY.
RAISING A CHILD IS HARD WORK!! AND A DEMON WILL BE EVEN MORE DIFFICULT!
I AGREE. I DON'T NEED ANY MORE NUISANCES AROUND...
YOU DON'T WANT ME?

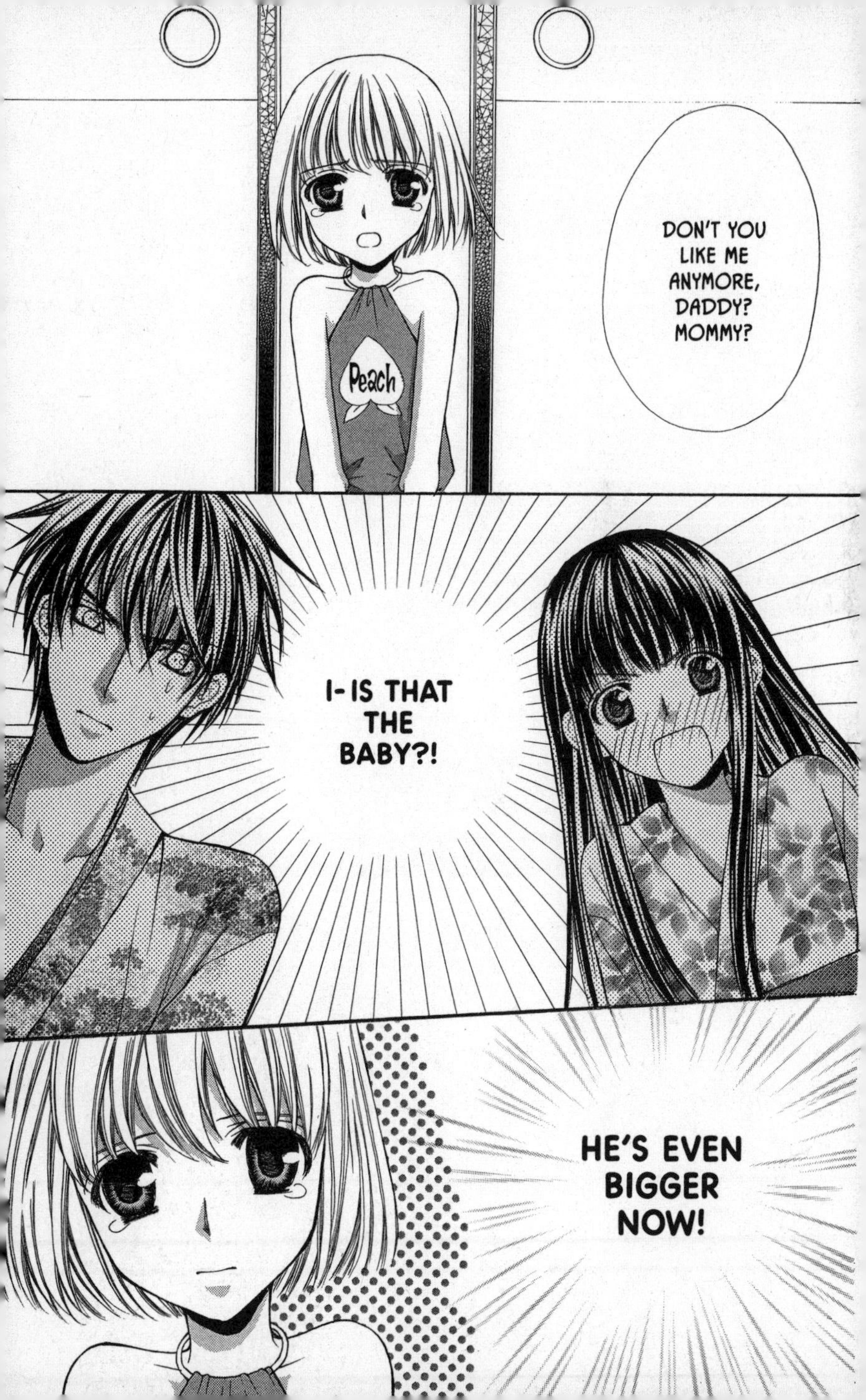

DON'T YOU LIKE ME ANYMORE, DADDY? MOMMY?
Peach
I- IS THAT THE BABY?!
HE'S EVEN BIGGER NOW!

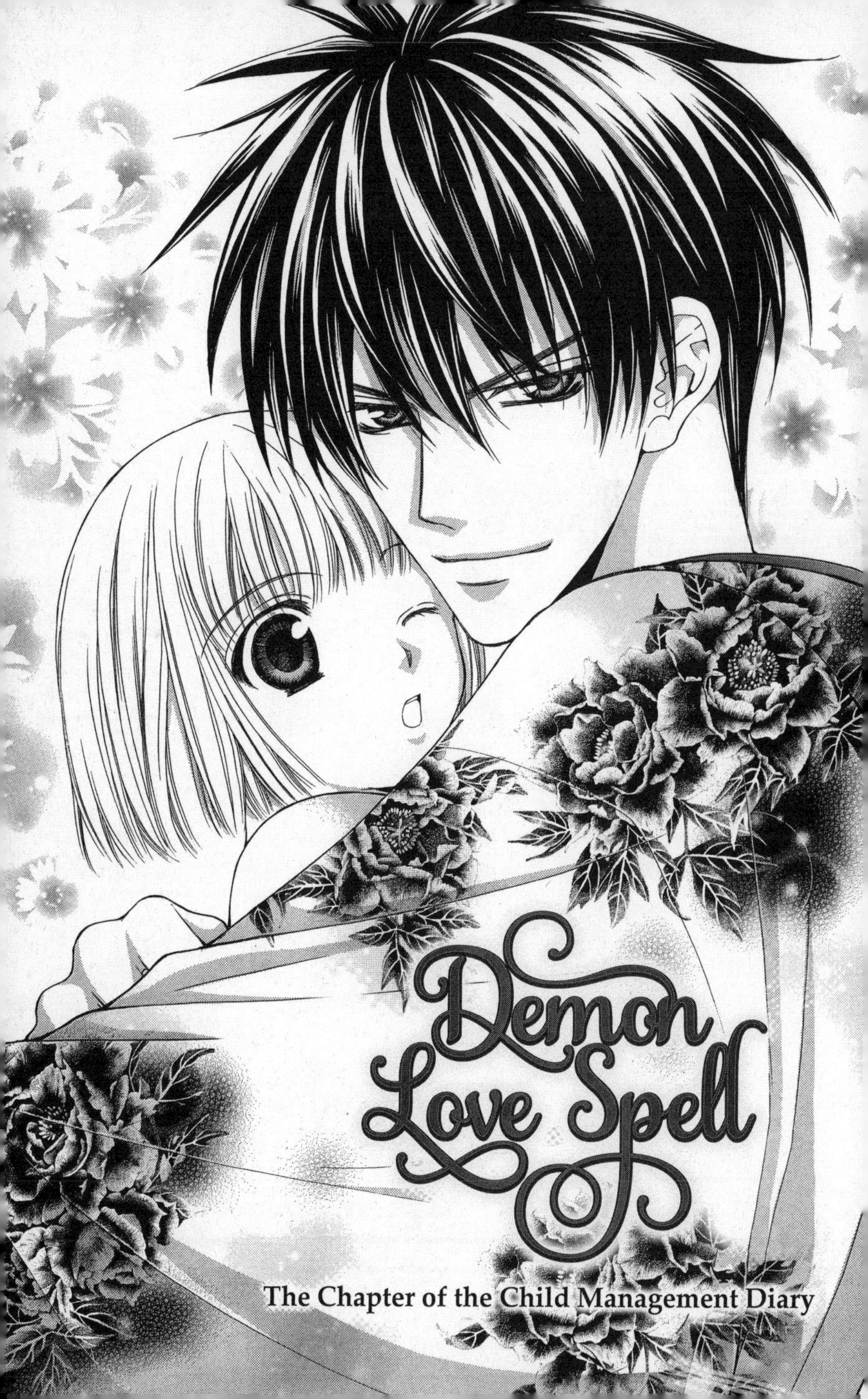
Demon Love Spell
The Chapter of the Child Management Diary

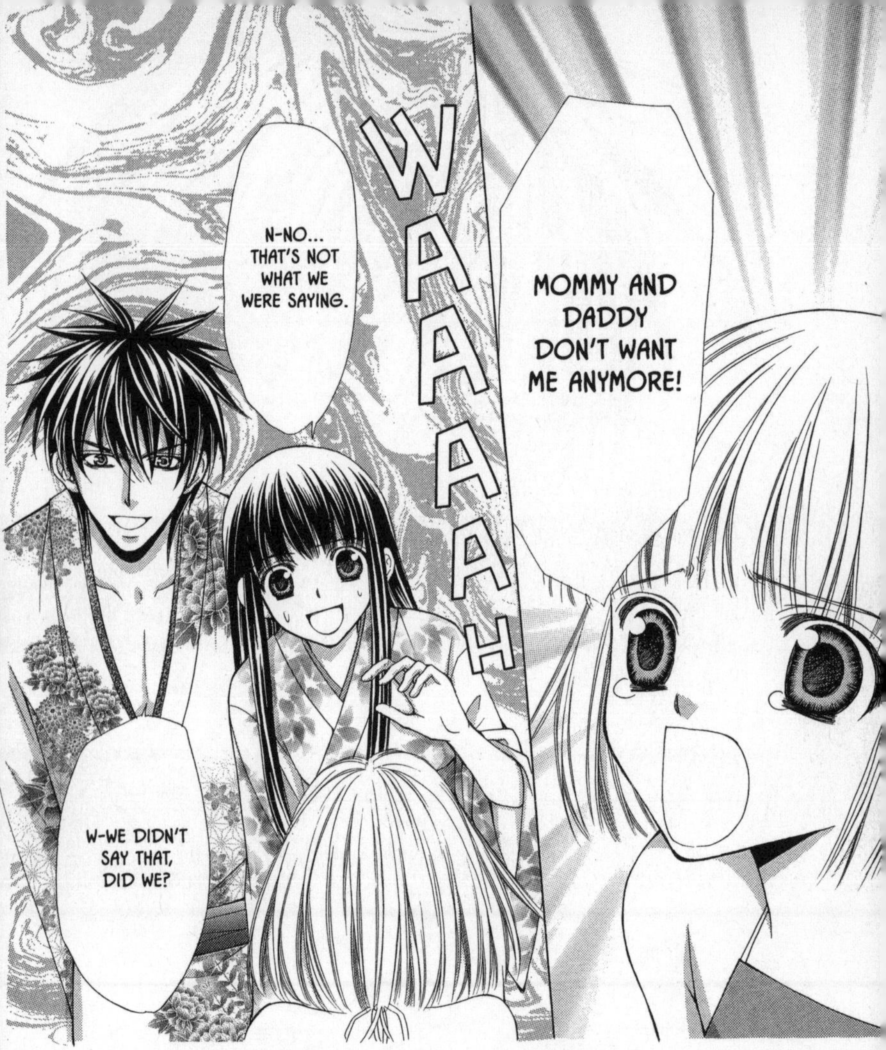
MOMMY AND DADDY DON'T WANT ME ANYMORE!
WAAAAAH
N-NO... THAT'S NOT WHAT WE WERE SAYING.
W-WE DIDN'T SAY THAT, DID WE?

Demon Love Spell

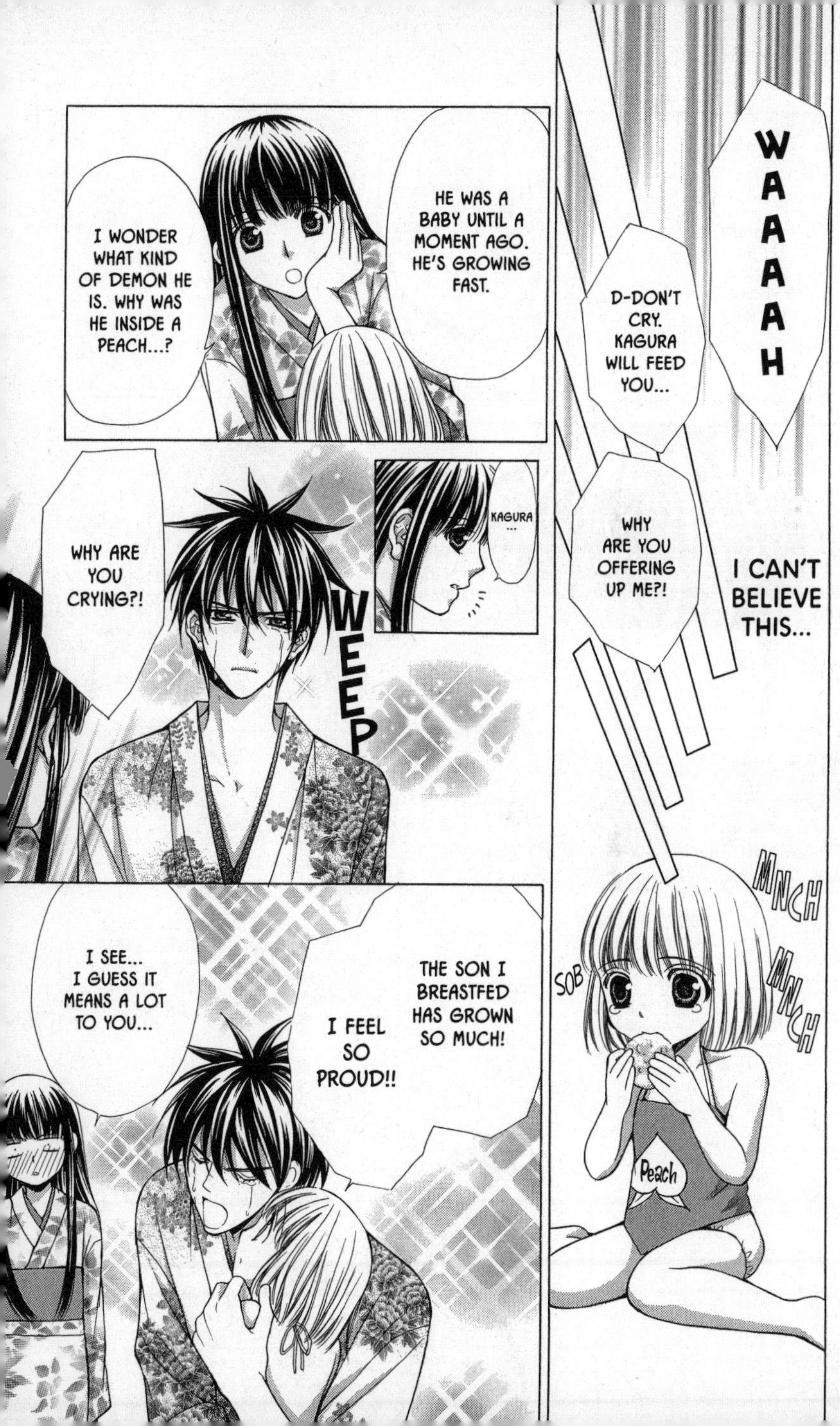
WAAAAH
D-DON'T CRY. KAGURA WILL FEED YOU...
WHY ARE YOU OFFERING UP ME?!
I CAN'T BELIEVE THIS...
MNCH
MNCH
SOB
Peach
HE WAS A BABY UNTIL A MOMENT AGO. HE'S GROWING FAST.
I WONDER WHAT KIND OF DEMON HE IS. WHY WAS HE INSIDE A PEACH...?
KAGURA...
WEEP
WHY ARE YOU CRYING?!
THE SON I BREASTFED HAS GROWN SO MUCH!
I FEEL SO PROUD!!
I SEE... I GUESS IT MEANS A LOT TO YOU...

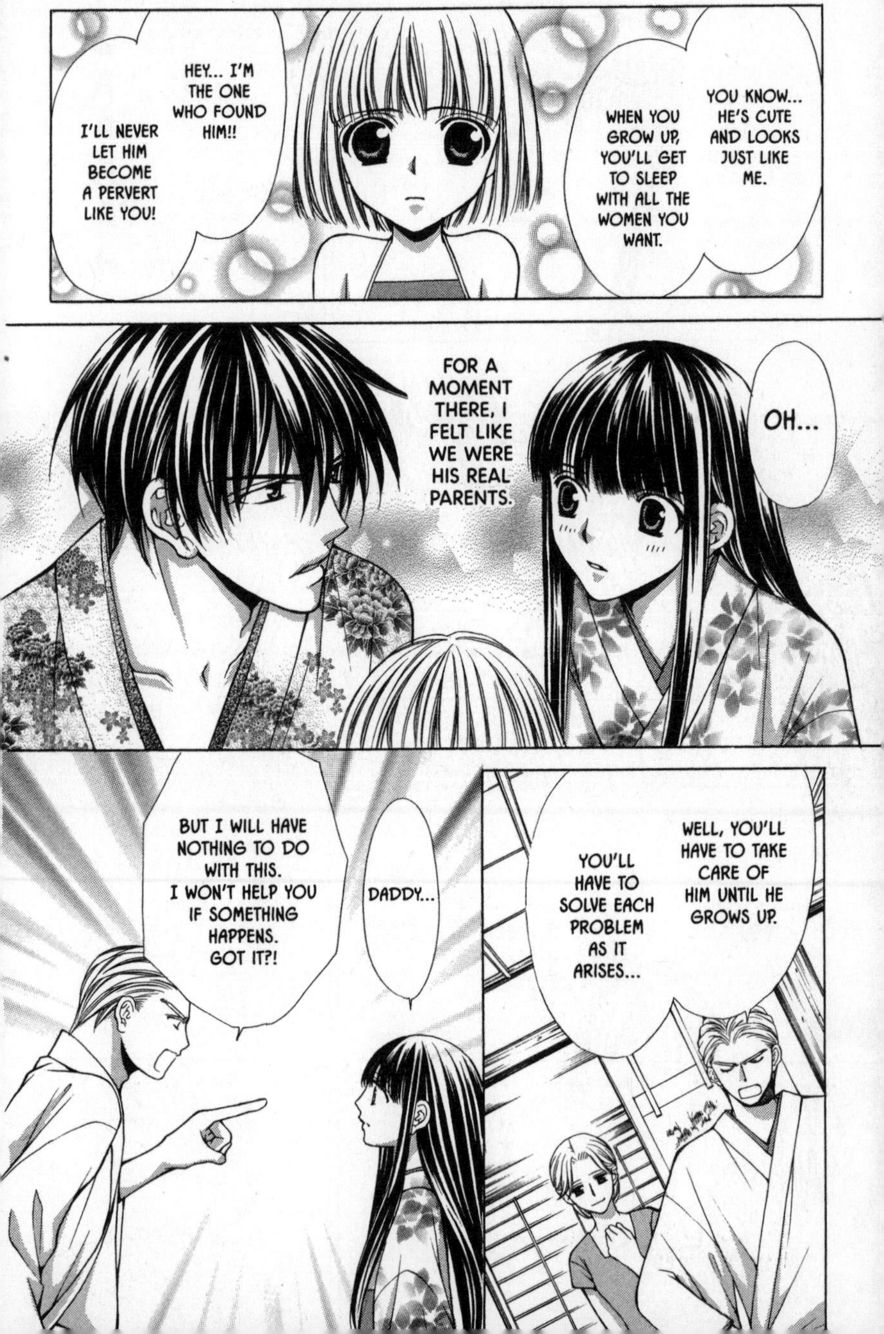
YOU KNOW... HE'S CUTE AND LOOKS JUST LIKE ME.
WHEN YOU GROW UP, YOU'LL GET TO SLEEP WITH ALL THE WOMEN YOU WANT.
HEY... I'M THE ONE WHO FOUND HIM!!
I'LL NEVER LET HIM BECOME A PERVERT LIKE YOU!
OH...
FOR A MOMENT THERE, I FELT LIKE WE WERE HIS REAL PARENTS.
WELL, YOU'LL HAVE TO TAKE CARE OF HIM UNTIL HE GROWS UP.
YOU'LL HAVE TO SOLVE EACH PROBLEM AS IT ARISES...
DADDY...
BUT I WILL HAVE NOTHING TO DO WITH THIS. I WON'T HELP YOU IF SOMETHING HAPPENS. GOT IT?!

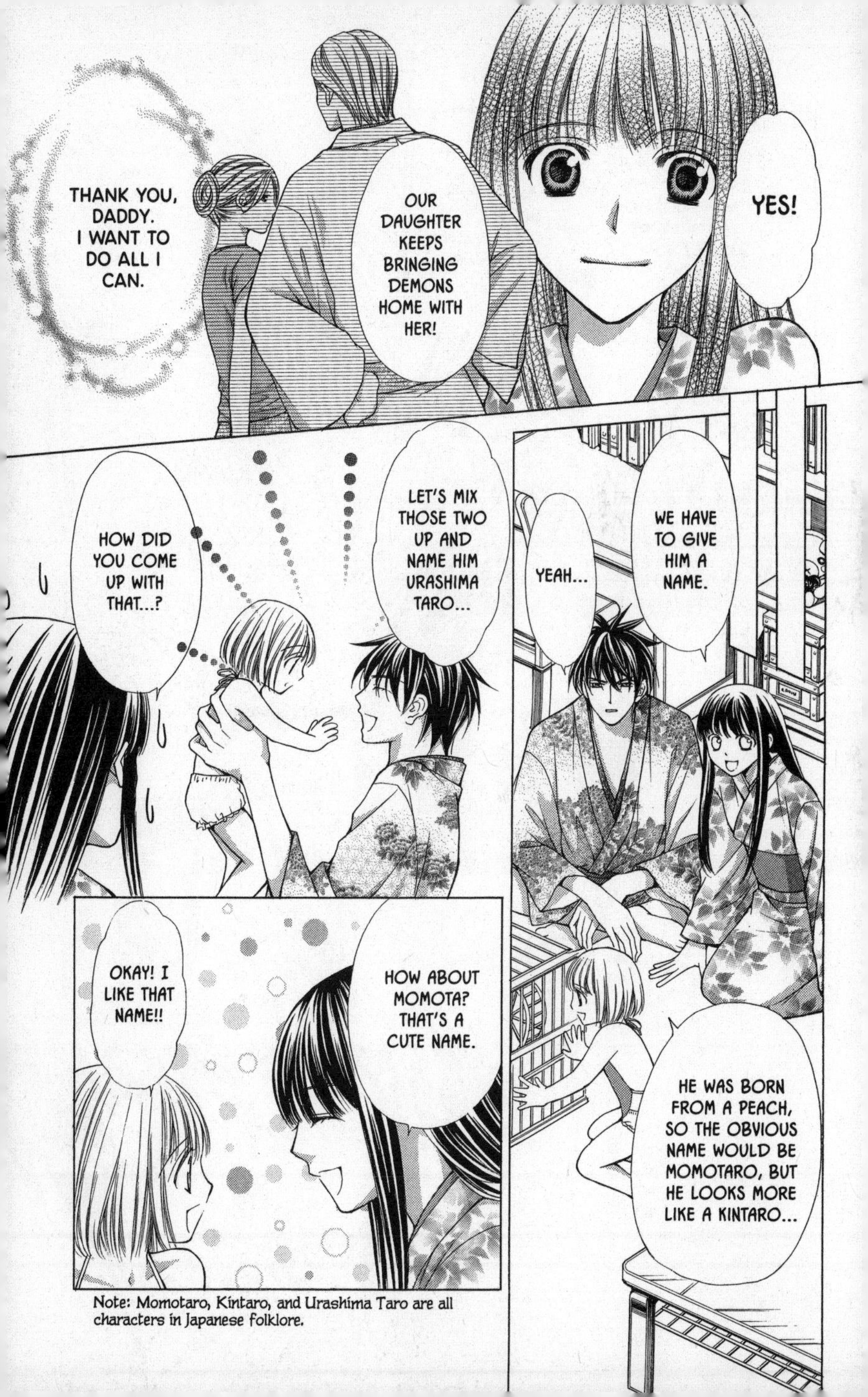
YES!
OUR DAUGHTER KEEPS BRINGING DEMONS HOME WITH HER!
THANK YOU, DADDY. I WANT TO DO ALL I CAN.
WE HAVE TO GIVE HIM A NAME.
YEAH...
HE WAS BORN FROM A PEACH, SO THE OBVIOUS NAME WOULD BE MOMOTARO, BUT HE LOOKS MORE LIKE A KINTARO...
LET'S MIX THOSE TWO UP AND NAME HIM URASHIMA TARO...
HOW DID YOU COME UP WITH THAT...?
HOW ABOUT MOMOTA? THAT'S A CUTE NAME.
OKAY! I LIKE THAT NAME!!

Note: Momotaro, Kintaro, and Urashima Taro are all characters in Japanese folklore.

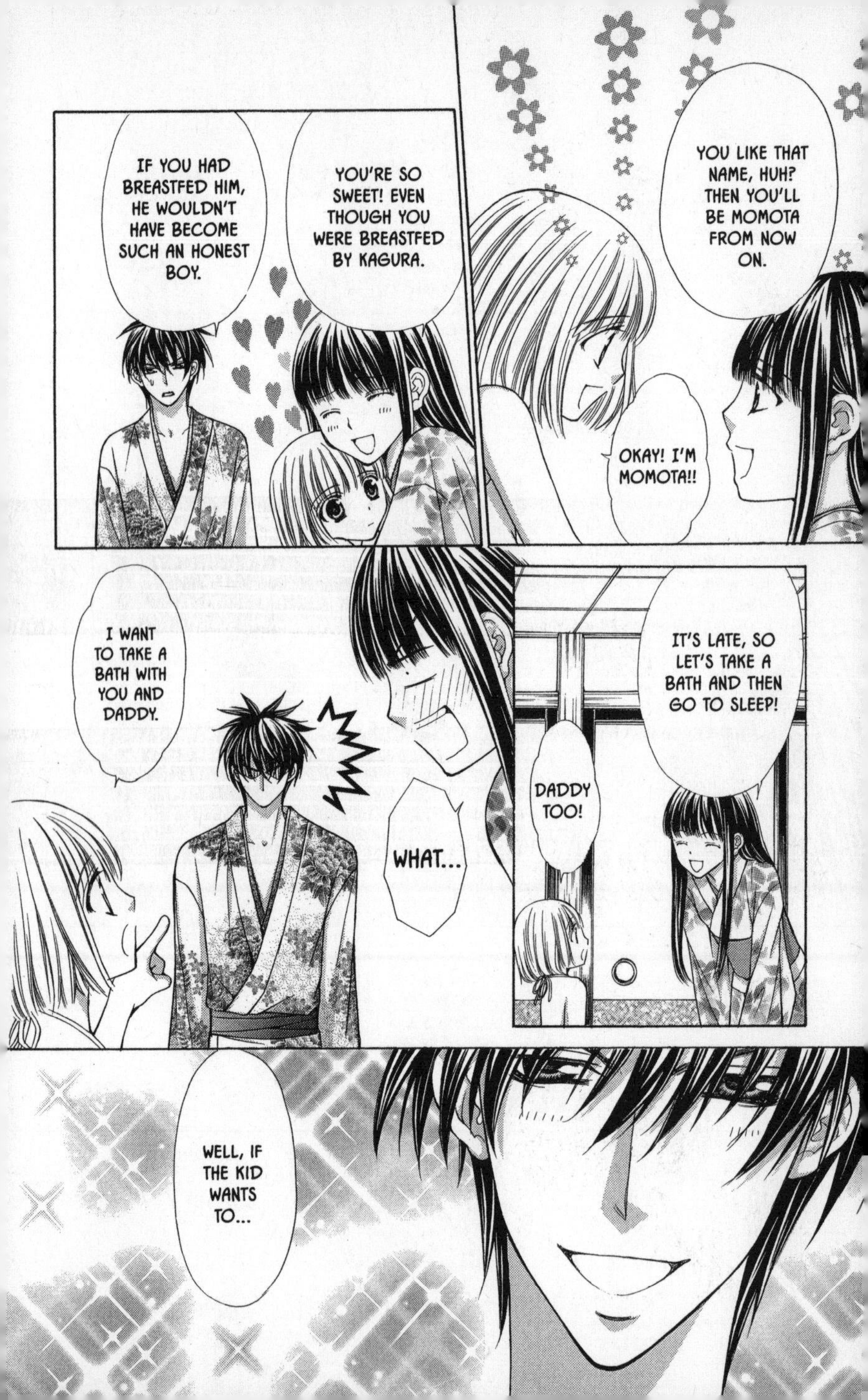
YOU LIKE THAT NAME, HUH? THEN YOU'LL BE MOMOTA FROM NOW ON.
OKAY! I'M MOMOTA!!
YOU'RE SO SWEET! EVEN THOUGH YOU WERE BREASTFED BY KAGURA.
IF YOU HAD BREASTFED HIM, HE WOULDN'T HAVE BECOME SUCH AN HONEST BOY.
IT'S LATE, SO LET'S TAKE A BATH AND THEN GO TO SLEEP!
DADDY TOO!
I WANT TO TAKE A BATH WITH YOU AND DADDY.
WHAT...
WELL, IF THE KID WANTS TO...

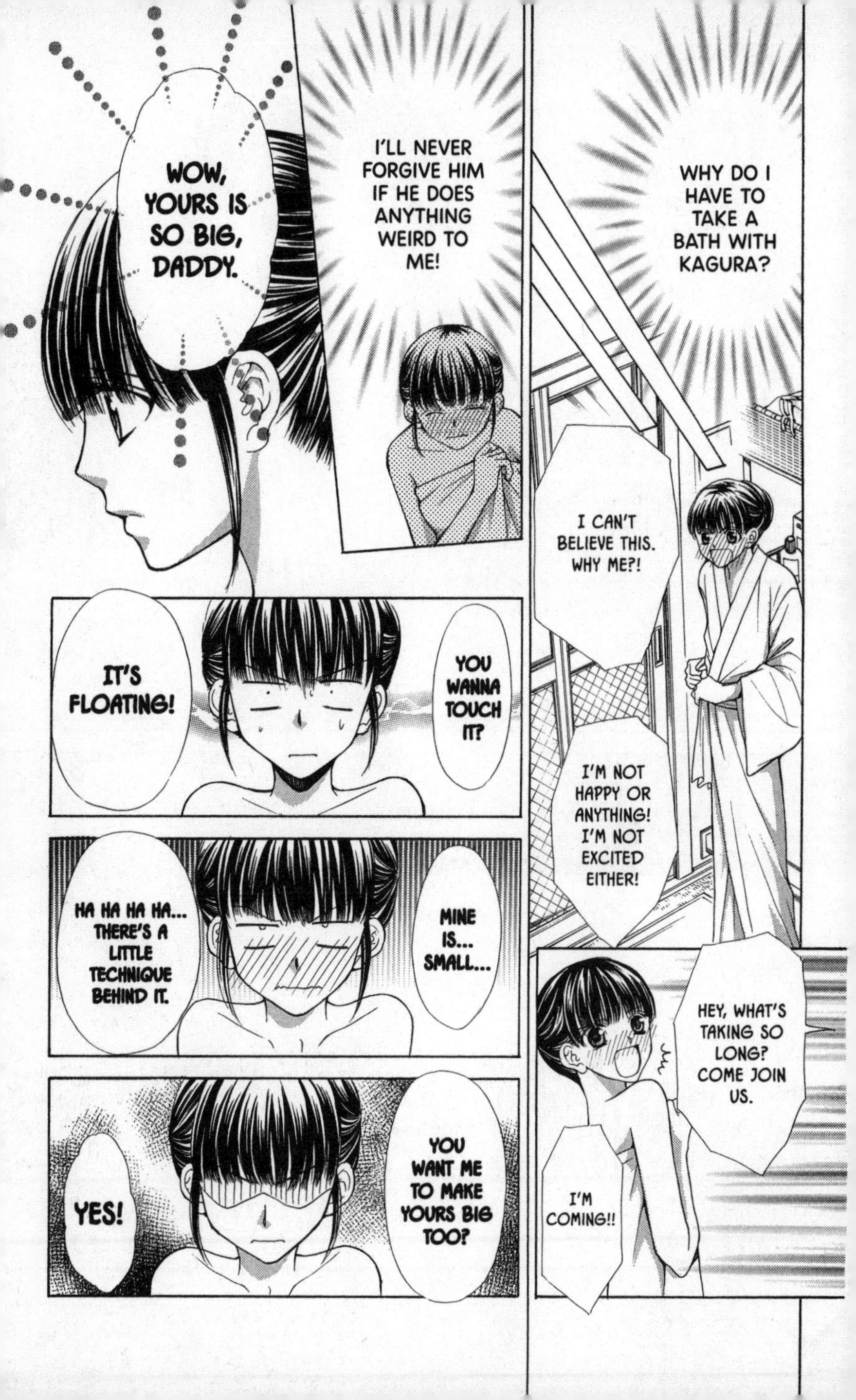
WHY DO I HAVE TO TAKE A BATH WITH KAGURA?
I CAN'T BELIEVE THIS. WHY ME?!
I'M NOT HAPPY OR ANYTHING! I'M NOT EXCITED EITHER!
HEY, WHAT'S TAKING SO LONG? COME JOIN US.
I'M COMING!!
I'LL NEVER FORGIVE HIM IF HE DOES ANYTHING WEIRD TO ME!
WOW, YOURS IS SO BIG, DADDY.
YOU WANNA TOUCH IT?
IT'S FLOATING!
MINE IS... SMALL...
HA HA HA HA... THERE'S A LITTLE TECHNIQUE BEHIND IT.
YOU WANT ME TO MAKE YOURS BIG TOO?
YES!

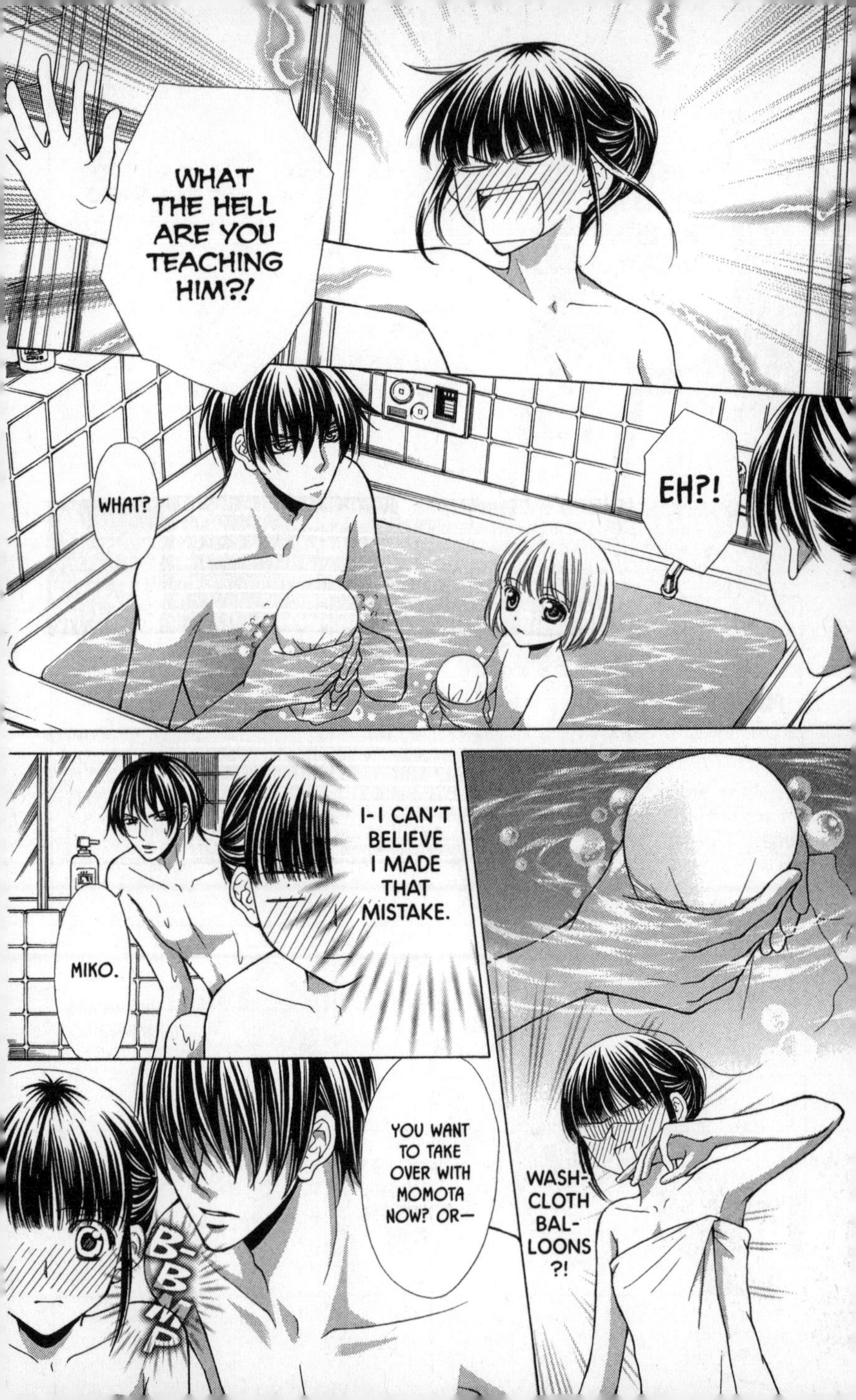
WHAT THE HELL ARE YOU TEACHING HIM?!
EH?!
WHAT?
I-I CAN'T BELIEVE I MADE THAT MISTAKE.
MIKO.
WASH-CLOTH BAL-LOONS?!
YOU WANT TO TAKE OVER WITH MOMOTA NOW? OR—
B-BMP

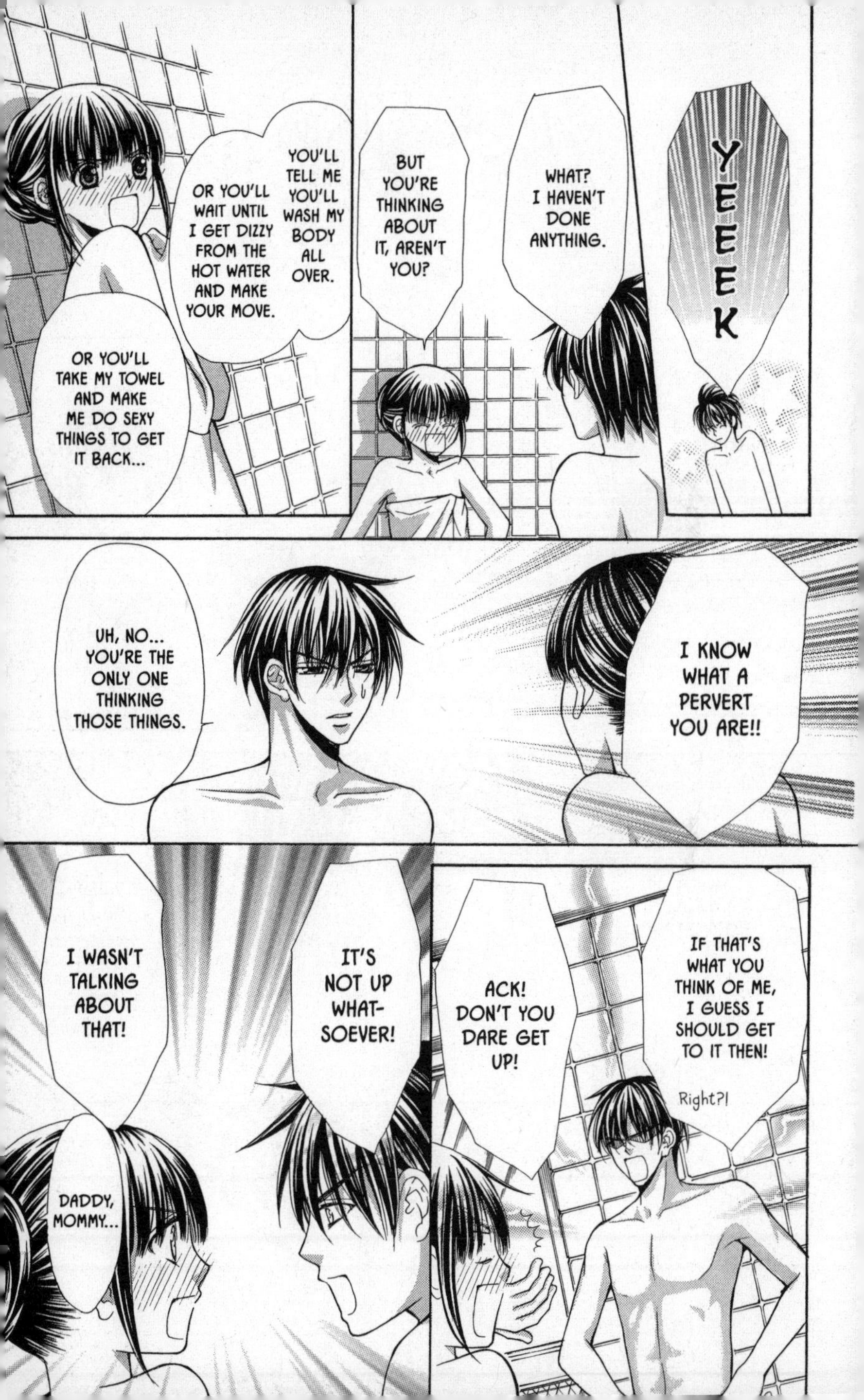
YEEEK
WHAT? I HAVEN'T DONE ANYTHING.
BUT YOU'RE THINKING ABOUT IT, AREN'T YOU?
YOU'LL TELL ME YOU'LL WASH MY BODY ALL OVER.
OR YOU'LL WAIT UNTIL I GET DIZZY FROM THE HOT WATER AND MAKE YOUR MOVE.
OR YOU'LL TAKE MY TOWEL AND MAKE ME DO SEXY THINGS TO GET IT BACK...
I KNOW WHAT A PERVERT YOU ARE!!
UH, NO... YOU'RE THE ONLY ONE THINKING THOSE THINGS.
IF THAT'S WHAT YOU THINK OF ME, I GUESS I SHOULD GET TO IT THEN!
Right?!
ACK! DON'T YOU DARE GET UP!
IT'S NOT UP WHAT-SOEVER!
I WASN'T TALKING ABOUT THAT!
DADDY, MOMMY...

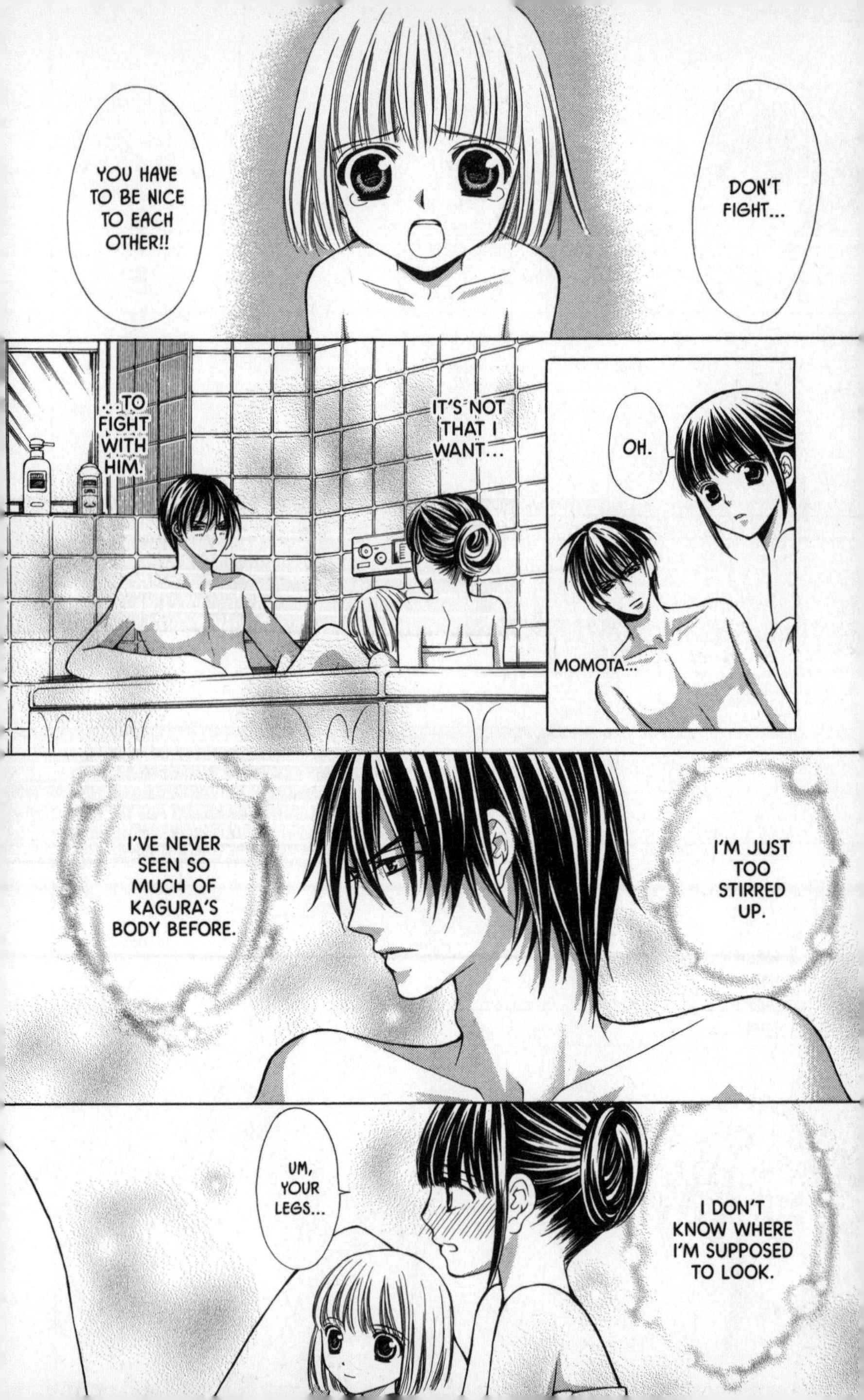
DON'T FIGHT...
YOU HAVE TO BE NICE TO EACH OTHER!!
OH.
MOMOTA...
IT'S NOT THAT I WANT...
...TO FIGHT WITH HIM.
I'M JUST TOO STIRRED UP.
I'VE NEVER SEEN SO MUCH OF KAGURA'S BODY BEFORE.
I DON'T KNOW WHERE I'M SUPPOSED TO LOOK.
UM, YOUR LEGS...

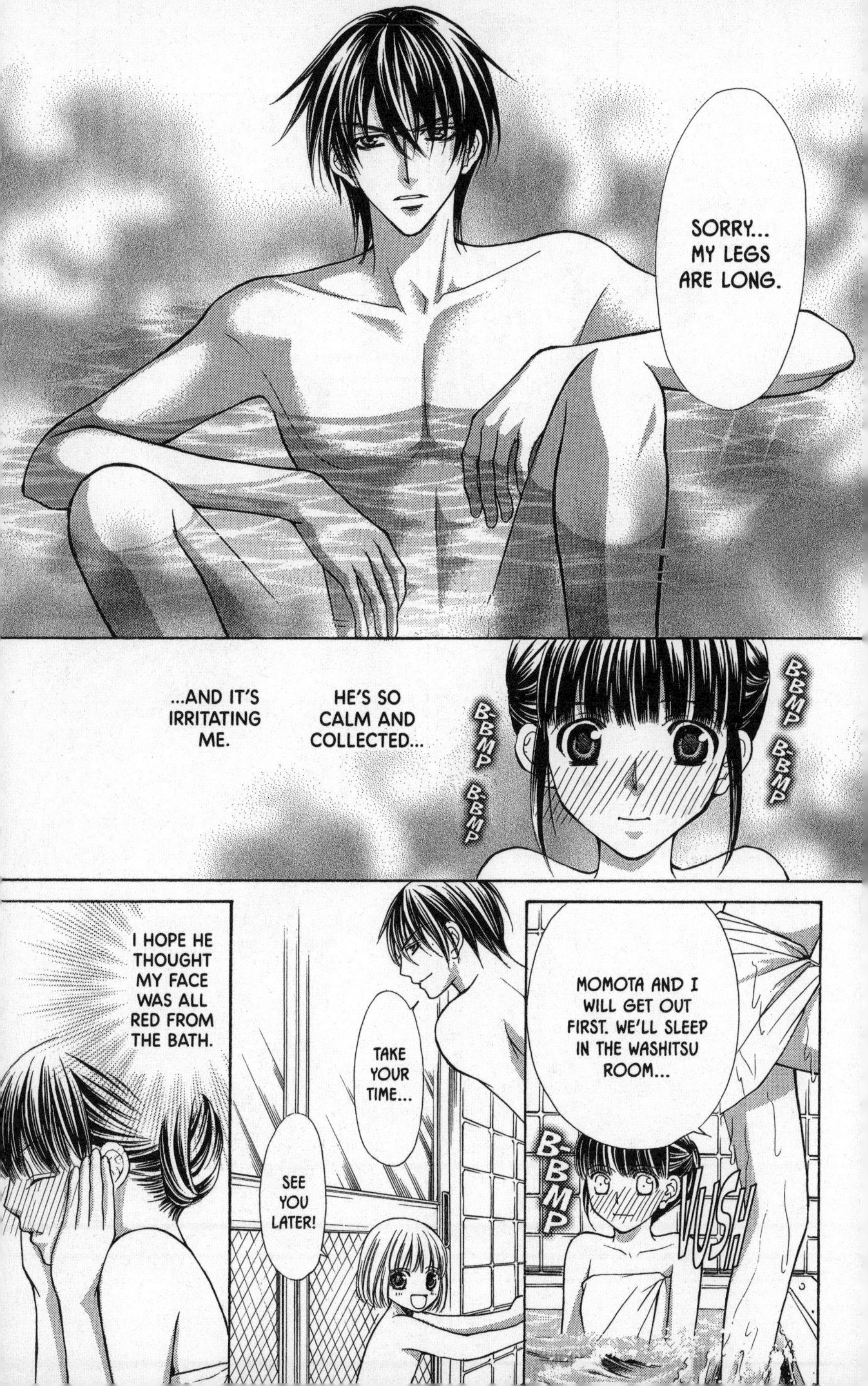
SORRY... MY LEGS ARE LONG.
B-BMP B-BMP
HE'S SO CALM AND COLLECTED...
B-BMP B-BMP
...AND IT'S IRRITATING ME.
MOMOTA AND I WILL GET OUT FIRST. WE'LL SLEEP IN THE WASHITSU ROOM...
VUSH
B-BMP
TAKE YOUR TIME...
SEE YOU LATER!
I HOPE HE THOUGHT MY FACE WAS ALL RED FROM THE BATH.

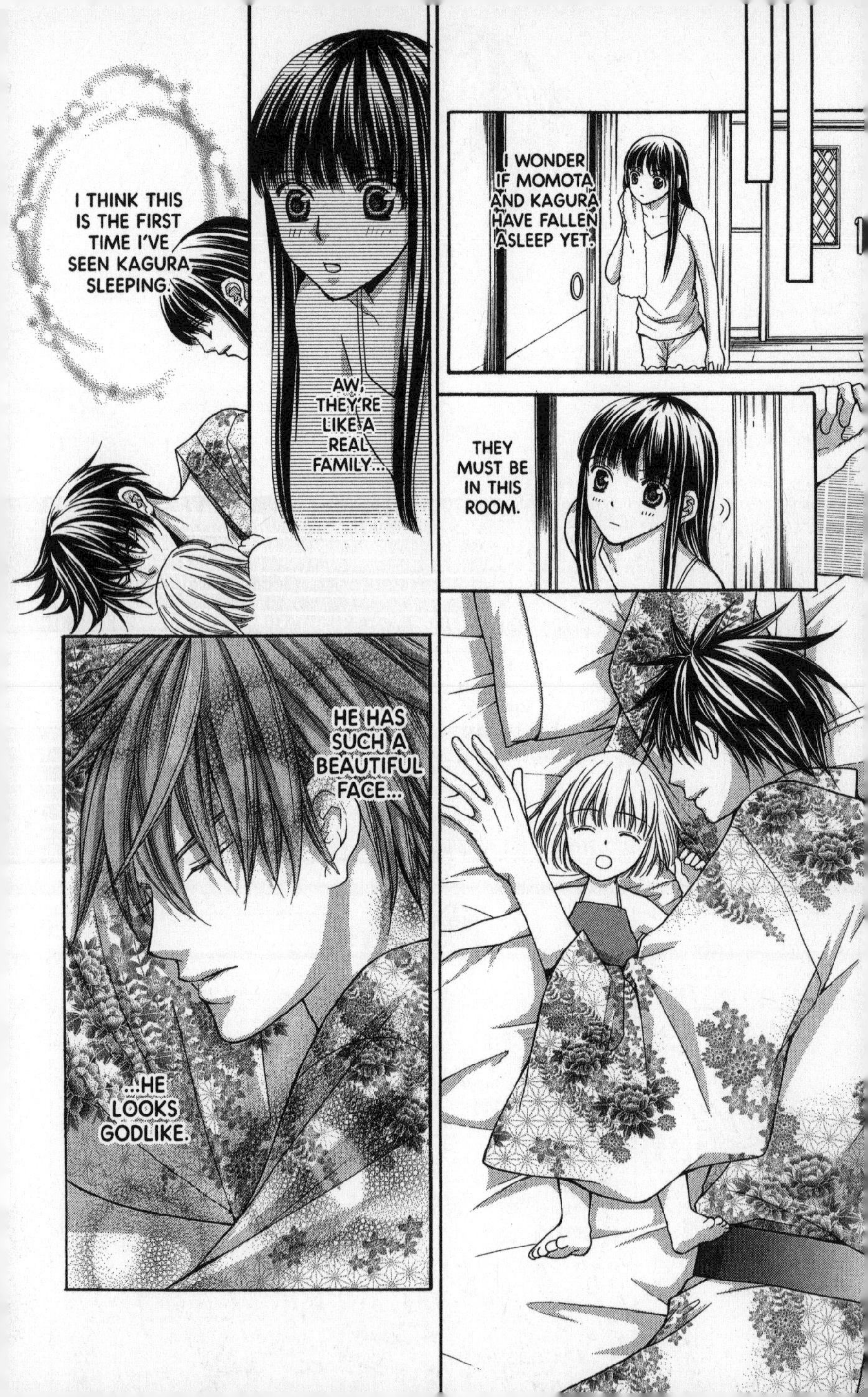

I WONDER IF MOMOTA AND KAGURA HAVE FALLEN ASLEEP YET.
THEY MUST BE IN THIS ROOM.
AW, THEY'RE LIKE A REAL FAMILY...
I THINK THIS IS THE FIRST TIME I'VE SEEN KAGURA SLEEPING.
HE HAS SUCH A BEAUTIFUL FACE...
...HE LOOKS GODLIKE.

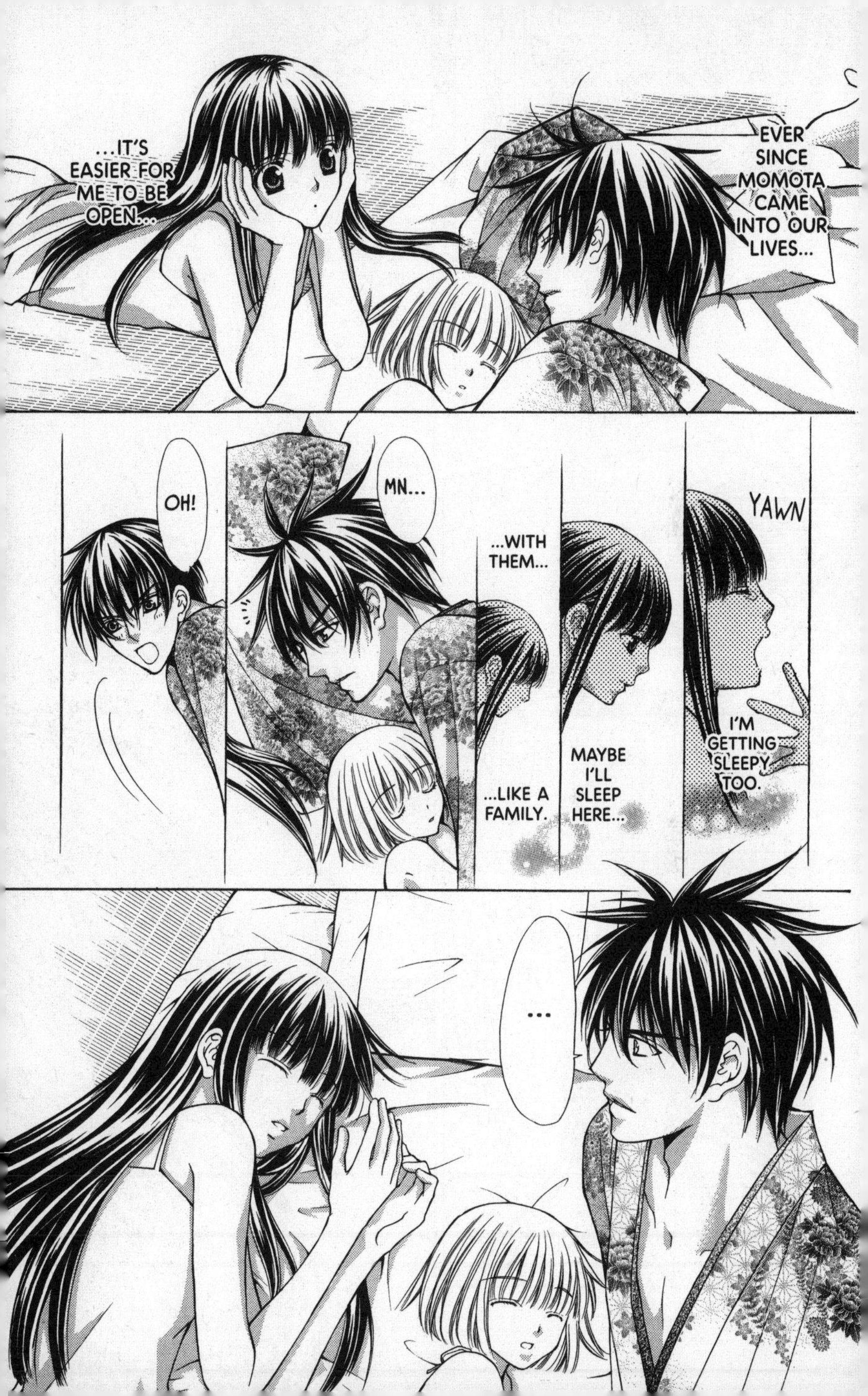
EVER SINCE MOMOTA CAME INTO OUR LIVES...
...IT'S EASIER FOR ME TO BE OPEN...
YAWN
I'M GETTING SLEEPY TOO.
MAYBE I'LL SLEEP HERE...
...WITH THEM...
...LIKE A FAMILY.
MN...
OH!
...

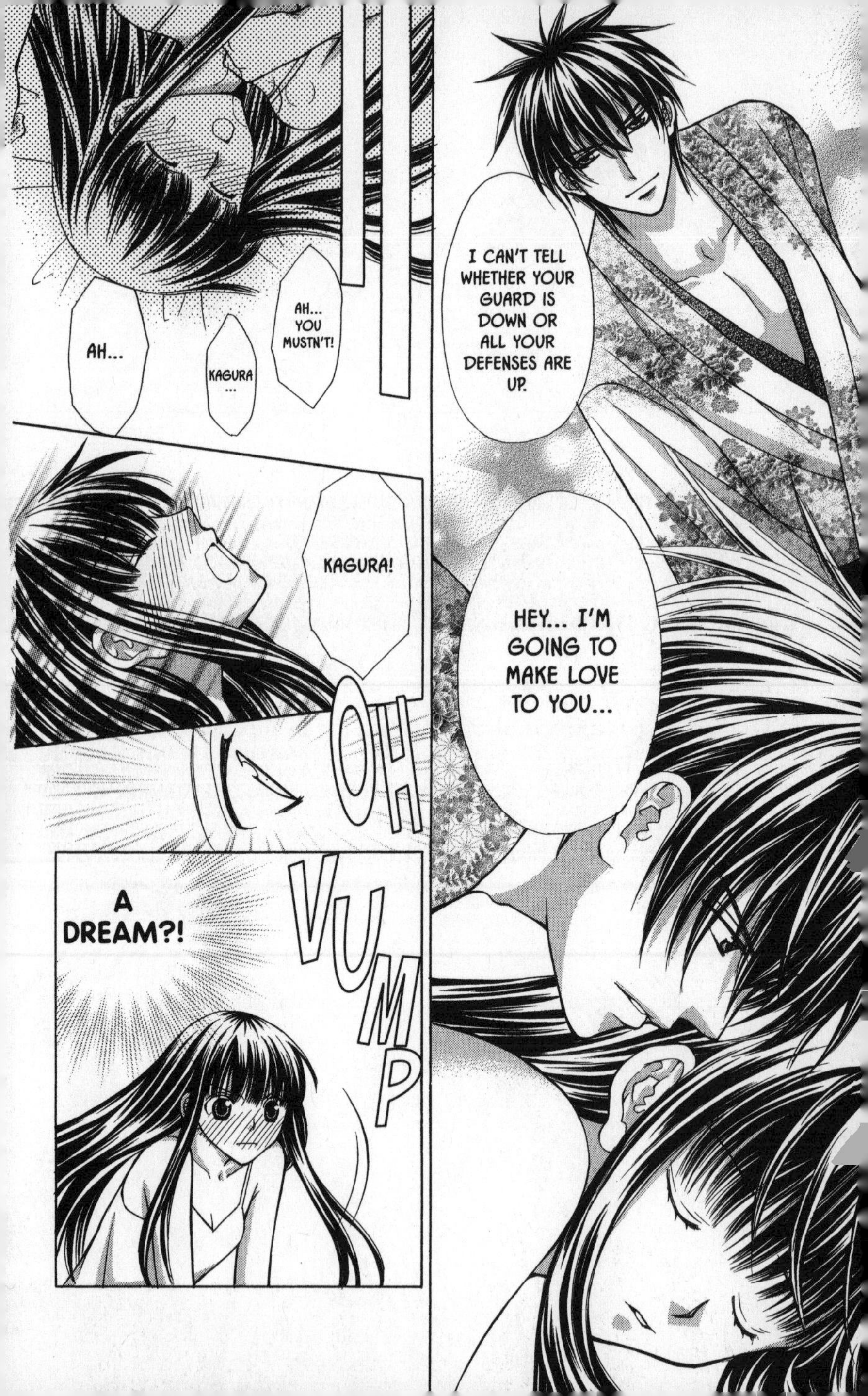
I CAN'T TELL WHETHER YOUR GUARD IS DOWN OR ALL YOUR DEFENSES ARE UP.
HEY... I'M GOING TO MAKE LOVE TO YOU...
AH... YOU MUSTN'T!
KAGURA...
AH...
KAGURA!
OH
VUMP
A DREAM?!

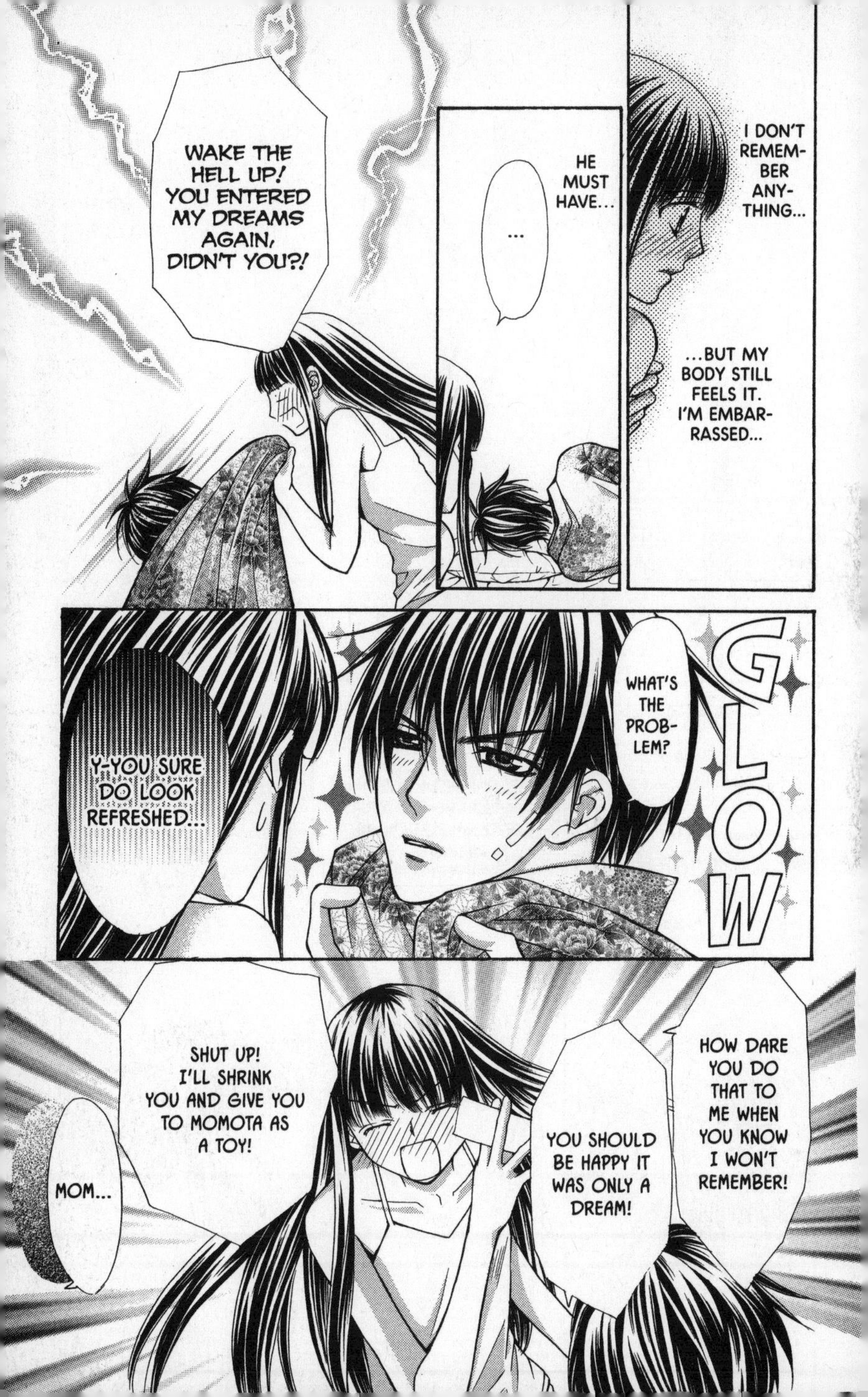
I DON'T REMEMBER ANYTHING...
...BUT MY BODY STILL FEELS IT. I'M EMBARRASSED...
HE MUST HAVE...
...
WAKE THE HELL UP! YOU ENTERED MY DREAMS AGAIN, DIDN'T YOU?!
GLOW
WHAT'S THE PROBLEM?
Y-YOU SURE DO LOOK REFRESHED...
HOW DARE YOU DO THAT TO ME WHEN YOU KNOW I WON'T REMEMBER!
YOU SHOULD BE HAPPY IT WAS ONLY A DREAM!
SHUT UP! I'LL SHRINK YOU AND GIVE YOU TO MOMOTA AS A TOY!
MOM...

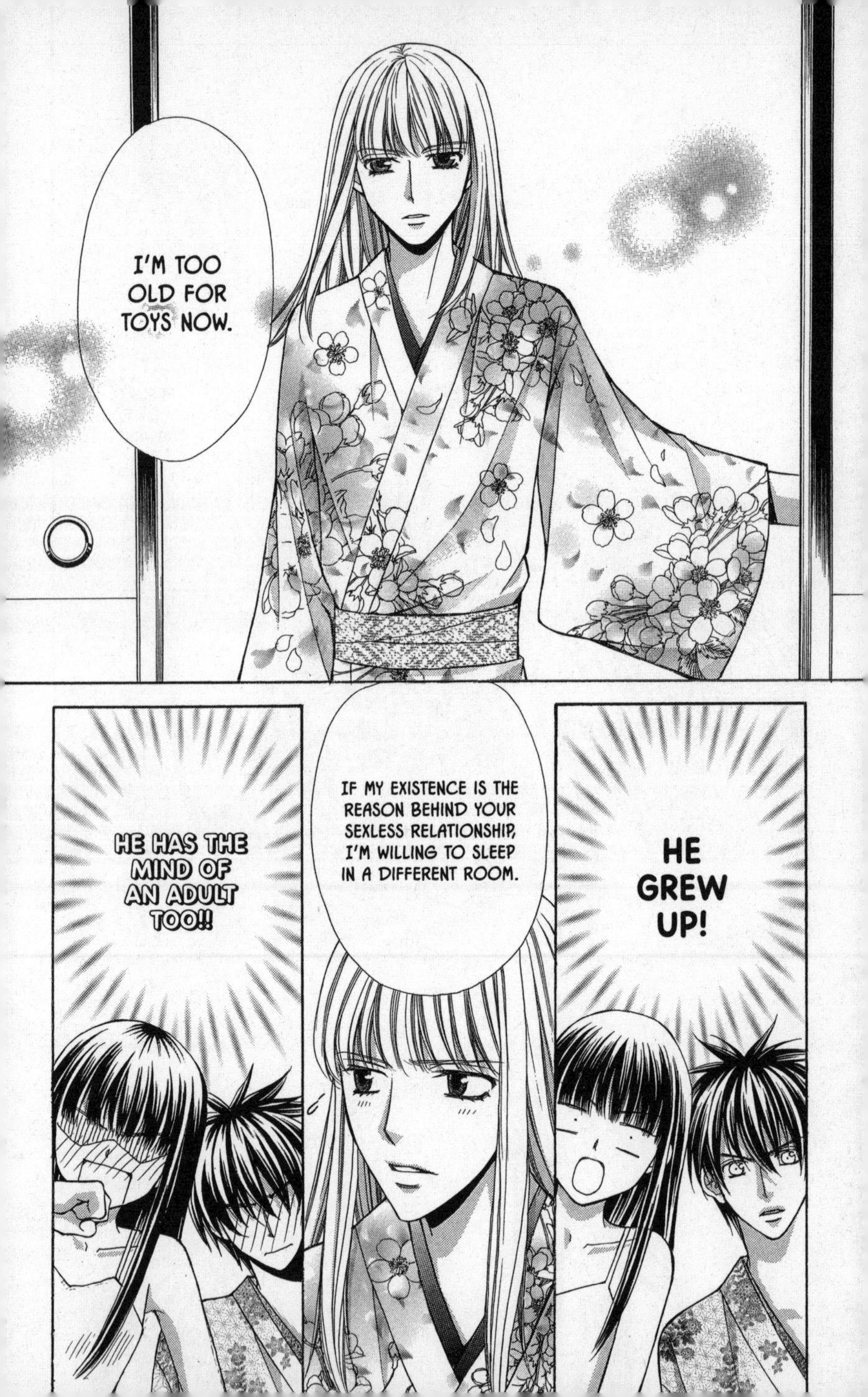
I'M TOO OLD FOR TOYS NOW.
HE GREW UP!
IF MY EXISTENCE IS THE REASON BEHIND YOUR SEXLESS RELATIONSHIP, I'M WILLING TO SLEEP IN A DIFFERENT ROOM.
HE HAS THE MIND OF AN ADULT TOO!!

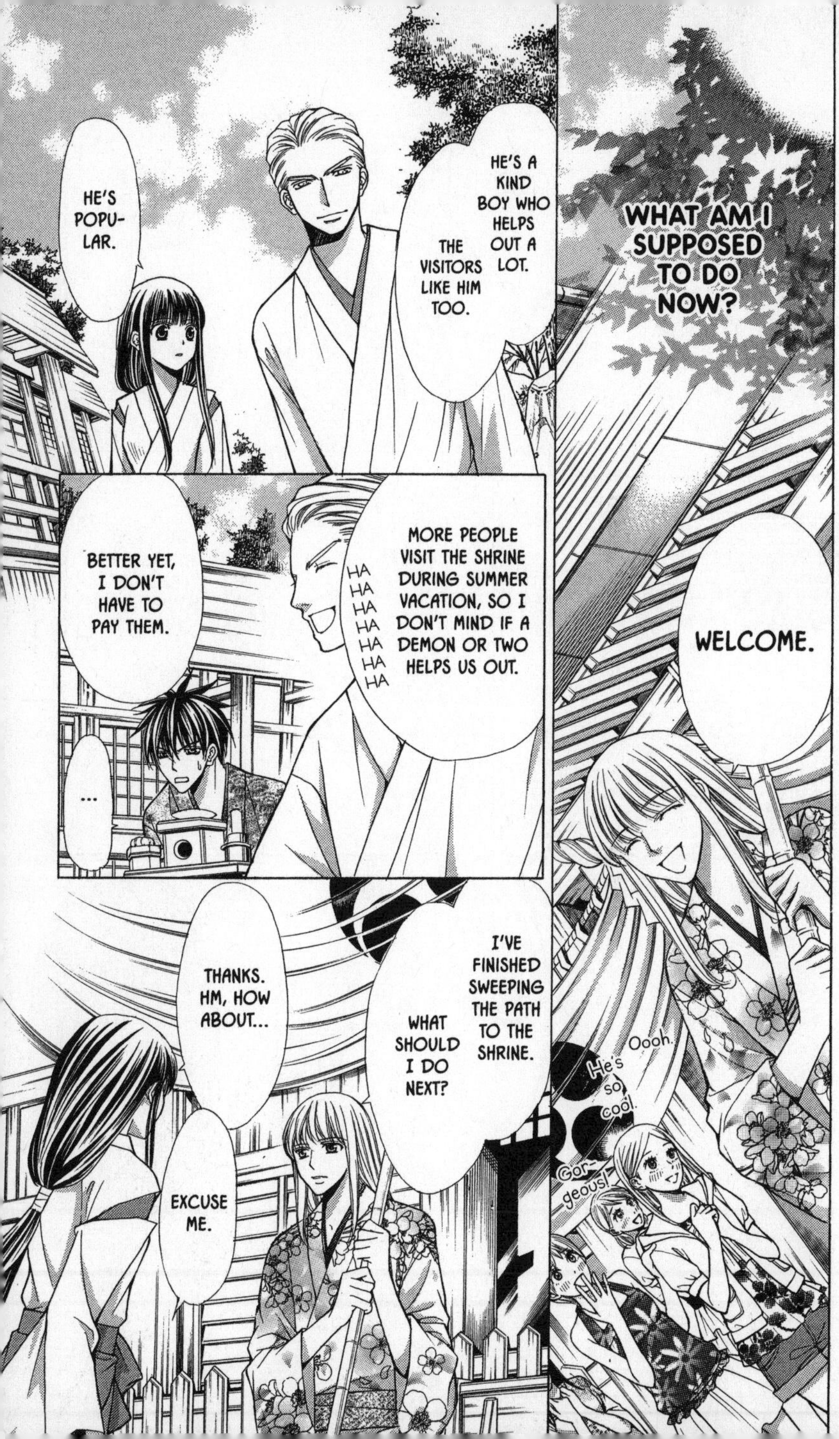
WHAT AM I SUPPOSED TO DO NOW?
WELCOME.
Oooh.
He's so cool.
Gorgeous!
HE'S A KIND BOY WHO HELPS OUT A LOT.
THE VISITORS LIKE HIM TOO.
HE'S POPU-LAR.
MORE PEOPLE VISIT THE SHRINE DURING SUMMER VACATION, SO I DON'T MIND IF A DEMON OR TWO HELPS US OUT.
HA HA HA HA HA HA HA
BETTER YET, I DON'T HAVE TO PAY THEM.
...
I'VE FINISHED SWEEPING THE PATH TO THE SHRINE.
WHAT SHOULD I DO NEXT?
THANKS. HM, HOW ABOUT...
EXCUSE ME.

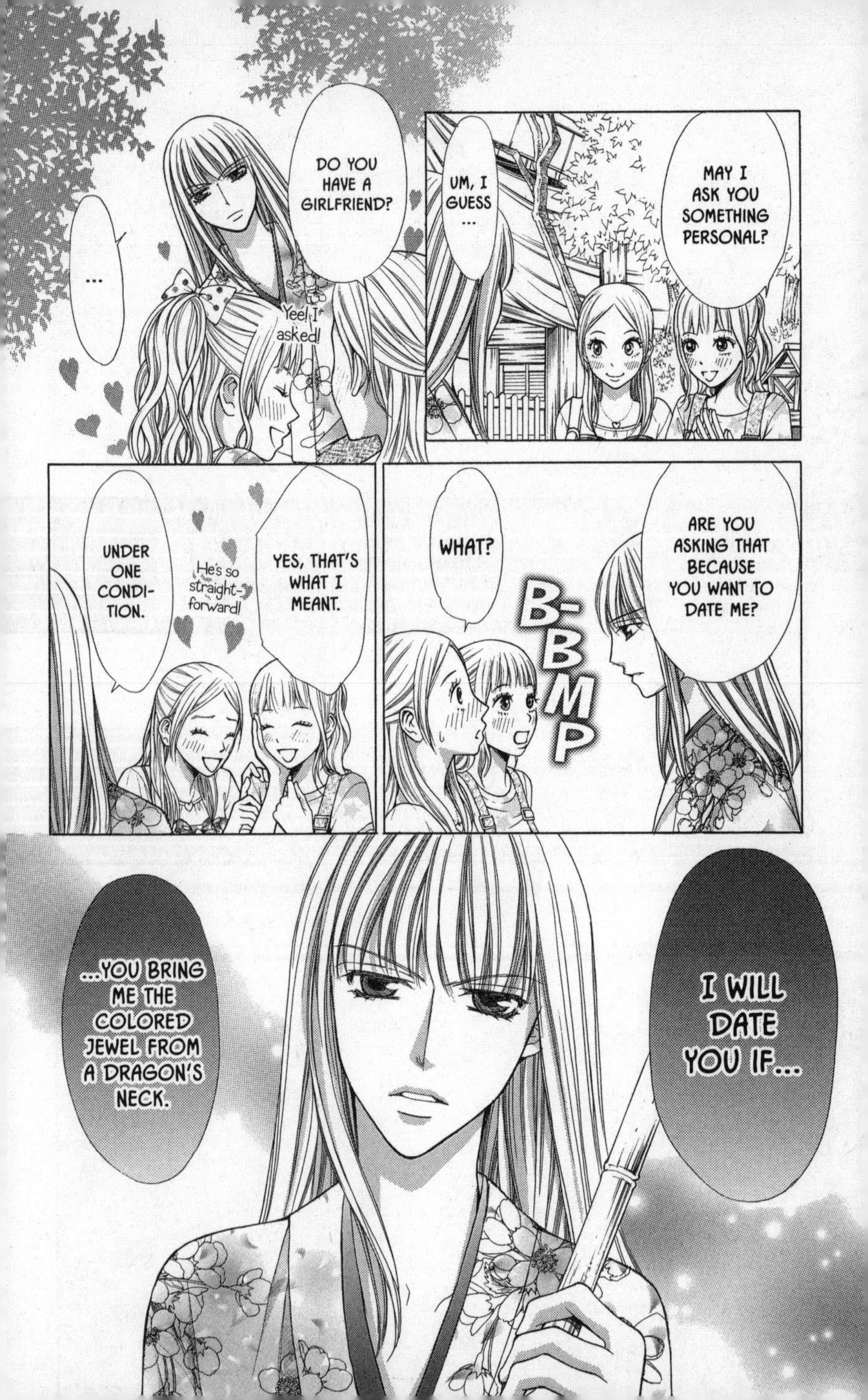
MAY I ASK YOU SOMETHING PERSONAL?
UM, I GUESS ...
DO YOU HAVE A GIRLFRIEND?
Yee! I asked!
...
ARE YOU ASKING THAT BECAUSE YOU WANT TO DATE ME?
WHAT?
B-BMP
YES, THAT'S WHAT I MEANT.
He's so straight-forward!
UNDER ONE CONDI-TION.
I WILL DATE YOU IF...
...YOU BRING ME THE COLORED JEWEL FROM A DRAGON'S NECK.

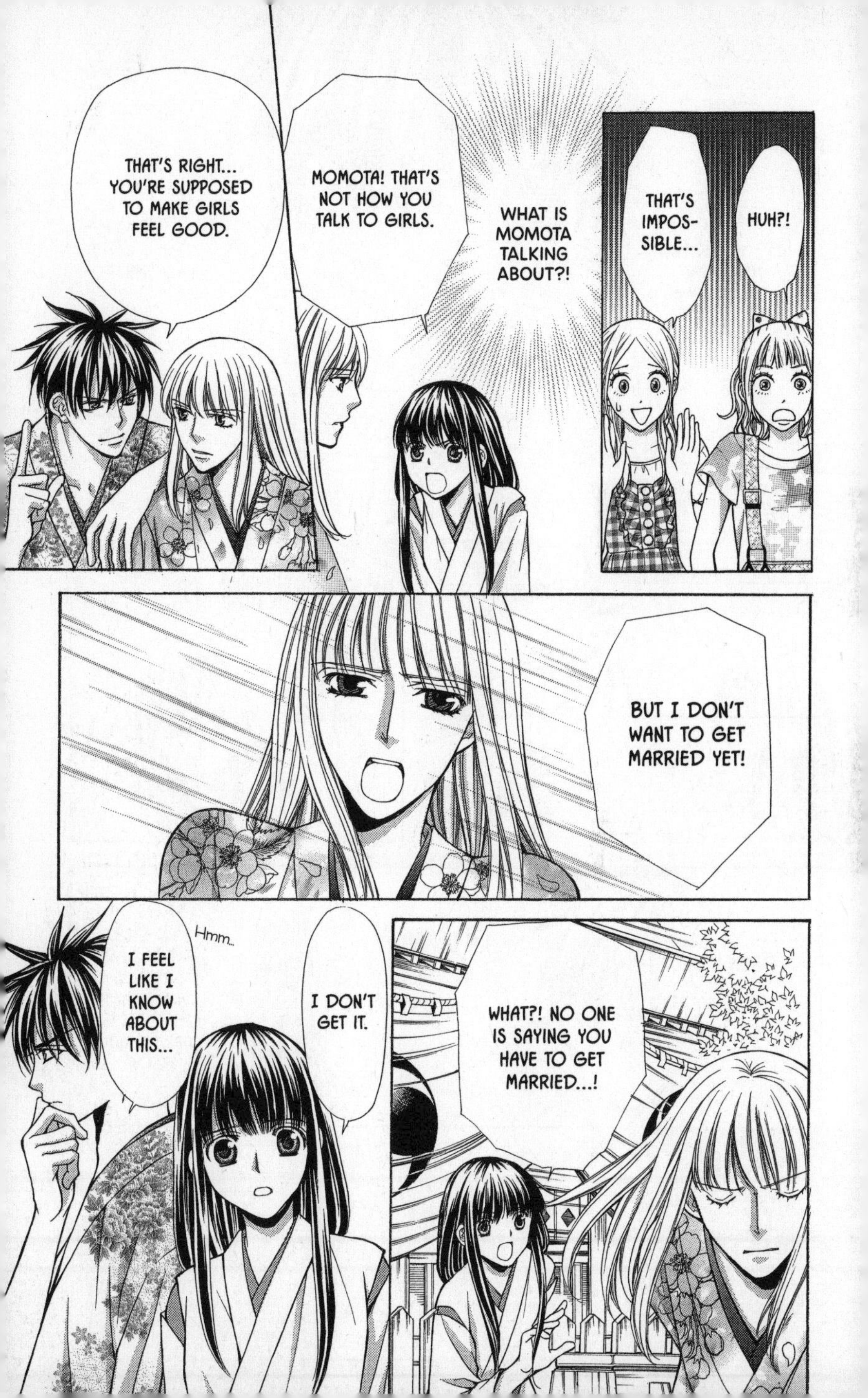
HUH?!
THAT'S IMPOSSIBLE...
WHAT IS MOMOTA TALKING ABOUT?!
MOMOTA! THAT'S NOT HOW YOU TALK TO GIRLS.
THAT'S RIGHT... YOU'RE SUPPOSED TO MAKE GIRLS FEEL GOOD.
BUT I DON'T WANT TO GET MARRIED YET!
WHAT?! NO ONE IS SAYING YOU HAVE TO GET MARRIED...!
I DON'T GET IT.
Hmm..
I FEEL LIKE I KNOW ABOUT THIS...

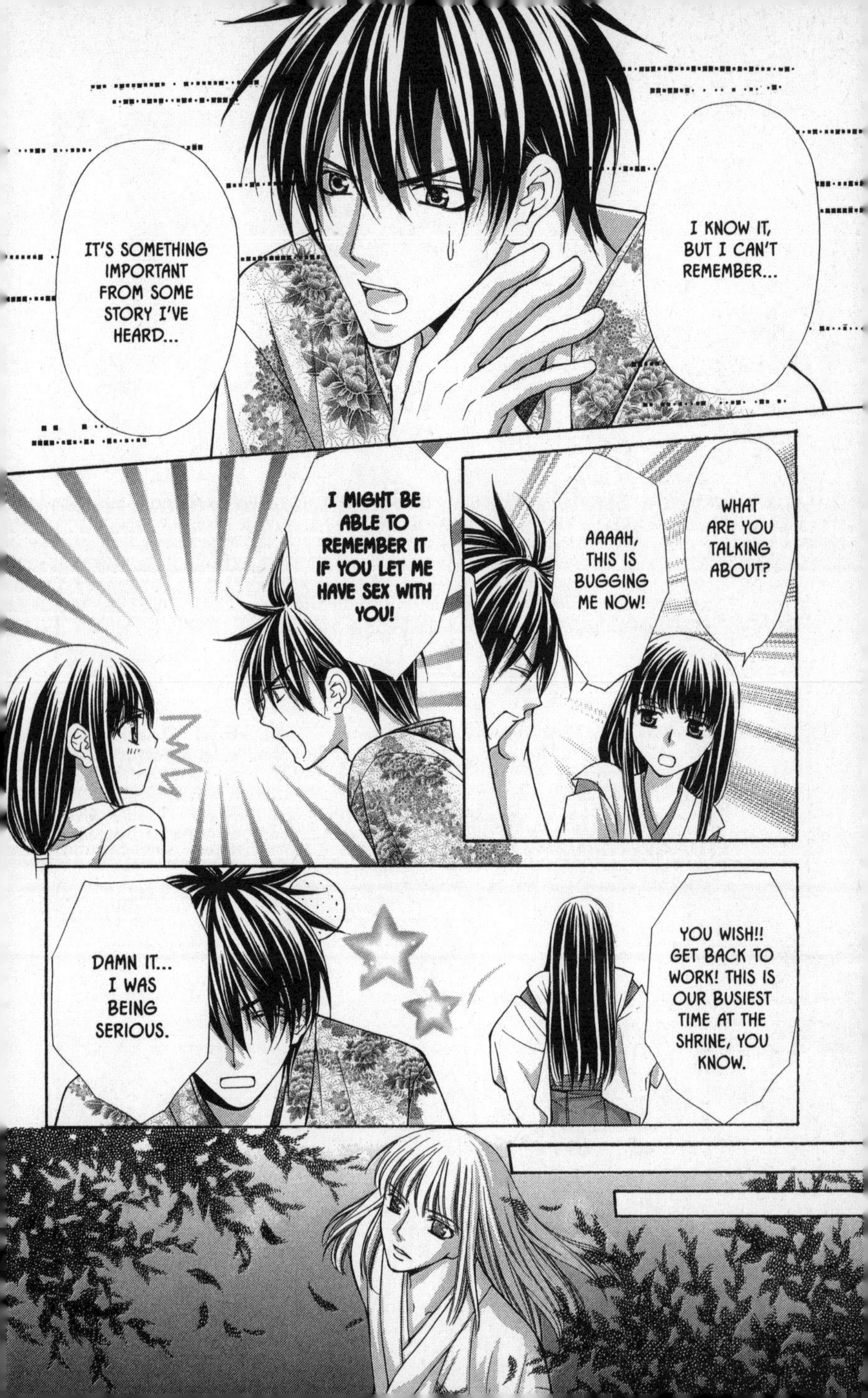
I KNOW IT, BUT I CAN'T REMEMBER...
IT'S SOMETHING IMPORTANT FROM SOME STORY I'VE HEARD...
WHAT ARE YOU TALKING ABOUT?
AAAAH, THIS IS BUGGING ME NOW!
I MIGHT BE ABLE TO REMEMBER IT IF YOU LET ME HAVE SEX WITH YOU!
YOU WISH!! GET BACK TO WORK! THIS IS OUR BUSIEST TIME AT THE SHRINE, YOU KNOW.
DAMN IT... I WAS BEING SERIOUS.

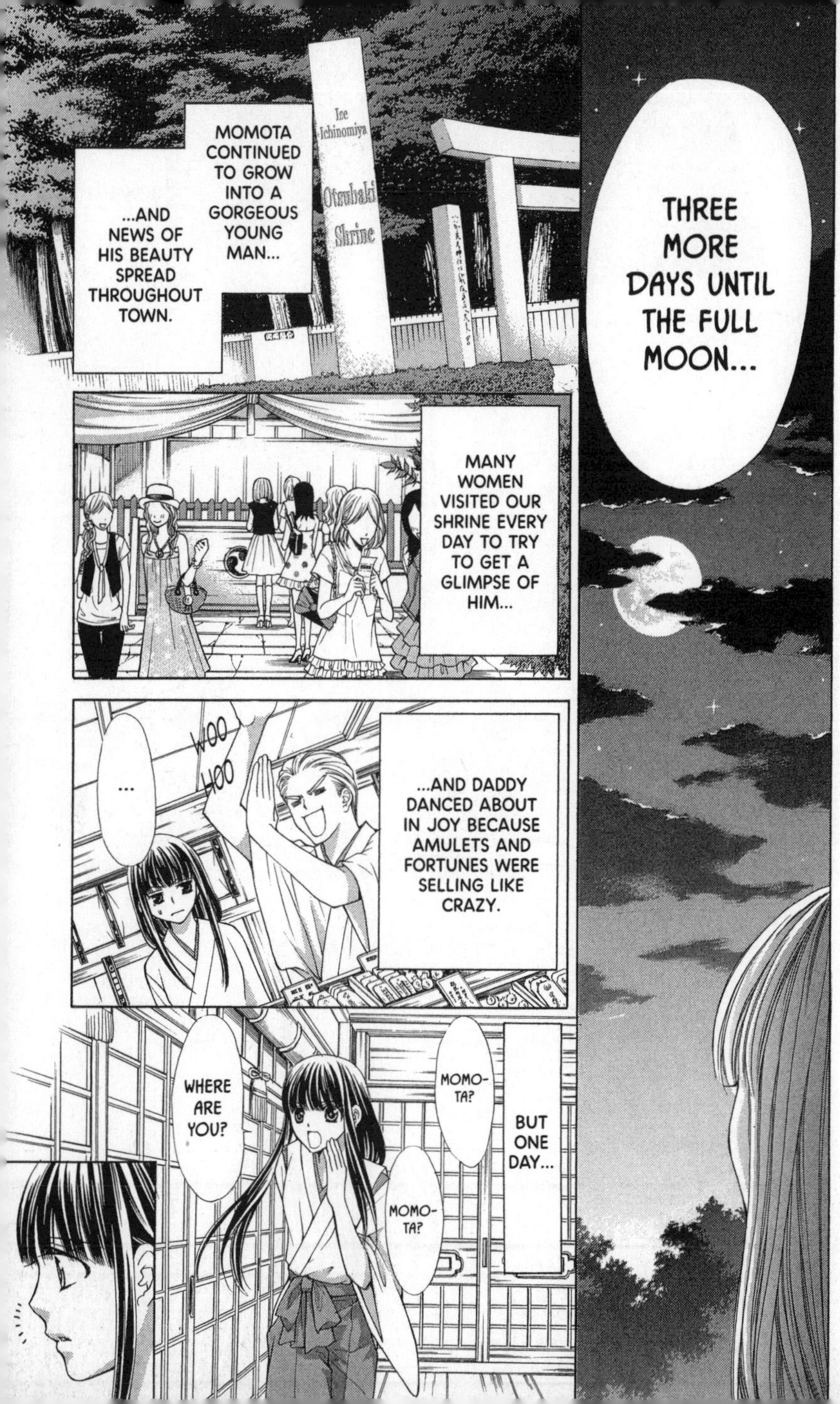

THREE MORE DAYS UNTIL THE FULL MOON...
MOMOTA CONTINUED TO GROW INTO A GORGEOUS YOUNG MAN...
Ise Ichinomiya Otsubaki Shrine
...AND NEWS OF HIS BEAUTY SPREAD THROUGHOUT TOWN.
MANY WOMEN VISITED OUR SHRINE EVERY DAY TO TRY TO GET A GLIMPSE OF HIM...
...AND DADDY DANCED ABOUT IN JOY BECAUSE AMULETS AND FORTUNES WERE SELLING LIKE CRAZY.
WOO HOO
...
BUT ONE DAY...
MOMO-TA?
MOMO-TA?
WHERE ARE YOU?

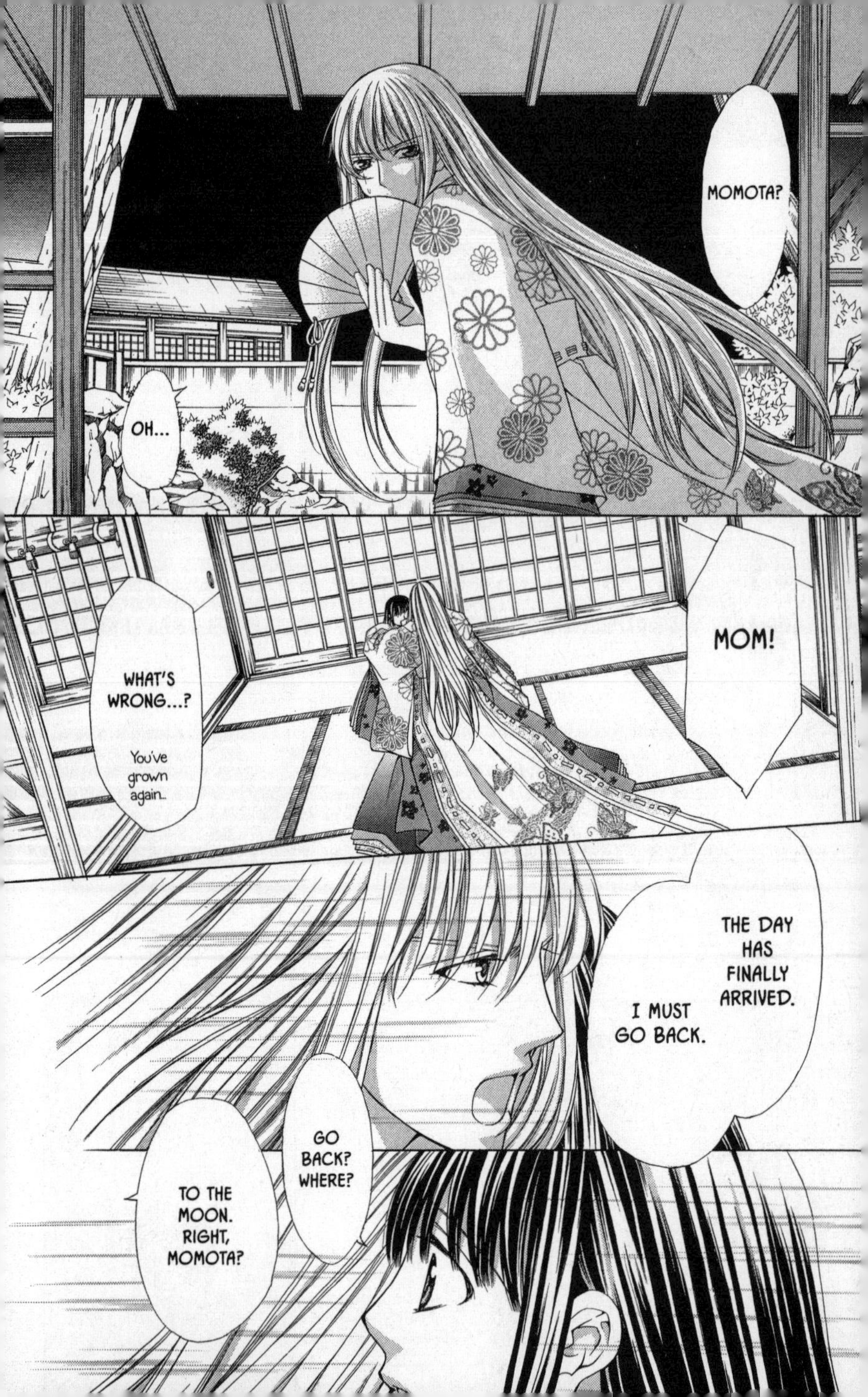
MOMOTA?
OH...
MOM!
WHAT'S WRONG...?
You've grown again..
THE DAY HAS FINALLY ARRIVED.
I MUST GO BACK.
GO BACK? WHERE?
TO THE MOON. RIGHT, MOMOTA?

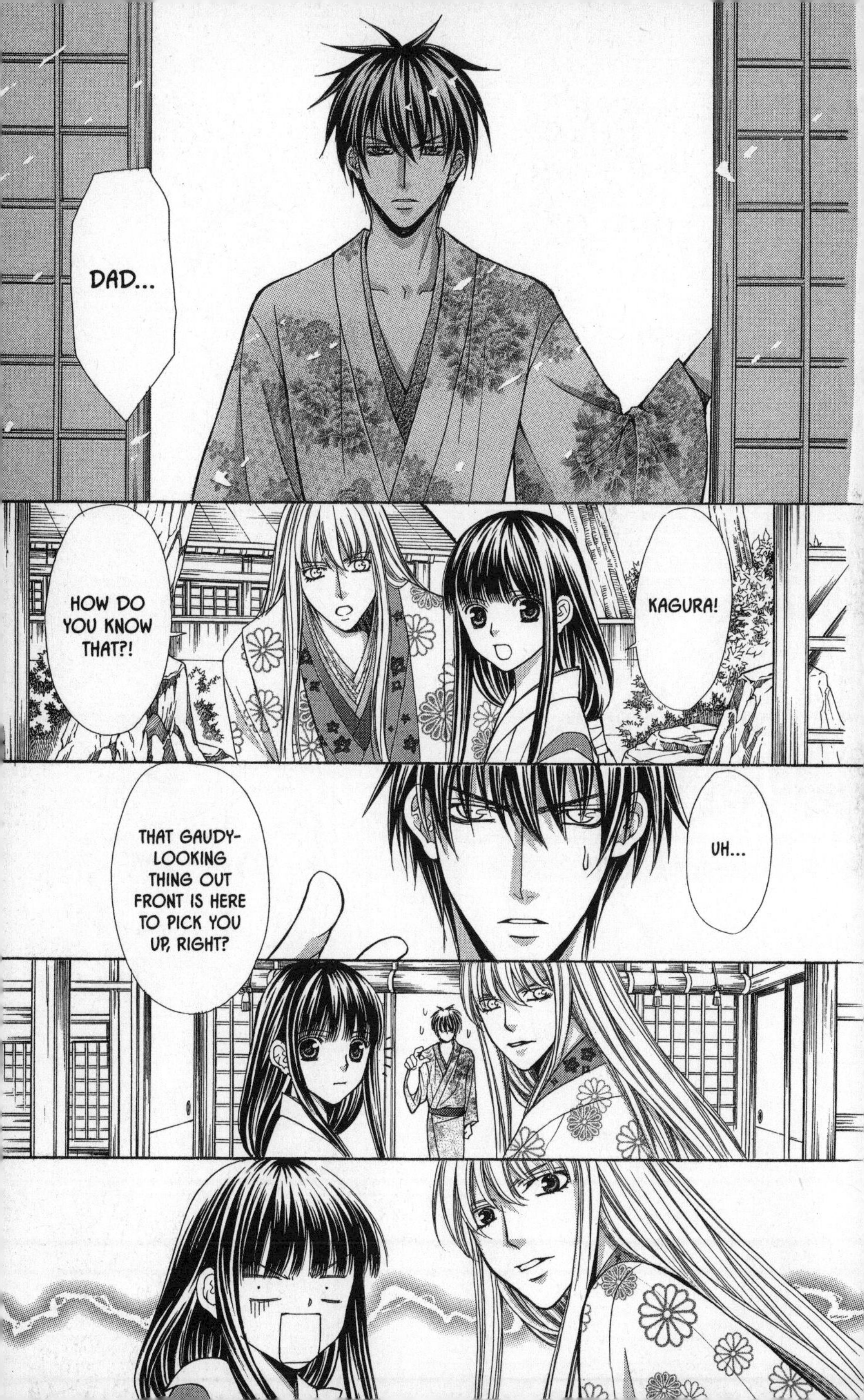
DAD...
KAGURA!
HOW DO YOU KNOW THAT?!
UH...
THAT GAUDY-LOOKING THING OUT FRONT IS HERE TO PICK YOU UP, RIGHT?

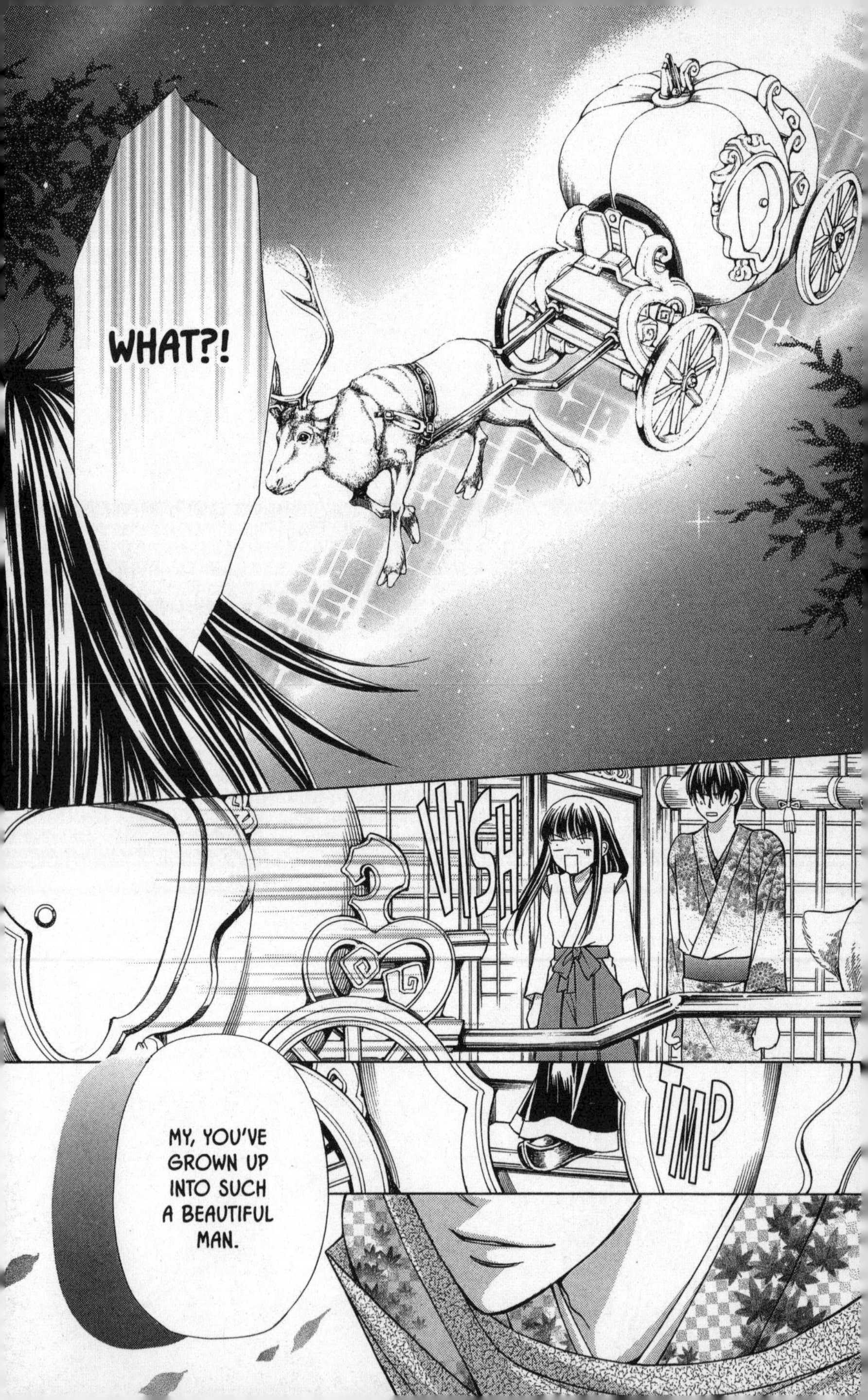
WHAT?!
VISH
TMP
MY, YOU'VE GROWN UP INTO SUCH A BEAUTIFUL MAN.

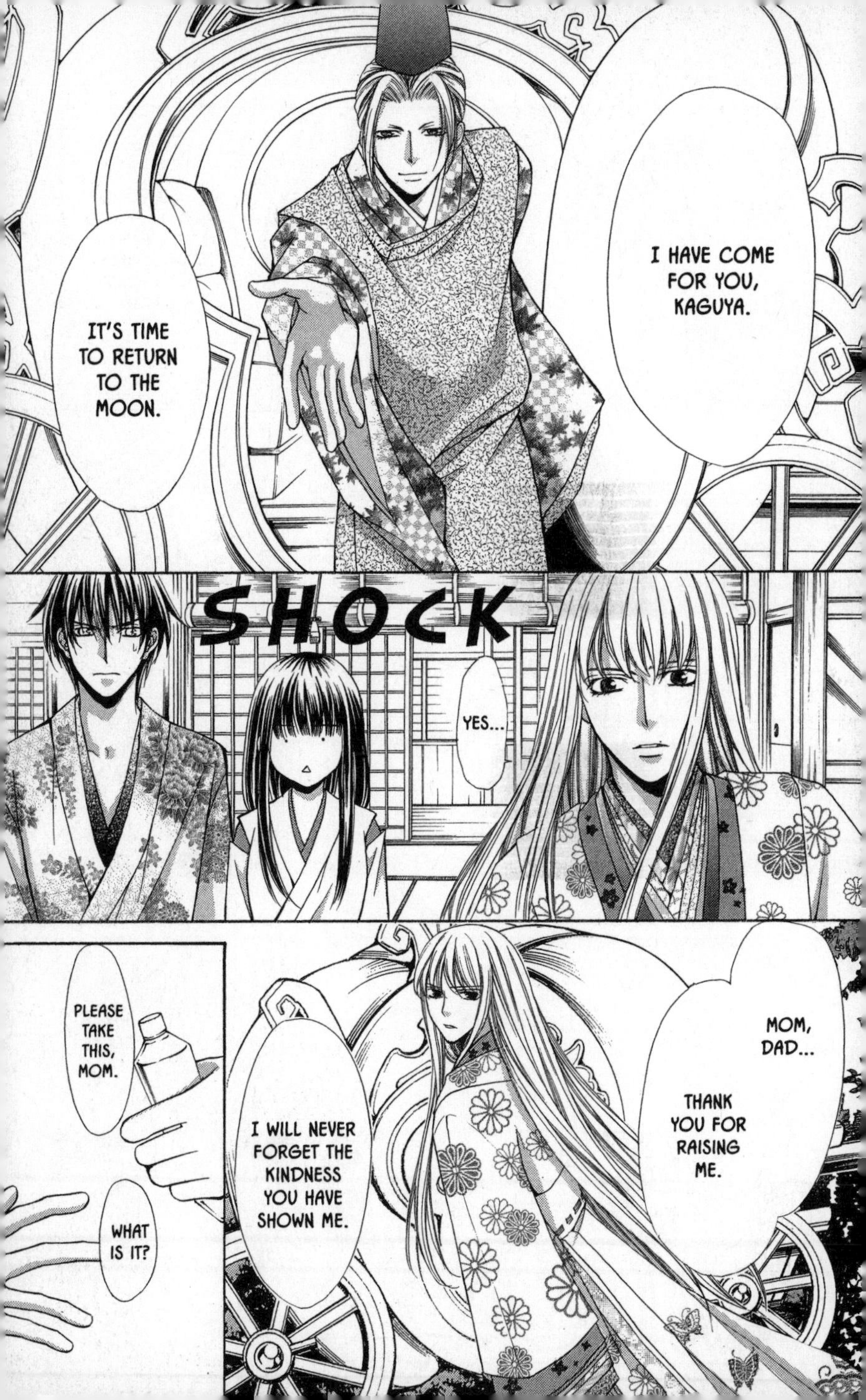
I HAVE COME FOR YOU, KAGUYA.
IT'S TIME TO RETURN TO THE MOON.
SHOCK
YES...
MOM, DAD...
THANK YOU FOR RAISING ME.
I WILL NEVER FORGET THE KINDNESS YOU HAVE SHOWN ME.
PLEASE TAKE THIS, MOM.
WHAT IS IT?

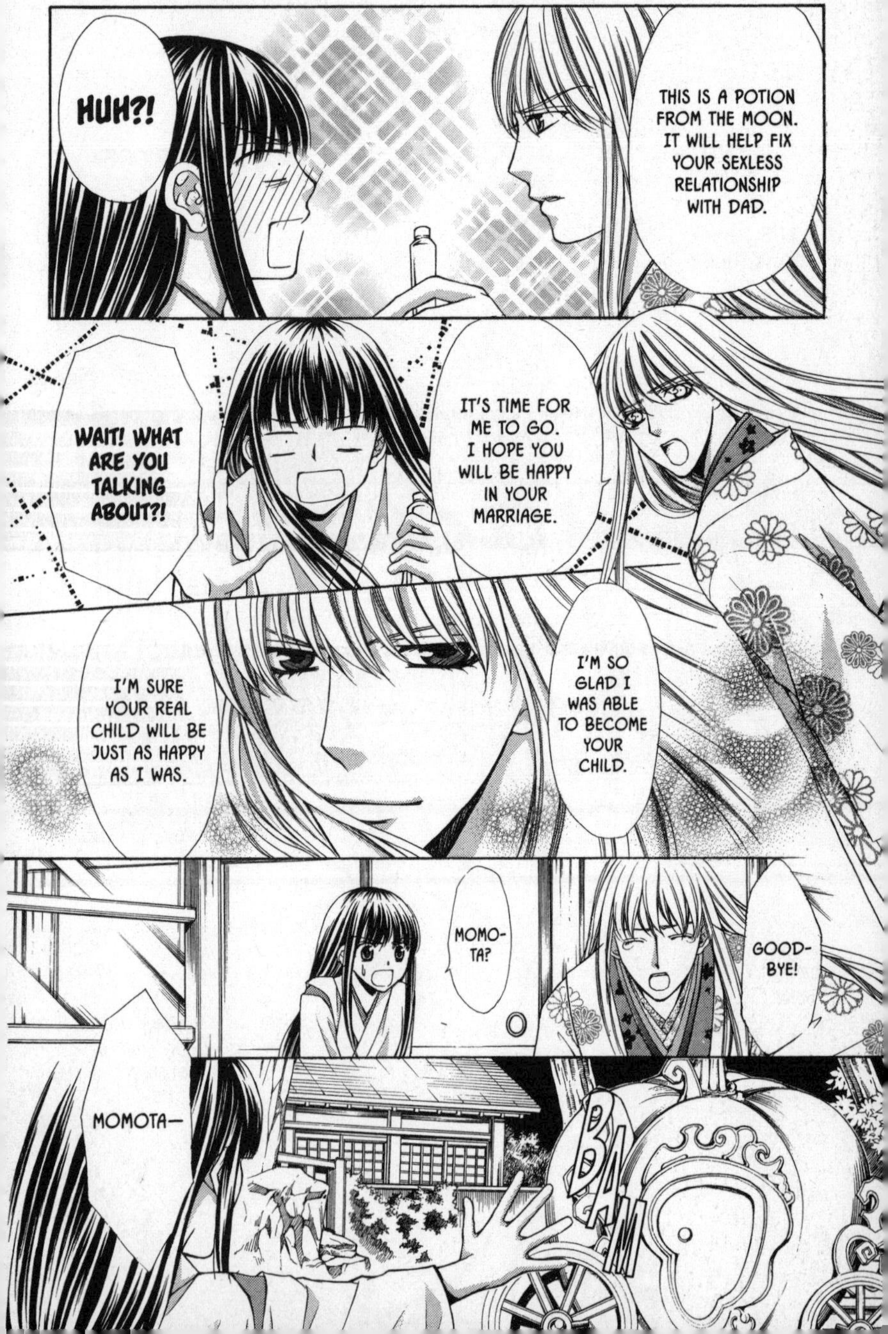
THIS IS A POTION FROM THE MOON. IT WILL HELP FIX YOUR SEXLESS RELATIONSHIP WITH DAD.
HUH?!
IT'S TIME FOR ME TO GO. I HOPE YOU WILL BE HAPPY IN YOUR MARRIAGE.
WAIT! WHAT ARE YOU TALKING ABOUT?!
I'M SO GLAD I WAS ABLE TO BECOME YOUR CHILD.
I'M SURE YOUR REAL CHILD WILL BE JUST AS HAPPY AS I WAS.
GOOD-BYE!
MOMO-TA?
BAM
MOMOTA—

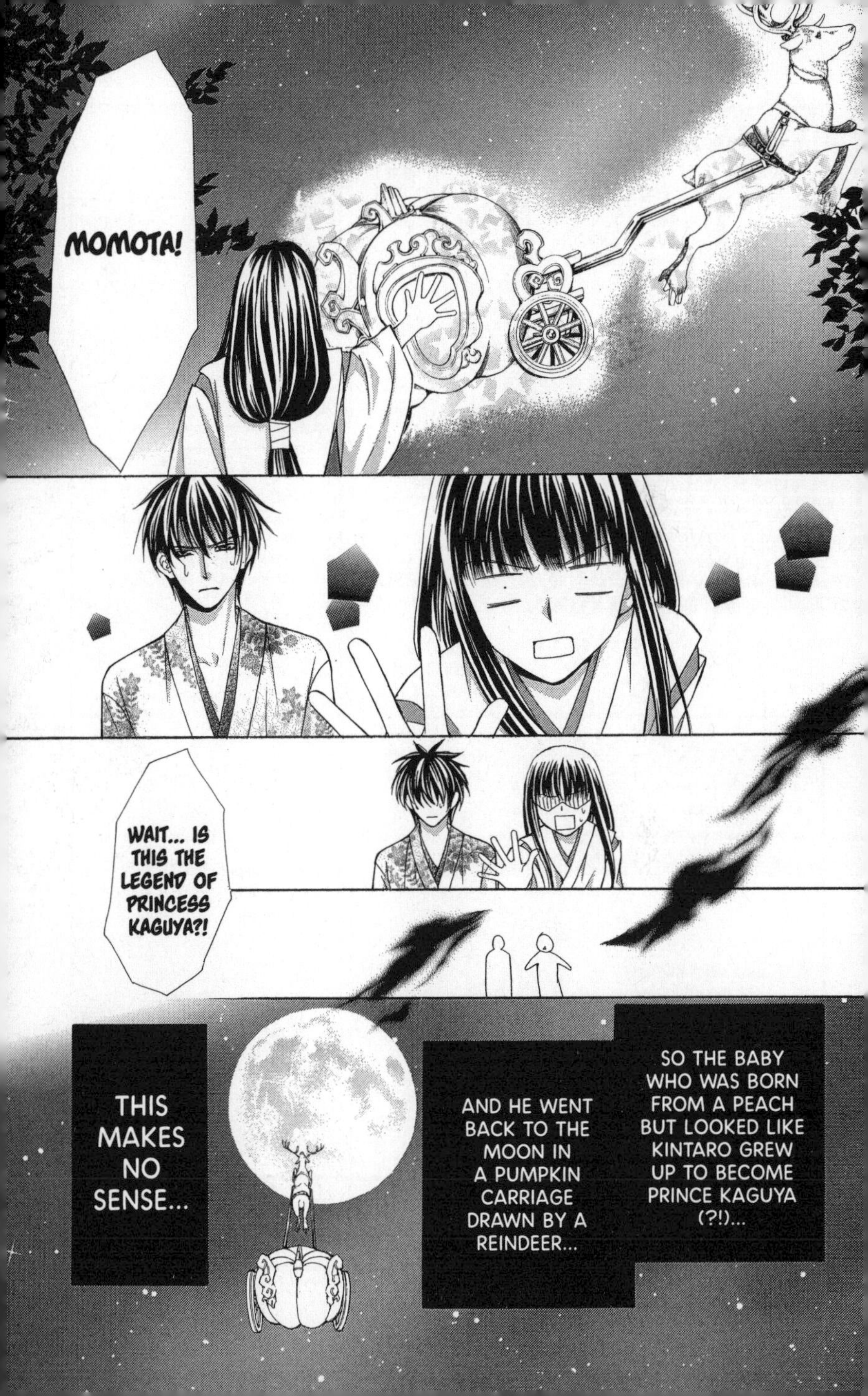
MOMOTA!
WAIT... IS THIS THE LEGEND OF PRINCESS KAGUYA?!
SO THE BABY WHO WAS BORN FROM A PEACH BUT LOOKED LIKE KINTARO GREW UP TO BECOME PRINCE KAGUYA (?!)...
AND HE WENT BACK TO THE MOON IN A PUMPKIN CARRIAGE DRAWN BY A REINDEER...
THIS MAKES NO SENSE...

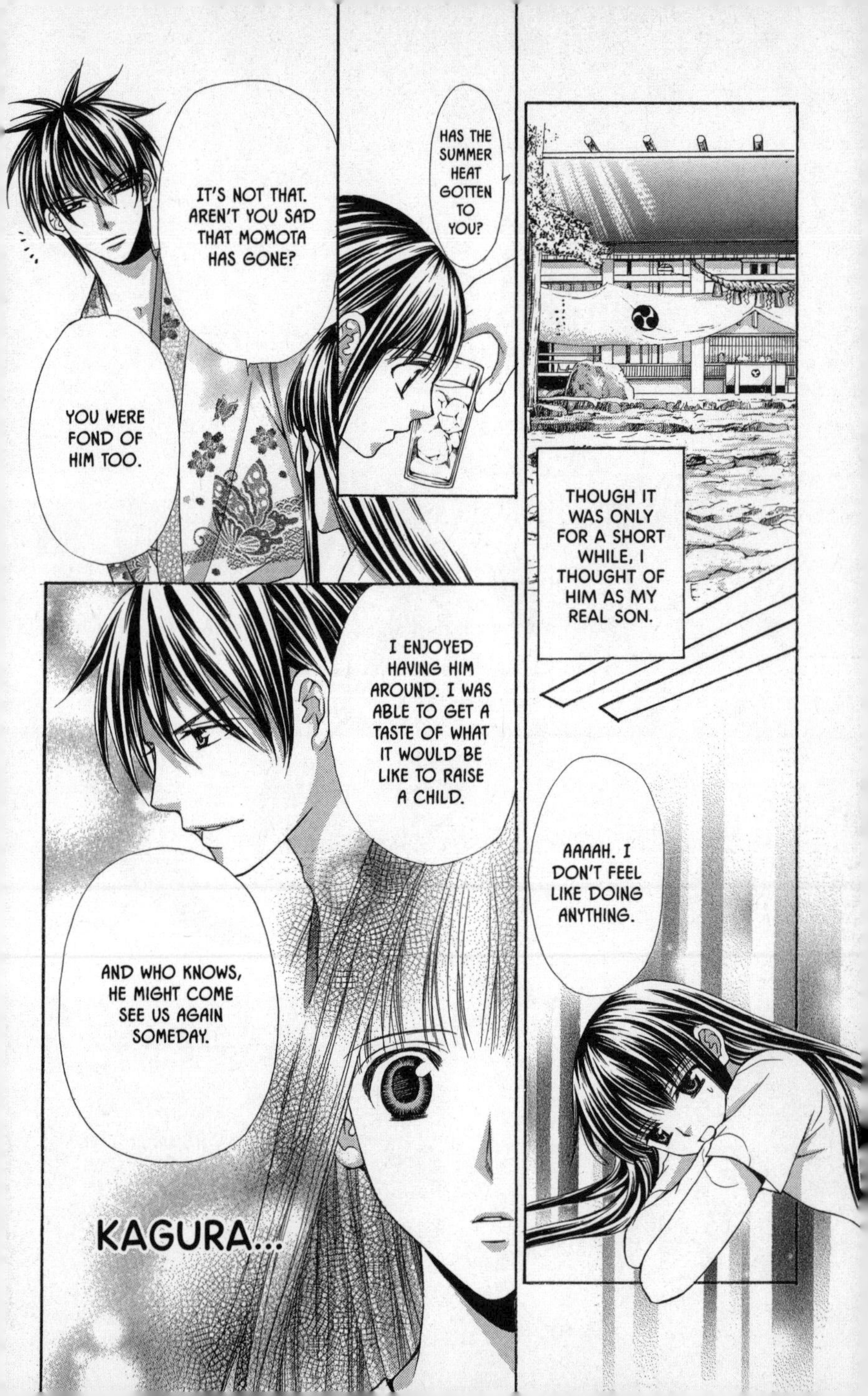
THOUGH IT WAS ONLY FOR A SHORT WHILE, I THOUGHT OF HIM AS MY REAL SON.
AAAAH. I DON'T FEEL LIKE DOING ANYTHING.
HAS THE SUMMER HEAT GOTTEN TO YOU?
IT'S NOT THAT. AREN'T YOU SAD THAT MOMOTA HAS GONE?
YOU WERE FOND OF HIM TOO.
I ENJOYED HAVING HIM AROUND. I WAS ABLE TO GET A TASTE OF WHAT IT WOULD BE LIKE TO RAISE A CHILD.
AND WHO KNOWS, HE MIGHT COME SEE US AGAIN SOMEDAY.
KAGURA...

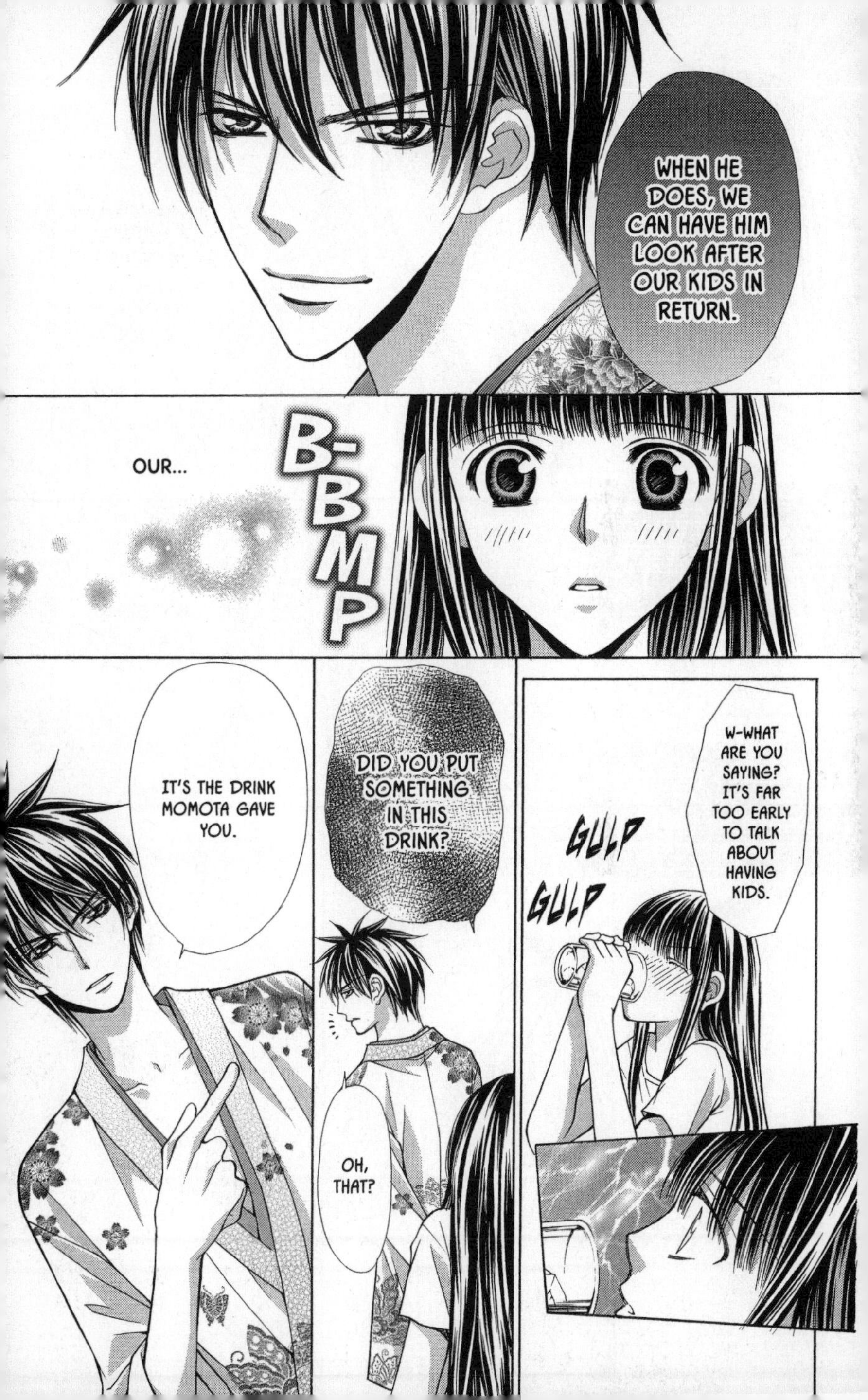
WHEN HE DOES, WE CAN HAVE HIM LOOK AFTER OUR KIDS IN RETURN.
B-BMP
OUR...
W-WHAT ARE YOU SAYING? IT'S FAR TOO EARLY TO TALK ABOUT HAVING KIDS.
GULP
GULP
DID YOU PUT SOMETHING IN THIS DRINK?
OH, THAT?
IT'S THE DRINK MOMOTA GAVE YOU.

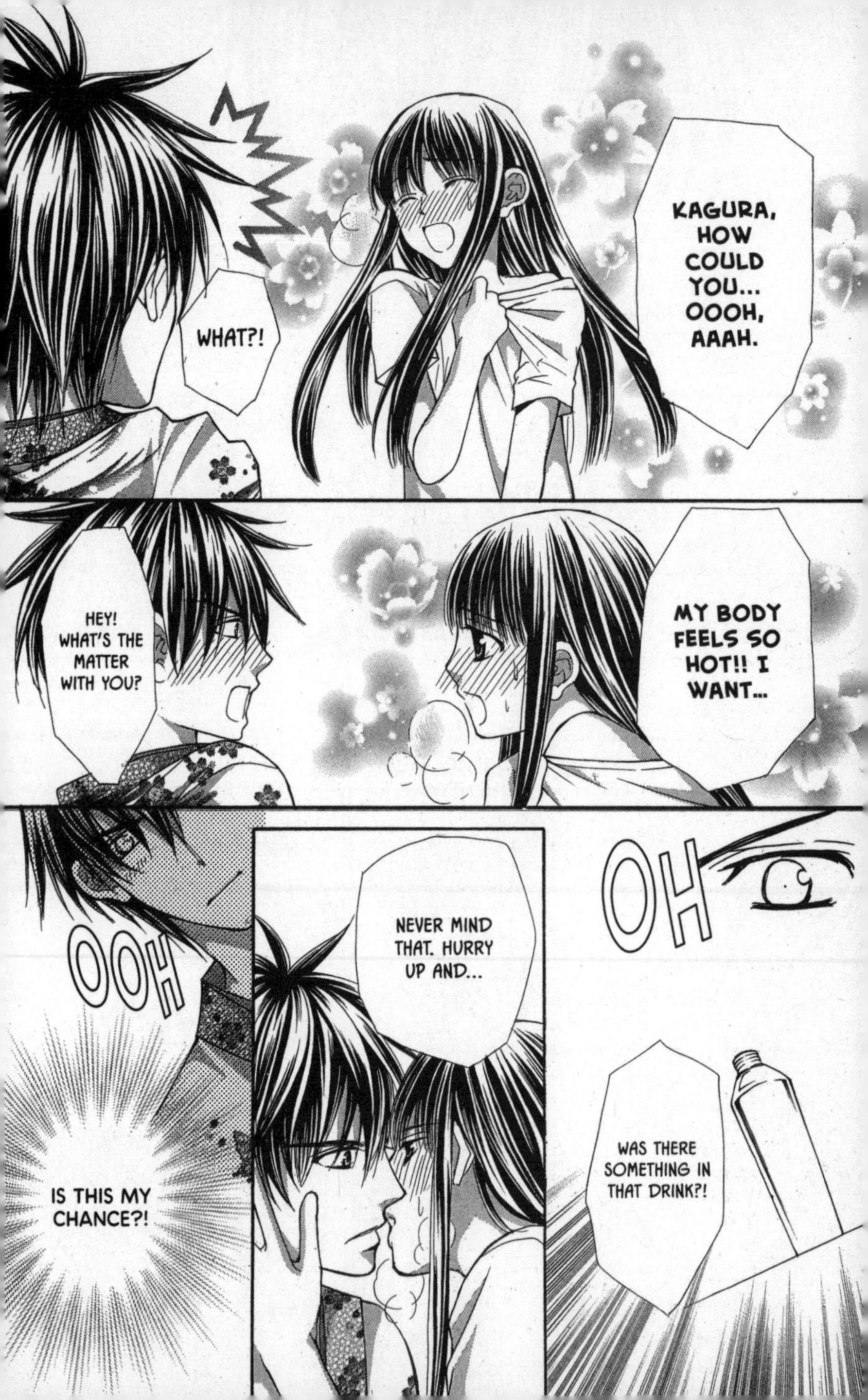
KAGURA, HOW COULD YOU... OOOH, AAAH.
WHAT?!
MY BODY FEELS SO HOT!! I WANT...
HEY! WHAT'S THE MATTER WITH YOU?
OH
WAS THERE SOMETHING IN THAT DRINK?!
NEVER MIND THAT. HURRY UP AND...
OOH
IS THIS MY CHANCE?!

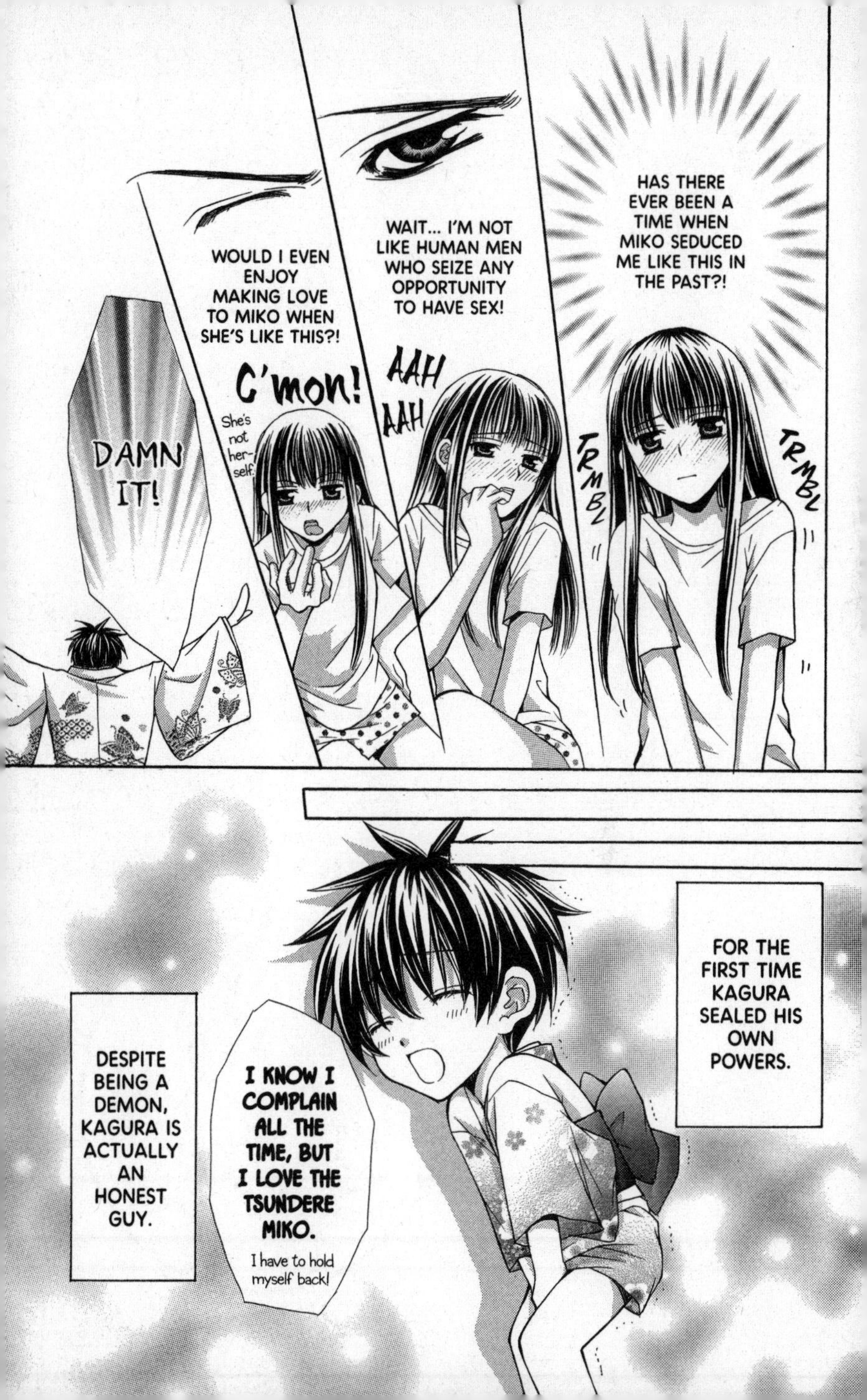
HAS THERE EVER BEEN A TIME WHEN MIKO SEDUCED ME LIKE THIS IN THE PAST?!
TRMBL
TRMBL
WAIT... I'M NOT LIKE HUMAN MEN WHO SEIZE ANY OPPORTUNITY TO HAVE SEX!
AAH AAH
WOULD I EVEN ENJOY MAKING LOVE TO MIKO WHEN SHE'S LIKE THIS?!
C'mon!
She's not her-self.
DAMN IT!
FOR THE FIRST TIME KAGURA SEALED HIS OWN POWERS.
I KNOW I COMPLAIN ALL THE TIME, BUT I LOVE THE TSUNDERE MIKO.
I have to hold myself back!
DESPITE BEING A DEMON, KAGURA IS ACTUALLY AN HONEST GUY.

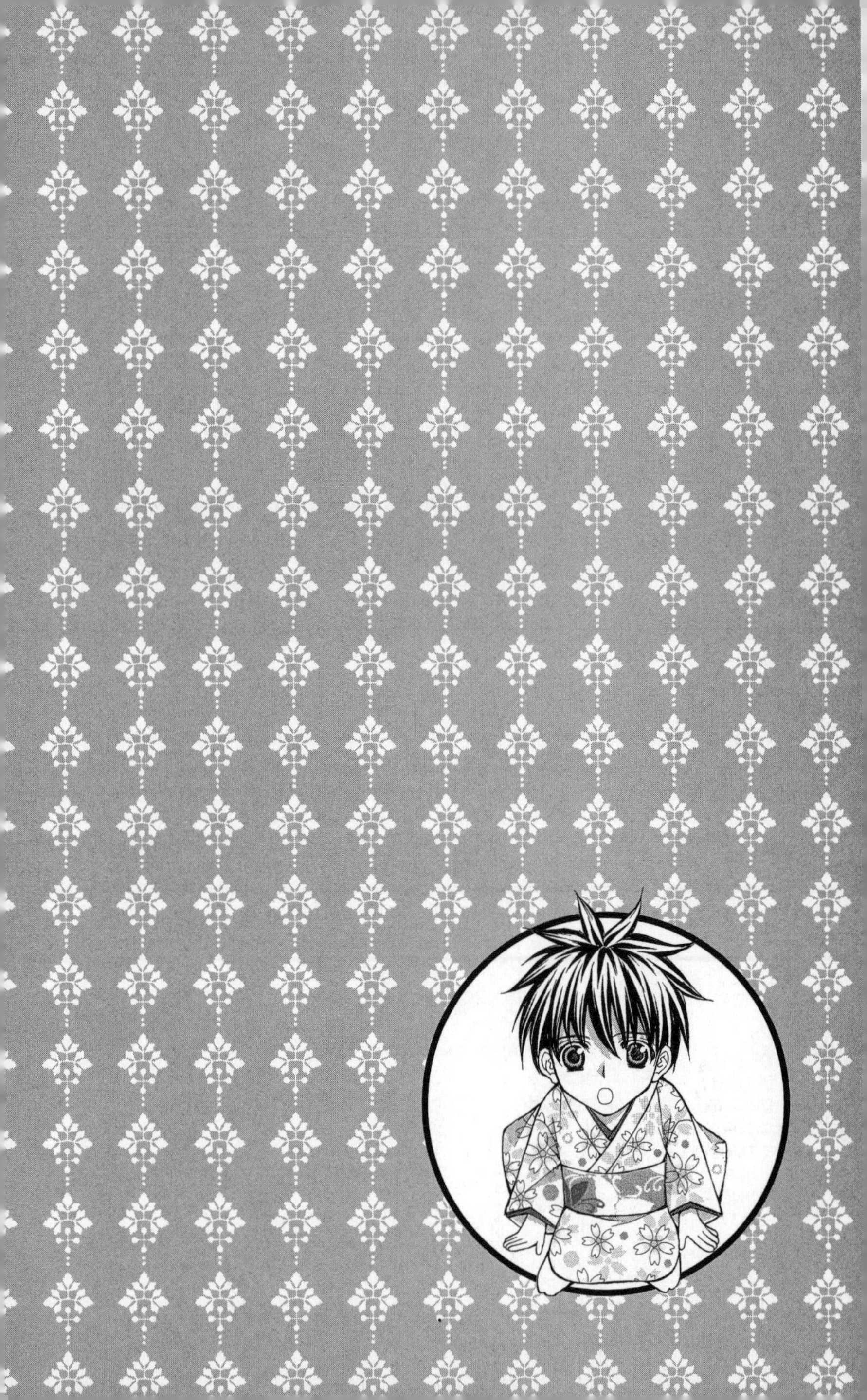

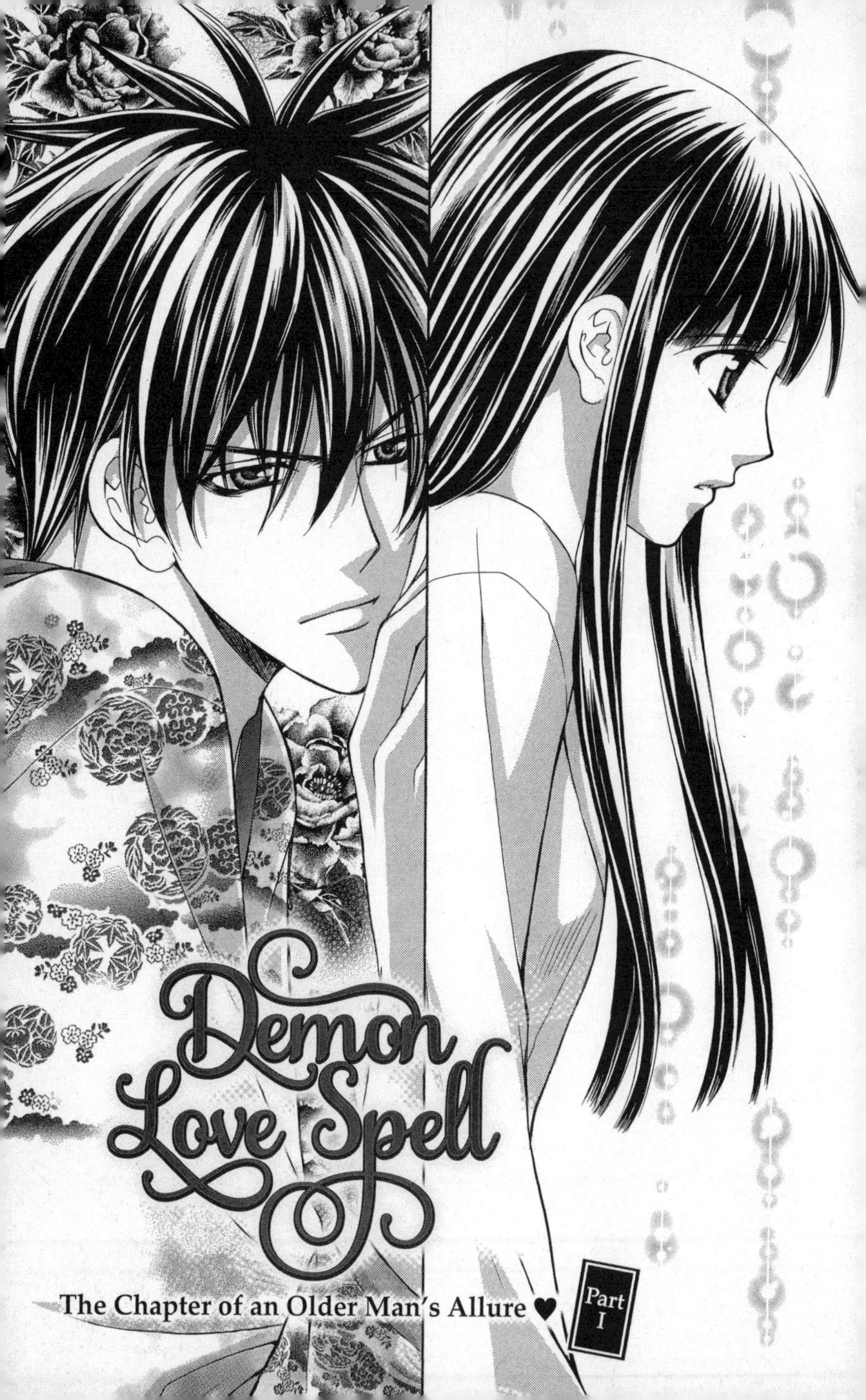
Demon Love Spell
The Chapter of an Older Man's Allure ♥
Part I

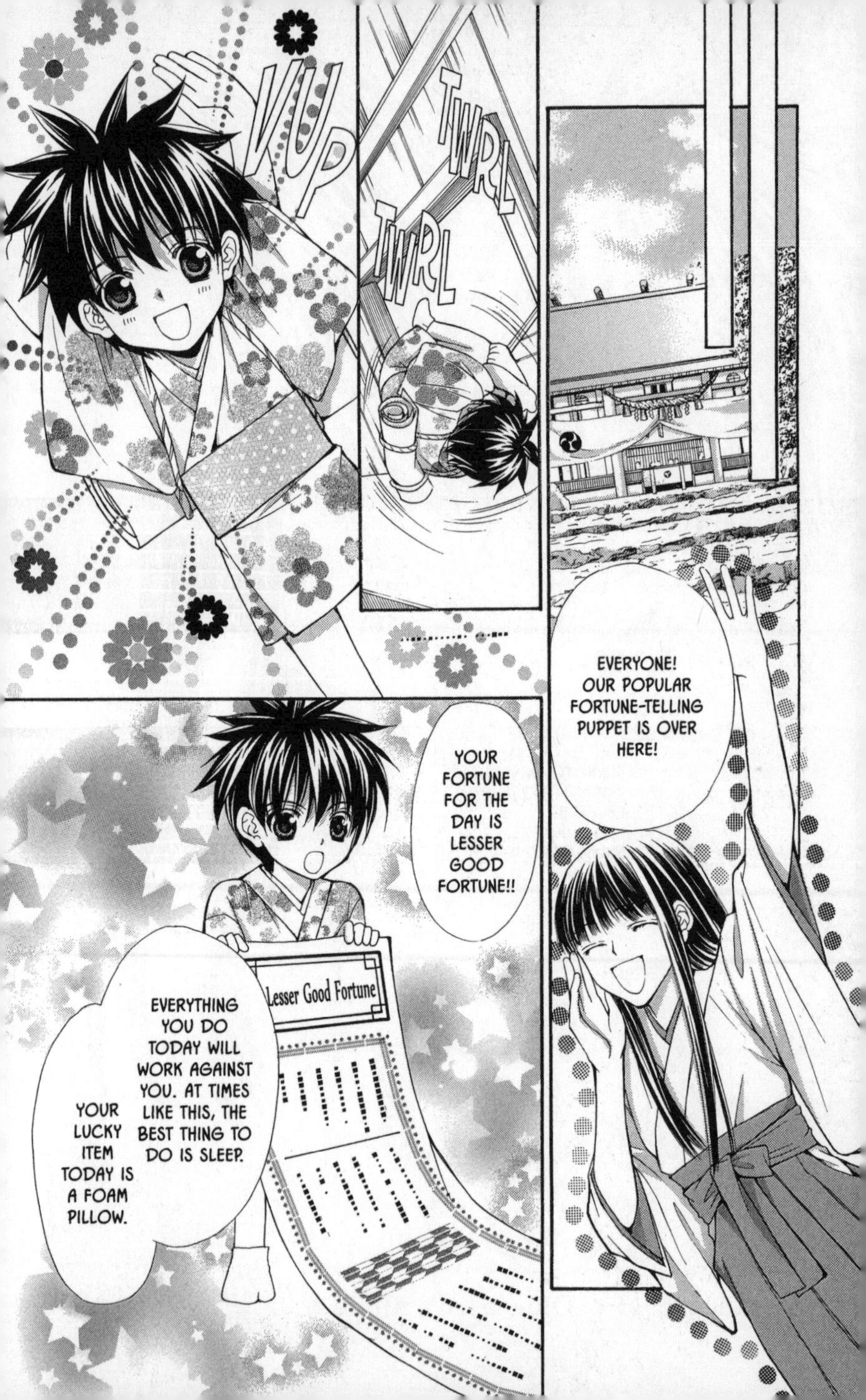
EVERYONE! OUR POPULAR FORTUNE-TELLING PUPPET IS OVER HERE!
TWRL
TWRL
VUP
YOUR FORTUNE FOR THE DAY IS LESSER GOOD FORTUNE!!
Lesser Good Fortune
EVERYTHING YOU DO TODAY WILL WORK AGAINST YOU. AT TIMES LIKE THIS, THE BEST THING TO DO IS SLEEP.
YOUR LUCKY ITEM TODAY IS A FOAM PILLOW.

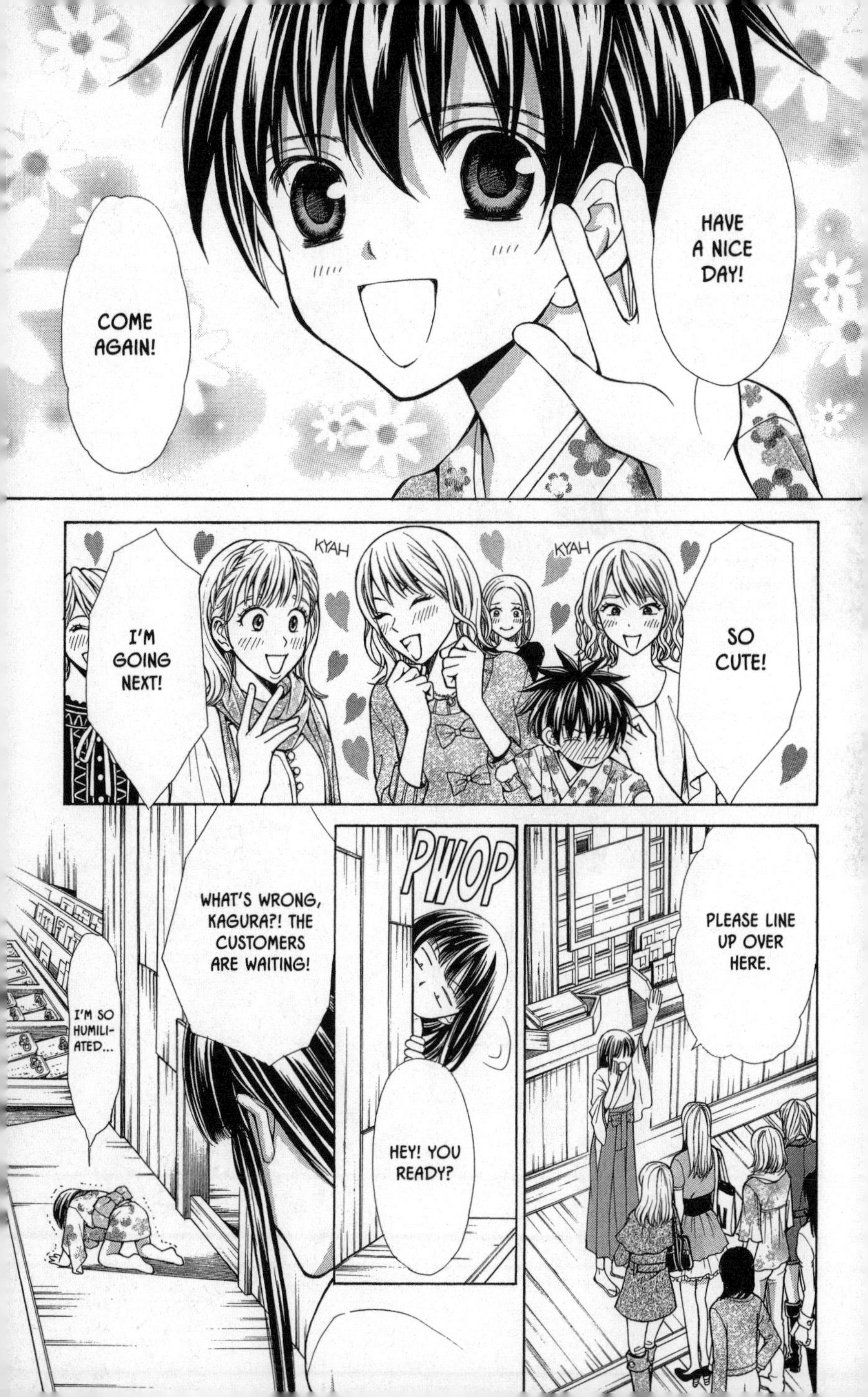
HAVE A NICE DAY!
COME AGAIN!
SO CUTE!
KYAH
KYAH
I'M GOING NEXT!
PLEASE LINE UP OVER HERE.
PWOP
HEY! YOU READY?
WHAT'S WRONG, KAGURA?! THE CUSTOMERS ARE WAITING!
I'M SO HUMILI-ATED...

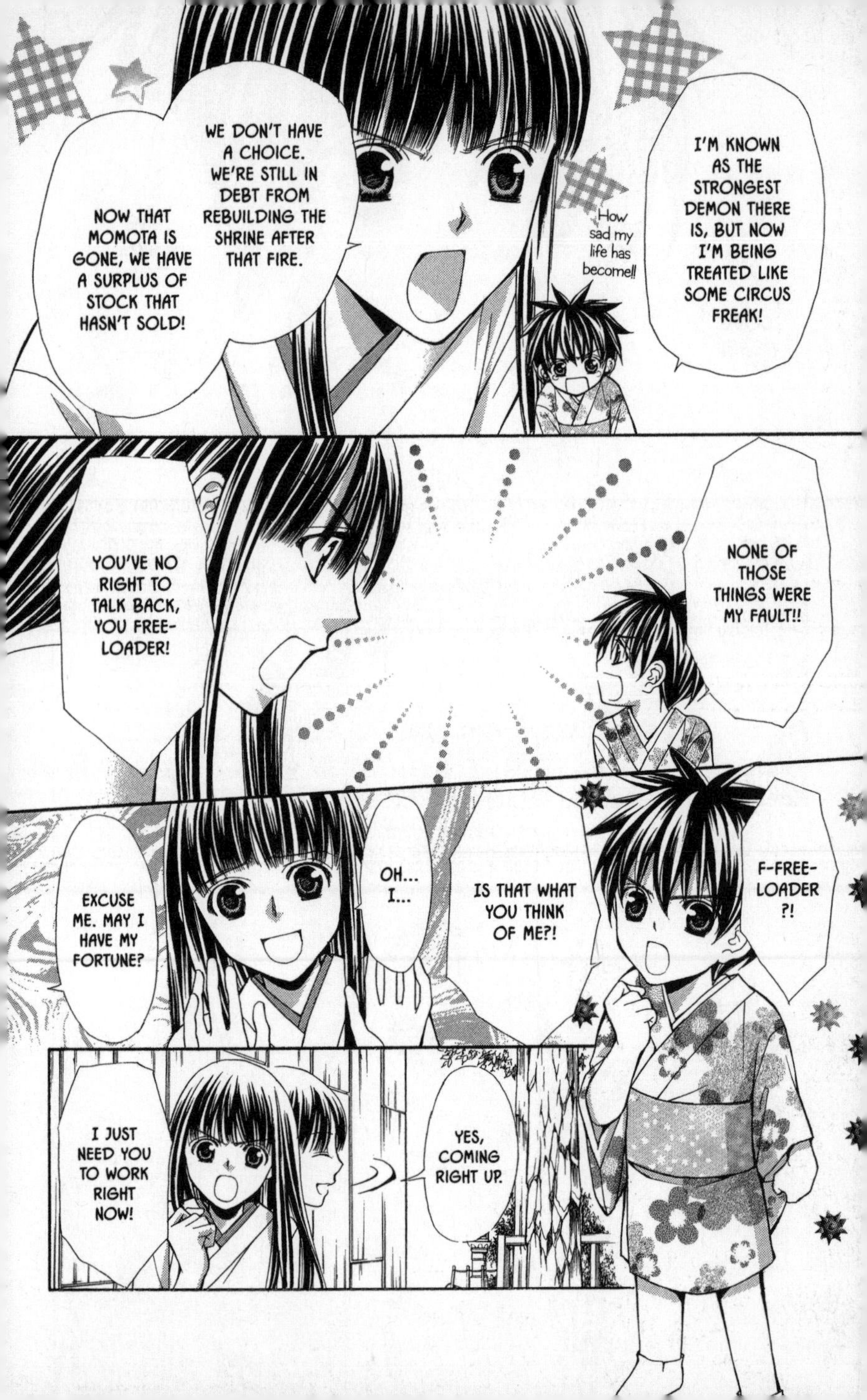
I'M KNOWN AS THE STRONGEST DEMON THERE IS, BUT NOW I'M BEING TREATED LIKE SOME CIRCUS FREAK!
How sad my life has become!!
WE DON'T HAVE A CHOICE. WE'RE STILL IN DEBT FROM REBUILDING THE SHRINE AFTER THAT FIRE.
NOW THAT MOMOTA IS GONE, WE HAVE A SURPLUS OF STOCK THAT HASN'T SOLD!
NONE OF THOSE THINGS WERE MY FAULT!!
YOU'VE NO RIGHT TO TALK BACK, YOU FREE-LOADER!
F-FREE-LOADER ?!
IS THAT WHAT YOU THINK OF ME?!
OH... I...
EXCUSE ME. MAY I HAVE MY FORTUNE?
YES, COMING RIGHT UP.
I JUST NEED YOU TO WORK RIGHT NOW!

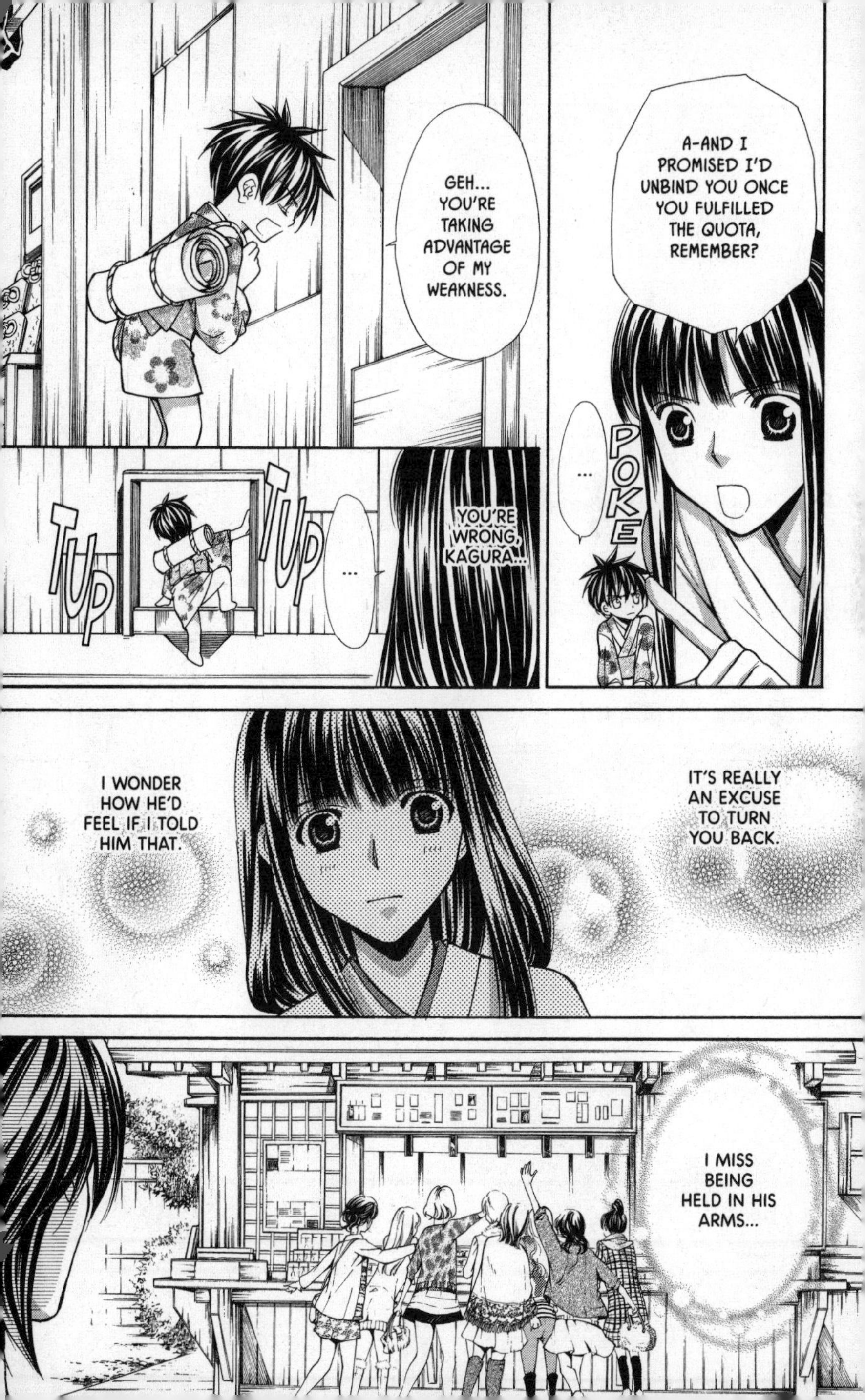
A-AND I PROMISED I'D UNBIND YOU ONCE YOU FULFILLED THE QUOTA, REMEMBER?
POKE
...
GEH... YOU'RE TAKING ADVANTAGE OF MY WEAKNESS.
YOU'RE WRONG, KAGURA...
...
TUP
TUP
IT'S REALLY AN EXCUSE TO TURN YOU BACK.
I WONDER HOW HE'D FEEL IF I TOLD HIM THAT.
I MISS BEING HELD IN HIS ARMS...

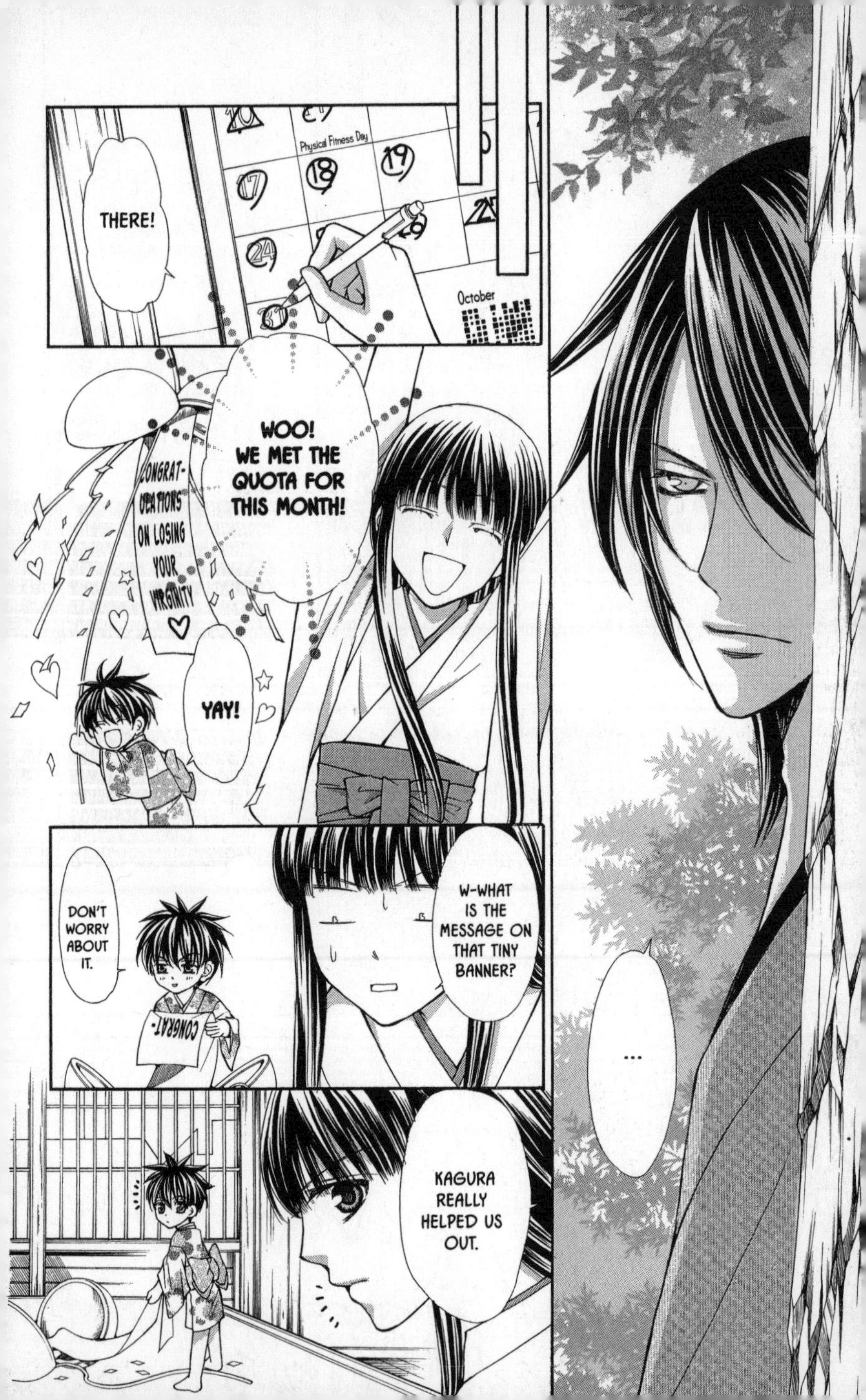
...
Physical Fitness Day
October
THERE!
WOO! WE MET THE QUOTA FOR THIS MONTH!
CONGRAT-ULATIONS ON LOSING YOUR VIRGINITY
YAY!
W-WHAT IS THE MESSAGE ON THAT TINY BANNER?
DON'T WORRY ABOUT IT.
CONGRAT-
KAGURA REALLY HELPED US OUT.

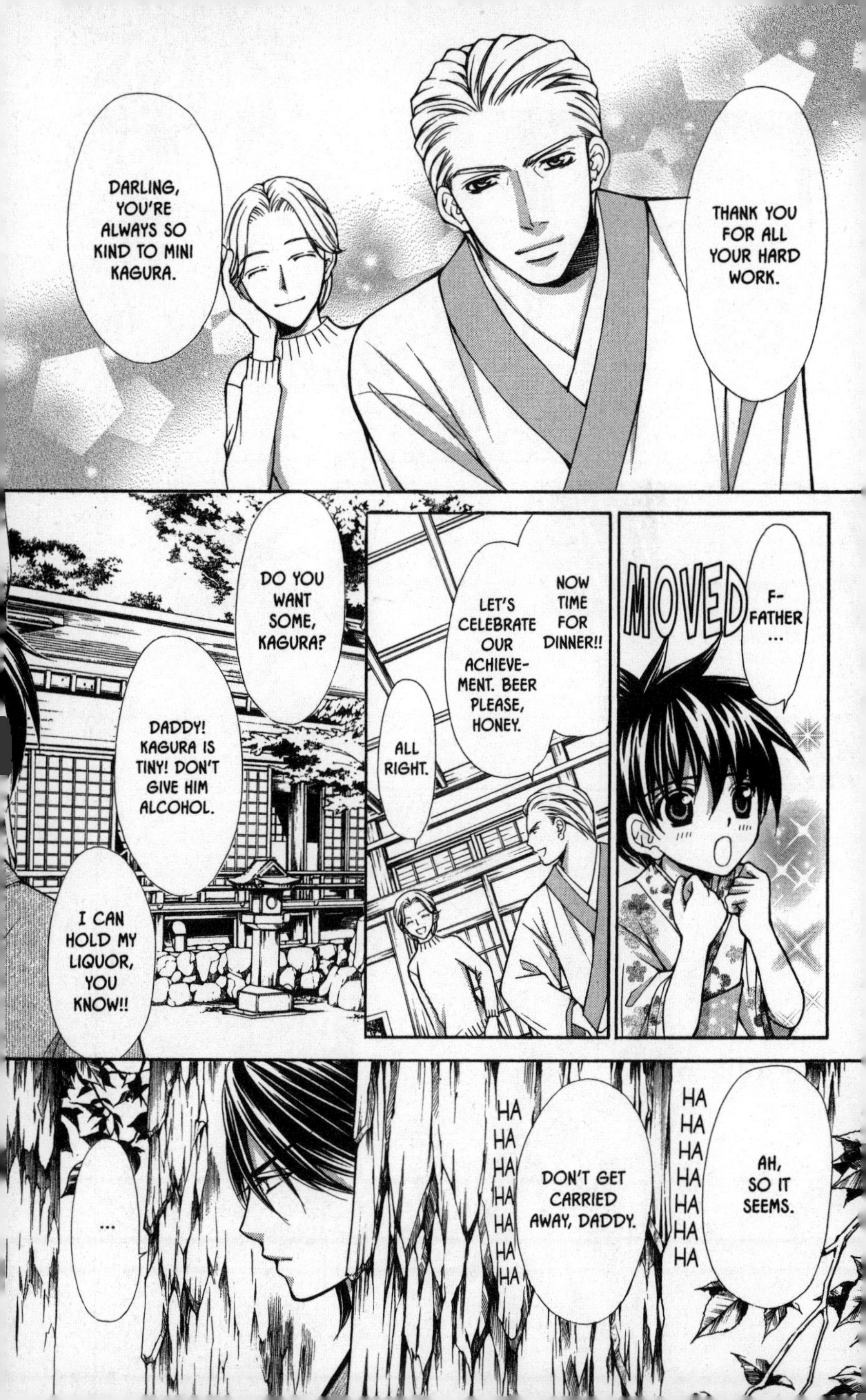
THANK YOU FOR ALL YOUR HARD WORK.
DARLING, YOU'RE ALWAYS SO KIND TO MINI KAGURA.
MOVED
F-FATHER...
NOW TIME FOR DINNER!!
LET'S CELEBRATE OUR ACHIEVEMENT. BEER PLEASE, HONEY.
ALL RIGHT.
DO YOU WANT SOME, KAGURA?
DADDY! KAGURA IS TINY! DON'T GIVE HIM ALCOHOL.
I CAN HOLD MY LIQUOR, YOU KNOW!!
AH, SO IT SEEMS.
HA HA HA HA HA HA HA
DON'T GET CARRIED AWAY, DADDY.
HA HA HA HA HA HA HA
...

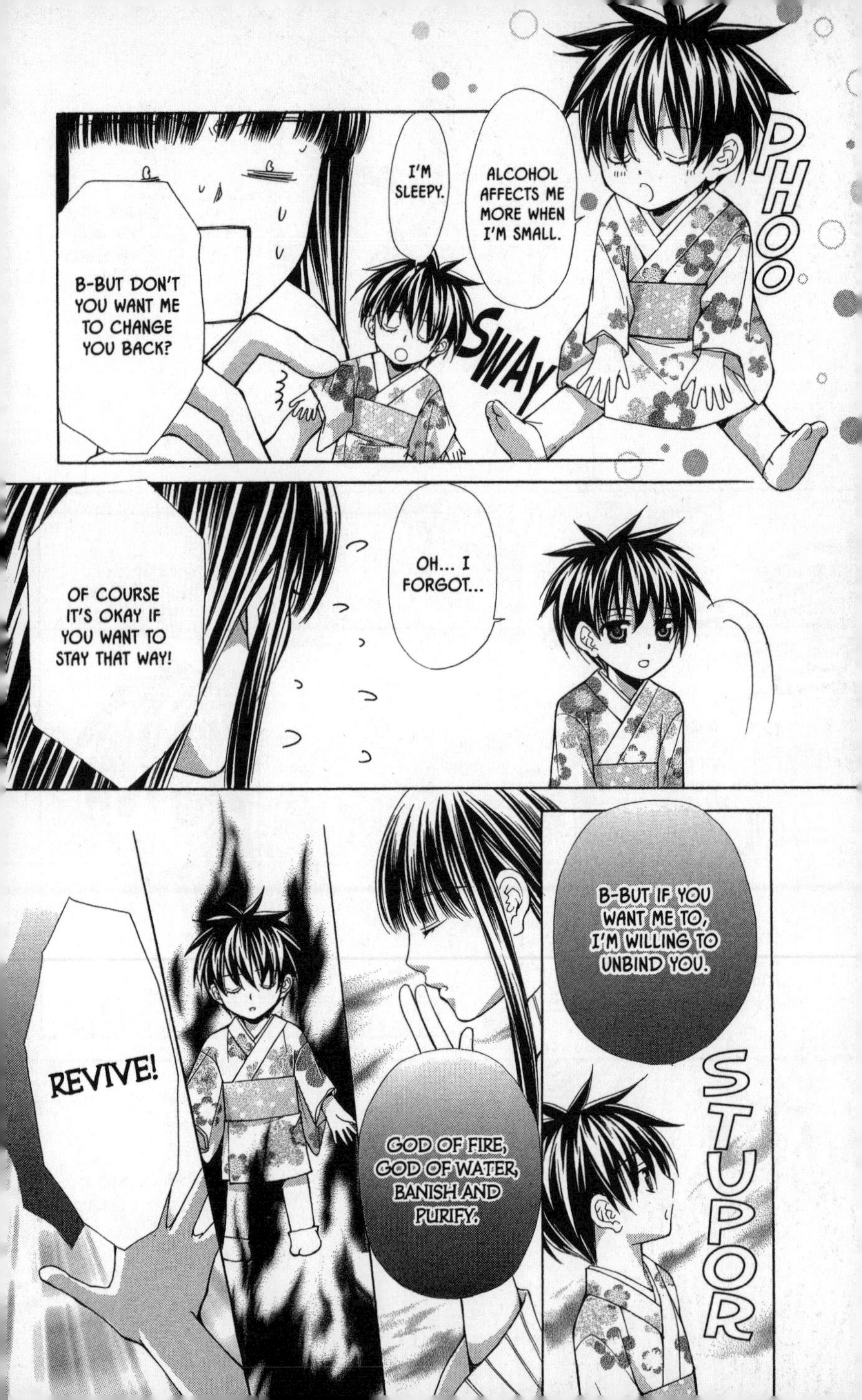
PHOO
ALCOHOL AFFECTS ME MORE WHEN I'M SMALL.
I'M SLEEPY.
SWAY
B-BUT DON'T YOU WANT ME TO CHANGE YOU BACK?
OH... I FORGOT...
OF COURSE IT'S OKAY IF YOU WANT TO STAY THAT WAY!
B-BUT IF YOU WANT ME TO, I'M WILLING TO UNBIND YOU.
STUPOR
GOD OF FIRE, GOD OF WATER, BANISH AND PURIFY.
REVIVE!

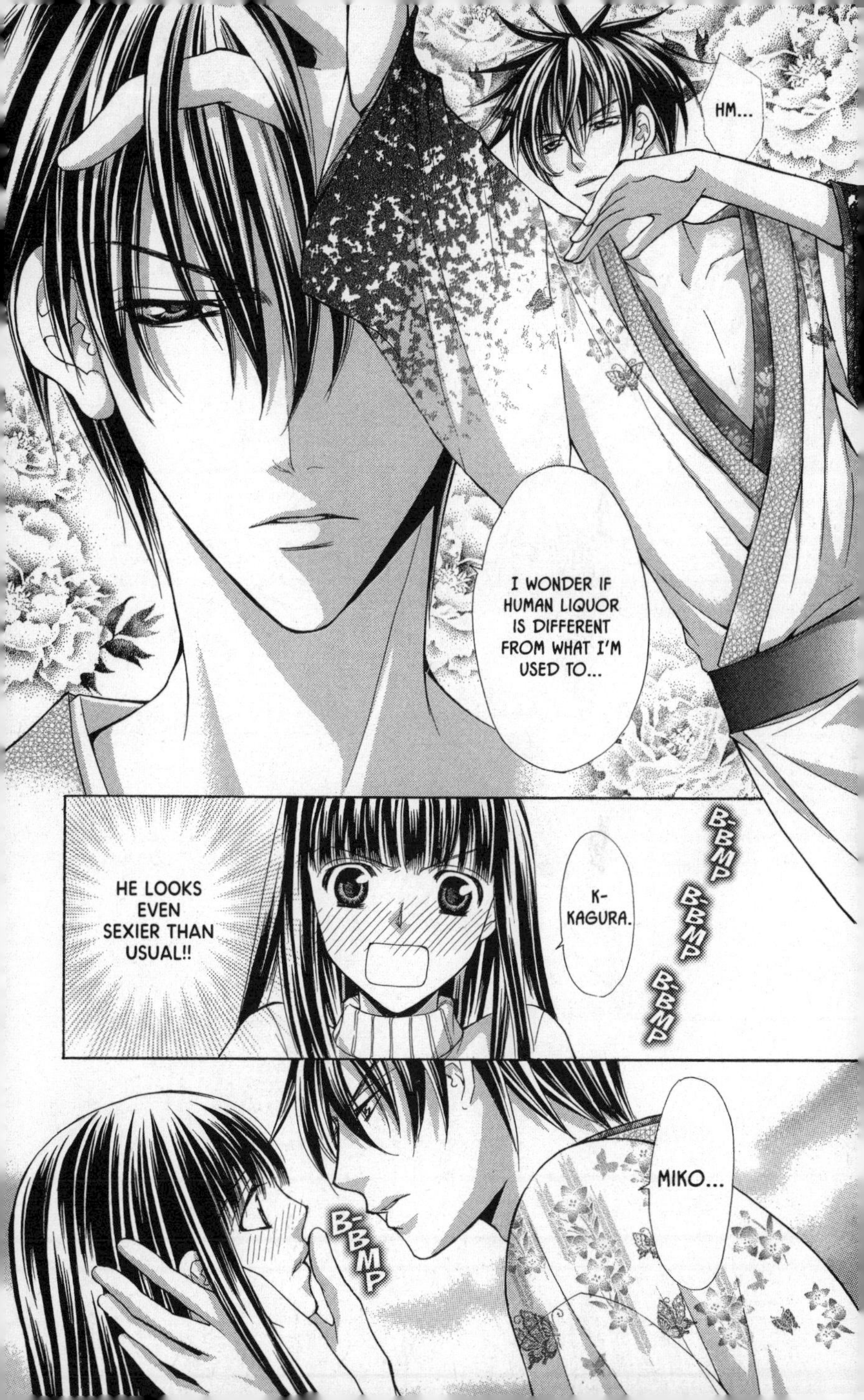
HM...
I WONDER IF HUMAN LIQUOR IS DIFFERENT FROM WHAT I'M USED TO...
B-BMP B-BMP B-BMP
K-KAGURA.
HE LOOKS EVEN SEXIER THAN USUAL!!
MIKO...
B-BMP

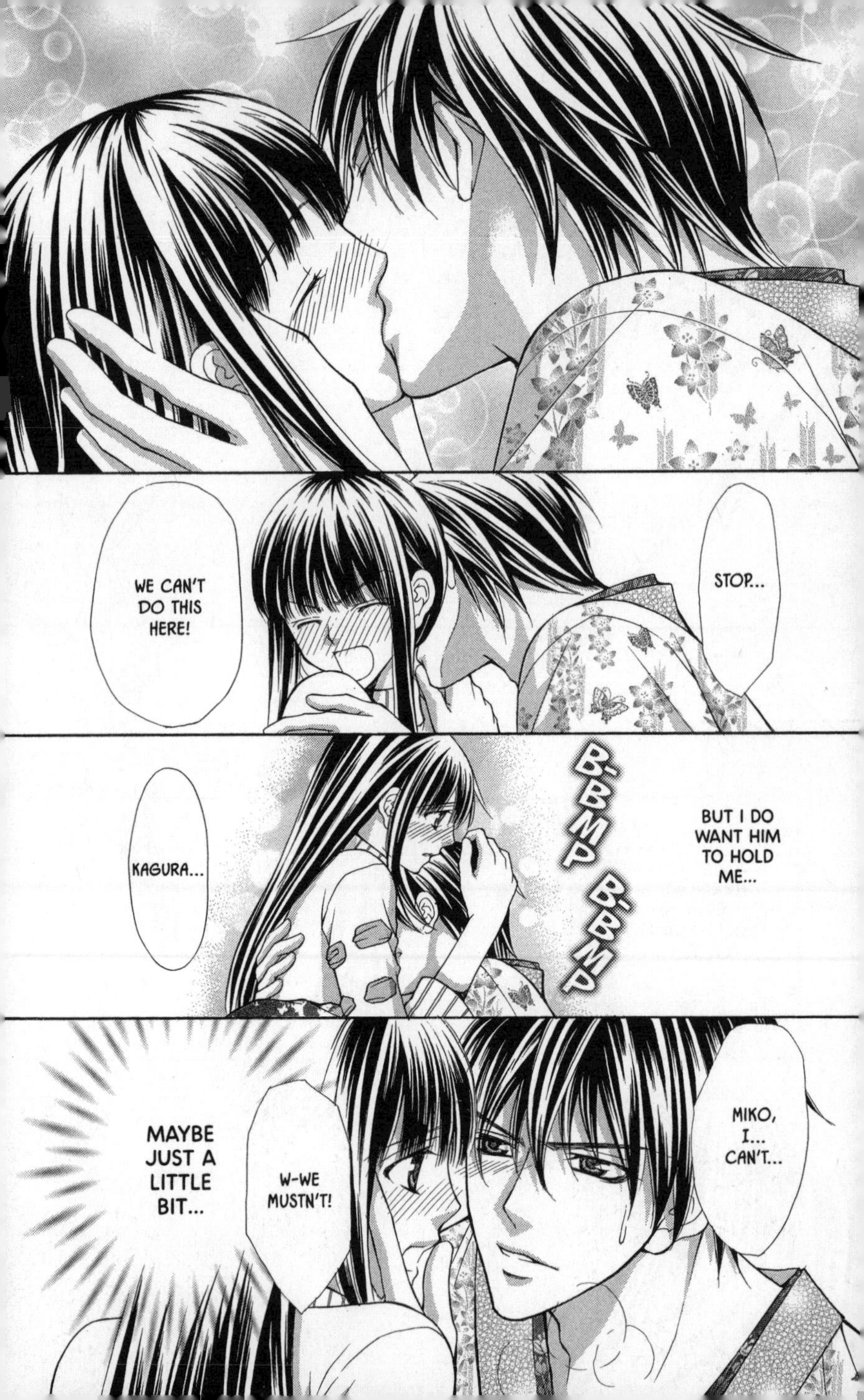
STOP...
WE CAN'T DO THIS HERE!
BUT I DO WANT HIM TO HOLD ME...
B-BMP B-BMP
KAGURA...
MIKO, I... CAN'T...
W-WE MUSTN'T!
MAYBE JUST A LITTLE BIT...

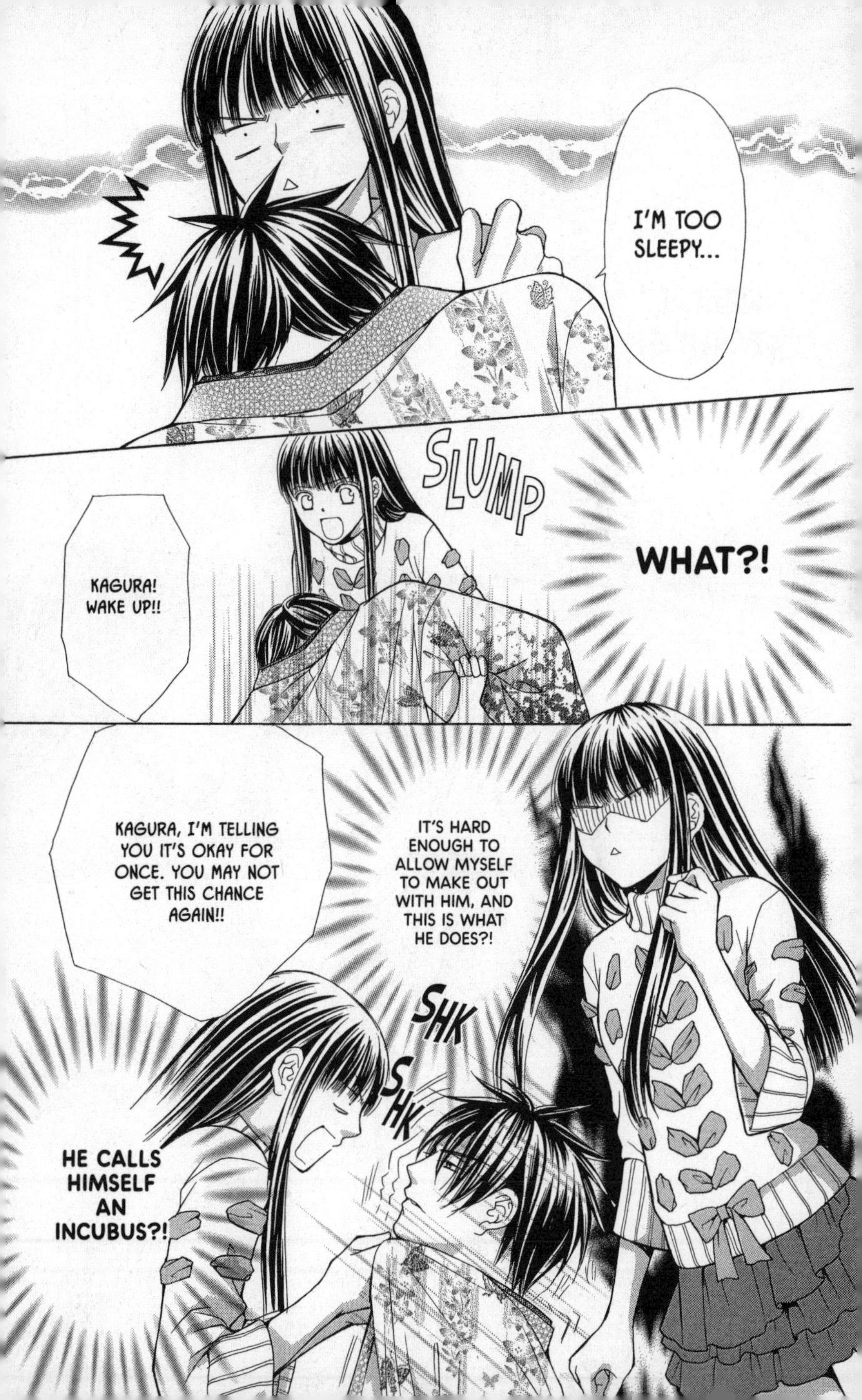
I'M TOO SLEEPY...
WHAT?!
SLUMP
KAGURA! WAKE UP!!
IT'S HARD ENOUGH TO ALLOW MYSELF TO MAKE OUT WITH HIM, AND THIS IS WHAT HE DOES?!
KAGURA, I'M TELLING YOU IT'S OKAY FOR ONCE. YOU MAY NOT GET THIS CHANCE AGAIN!!
SHK
SHK
HE CALLS HIMSELF AN INCUBUS?!

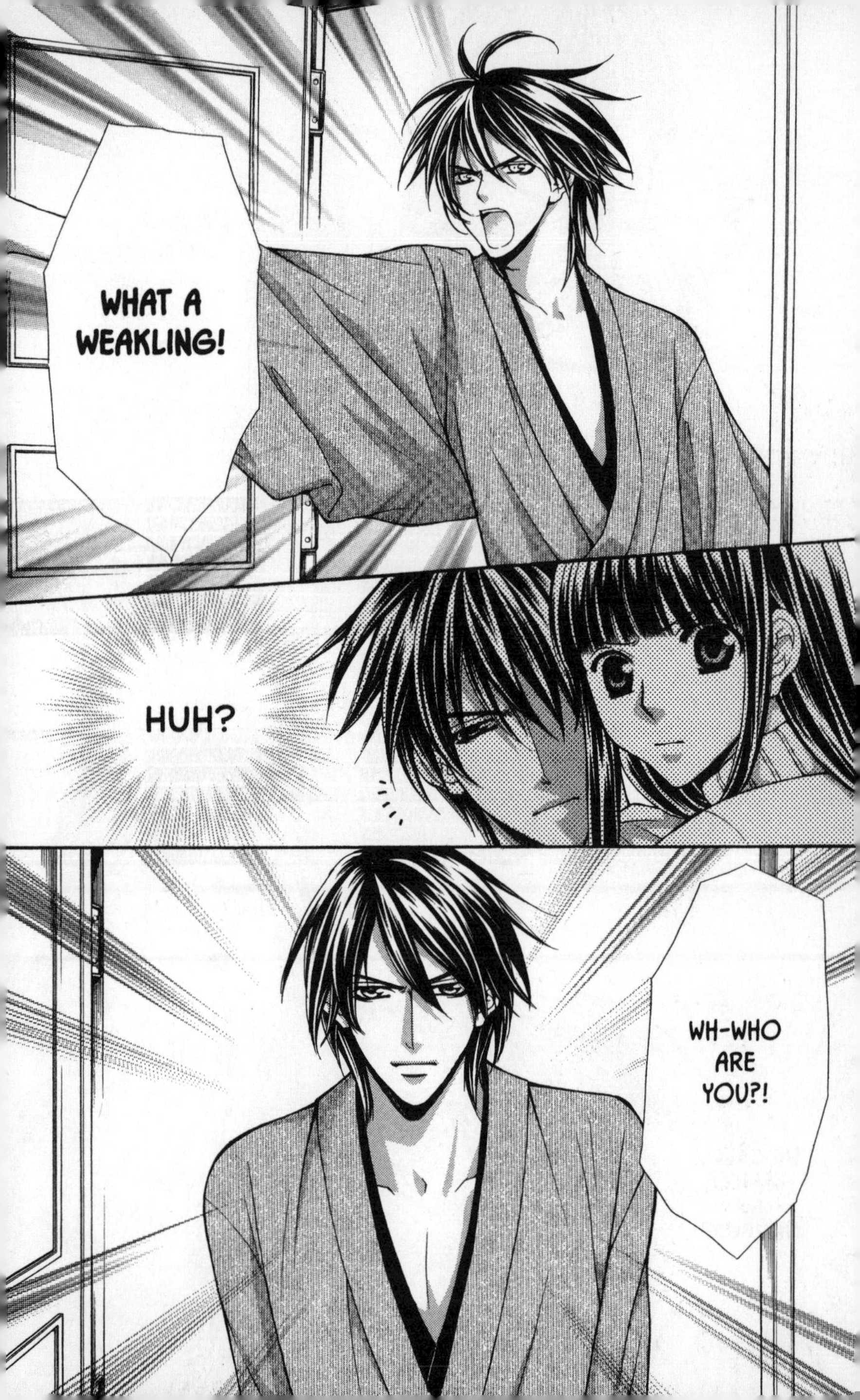
WHAT A WEAKLING!
HUH?
WH-WHO ARE YOU?!

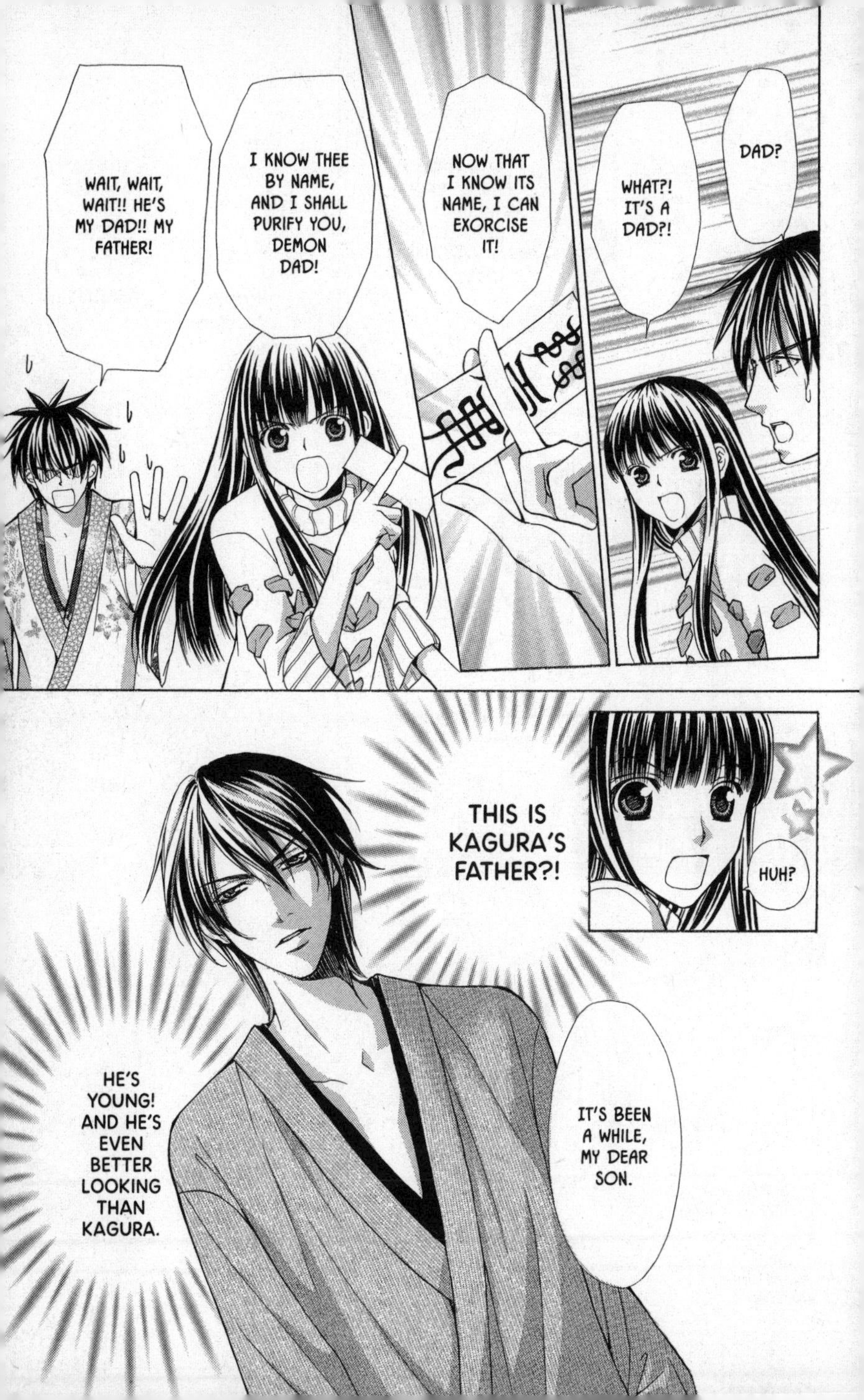
DAD?
WHAT?! IT'S A DAD?!
NOW THAT I KNOW ITS NAME, I CAN EXORCISE IT!
I KNOW THEE BY NAME, AND I SHALL PURIFY YOU, DEMON DAD!
WAIT, WAIT, WAIT!! HE'S MY DAD!! MY FATHER!
HUH?
THIS IS KAGURA'S FATHER?!
IT'S BEEN A WHILE, MY DEAR SON.
HE'S YOUNG! AND HE'S EVEN BETTER LOOKING THAN KAGURA.

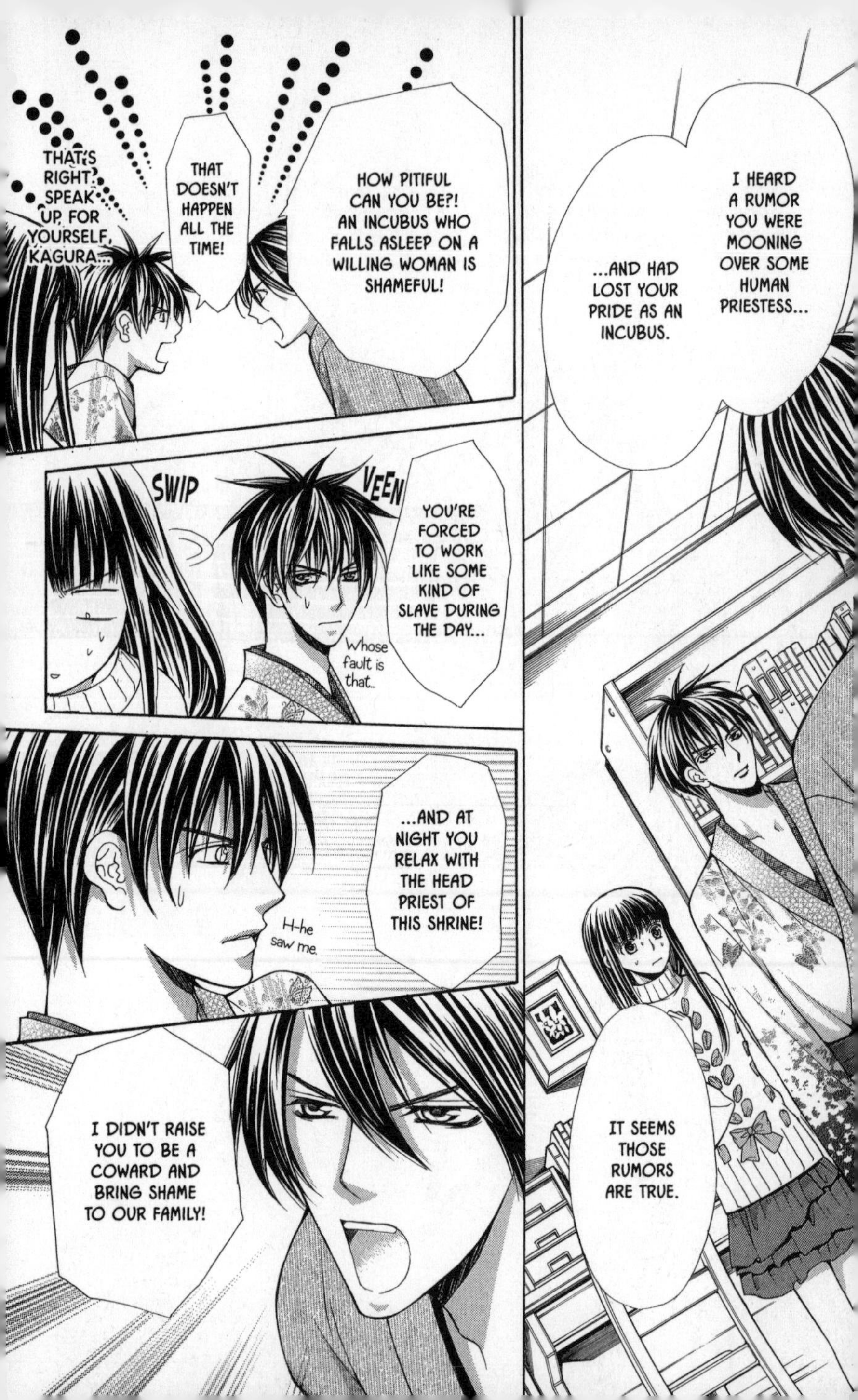
I HEARD A RUMOR YOU WERE MOONING OVER SOME HUMAN PRIESTESS...
...AND HAD LOST YOUR PRIDE AS AN INCUBUS.
IT SEEMS THOSE RUMORS ARE TRUE.
HOW PITIFUL CAN YOU BE?! AN INCUBUS WHO FALLS ASLEEP ON A WILLING WOMAN IS SHAMEFUL!
THAT DOESN'T HAPPEN ALL THE TIME!
THAT'S RIGHT. SPEAK UP FOR YOURSELF, KAGURA...
YOU'RE FORCED TO WORK LIKE SOME KIND OF SLAVE DURING THE DAY...
VEEN
Whose fault is that..
SWIP
...AND AT NIGHT YOU RELAX WITH THE HEAD PRIEST OF THIS SHRINE!
H-he saw me.
I DIDN'T RAISE YOU TO BE A COWARD AND BRING SHAME TO OUR FAMILY!

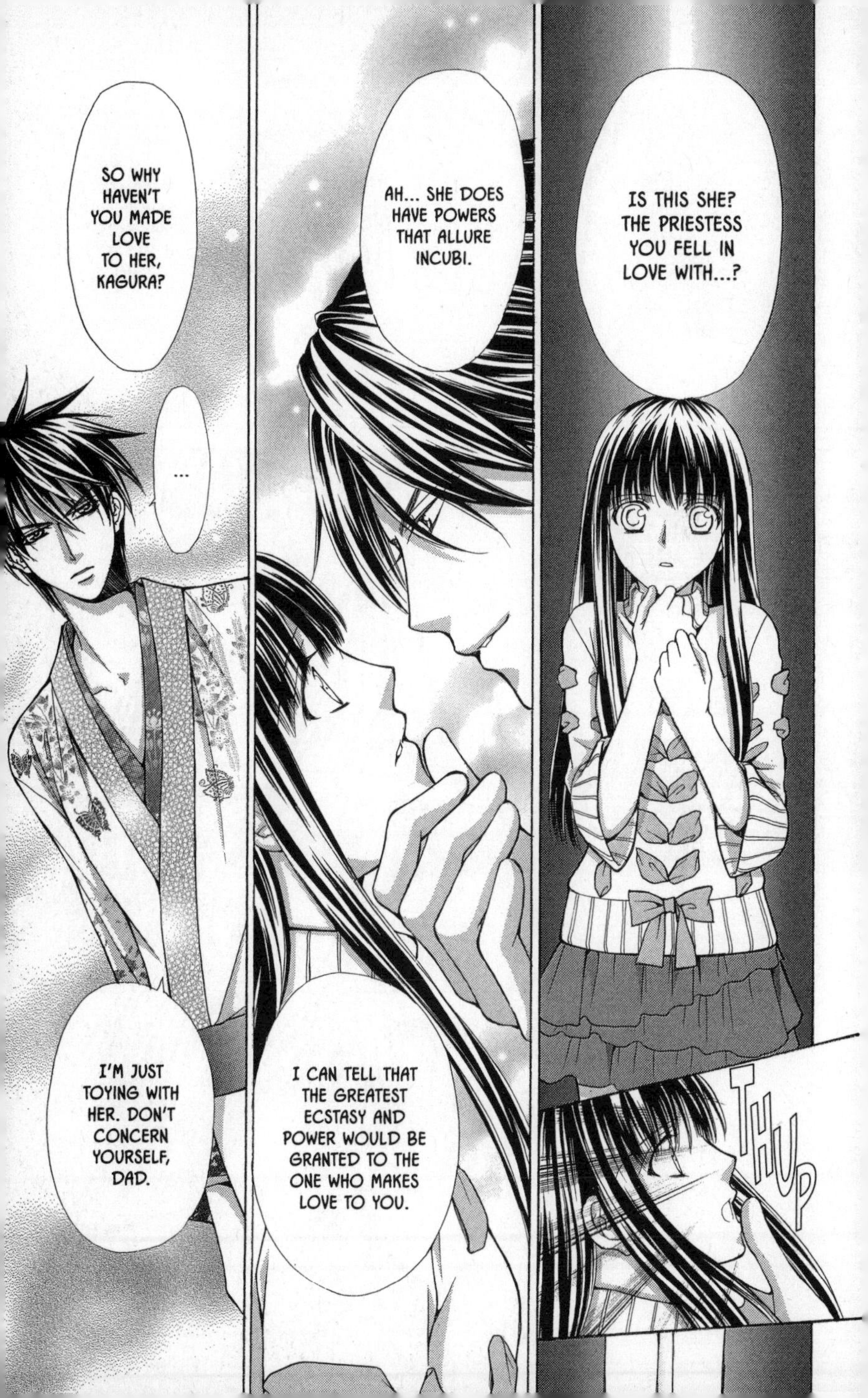
IS THIS SHE? THE PRIESTESS YOU FELL IN LOVE WITH...?
THUP
AH... SHE DOES HAVE POWERS THAT ALLURE INCUBI.
I CAN TELL THAT THE GREATEST ECSTASY AND POWER WOULD BE GRANTED TO THE ONE WHO MAKES LOVE TO YOU.
SO WHY HAVEN'T YOU MADE LOVE TO HER, KAGURA?
...
I'M JUST TOYING WITH HER. DON'T CONCERN YOURSELF, DAD.

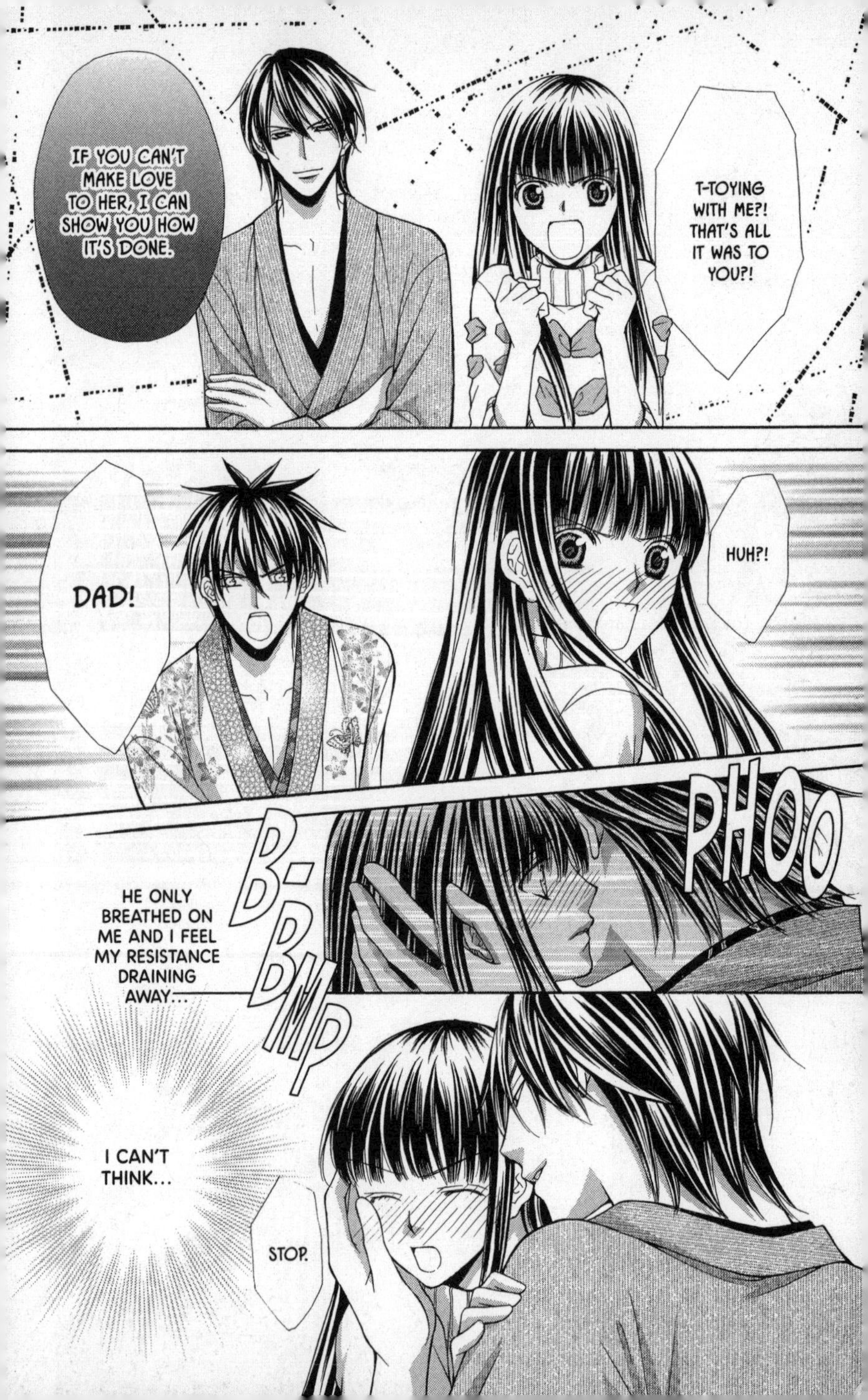
T-TOYING WITH ME?! THAT'S ALL IT WAS TO YOU?!
IF YOU CAN'T MAKE LOVE TO HER, I CAN SHOW YOU HOW IT'S DONE.
HUH?!
DAD!
PHOO
B-BMP
HE ONLY BREATHED ON ME AND I FEEL MY RESISTANCE DRAINING AWAY...
I CAN'T THINK...
STOP.

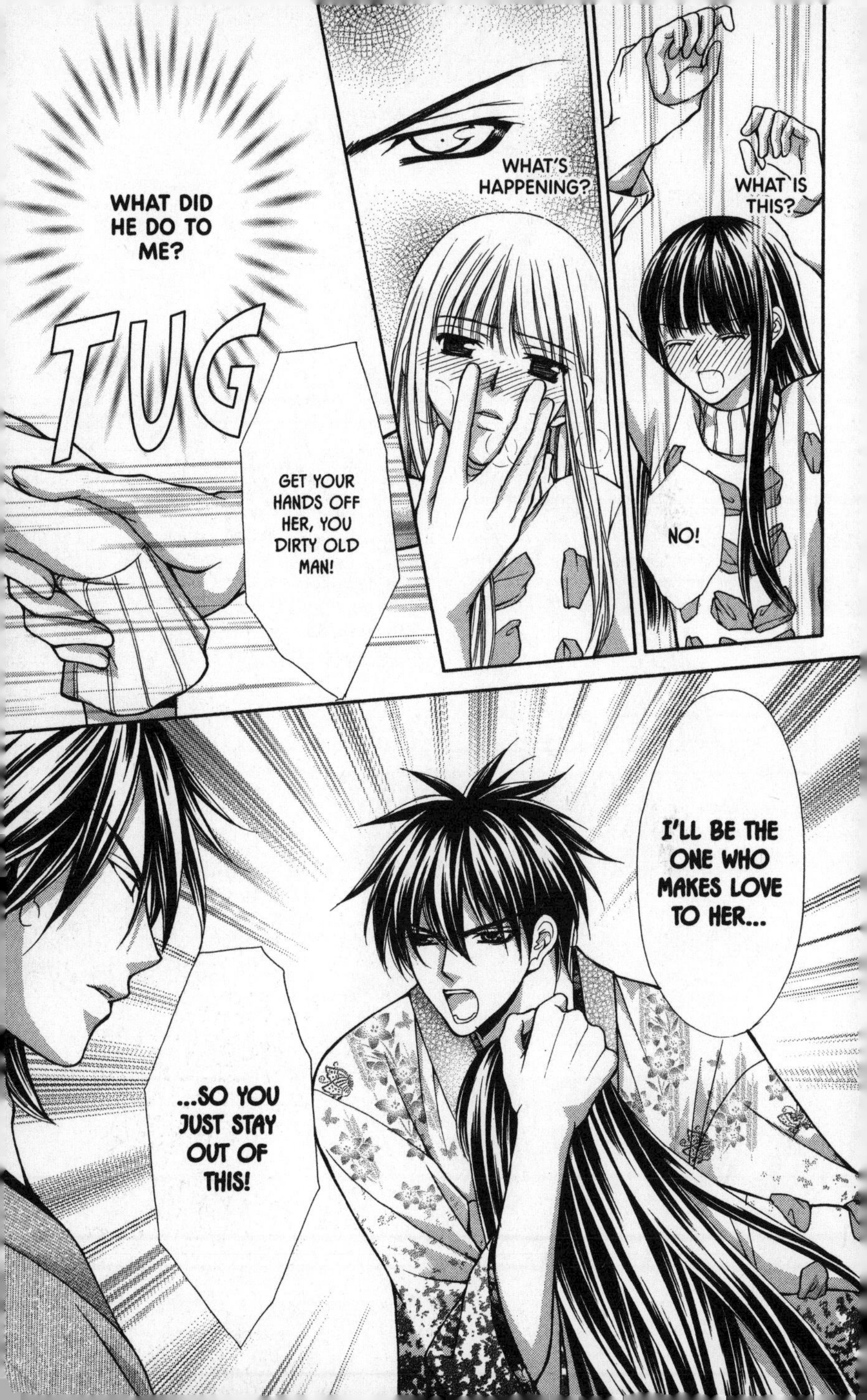
WHAT IS THIS?
NO!
WHAT'S HAPPENING?
WHAT DID HE DO TO ME?
TUG
GET YOUR HANDS OFF HER, YOU DIRTY OLD MAN!
I'LL BE THE ONE WHO MAKES LOVE TO HER...
...SO YOU JUST STAY OUT OF THIS!

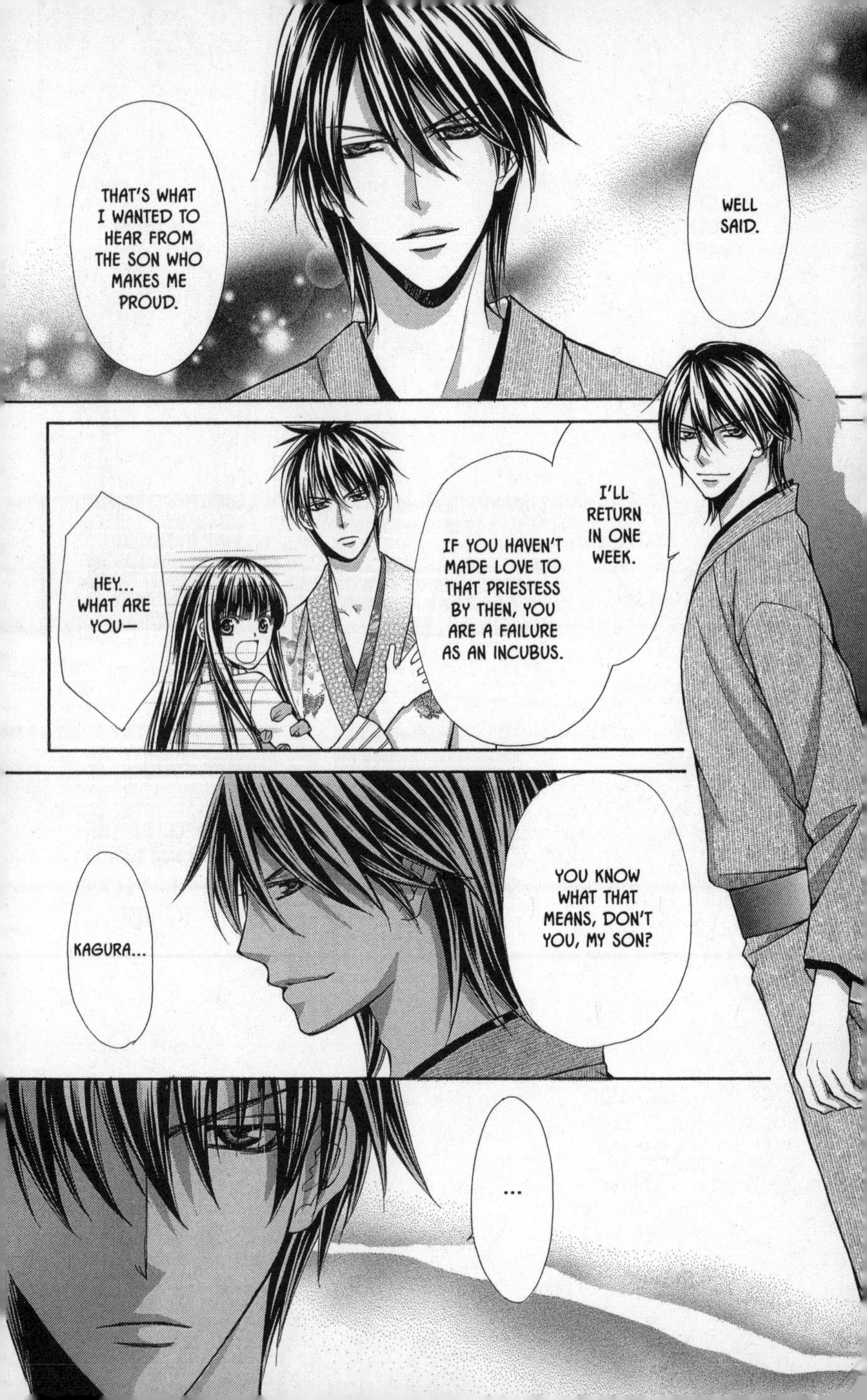
WELL SAID.
THAT'S WHAT I WANTED TO HEAR FROM THE SON WHO MAKES ME PROUD.
I'LL RETURN IN ONE WEEK.
IF YOU HAVEN'T MADE LOVE TO THAT PRIESTESS BY THEN, YOU ARE A FAILURE AS AN INCUBUS.
HEY... WHAT ARE YOU—
YOU KNOW WHAT THAT MEANS, DON'T YOU, MY SON?
KAGURA...
...

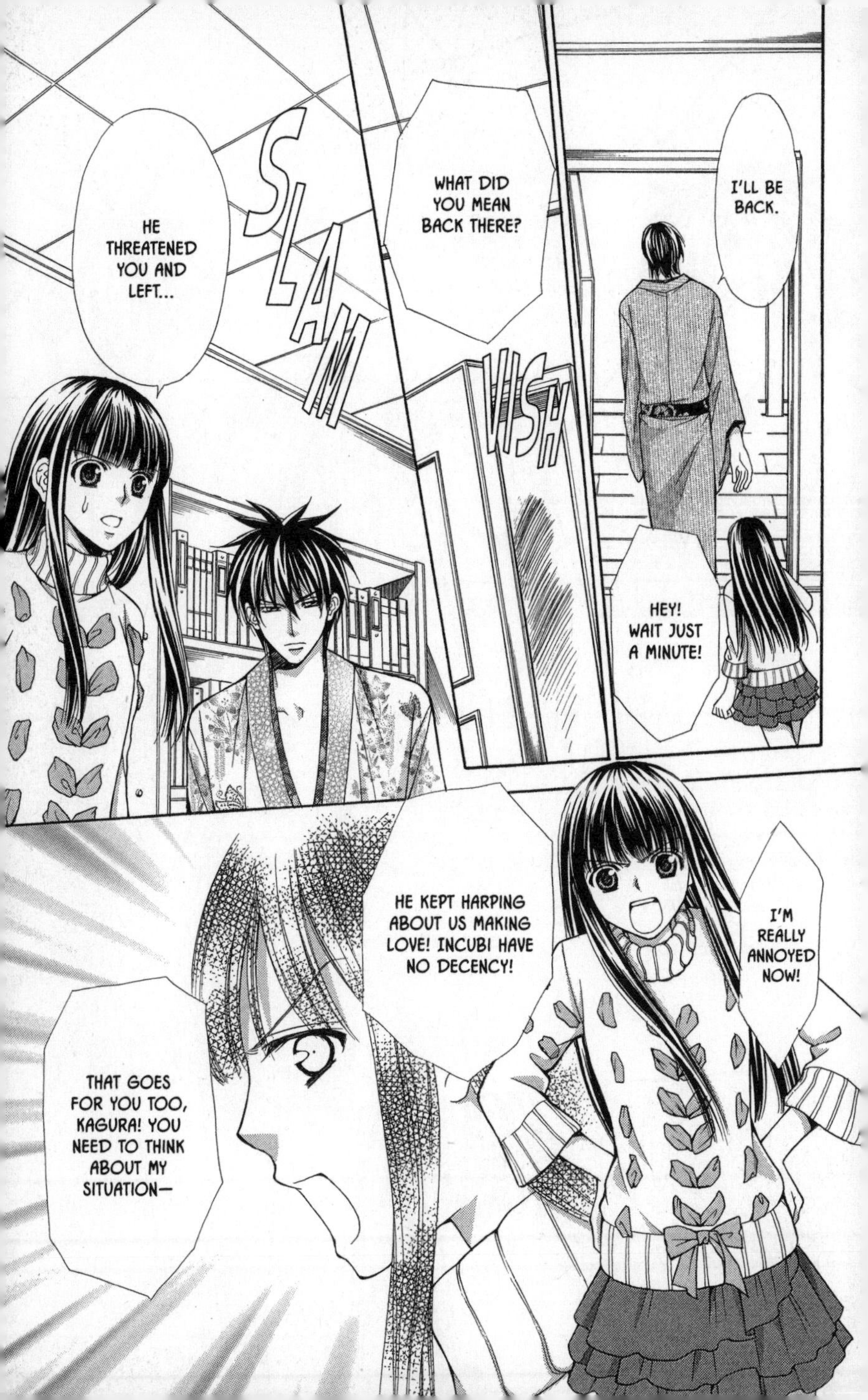
I'LL BE BACK.
HEY! WAIT JUST A MINUTE!
VISH
WHAT DID YOU MEAN BACK THERE?
SLAM
HE THREATENED YOU AND LEFT...
I'M REALLY ANNOYED NOW!
HE KEPT HARPING ABOUT US MAKING LOVE! INCUBI HAVE NO DECENCY!
THAT GOES FOR YOU TOO, KAGURA! YOU NEED TO THINK ABOUT MY SITUATION—

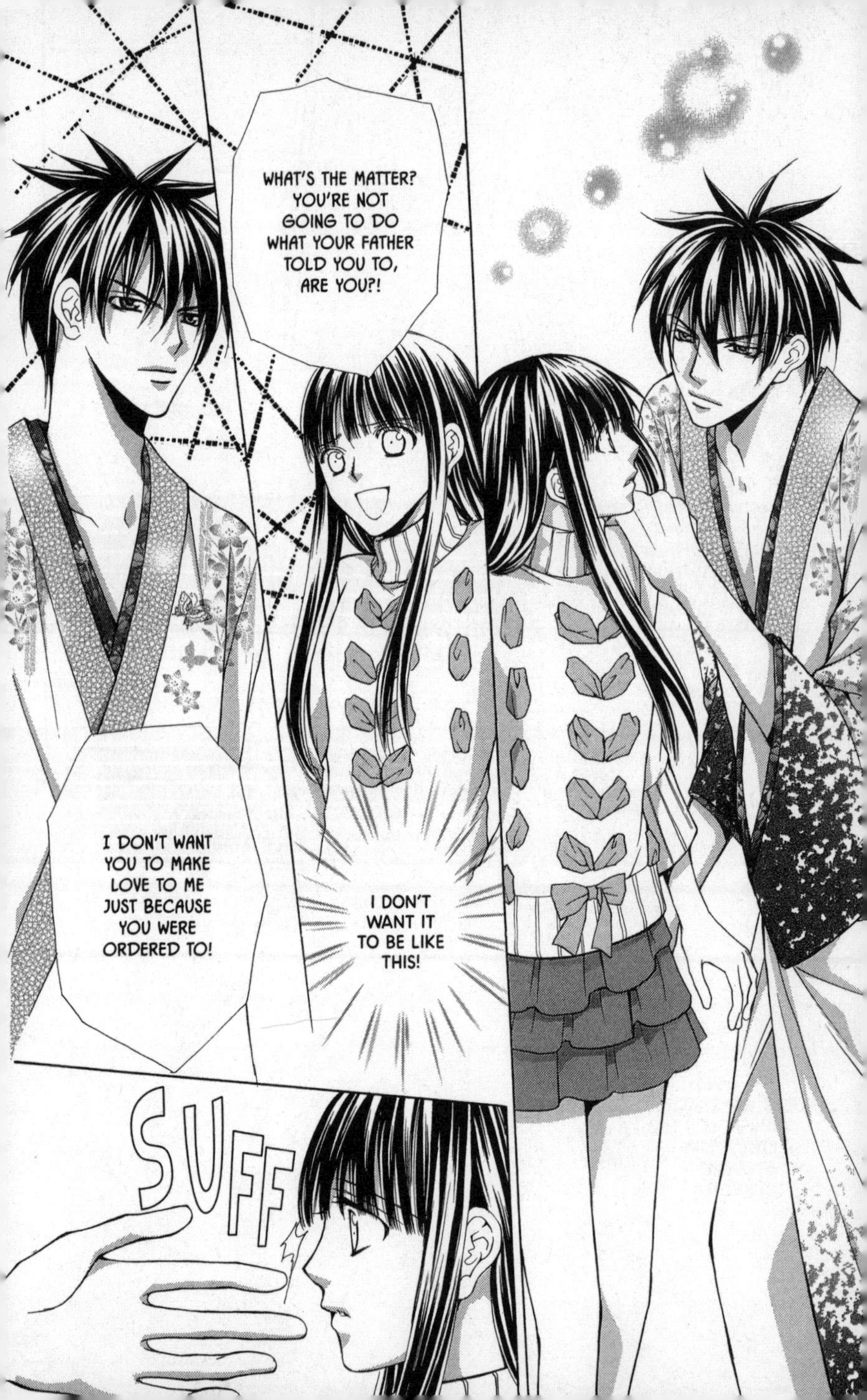
WHAT'S THE MATTER? YOU'RE NOT GOING TO DO WHAT YOUR FATHER TOLD YOU TO, ARE YOU?!
I DON'T WANT IT TO BE LIKE THIS!
I DON'T WANT YOU TO MAKE LOVE TO ME JUST BECAUSE YOU WERE ORDERED TO!
SUFF

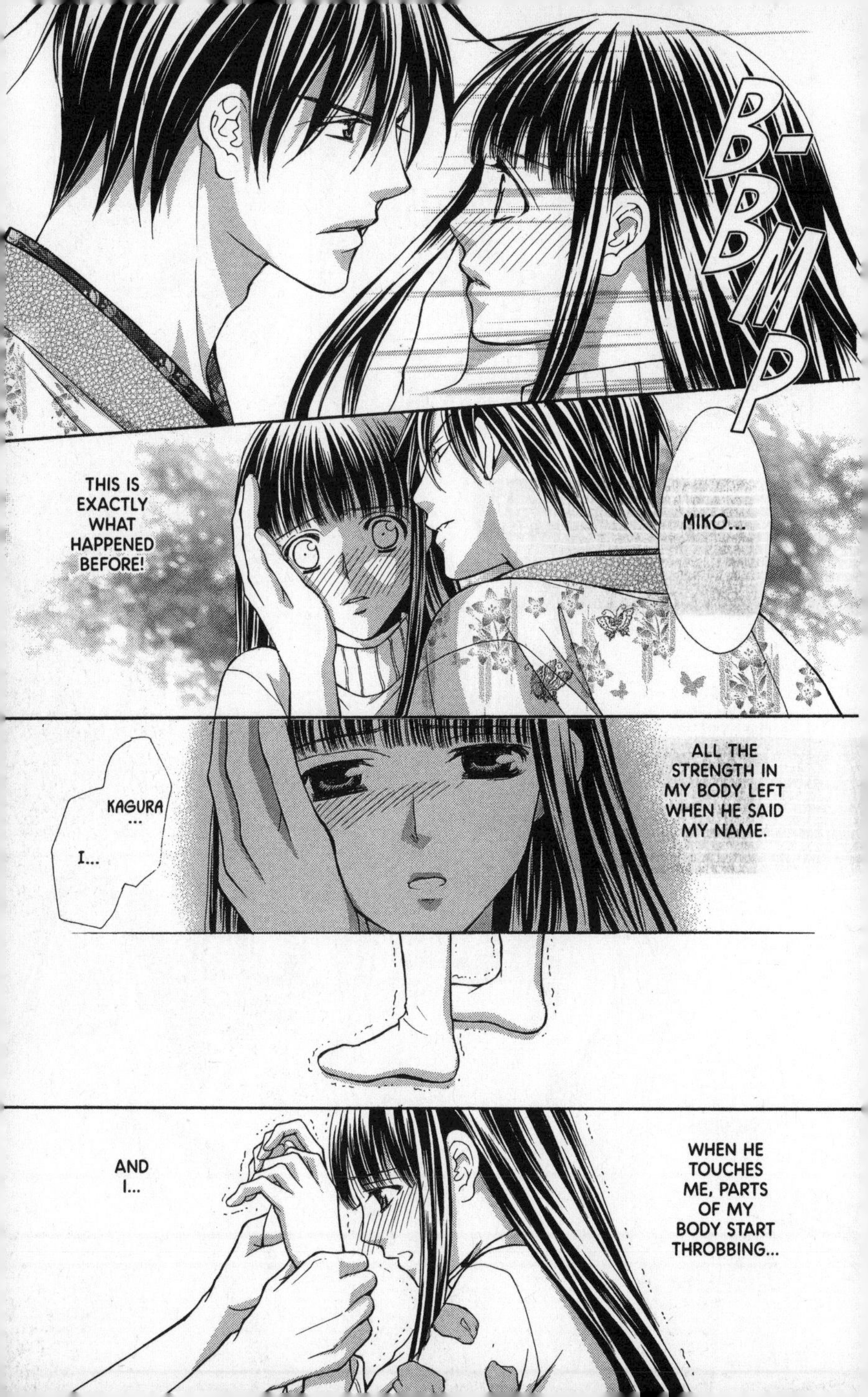
B-BMP
MIKO...
THIS IS EXACTLY WHAT HAPPENED BEFORE!
ALL THE STRENGTH IN MY BODY LEFT WHEN HE SAID MY NAME.
KAGURA ...
I...
WHEN HE TOUCHES ME, PARTS OF MY BODY START THROBBING...
AND I...

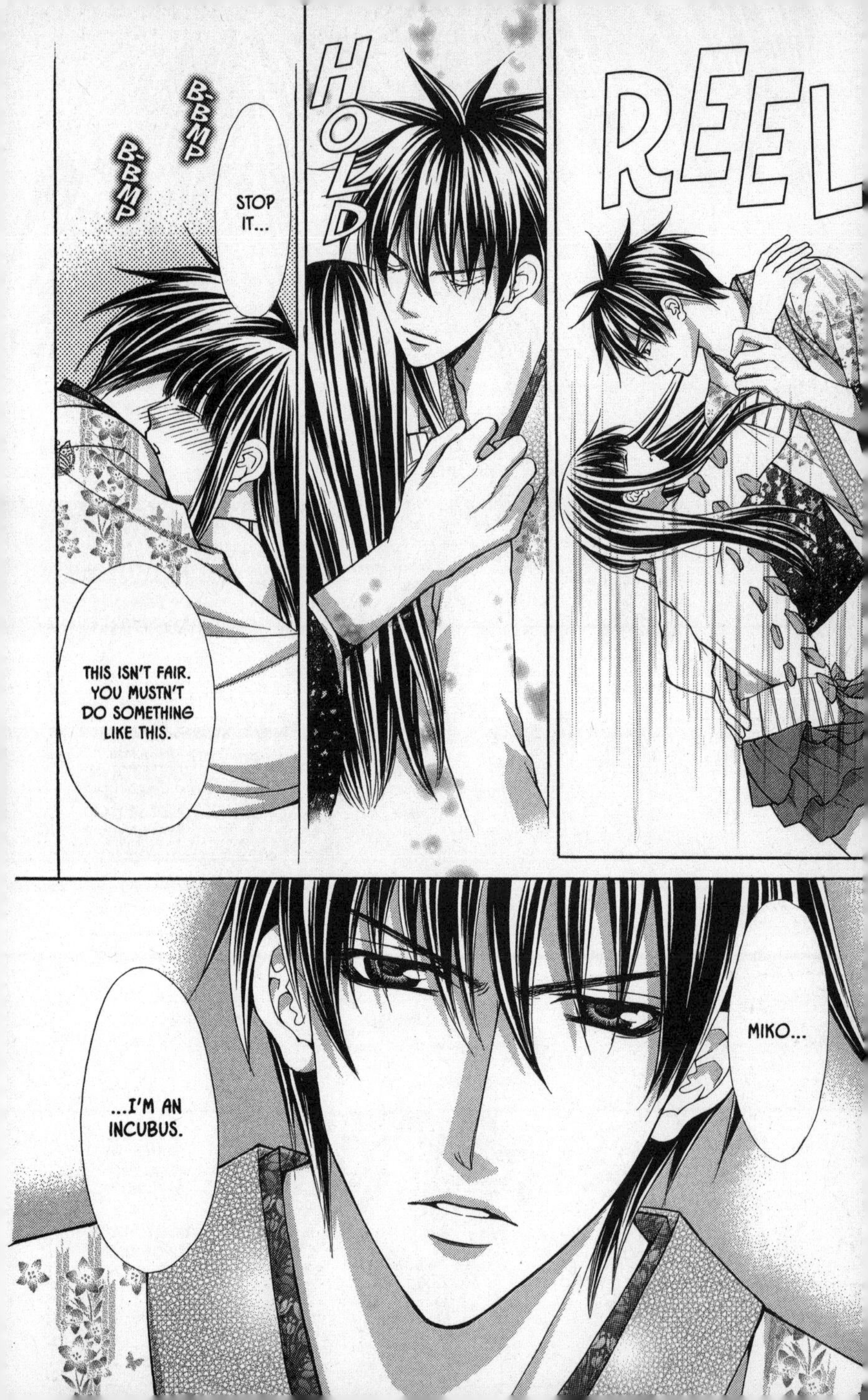
REEL
HOLD
STOP IT...
B-BMP
B-BMP
THIS ISN'T FAIR. YOU MUSTN'T DO SOMETHING LIKE THIS.
MIKO...
...I'M AN INCUBUS.

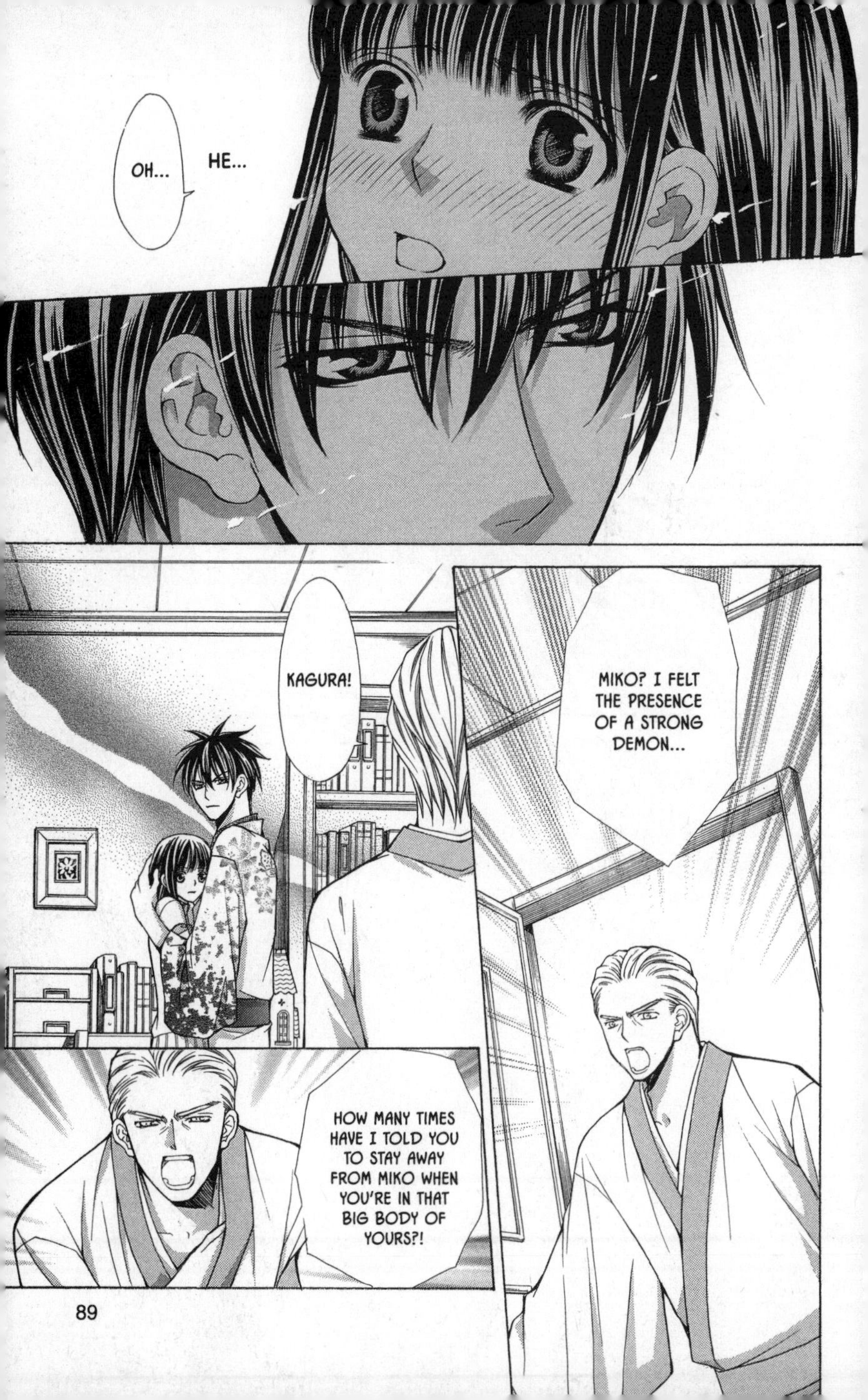
OH...
HE...
MIKO? I FELT THE PRESENCE OF A STRONG DEMON...
KAGURA!
HOW MANY TIMES HAVE I TOLD YOU TO STAY AWAY FROM MIKO WHEN YOU'RE IN THAT BIG BODY OF YOURS?!

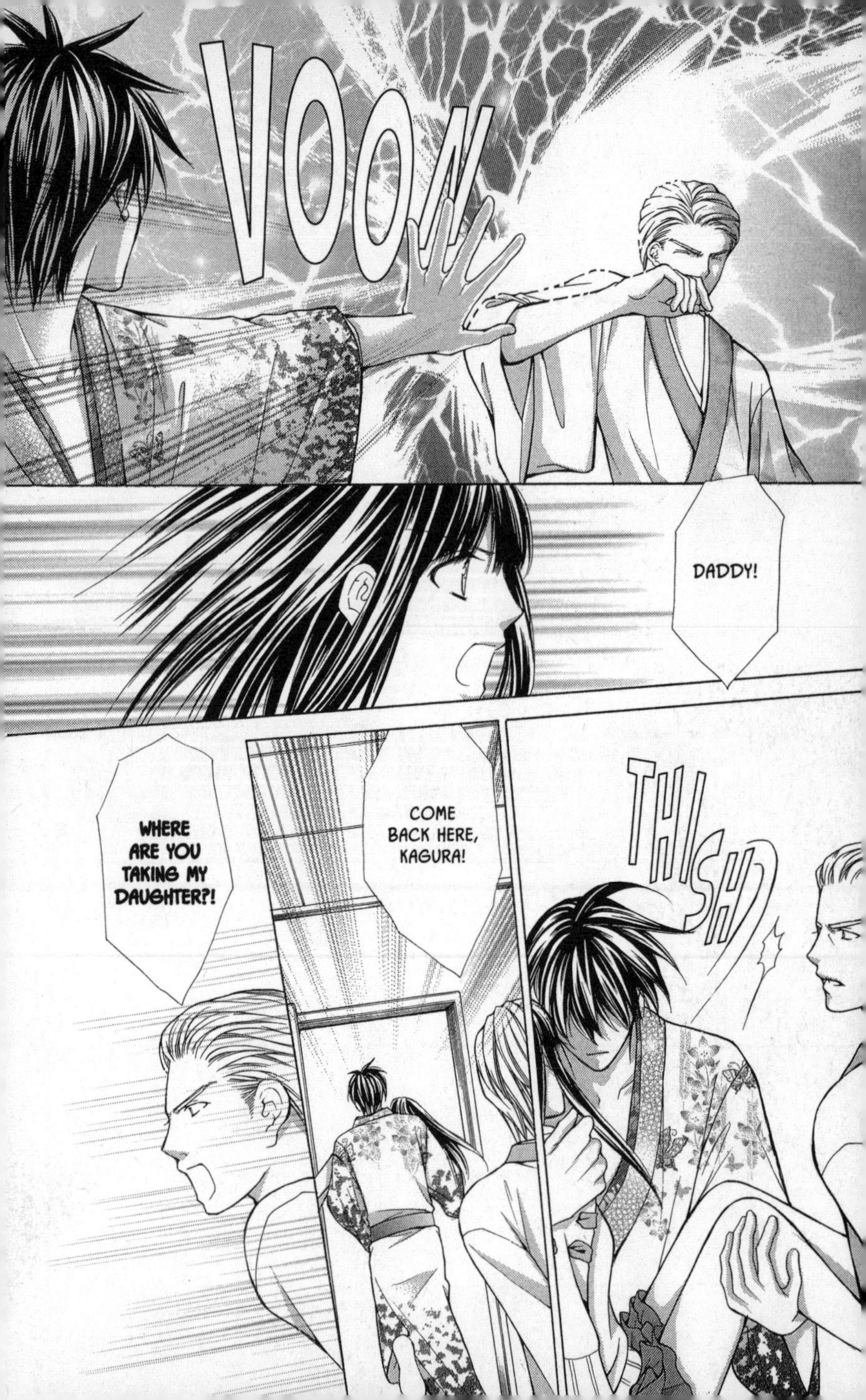
VOOM
DADDY!
THISH
COME BACK HERE, KAGURA!
WHERE ARE YOU TAKING MY DAUGHTER?!

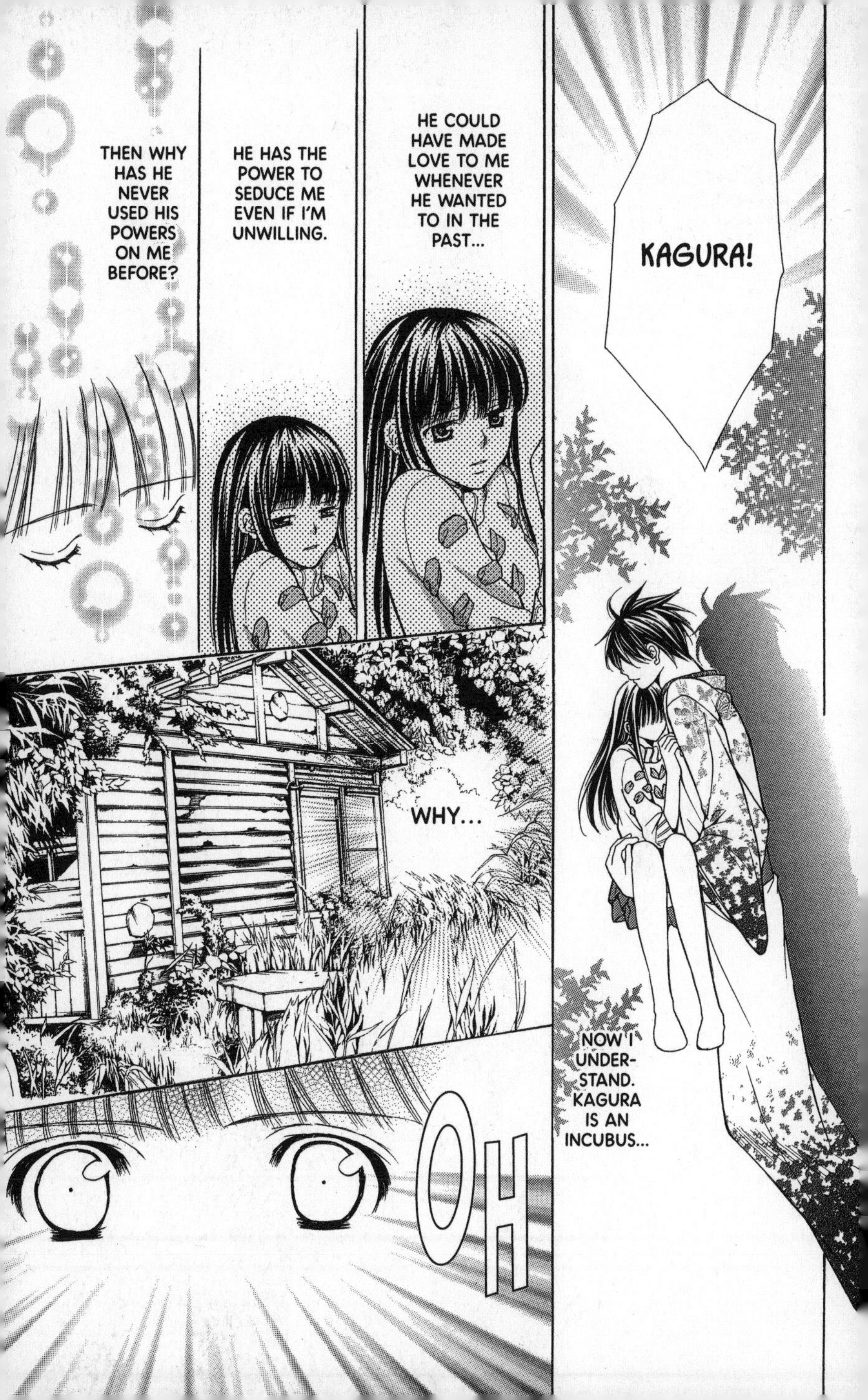
KAGURA!
NOW I UNDERSTAND. KAGURA IS AN INCUBUS...
HE COULD HAVE MADE LOVE TO ME WHENEVER HE WANTED TO IN THE PAST...
HE HAS THE POWER TO SEDUCE ME EVEN IF I'M UNWILLING.
THEN WHY HAS HE NEVER USED HIS POWERS ON ME BEFORE?
WHY...
OH

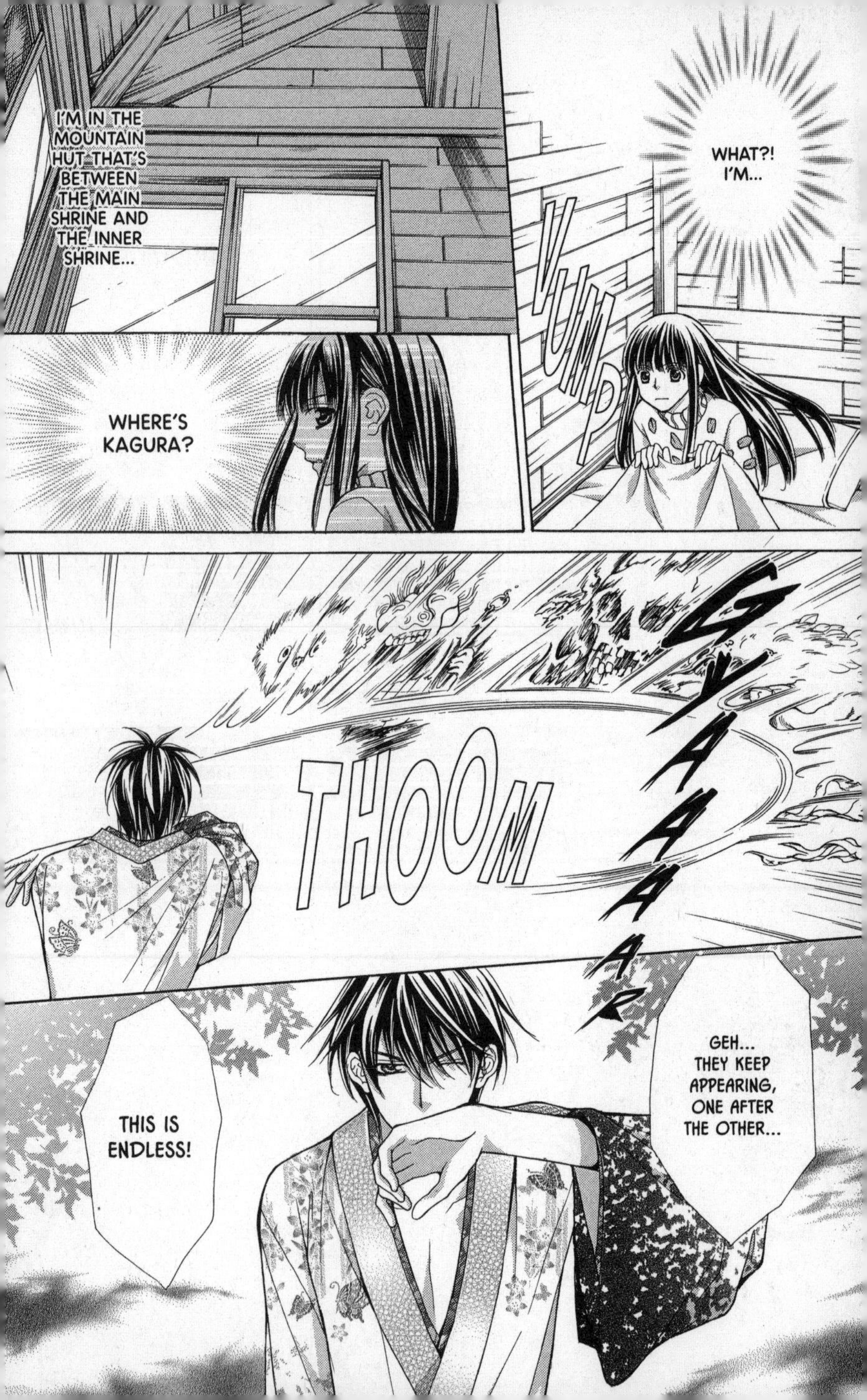
WHAT?! I'M...
VUMP
I'M IN THE MOUNTAIN HUT THAT'S BETWEEN THE MAIN SHRINE AND THE INNER SHRINE...
WHERE'S KAGURA?
GYAAAAAR
THOOM
GEH... THEY KEEP APPEARING, ONE AFTER THE OTHER...
THIS IS ENDLESS!

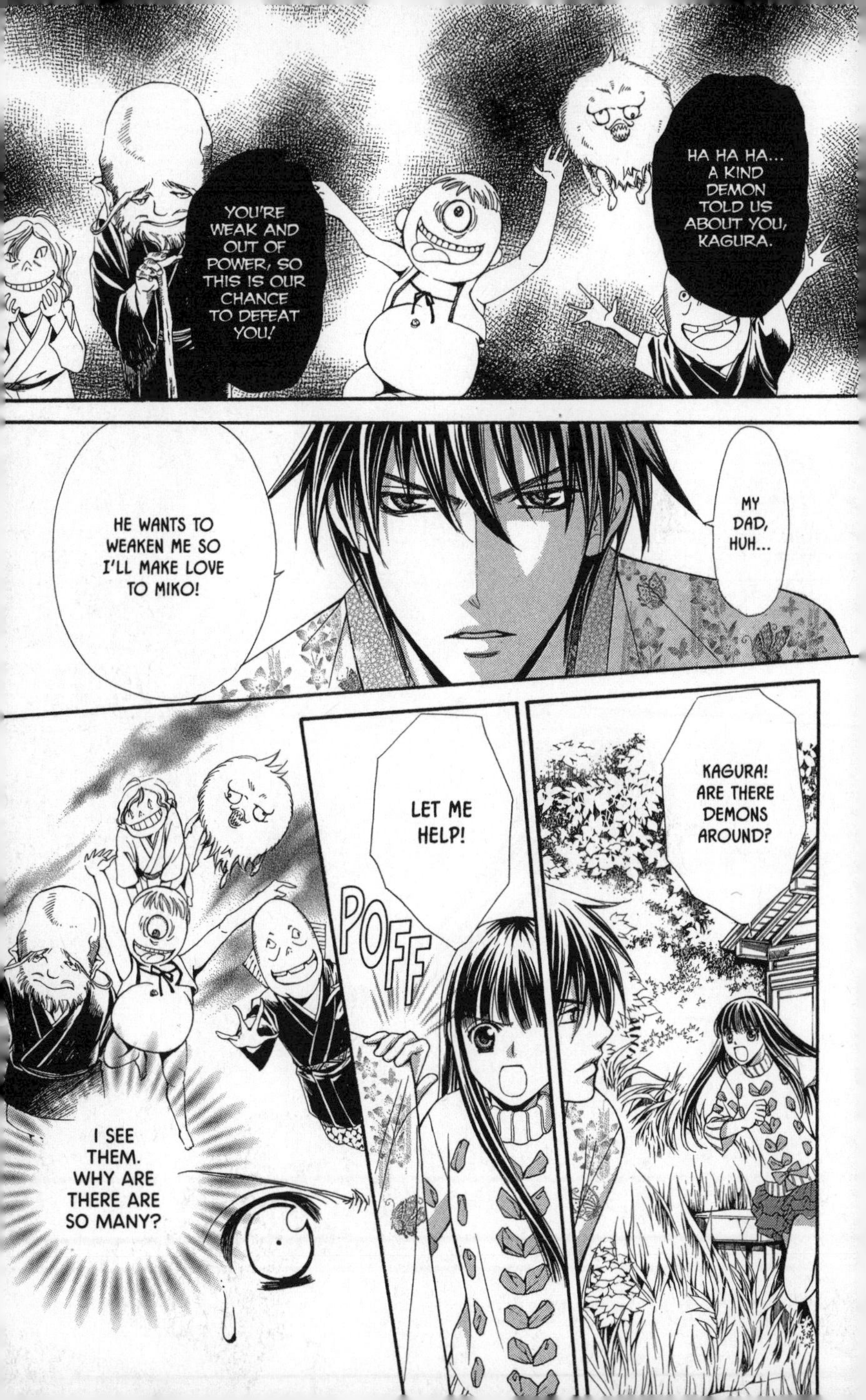
HA HA HA... A KIND DEMON TOLD US ABOUT YOU, KAGURA.
YOU'RE WEAK AND OUT OF POWER, SO THIS IS OUR CHANCE TO DEFEAT YOU!
MY DAD, HUH...
HE WANTS TO WEAKEN ME SO I'LL MAKE LOVE TO MIKO!
KAGURA! ARE THERE DEMONS AROUND?
LET ME HELP!
POFF
I SEE THEM. WHY ARE THERE ARE SO MANY?

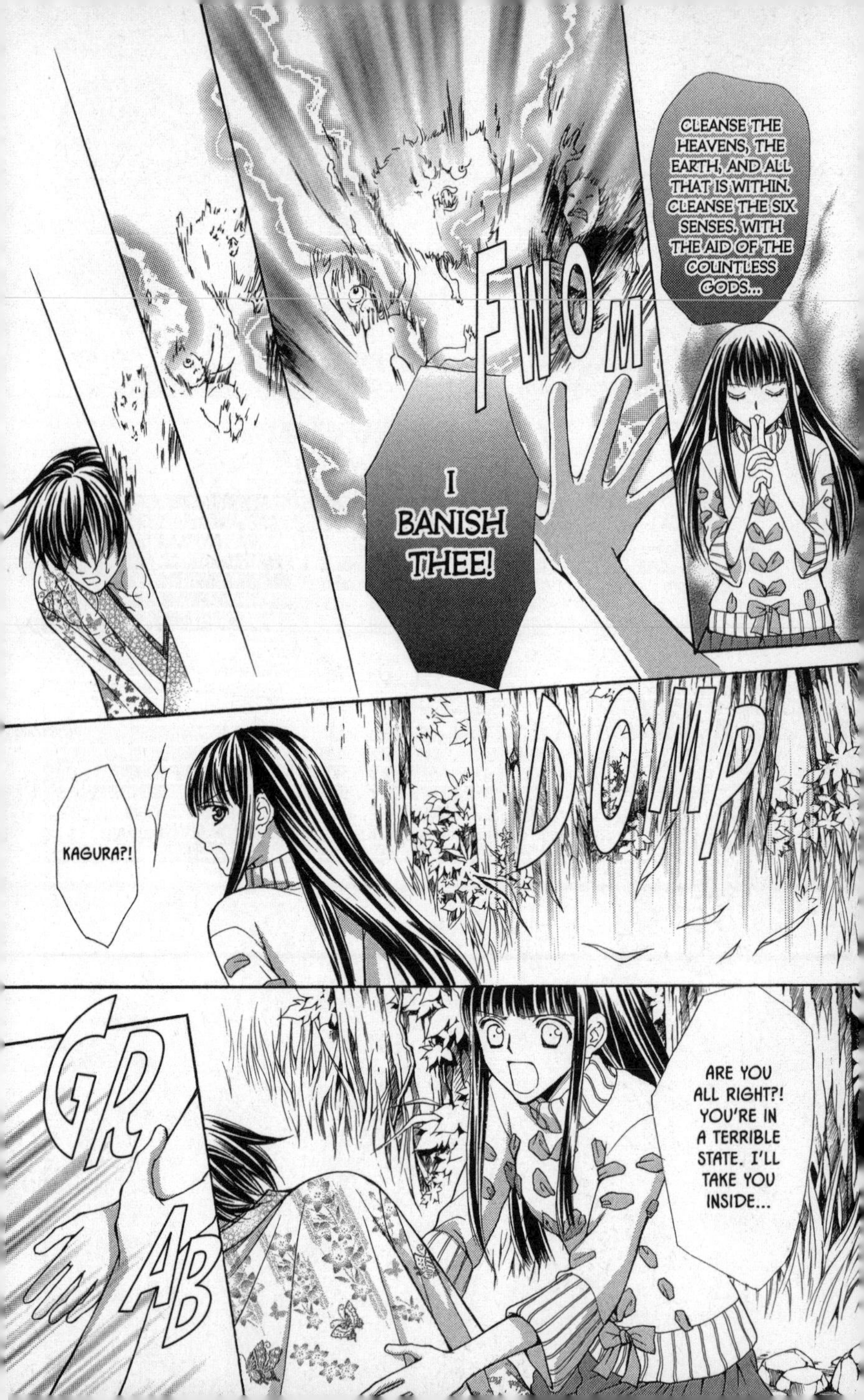
CLEANSE THE HEAVENS, THE EARTH, AND ALL THAT IS WITHIN. CLEANSE THE SIX SENSES. WITH THE AID OF THE COUNTLESS GODS...
FWOM
I BANISH THEE!
DOMP
KAGURA?!
ARE YOU ALL RIGHT?! YOU'RE IN A TERRIBLE STATE. I'LL TAKE YOU INSIDE...
GRAB

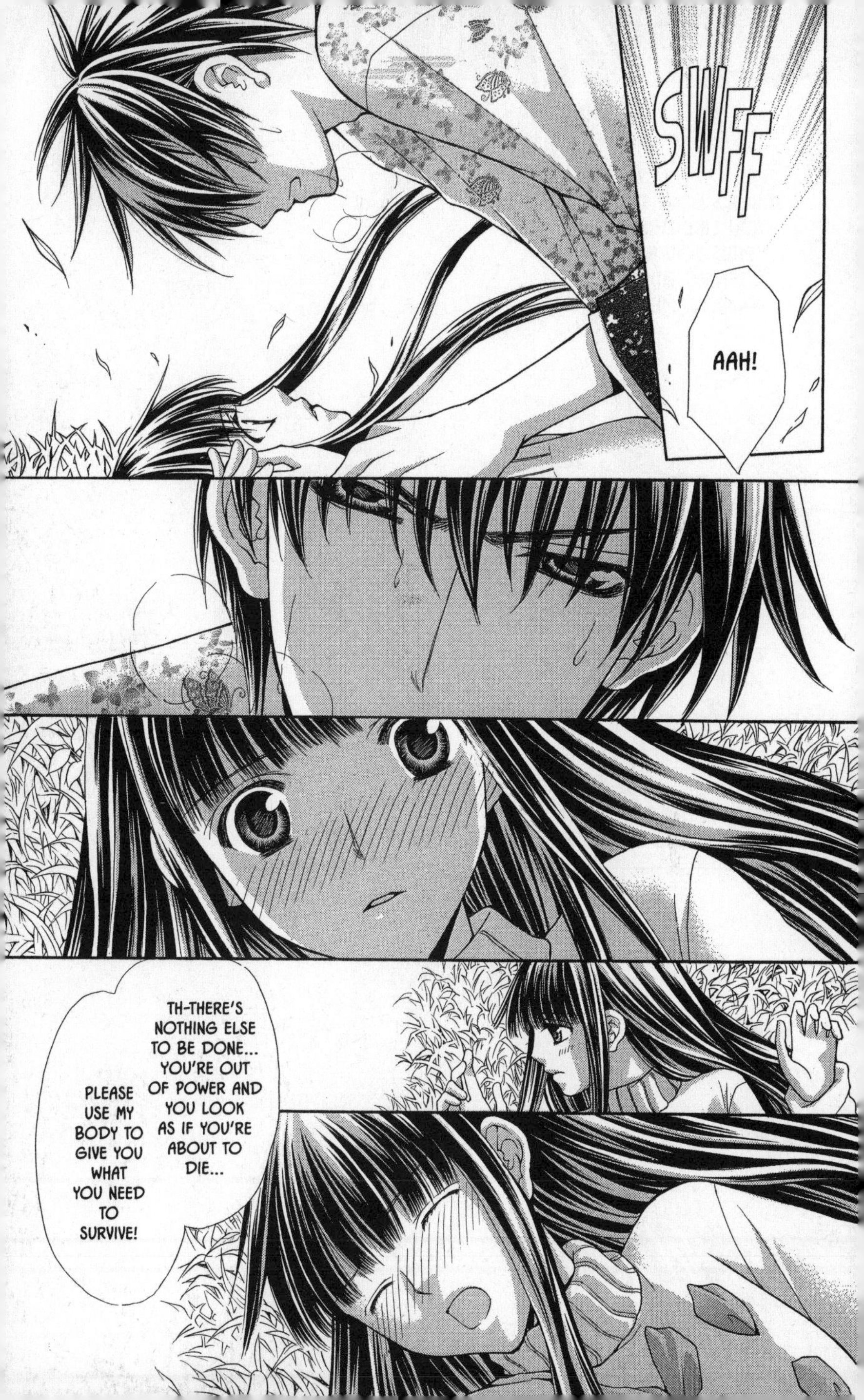
SWFF
AAH!
TH-THERE'S NOTHING ELSE TO BE DONE... YOU'RE OUT OF POWER AND YOU LOOK AS IF YOU'RE ABOUT TO DIE...
PLEASE USE MY BODY TO GIVE YOU WHAT YOU NEED TO SURVIVE!

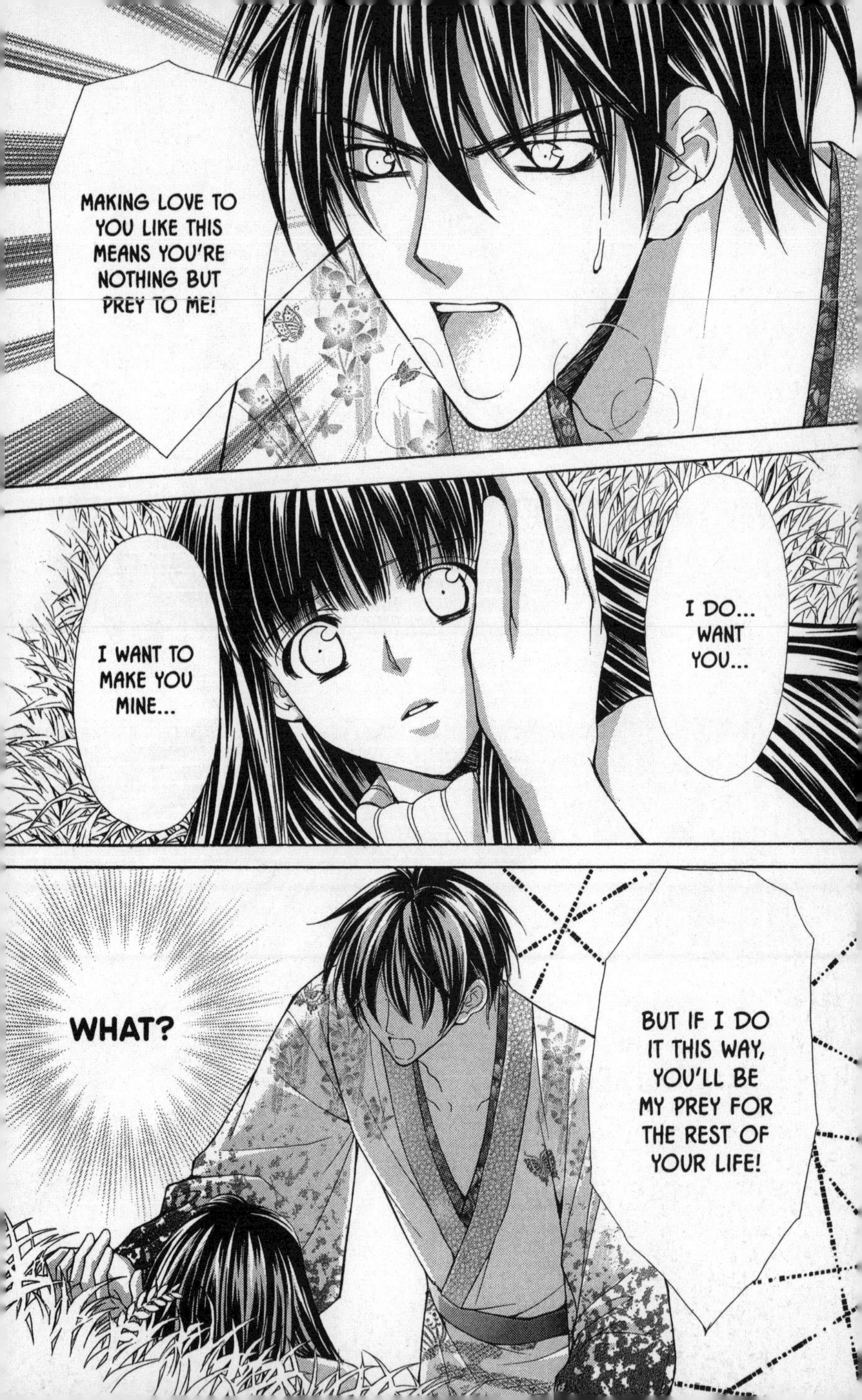
MAKING LOVE TO YOU LIKE THIS MEANS YOU'RE NOTHING BUT PREY TO ME!
I DO... WANT YOU...
I WANT TO MAKE YOU MINE...
BUT IF I DO IT THIS WAY, YOU'LL BE MY PREY FOR THE REST OF YOUR LIFE!
WHAT?

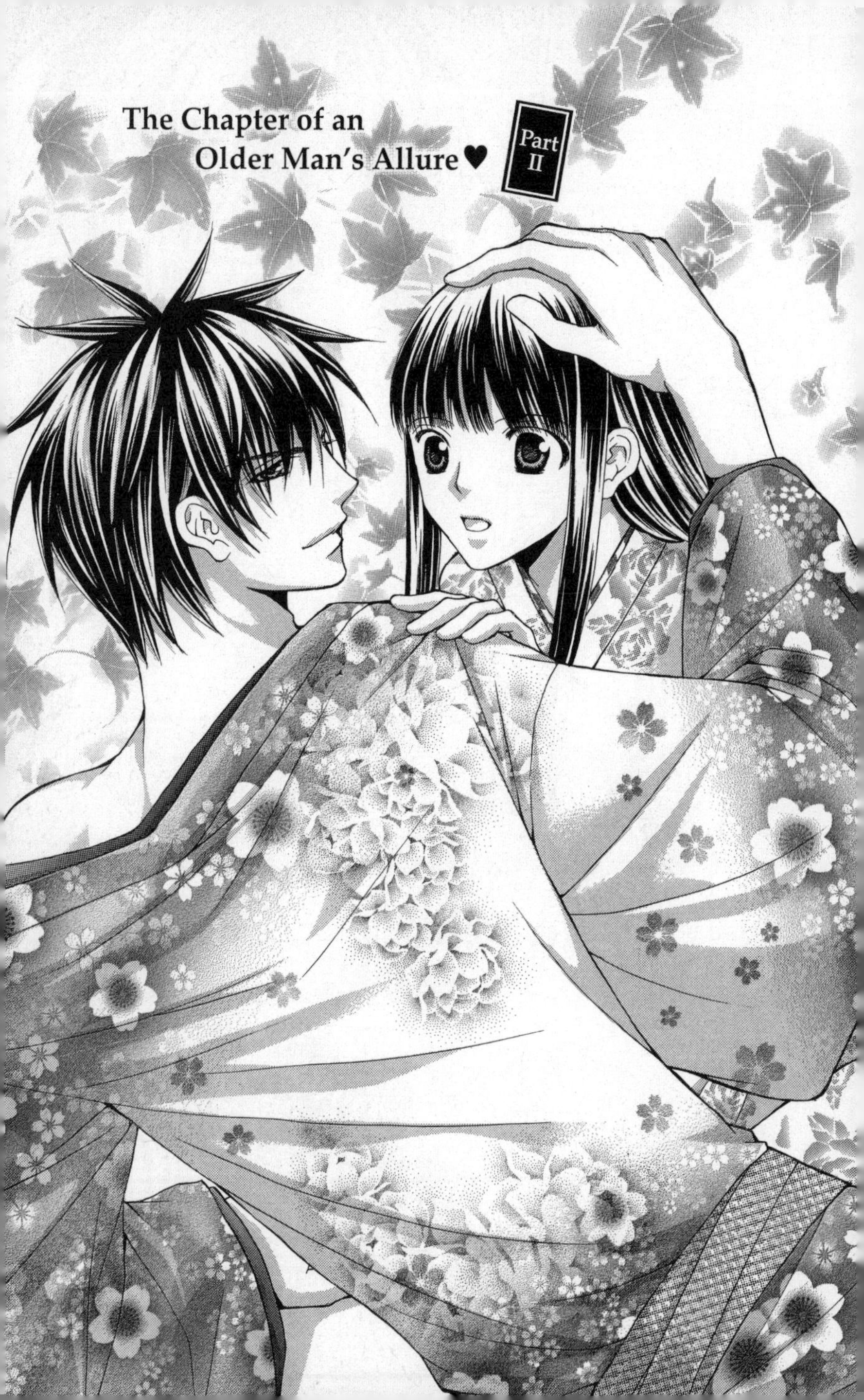
The Chapter of an
Older Man's Allure♥
Part II

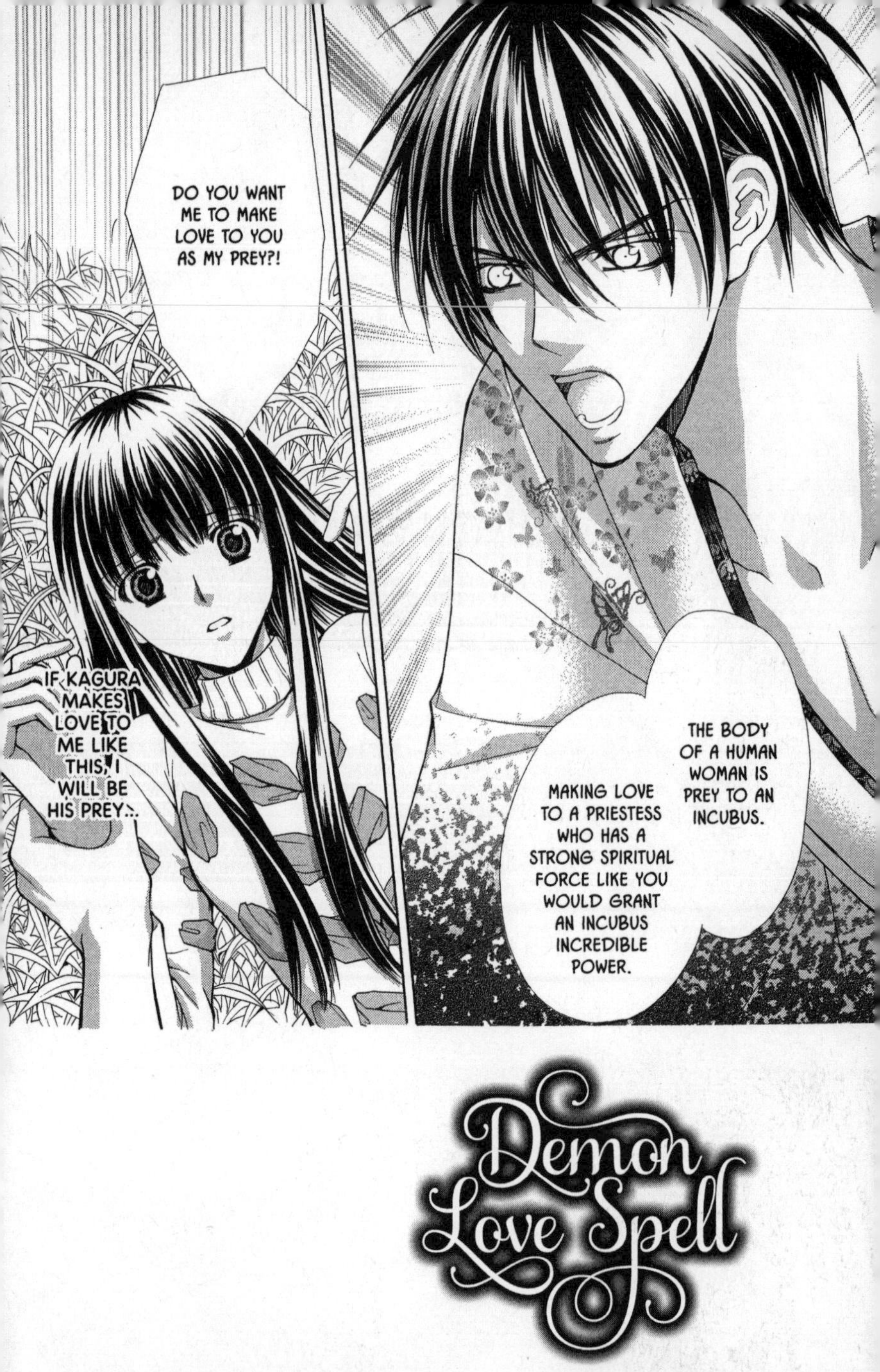
THE BODY OF A HUMAN WOMAN IS PREY TO AN INCUBUS.
MAKING LOVE TO A PRIESTESS WHO HAS A STRONG SPIRITUAL FORCE LIKE YOU WOULD GRANT AN INCUBUS INCREDIBLE POWER.
DO YOU WANT ME TO MAKE LOVE TO YOU AS MY PREY?!
IF KAGURA MAKES LOVE TO ME LIKE THIS, I WILL BE HIS PREY...

Demon Love Spell

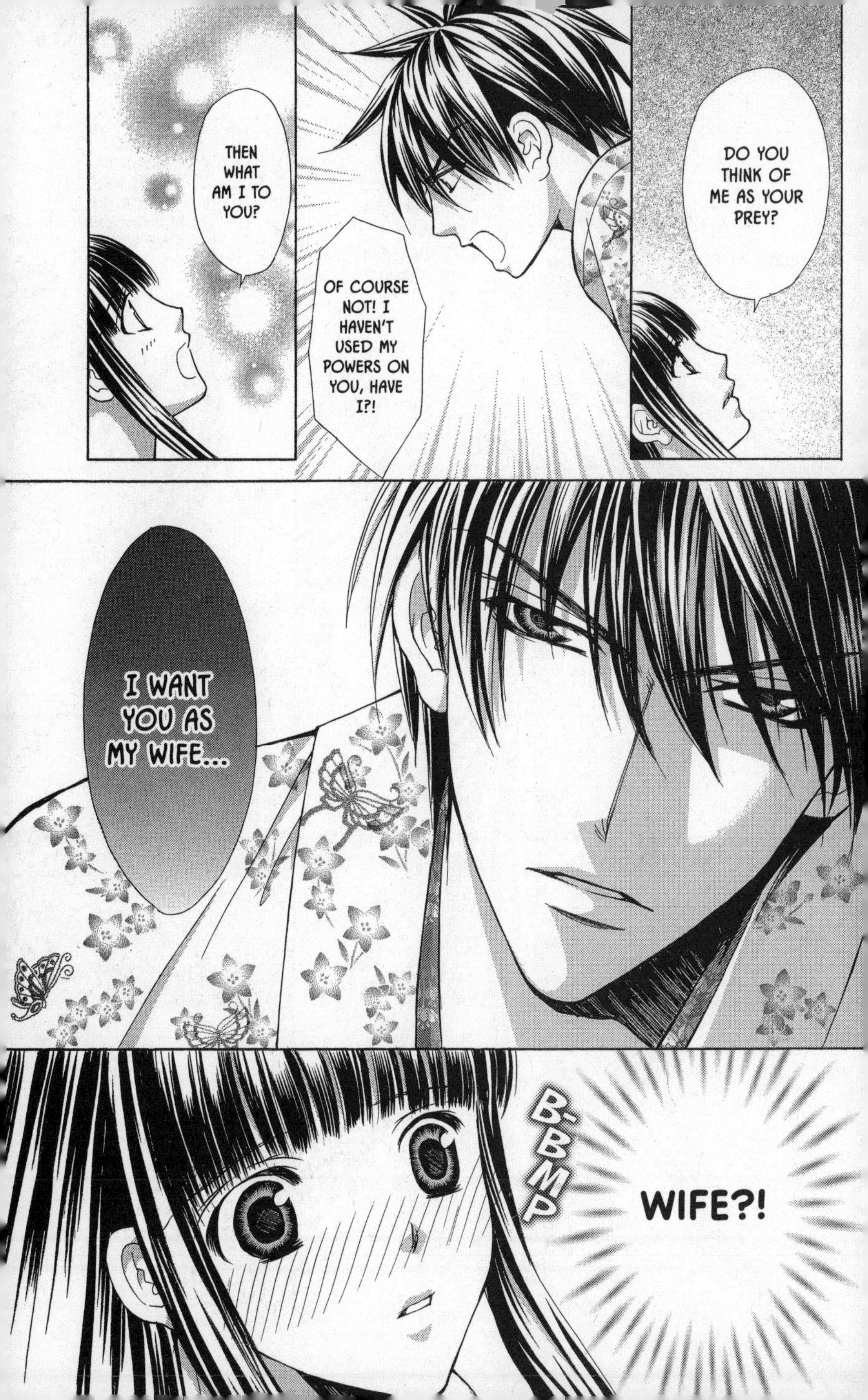
DO YOU THINK OF ME AS YOUR PREY?
OF COURSE NOT! I HAVEN'T USED MY POWERS ON YOU, HAVE I?!
THEN WHAT AM I TO YOU?
I WANT YOU AS MY WIFE...
WIFE?!
B-BMP

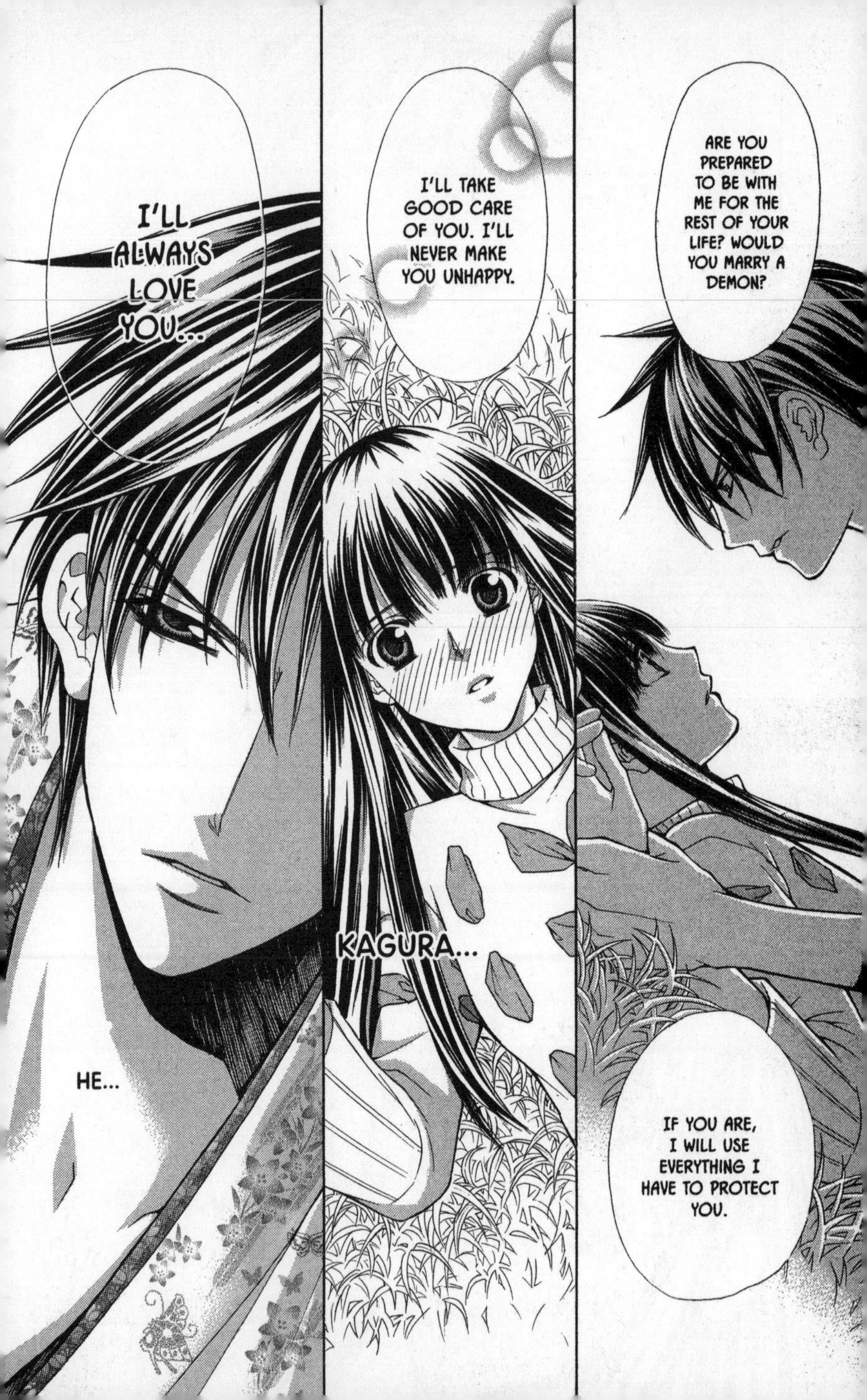
ARE YOU PREPARED TO BE WITH ME FOR THE REST OF YOUR LIFE? WOULD YOU MARRY A DEMON?
IF YOU ARE, I WILL USE EVERYTHING I HAVE TO PROTECT YOU.
I'LL TAKE GOOD CARE OF YOU. I'LL NEVER MAKE YOU UNHAPPY.
KAGURA...
I'LL ALWAYS LOVE YOU...
HE...

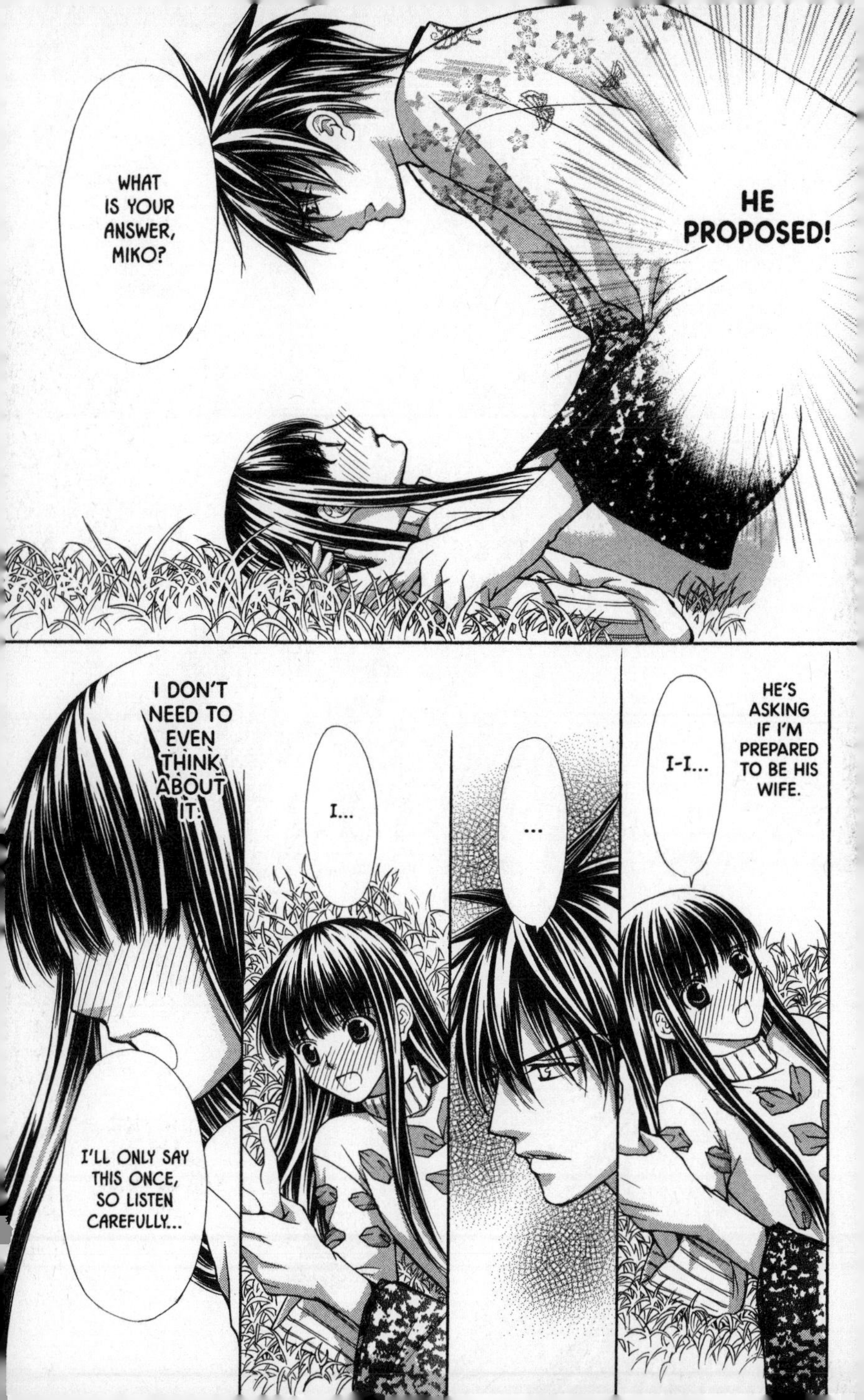
HE PROPOSED!
WHAT IS YOUR ANSWER, MIKO?
HE'S ASKING IF I'M PREPARED TO BE HIS WIFE.
I-I...
...
I...
I DON'T NEED TO EVEN THINK ABOUT IT.
I'LL ONLY SAY THIS ONCE, SO LISTEN CAREFULLY...

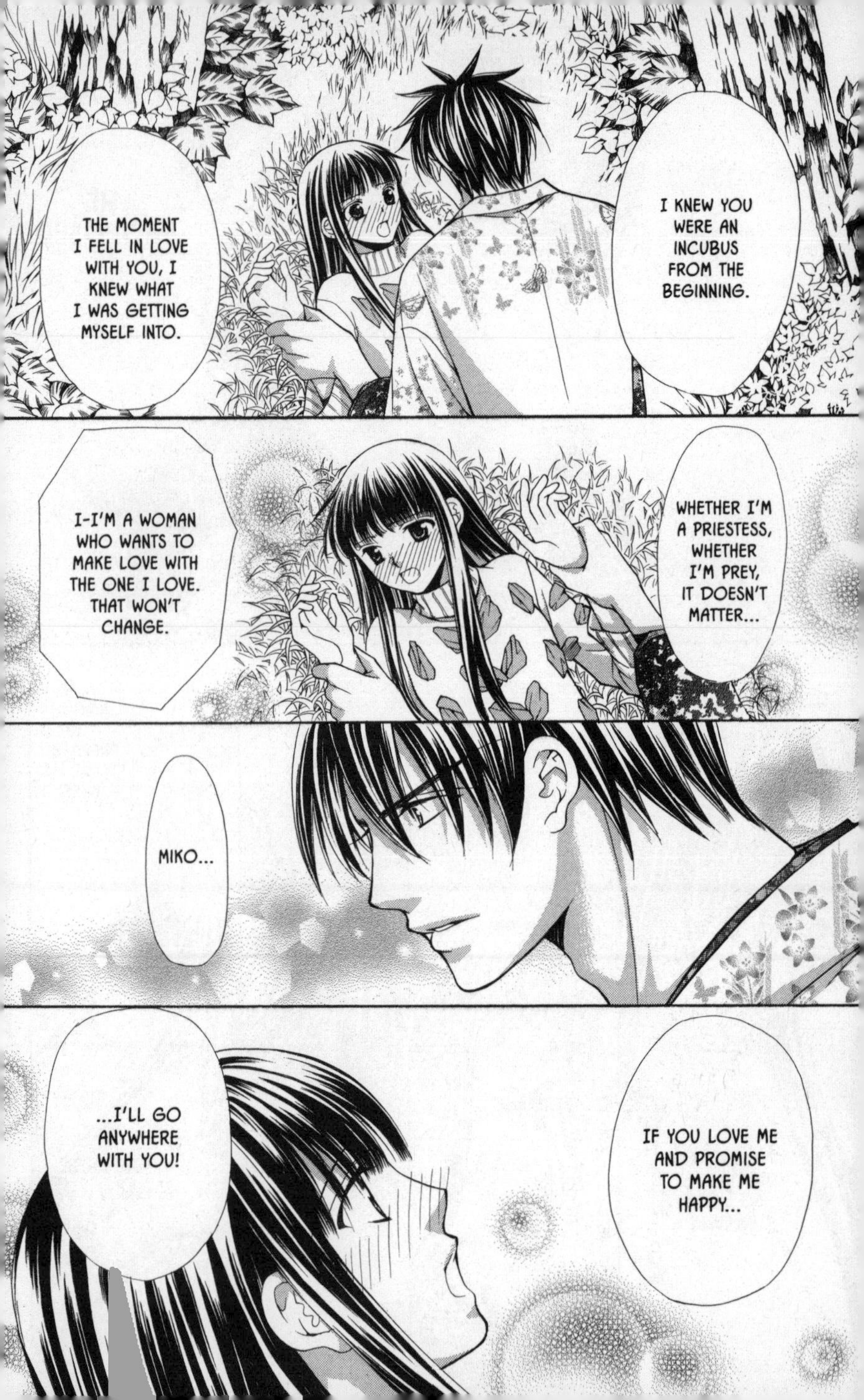
I KNEW YOU WERE AN INCUBUS FROM THE BEGINNING.
THE MOMENT I FELL IN LOVE WITH YOU, I KNEW WHAT I WAS GETTING MYSELF INTO.
WHETHER I'M A PRIESTESS, WHETHER I'M PREY, IT DOESN'T MATTER...
I-I'M A WOMAN WHO WANTS TO MAKE LOVE WITH THE ONE I LOVE. THAT WON'T CHANGE.
MIKO...
IF YOU LOVE ME AND PROMISE TO MAKE ME HAPPY...
...I'LL GO ANYWHERE WITH YOU!

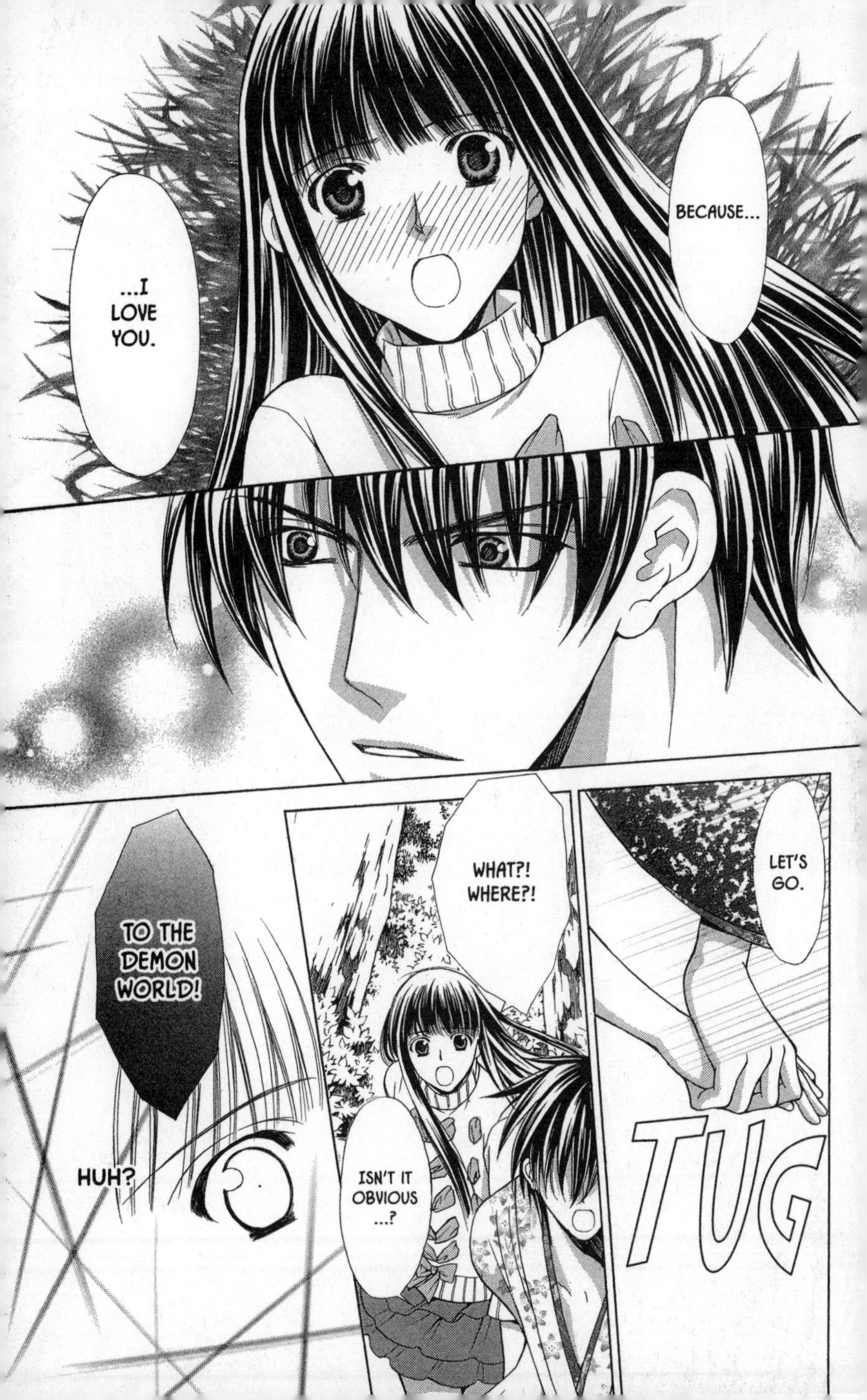
BECAUSE...
...I LOVE YOU.
LET'S GO.
TUG
WHAT?! WHERE?!
ISN'T IT OBVIOUS ...?
TO THE DEMON WORLD!
HUH?

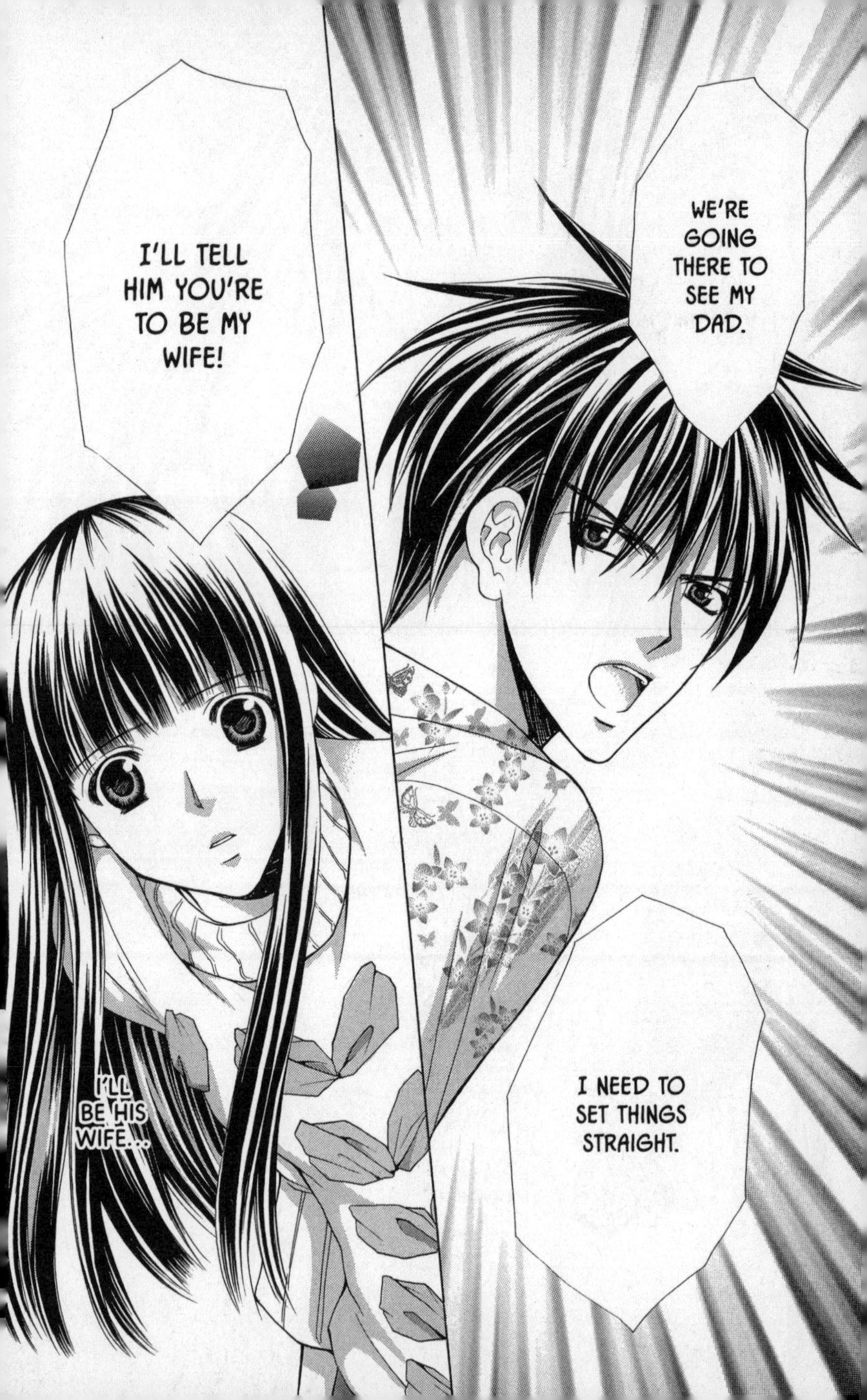
WE'RE GOING THERE TO SEE MY DAD.
I NEED TO SET THINGS STRAIGHT.
I'LL TELL HIM YOU'RE TO BE MY WIFE!
I'LL BE HIS WIFE...

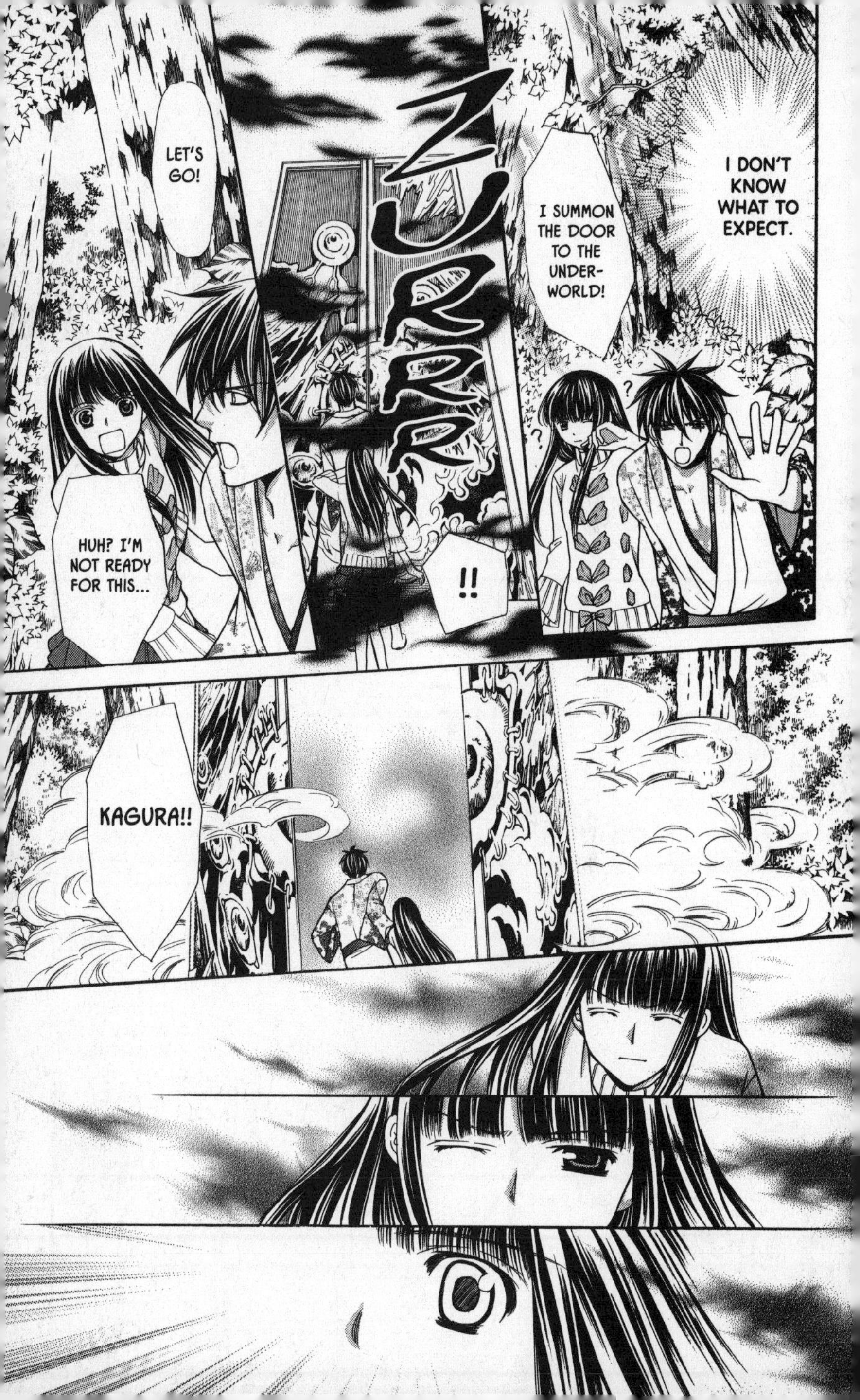
I DON'T KNOW WHAT TO EXPECT.
I SUMMON THE DOOR TO THE UNDER-WORLD!
!!
ZURRR
LET'S GO!
HUH? I'M NOT READY FOR THIS...
KAGURA!!

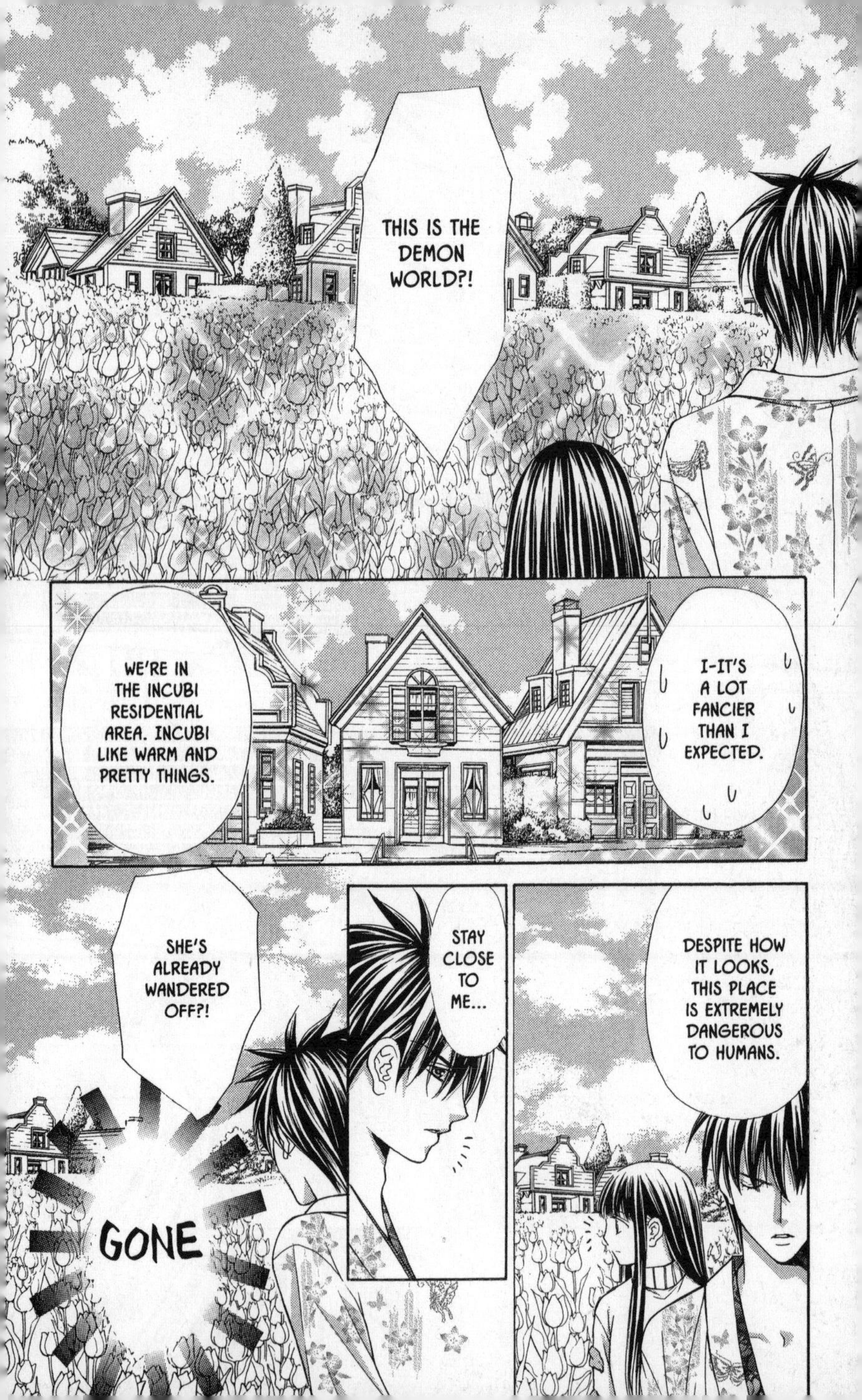
THIS IS THE DEMON WORLD?!
I-IT'S A LOT FANCIER THAN I EXPECTED.
WE'RE IN THE INCUBI RESIDENTIAL AREA. INCUBI LIKE WARM AND PRETTY THINGS.
DESPITE HOW IT LOOKS, THIS PLACE IS EXTREMELY DANGEROUS TO HUMANS.
STAY CLOSE TO ME...
SHE'S ALREADY WANDERED OFF?!
GONE

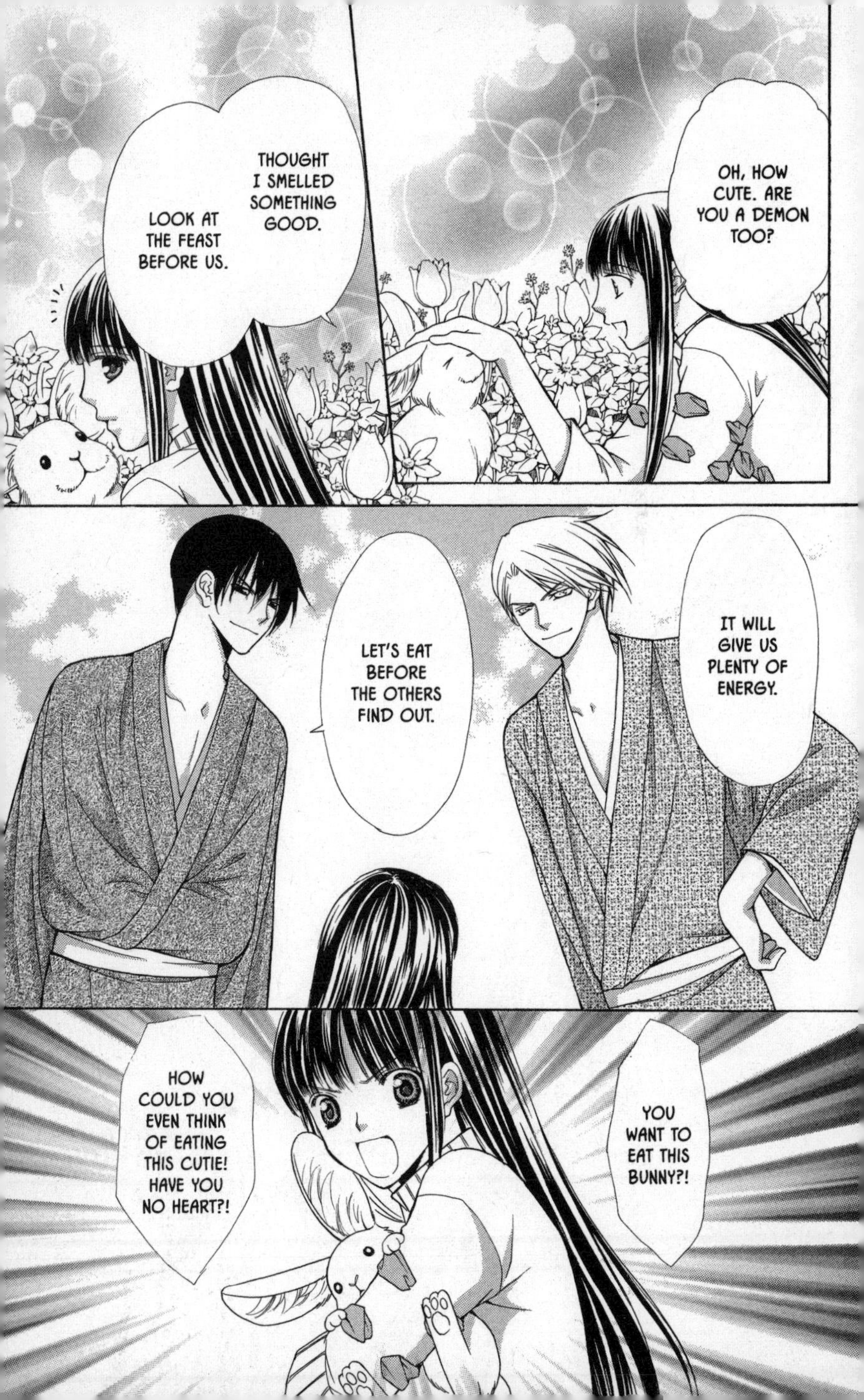
OH, HOW CUTE. ARE YOU A DEMON TOO?
THOUGHT I SMELLED SOMETHING GOOD.
LOOK AT THE FEAST BEFORE US.
IT WILL GIVE US PLENTY OF ENERGY.
LET'S EAT BEFORE THE OTHERS FIND OUT.
YOU WANT TO EAT THIS BUNNY?!
HOW COULD YOU EVEN THINK OF EATING THIS CUTIE! HAVE YOU NO HEART?!

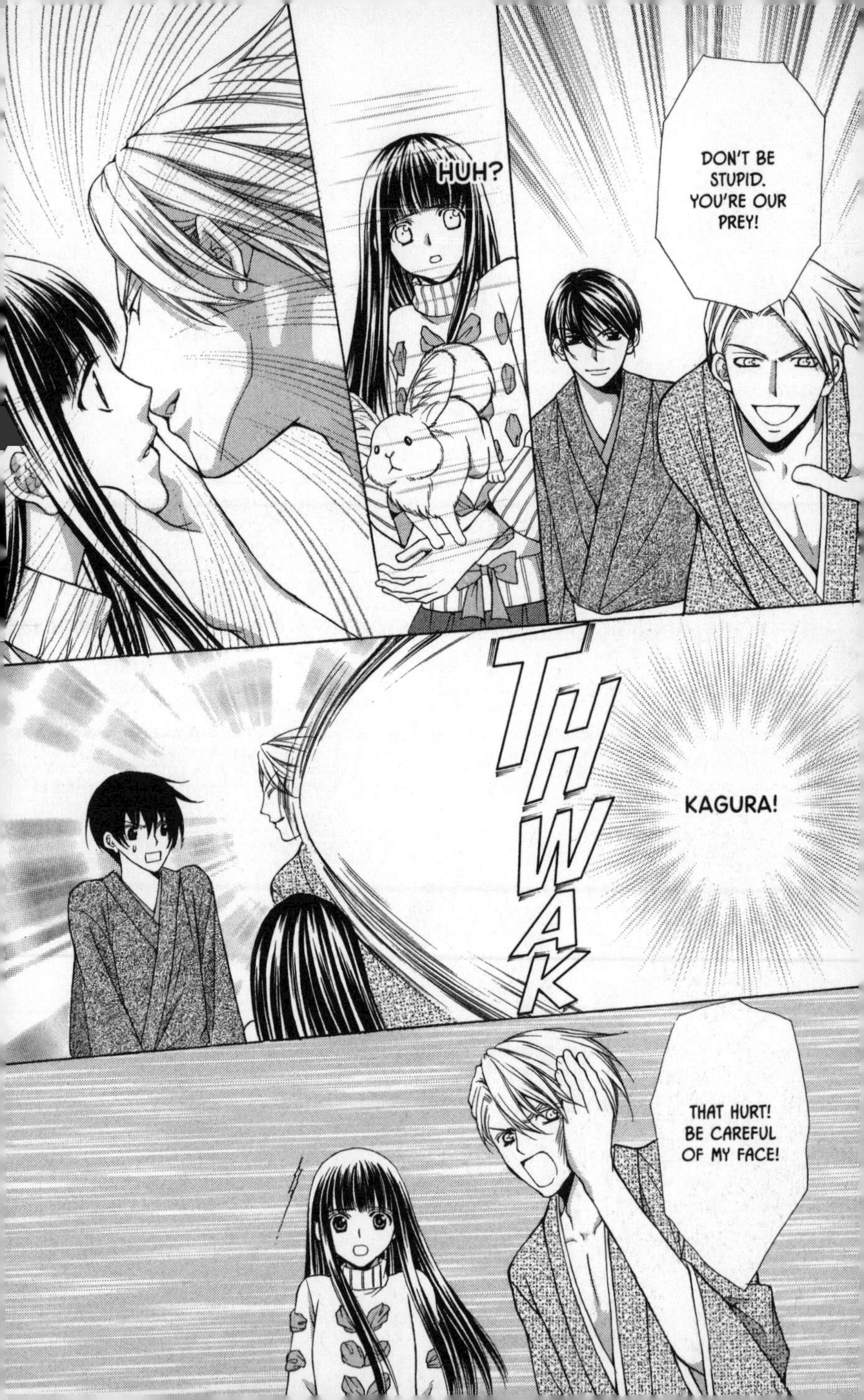
DON'T BE STUPID. YOU'RE OUR PREY!
HUH?
KAGURA!
THWAK
THAT HURT! BE CAREFUL OF MY FACE!

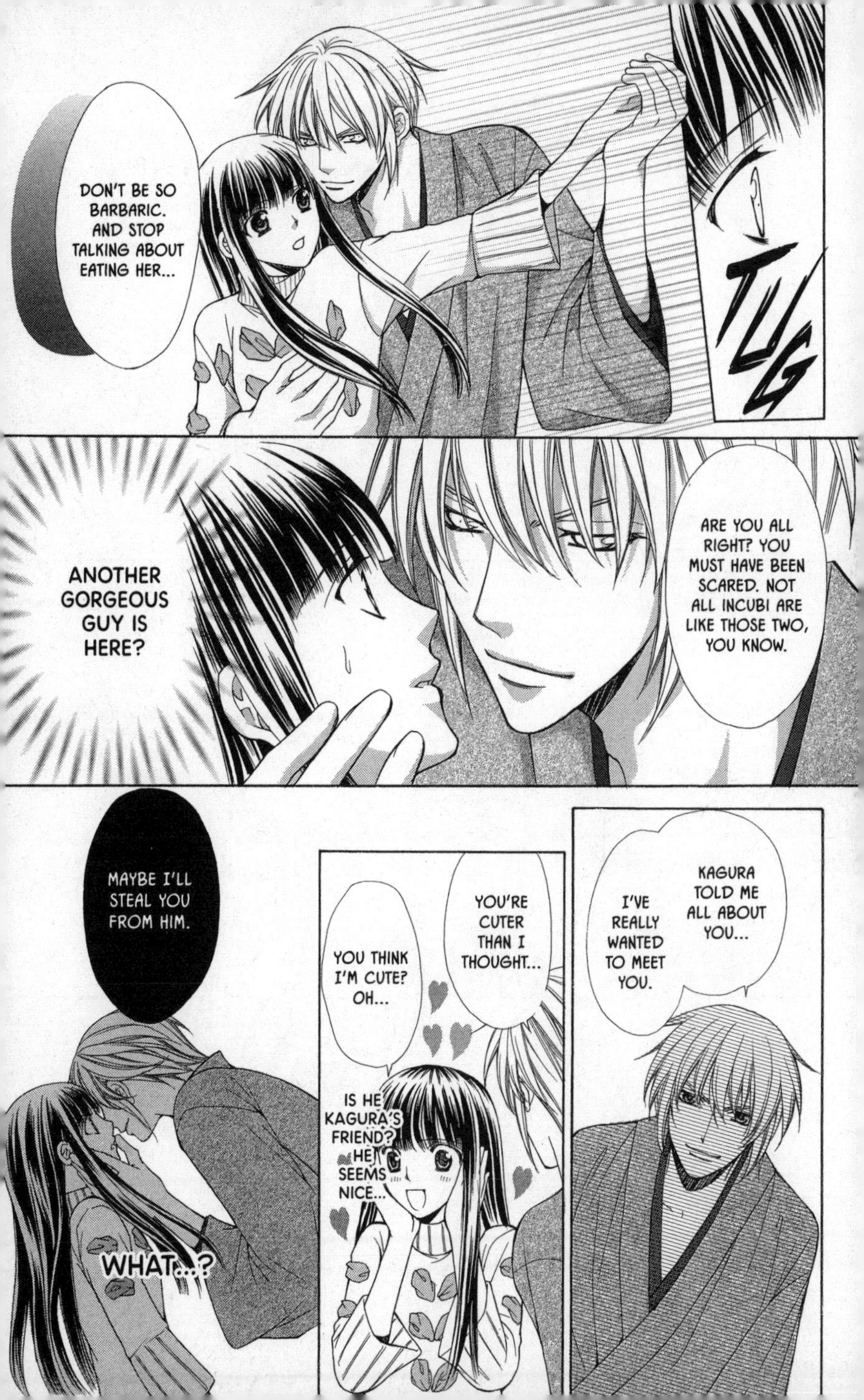
TUG
DON'T BE SO BARBARIC. AND STOP TALKING ABOUT EATING HER...
ARE YOU ALL RIGHT? YOU MUST HAVE BEEN SCARED. NOT ALL INCUBI ARE LIKE THOSE TWO, YOU KNOW.
ANOTHER GORGEOUS GUY IS HERE?
KAGURA TOLD ME ALL ABOUT YOU...
I'VE REALLY WANTED TO MEET YOU.
YOU'RE CUTER THAN I THOUGHT...
YOU THINK I'M CUTE? OH...
IS HE KAGURA'S FRIEND? HE SEEMS NICE...
MAYBE I'LL STEAL YOU FROM HIM.
WHAT...?

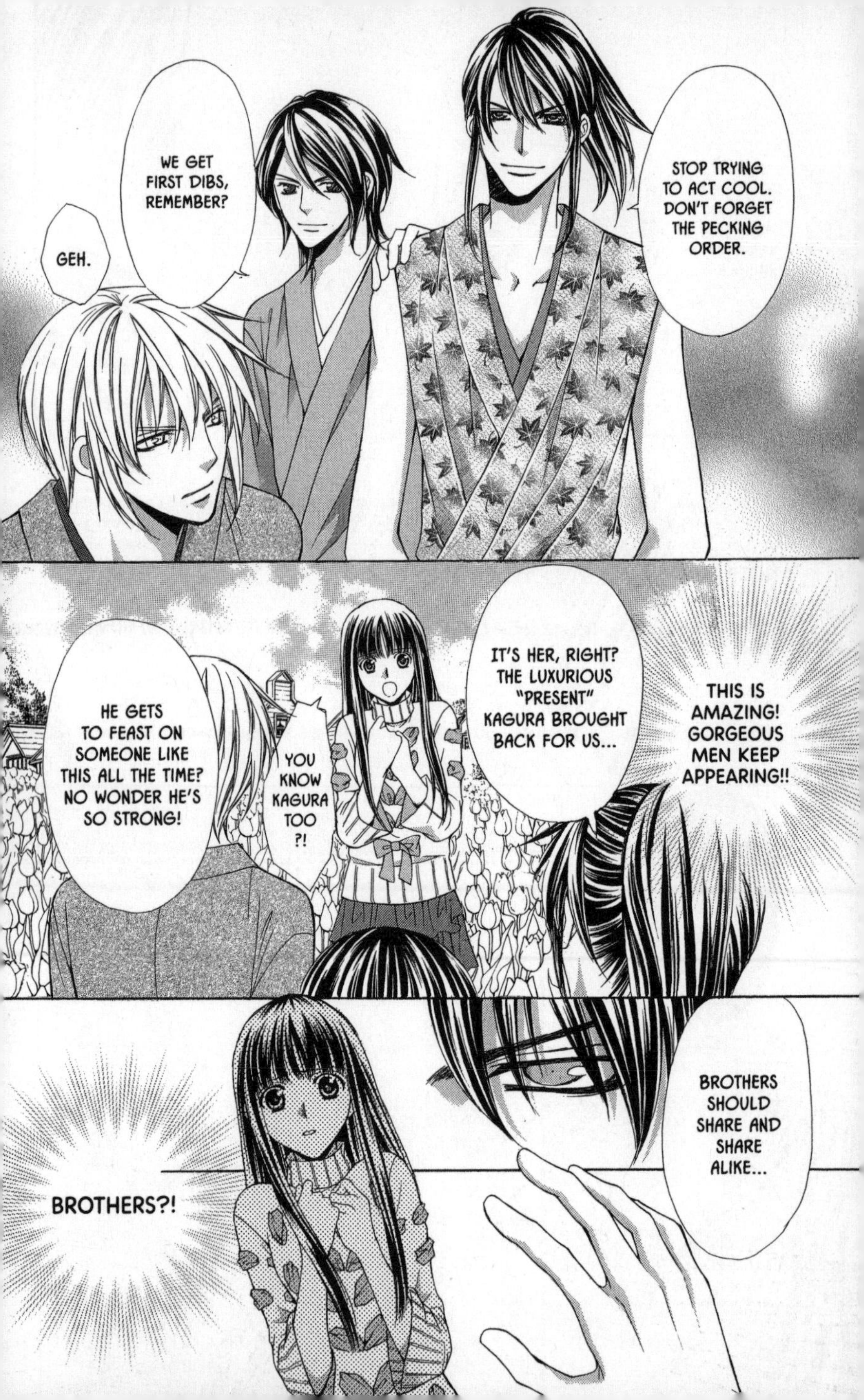
STOP TRYING TO ACT COOL. DON'T FORGET THE PECKING ORDER.
WE GET FIRST DIBS, REMEMBER?
GEH.
THIS IS AMAZING! GORGEOUS MEN KEEP APPEARING!!
IT'S HER, RIGHT? THE LUXURIOUS "PRESENT" KAGURA BROUGHT BACK FOR US...
YOU KNOW KAGURA TOO ?!
HE GETS TO FEAST ON SOMEONE LIKE THIS ALL THE TIME? NO WONDER HE'S SO STRONG!
BROTHERS SHOULD SHARE AND SHARE ALIKE...
BROTHERS?!

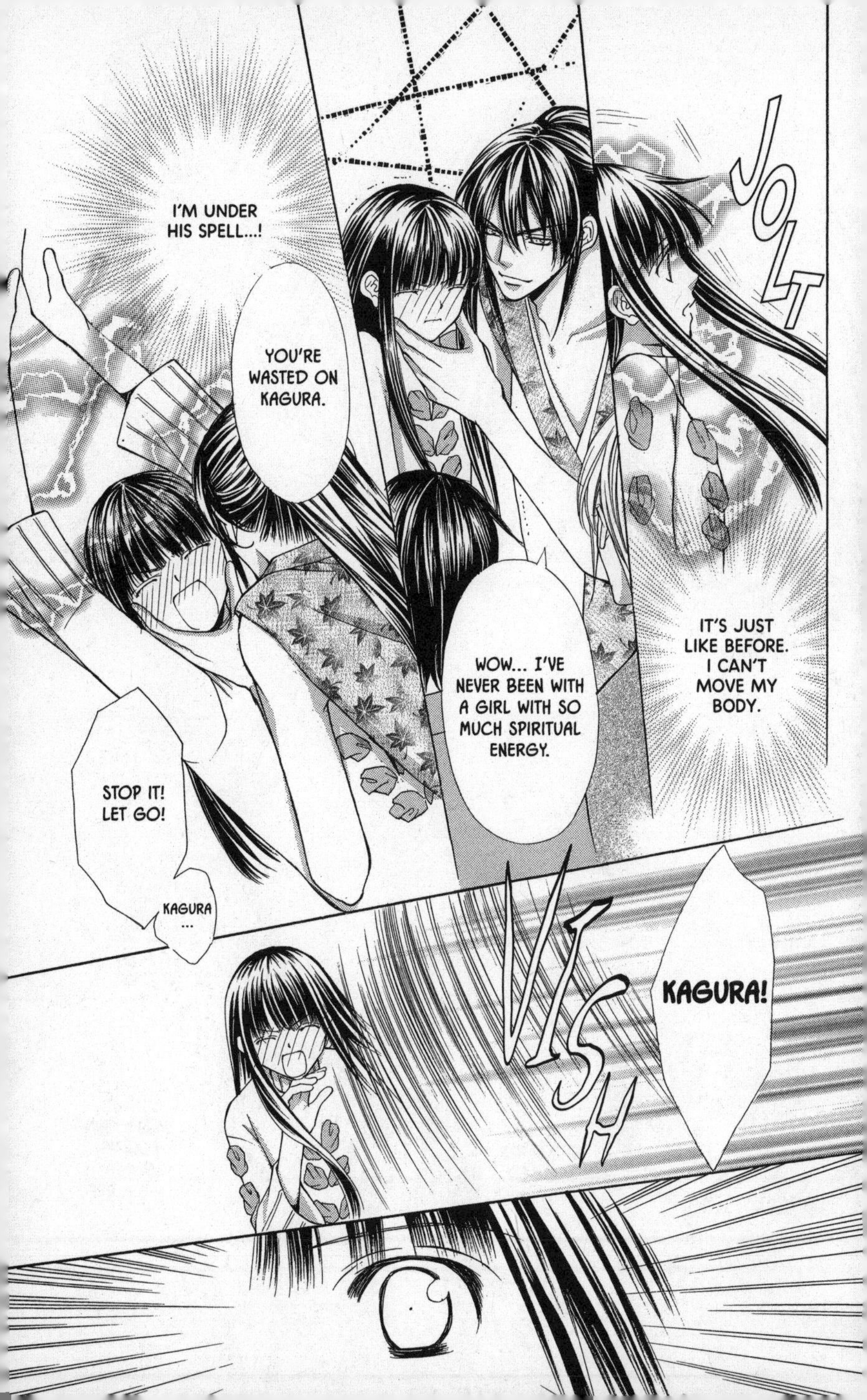
JOLT
YOU'RE WASTED ON KAGURA.
I'M UNDER HIS SPELL...!
IT'S JUST LIKE BEFORE. I CAN'T MOVE MY BODY.
WOW... I'VE NEVER BEEN WITH A GIRL WITH SO MUCH SPIRITUAL ENERGY.
STOP IT! LET GO!
KAGURA ...
KAGURA!
VISH

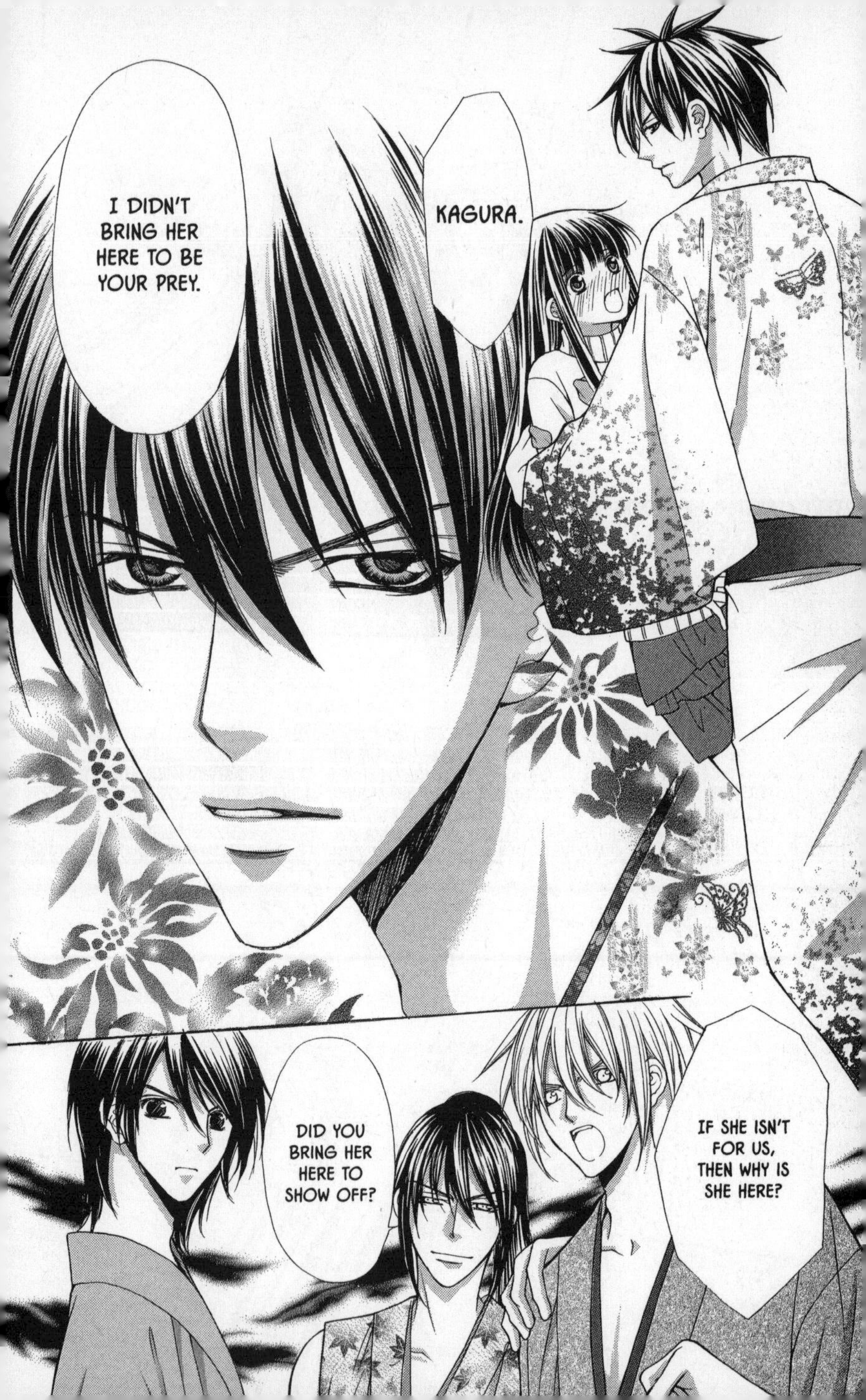
KAGURA.
I DIDN'T BRING HER HERE TO BE YOUR PREY.
IF SHE ISN'T FOR US, THEN WHY IS SHE HERE?
DID YOU BRING HER HERE TO SHOW OFF?

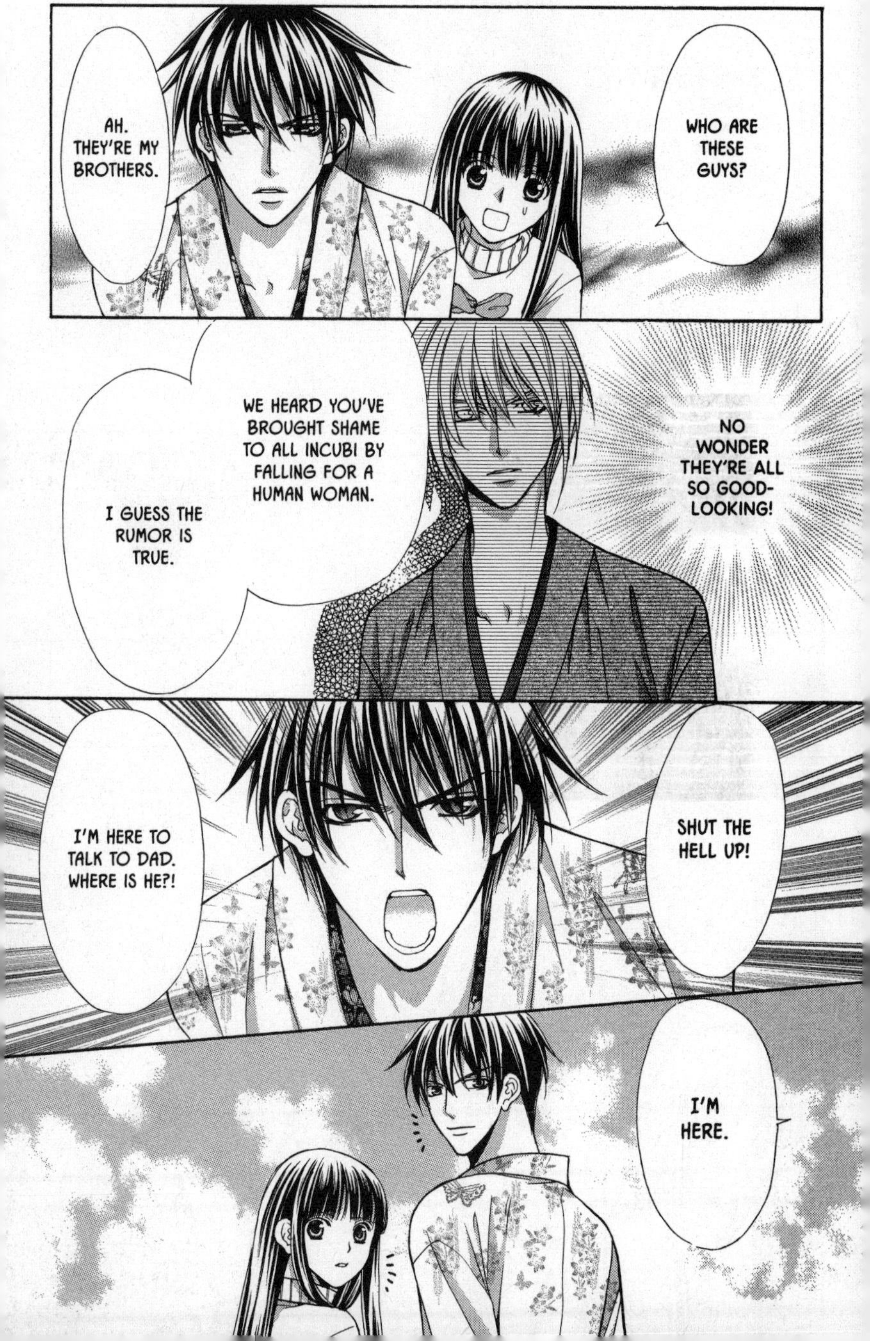
WHO ARE THESE GUYS?
AH. THEY'RE MY BROTHERS.
NO WONDER THEY'RE ALL SO GOOD-LOOKING!
WE HEARD YOU'VE BROUGHT SHAME TO ALL INCUBI BY FALLING FOR A HUMAN WOMAN.
I GUESS THE RUMOR IS TRUE.
SHUT THE HELL UP!
I'M HERE TO TALK TO DAD. WHERE IS HE?!
I'M HERE.

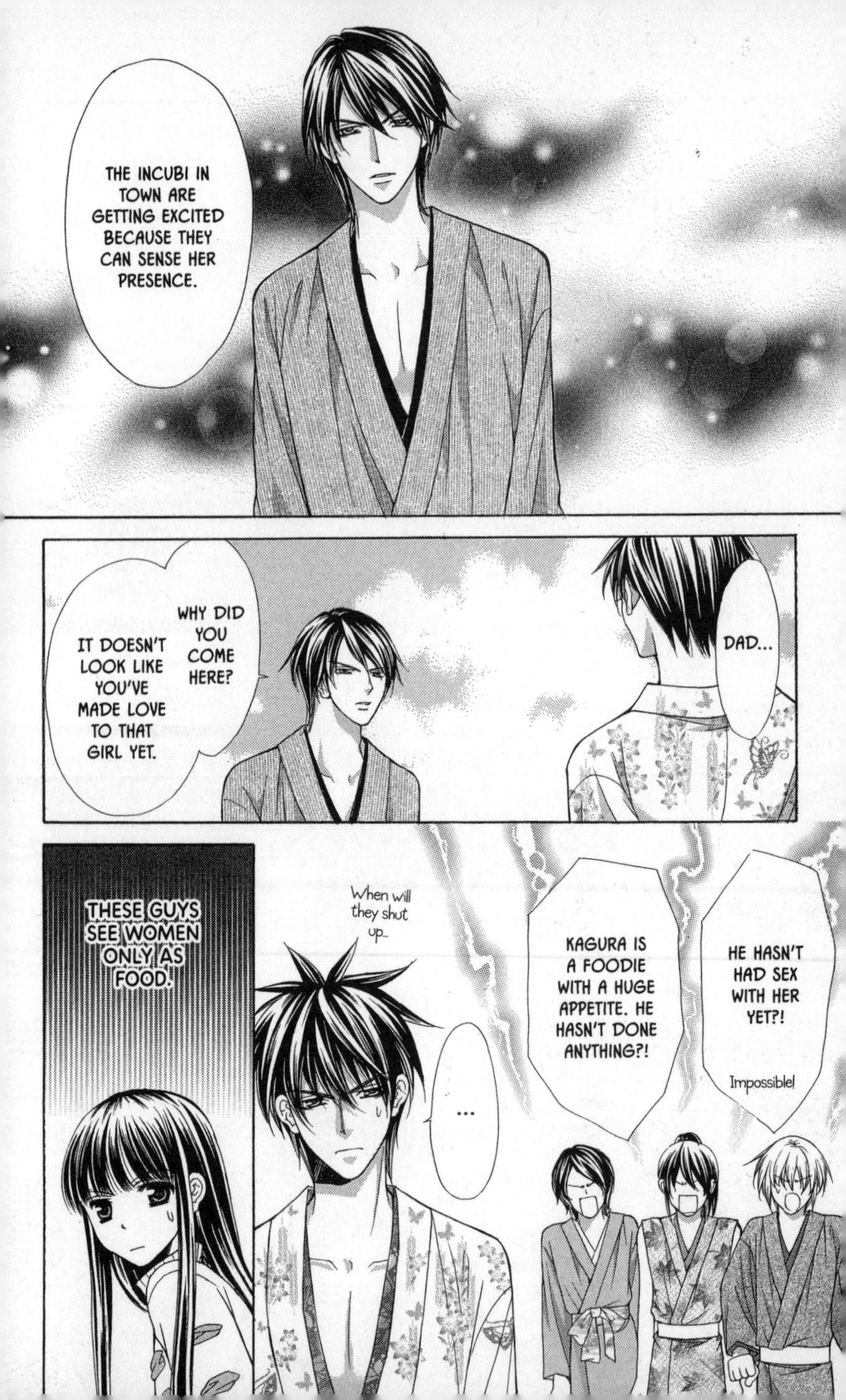
THE INCUBI IN TOWN ARE GETTING EXCITED BECAUSE THEY CAN SENSE HER PRESENCE.
DAD...
WHY DID YOU COME HERE?
IT DOESN'T LOOK LIKE YOU'VE MADE LOVE TO THAT GIRL YET.
HE HASN'T HAD SEX WITH HER YET?!
Impossible!
KAGURA IS A FOODIE WITH A HUGE APPETITE. HE HASN'T DONE ANYTHING?!
When will they shut up...
...
THESE GUYS SEE WOMEN ONLY AS FOOD.

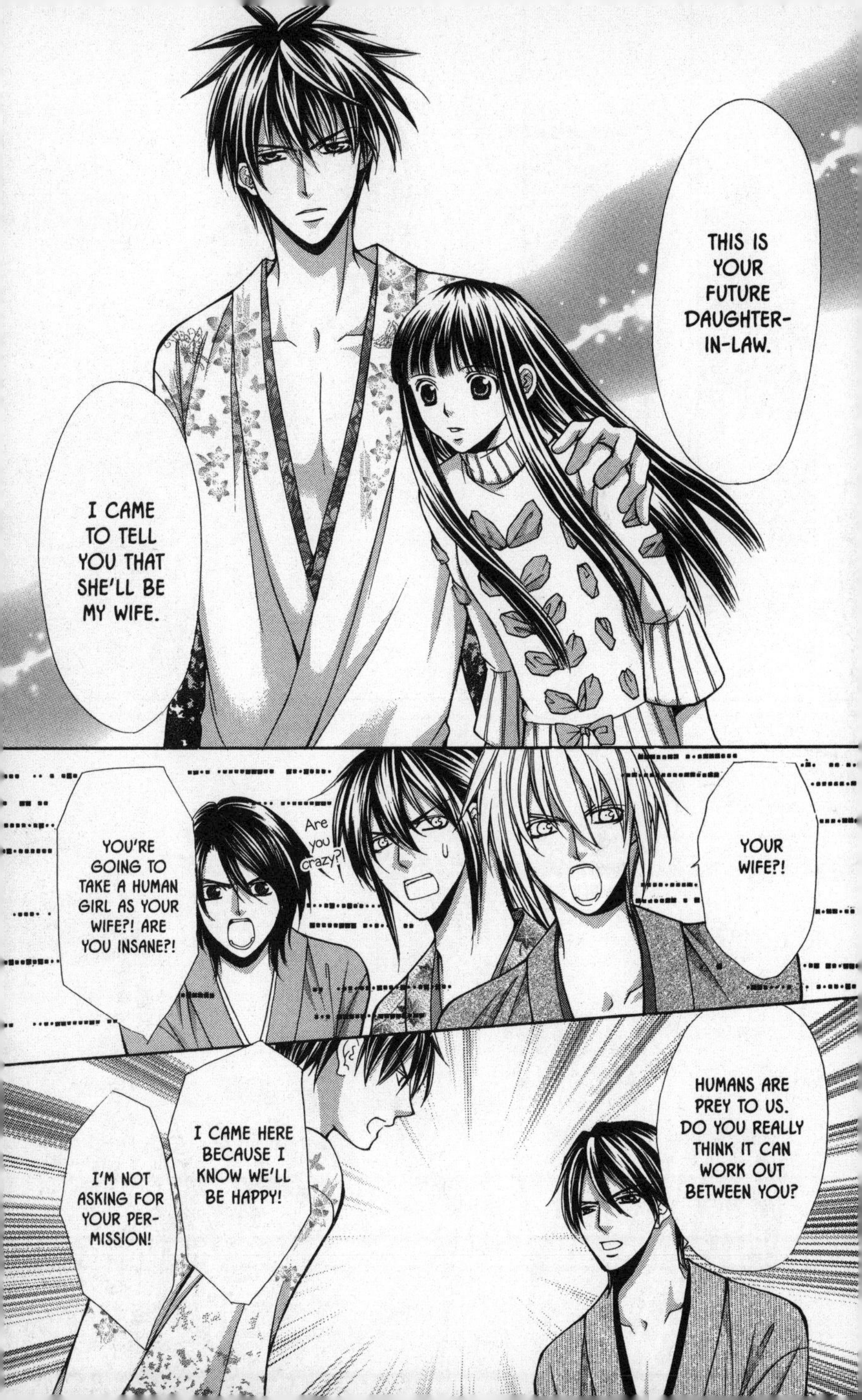
THIS IS YOUR FUTURE DAUGHTER-IN-LAW.
I CAME TO TELL YOU THAT SHE'LL BE MY WIFE.
YOUR WIFE?!
Are you crazy?!
YOU'RE GOING TO TAKE A HUMAN GIRL AS YOUR WIFE?! ARE YOU INSANE?!
HUMANS ARE PREY TO US. DO YOU REALLY THINK IT CAN WORK OUT BETWEEN YOU?
I CAME HERE BECAUSE I KNOW WE'LL BE HAPPY!
I'M NOT ASKING FOR YOUR PERMISSION!

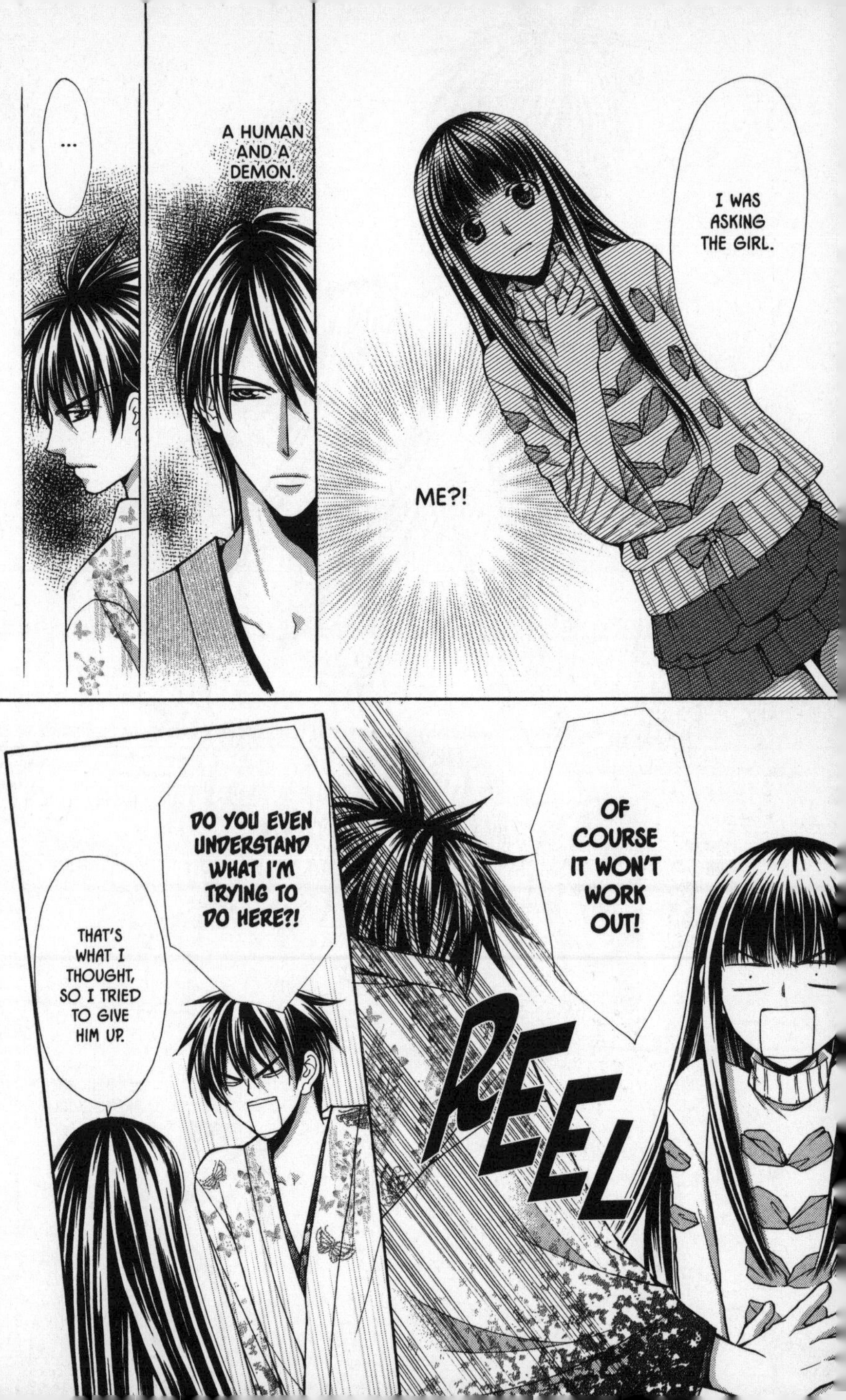
I WAS ASKING THE GIRL.
ME?!
A HUMAN AND A DEMON.
...
OF COURSE IT WON'T WORK OUT!
REEL
DO YOU EVEN UNDERSTAND WHAT I'M TRYING TO DO HERE?!
THAT'S WHAT I THOUGHT, SO I TRIED TO GIVE HIM UP.

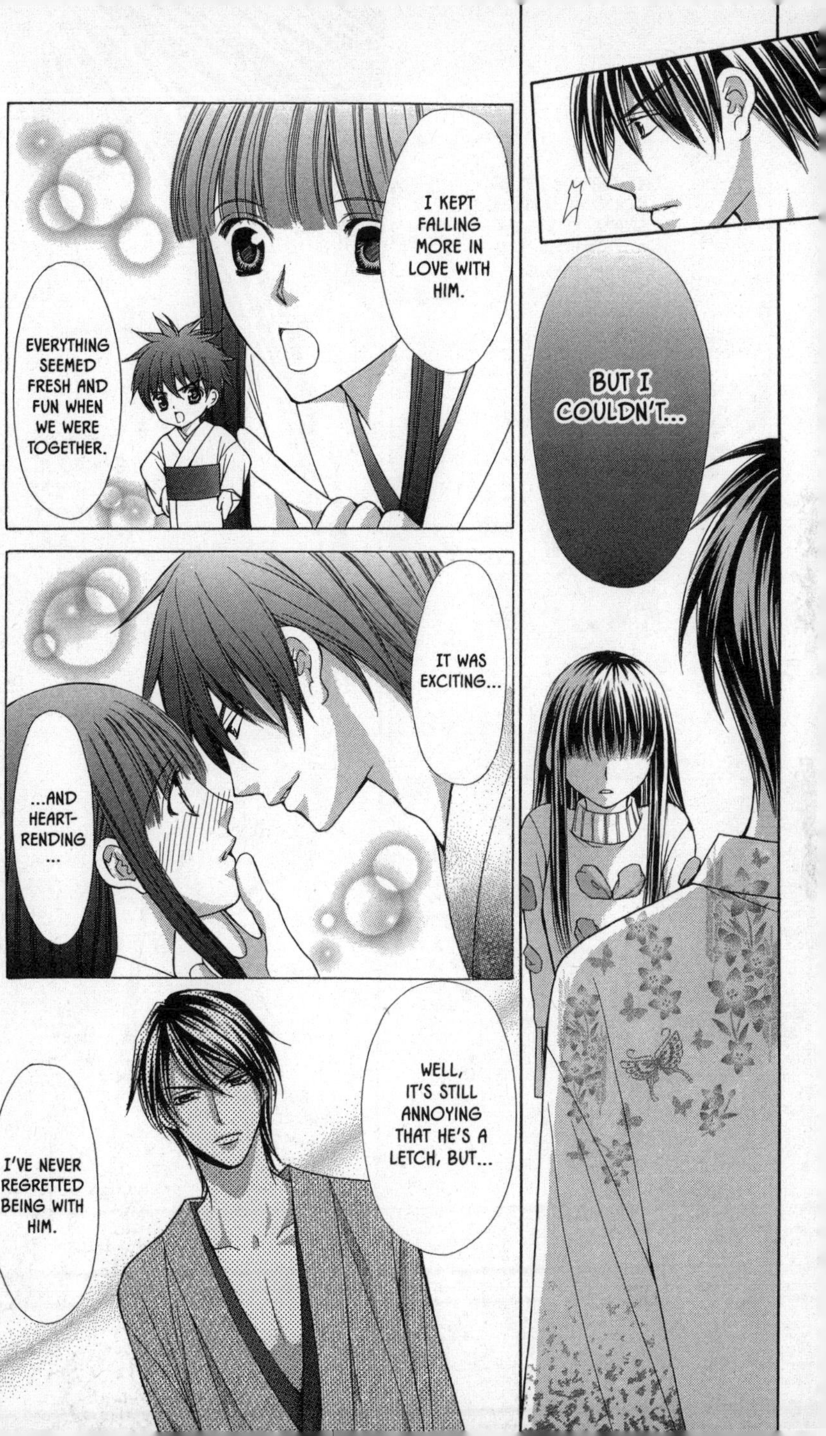
BUT I COULDN'T...
I KEPT FALLING MORE IN LOVE WITH HIM.
EVERYTHING SEEMED FRESH AND FUN WHEN WE WERE TOGETHER.
IT WAS EXCITING...
...AND HEART-RENDING...
WELL, IT'S STILL ANNOYING THAT HE'S A LETCH, BUT...
I'VE NEVER REGRETTED BEING WITH HIM.

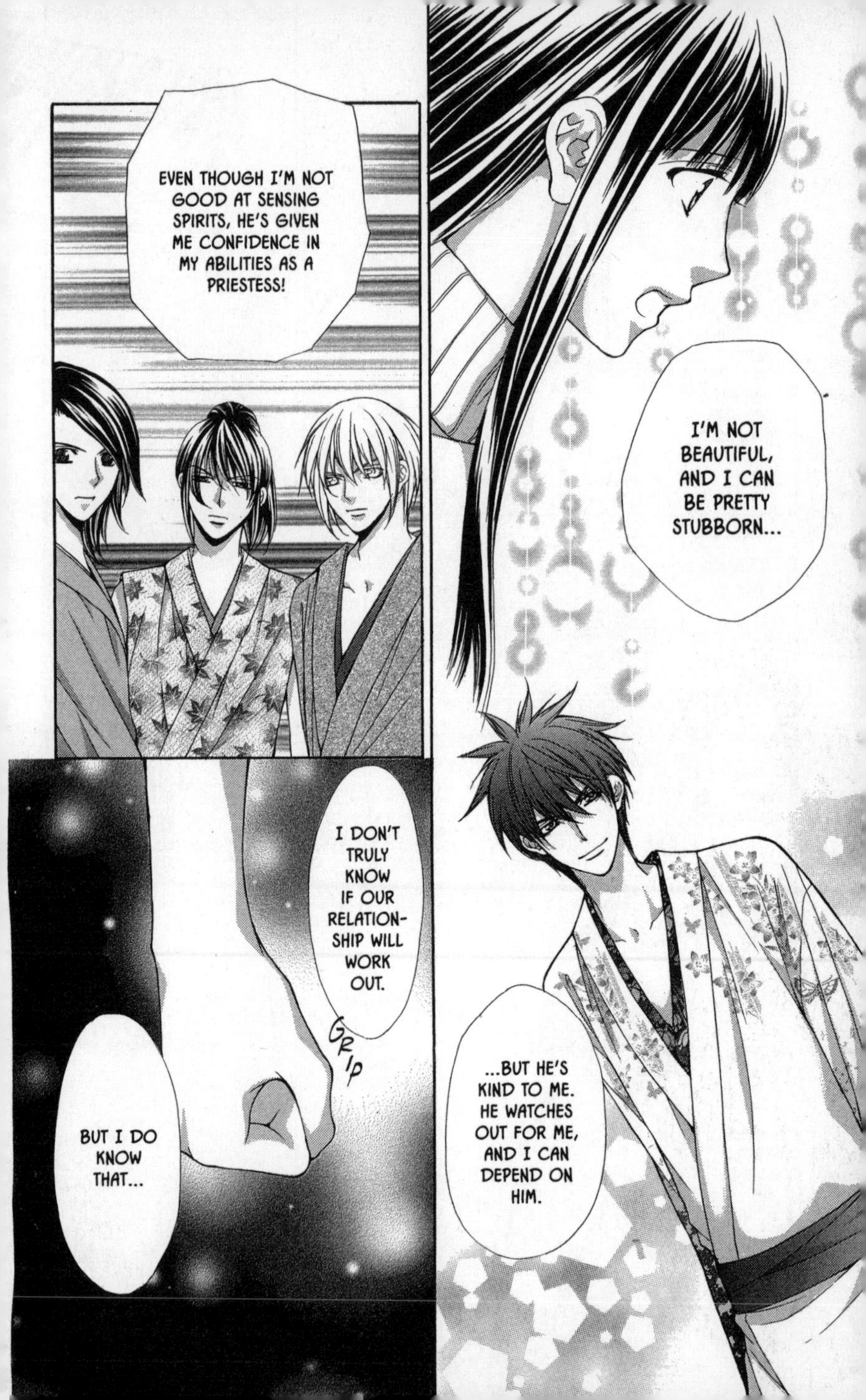
I'M NOT BEAUTIFUL, AND I CAN BE PRETTY STUBBORN...
...BUT HE'S KIND TO ME. HE WATCHES OUT FOR ME, AND I CAN DEPEND ON HIM.
EVEN THOUGH I'M NOT GOOD AT SENSING SPIRITS, HE'S GIVEN ME CONFIDENCE IN MY ABILITIES AS A PRIESTESS!
I DON'T TRULY KNOW IF OUR RELATION-SHIP WILL WORK OUT.
GRIP
BUT I DO KNOW THAT...

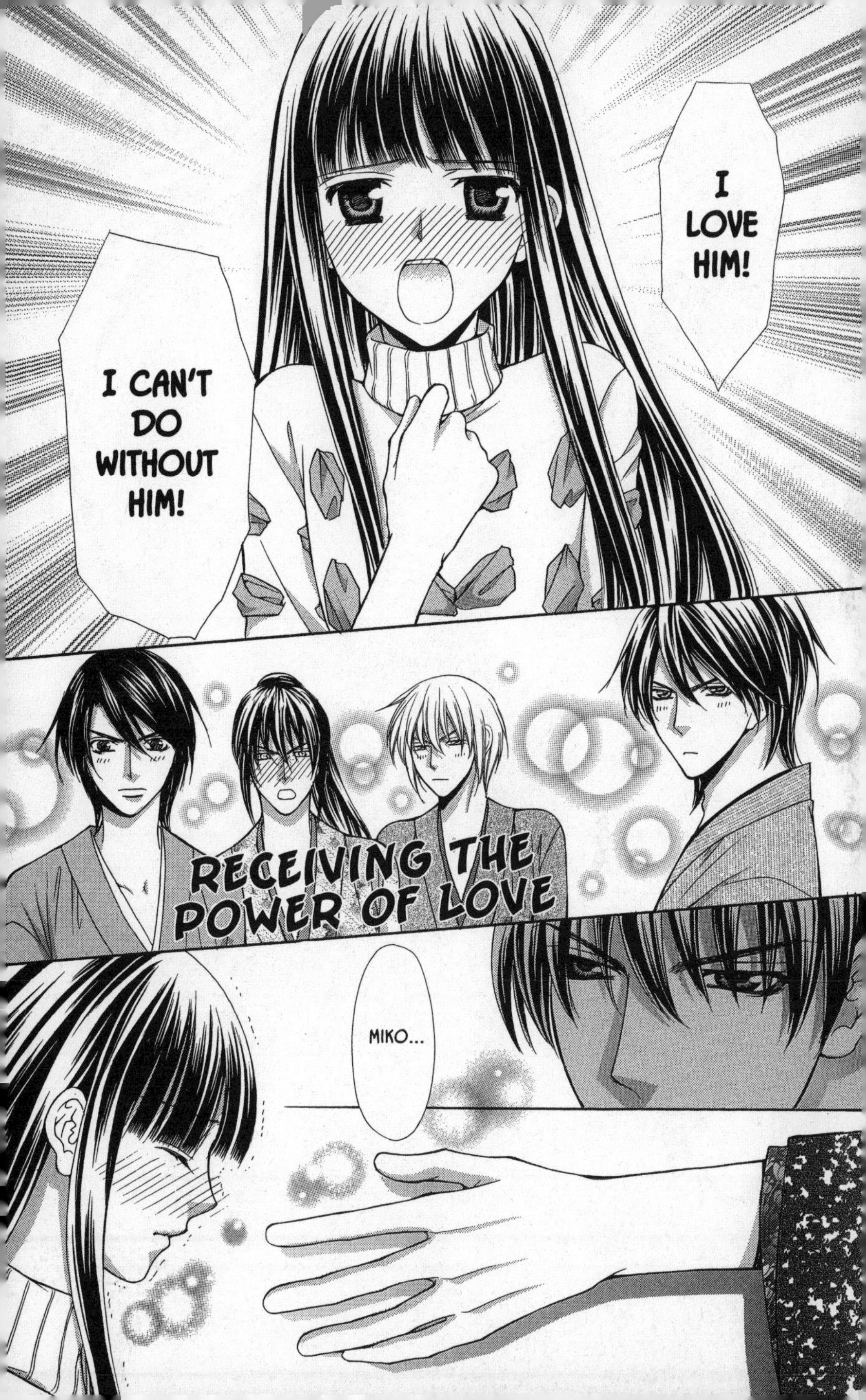
I LOVE HIM!
I CAN'T DO WITHOUT HIM!
RECEIVING THE POWER OF LOVE
MIKO...

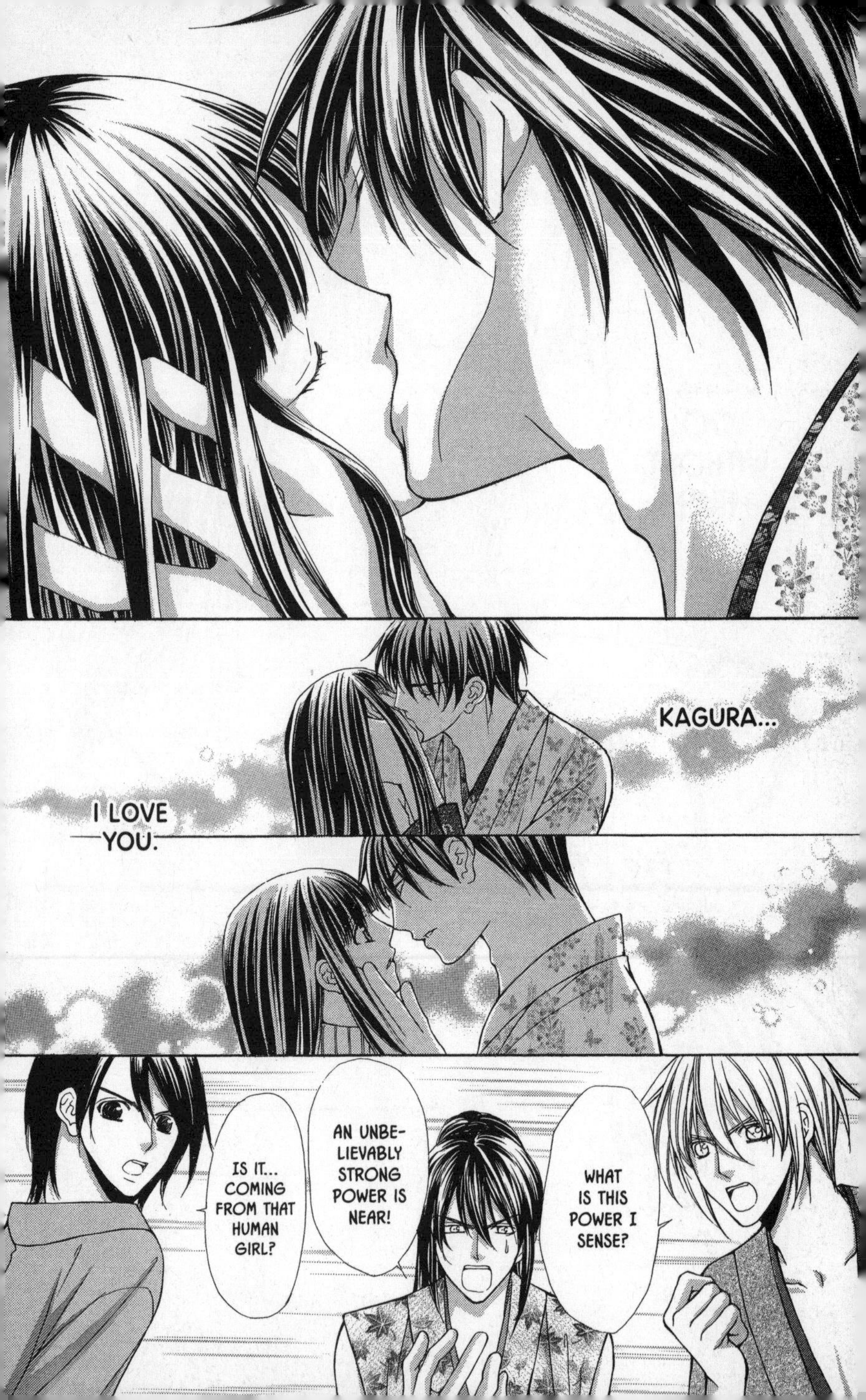
KAGURA...
I LOVE YOU.
WHAT IS THIS POWER I SENSE?
AN UNBE-LIEVABLY STRONG POWER IS NEAR!
IS IT... COMING FROM THAT HUMAN GIRL?

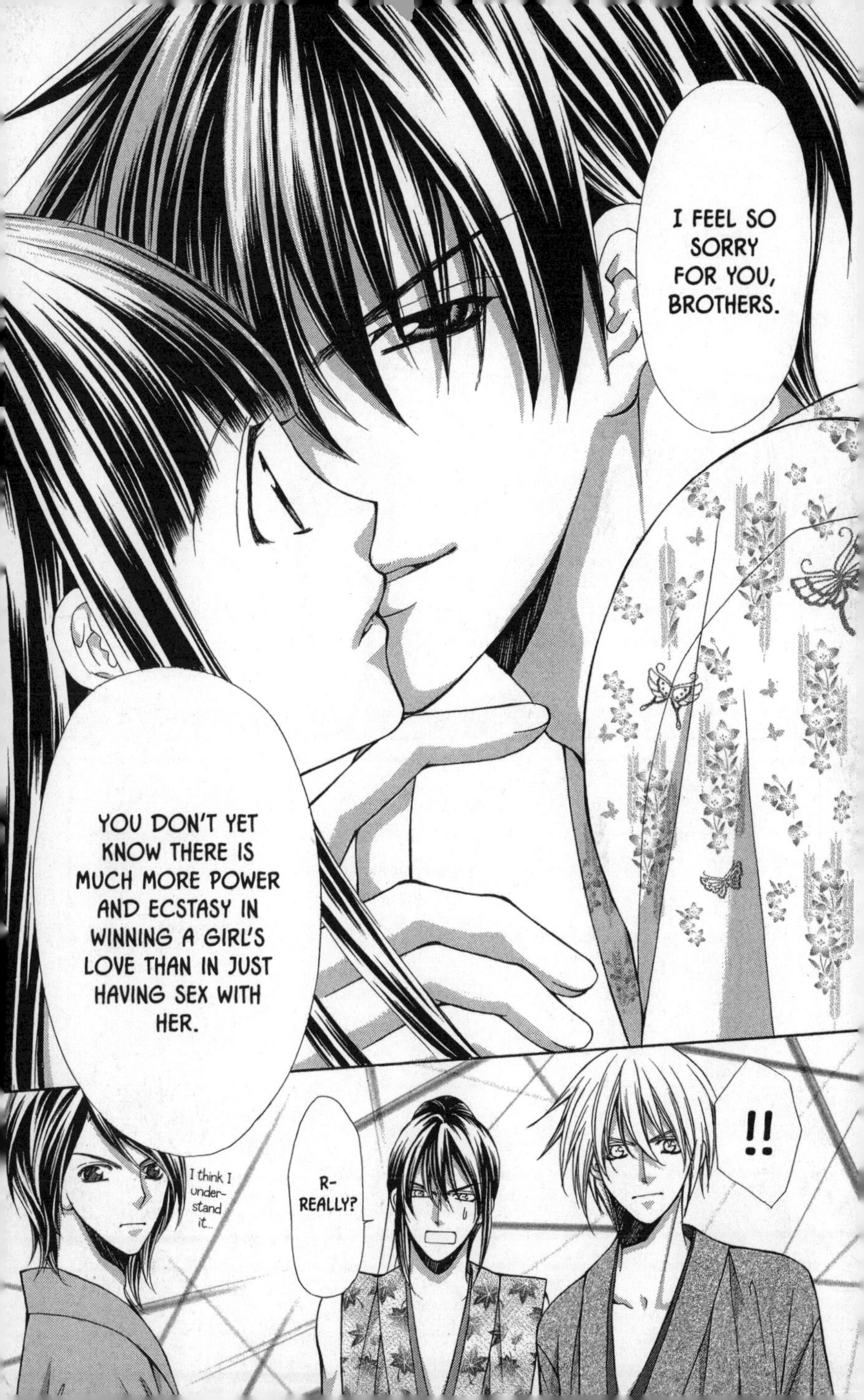
I FEEL SO SORRY FOR YOU, BROTHERS.
YOU DON'T YET KNOW THERE IS MUCH MORE POWER AND ECSTASY IN WINNING A GIRL'S LOVE THAN IN JUST HAVING SEX WITH HER.
!!
R-REALLY?
I think I understand it...

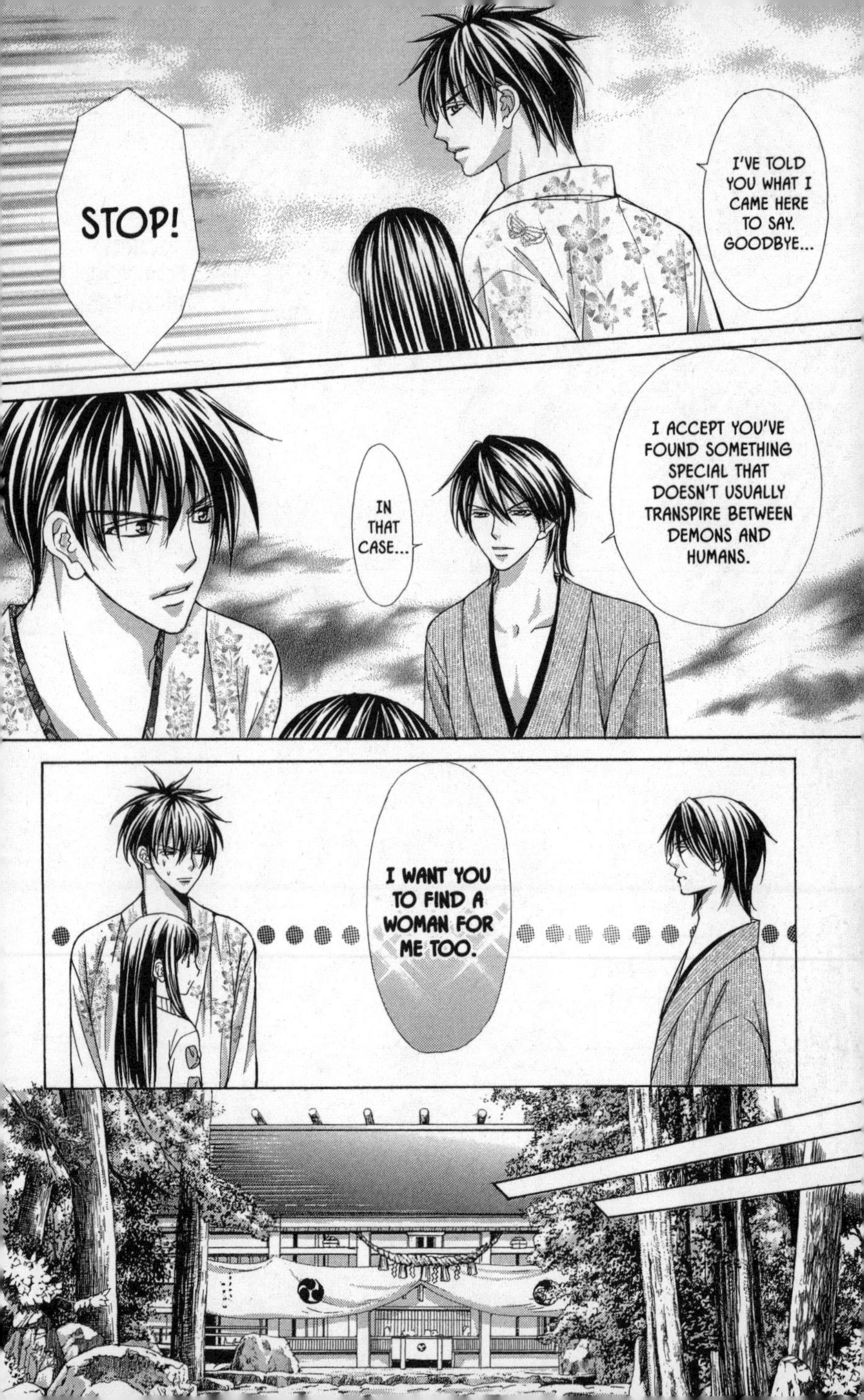
I'VE TOLD YOU WHAT I CAME HERE TO SAY. GOODBYE...
STOP!
I ACCEPT YOU'VE FOUND SOMETHING SPECIAL THAT DOESN'T USUALLY TRANSPIRE BETWEEN DEMONS AND HUMANS.
IN THAT CASE...
I WANT YOU TO FIND A WOMAN FOR ME TOO.

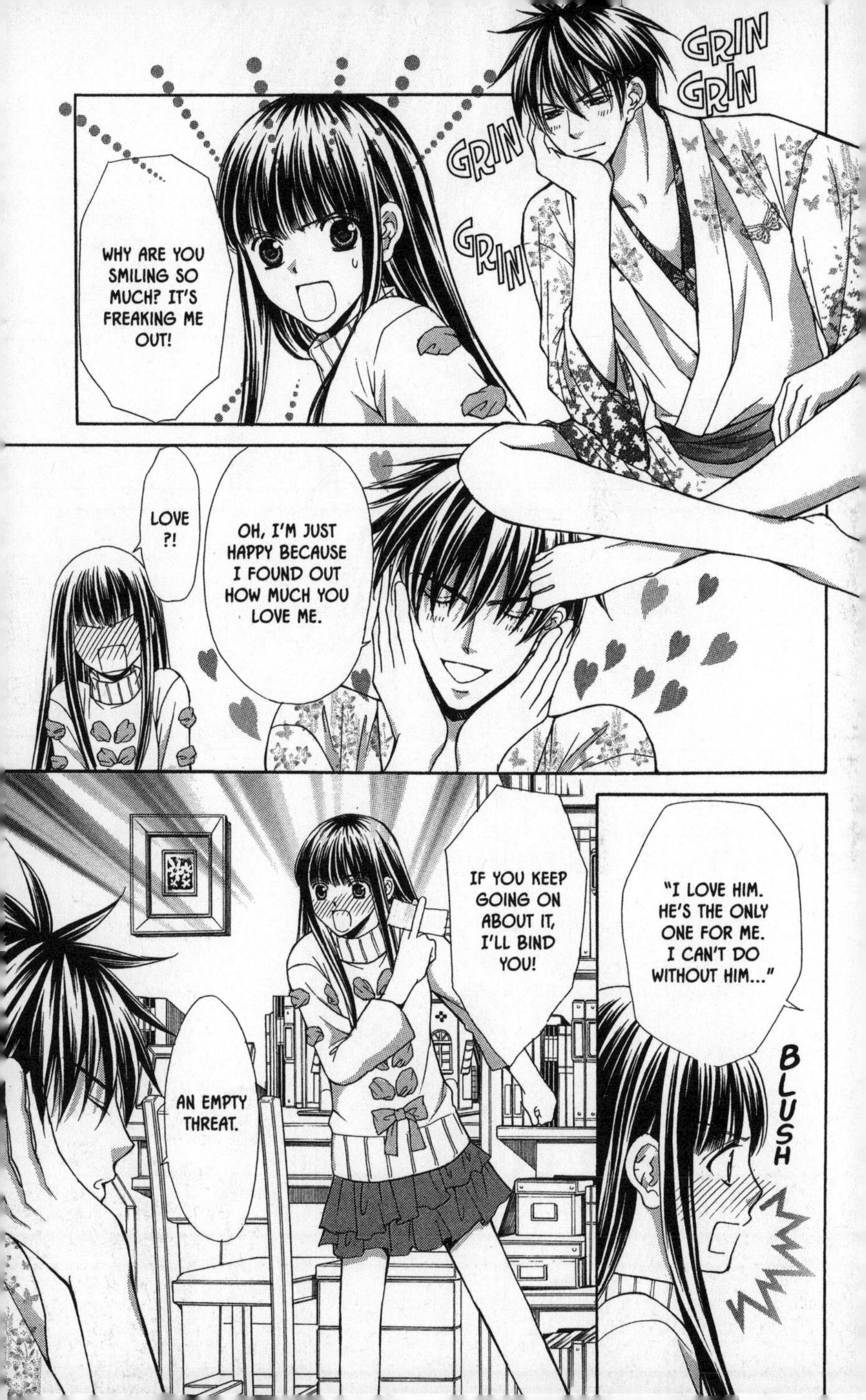
GRIN GRIN
GRIN
GRIN
WHY ARE YOU SMILING SO MUCH? IT'S FREAKING ME OUT!
OH, I'M JUST HAPPY BECAUSE I FOUND OUT HOW MUCH YOU LOVE ME.
LOVE ?!
"I LOVE HIM. HE'S THE ONLY ONE FOR ME. I CAN'T DO WITHOUT HIM..."
BLUSH
IF YOU KEEP GOING ON ABOUT IT, I'LL BIND YOU!
AN EMPTY THREAT.

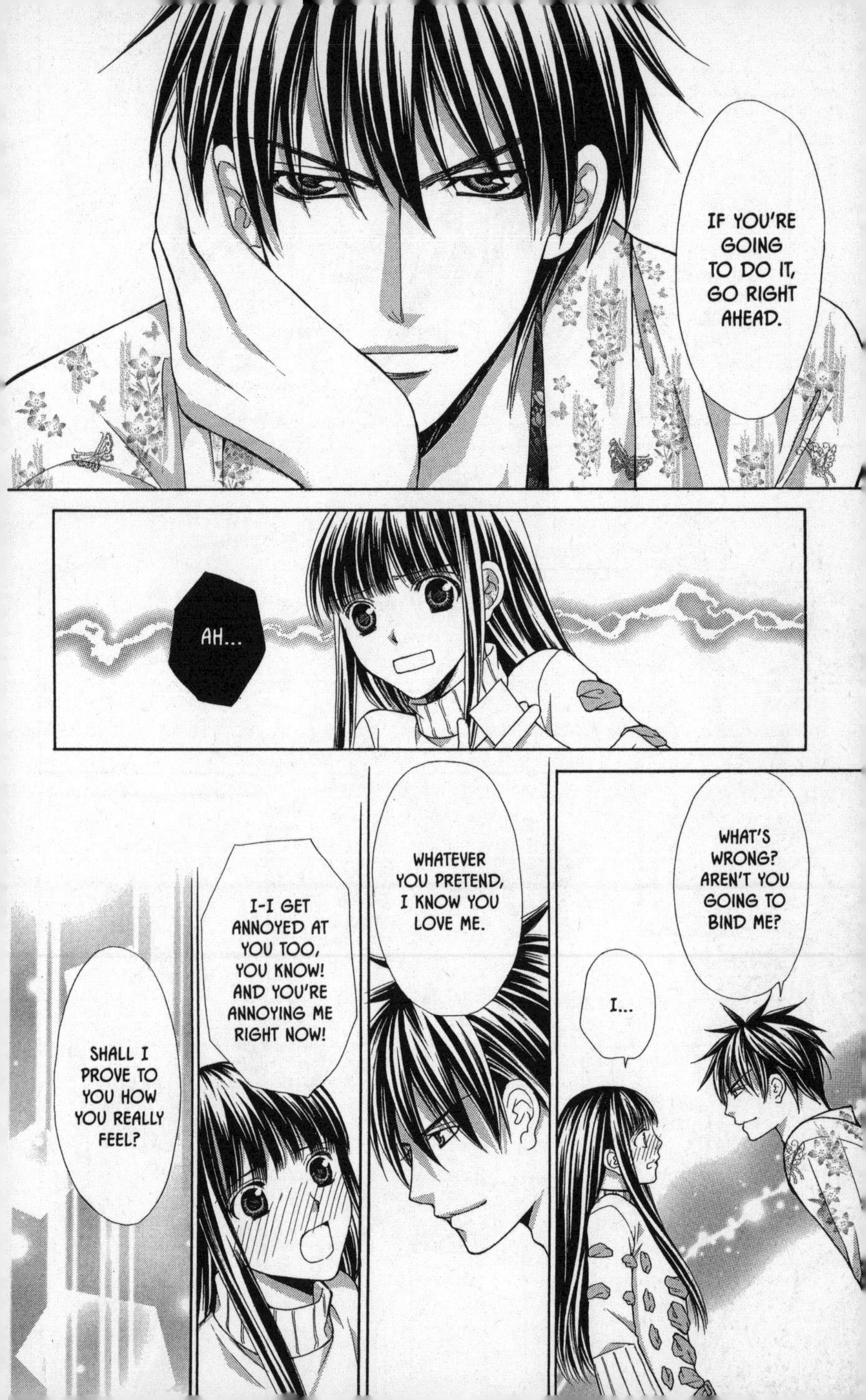
IF YOU'RE GOING TO DO IT, GO RIGHT AHEAD.
AH...
WHAT'S WRONG? AREN'T YOU GOING TO BIND ME?
I...
WHATEVER YOU PRETEND, I KNOW YOU LOVE ME.
I-I GET ANNOYED AT YOU TOO, YOU KNOW! AND YOU'RE ANNOYING ME RIGHT NOW!
SHALL I PROVE TO YOU HOW YOU REALLY FEEL?

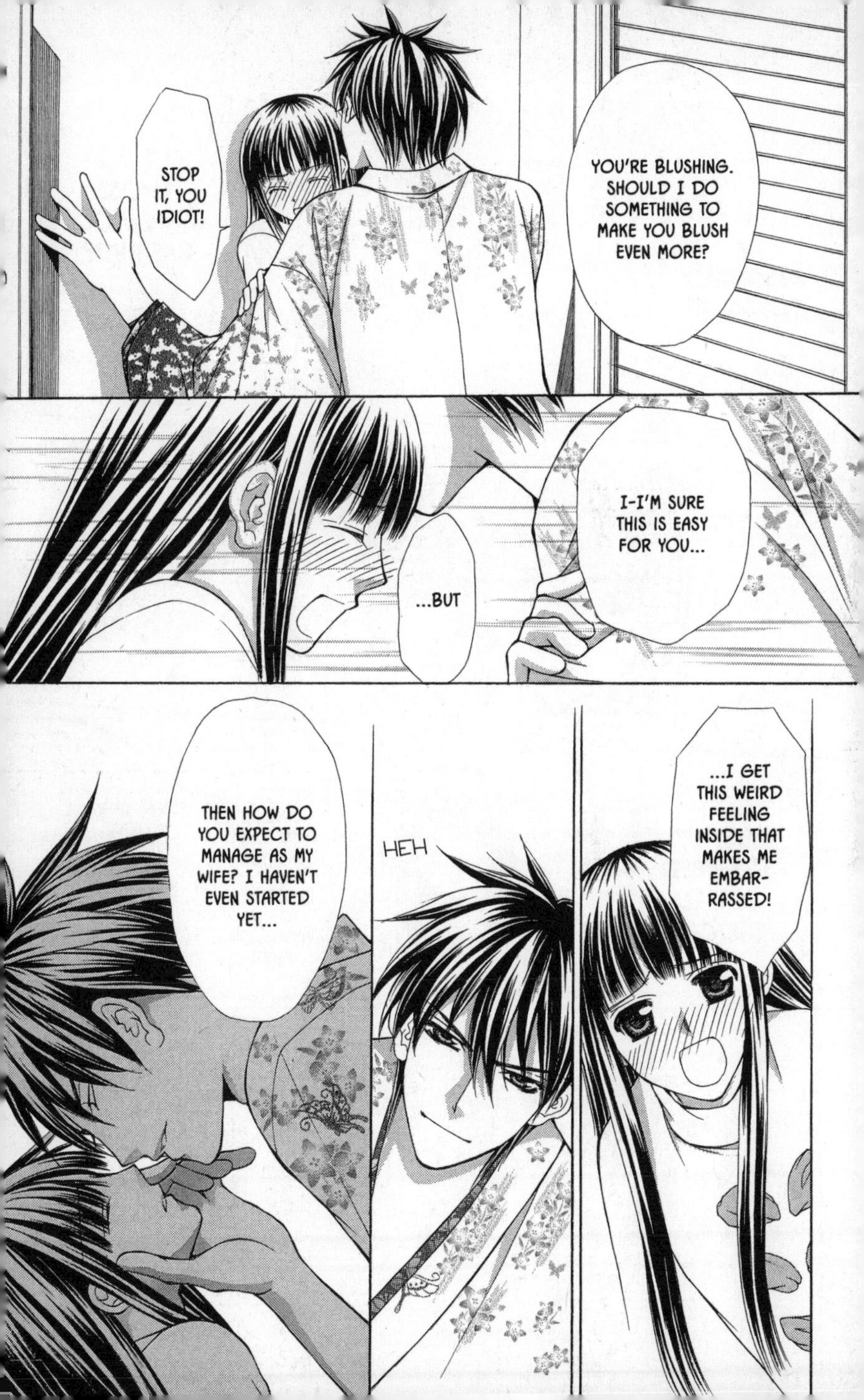
YOU'RE BLUSHING. SHOULD I DO SOMETHING TO MAKE YOU BLUSH EVEN MORE?
STOP IT, YOU IDIOT!
I-I'M SURE THIS IS EASY FOR YOU...
...BUT
...I GET THIS WEIRD FEELING INSIDE THAT MAKES ME EMBAR-RASSED!
HEH
THEN HOW DO YOU EXPECT TO MANAGE AS MY WIFE? I HAVEN'T EVEN STARTED YET...

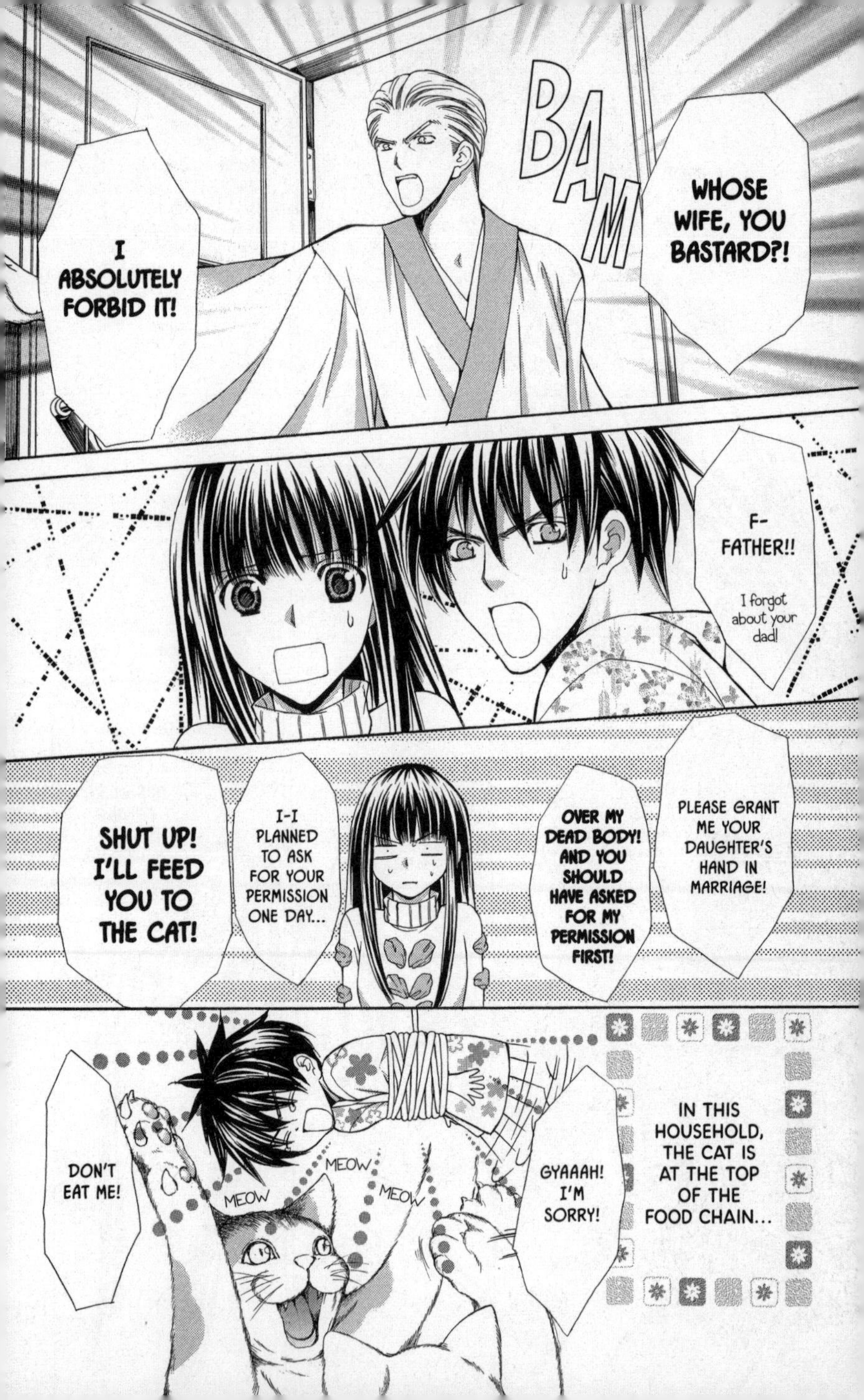
BAM
WHOSE WIFE, YOU BASTARD?!
I ABSOLUTELY FORBID IT!
F- FATHER!!
I forgot about your dad!
PLEASE GRANT ME YOUR DAUGHTER'S HAND IN MARRIAGE!
OVER MY DEAD BODY! AND YOU SHOULD HAVE ASKED FOR MY PERMISSION FIRST!
I-I PLANNED TO ASK FOR YOUR PERMISSION ONE DAY...
SHUT UP! I'LL FEED YOU TO THE CAT!
IN THIS HOUSEHOLD, THE CAT IS AT THE TOP OF THE FOOD CHAIN...
GYAAAH! I'M SORRY!
MEOW
MEOW
MEOW
DON'T EAT ME!

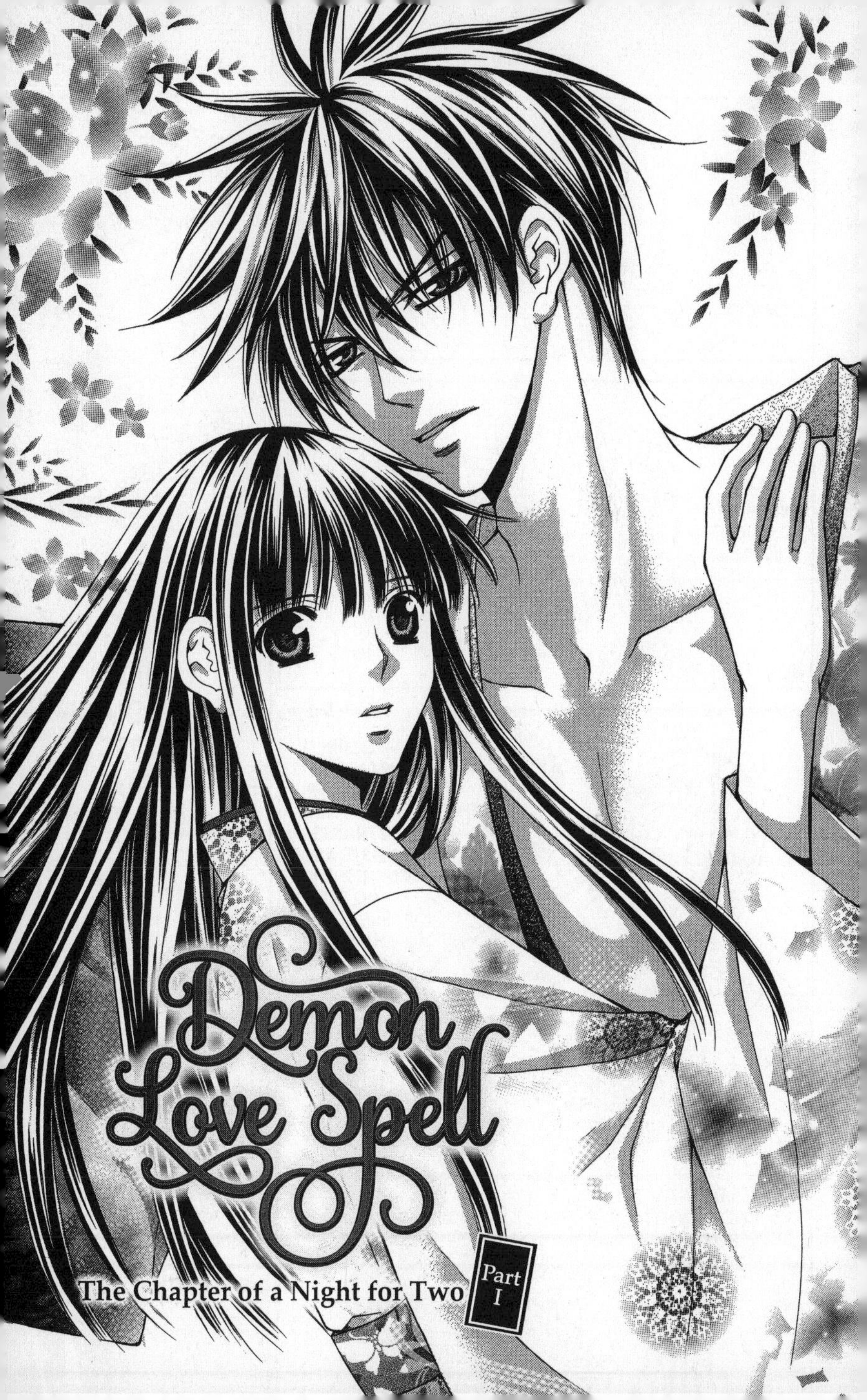
Demon Love Spell
The Chapter of a Night for Two
Part I

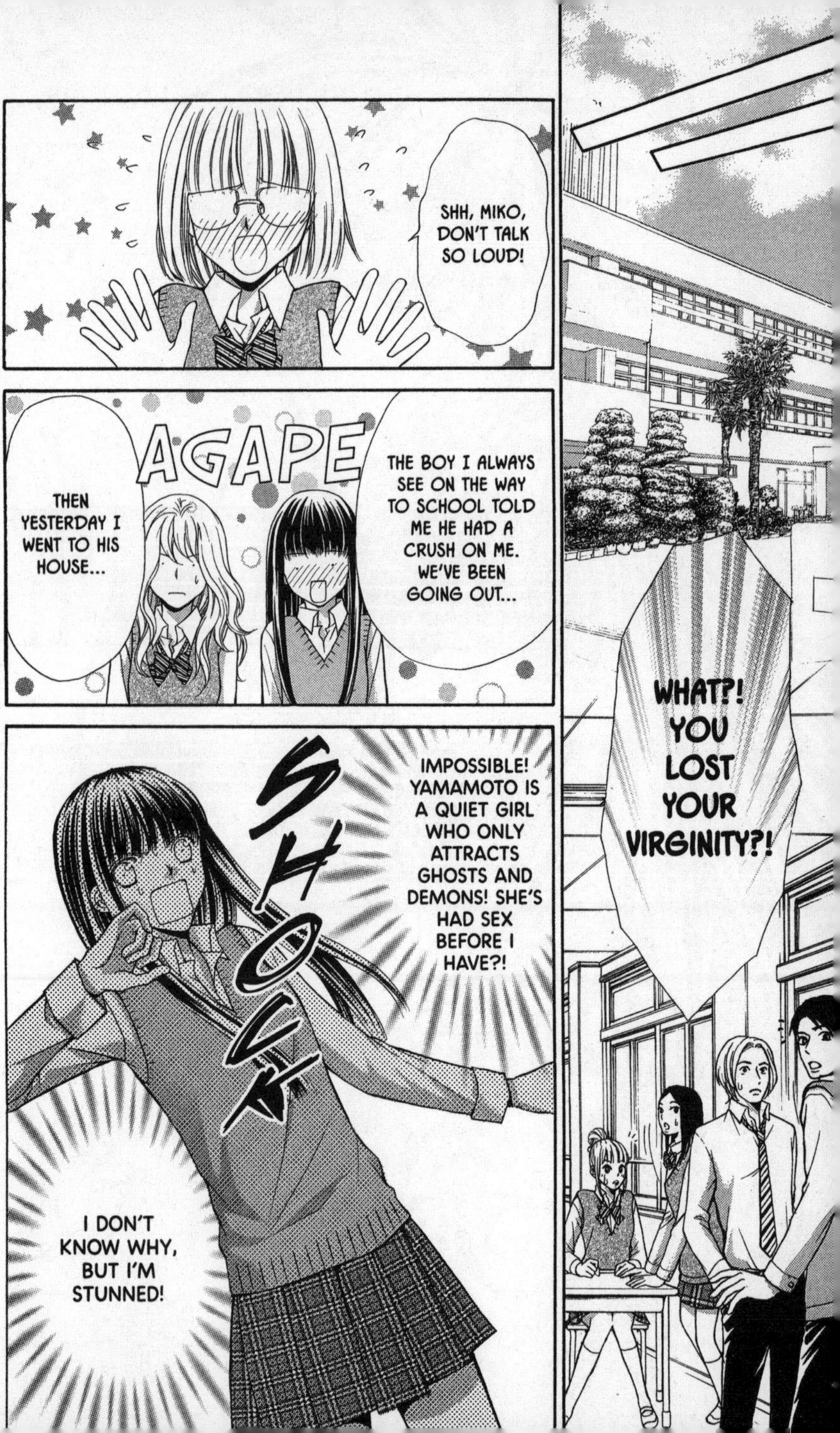
WHAT?! YOU LOST YOUR VIRGINITY?!
SHH, MIKO, DON'T TALK SO LOUD!
THE BOY I ALWAYS SEE ON THE WAY TO SCHOOL TOLD ME HE HAD A CRUSH ON ME. WE'VE BEEN GOING OUT...
AGAPE
THEN YESTERDAY I WENT TO HIS HOUSE...
SHOCK
IMPOSSIBLE! YAMAMOTO IS A QUIET GIRL WHO ONLY ATTRACTS GHOSTS AND DEMONS! SHE'S HAD SEX BEFORE I HAVE?!
I DON'T KNOW WHY, BUT I'M STUNNED!

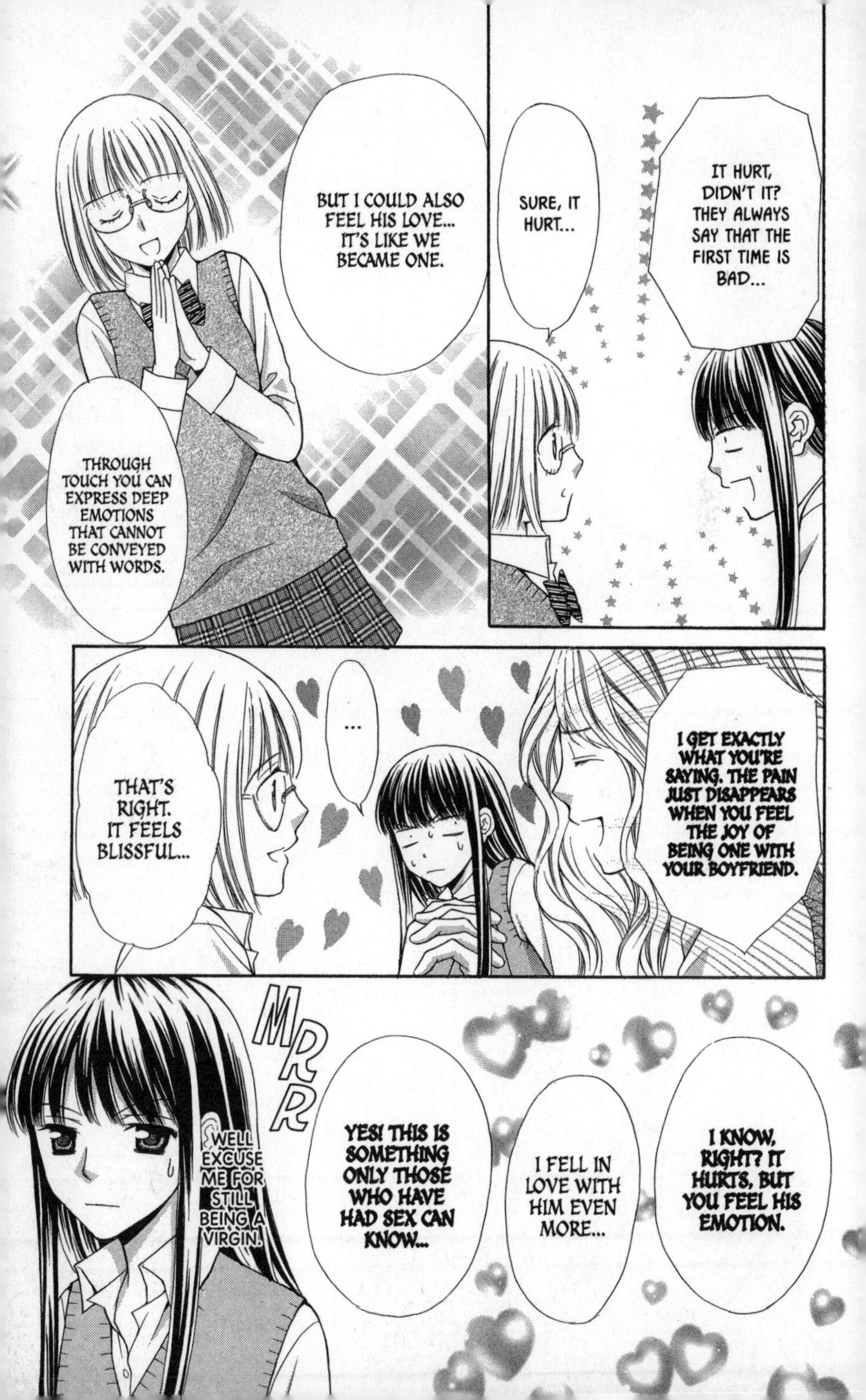
IT HURT, DIDN'T IT? THEY ALWAYS SAY THAT THE FIRST TIME IS BAD...
SURE, IT HURT...
BUT I COULD ALSO FEEL HIS LOVE... IT'S LIKE WE BECAME ONE.
THROUGH TOUCH YOU CAN EXPRESS DEEP EMOTIONS THAT CANNOT BE CONVEYED WITH WORDS.
I GET EXACTLY WHAT YOU'RE SAYING. THE PAIN JUST DISAPPEARS WHEN YOU FEEL THE JOY OF BEING ONE WITH YOUR BOYFRIEND.
...
THAT'S RIGHT. IT FEELS BLISSFUL...
I KNOW, RIGHT? IT HURTS, BUT YOU FEEL HIS EMOTION.
I FELL IN LOVE WITH HIM EVEN MORE...
YES! THIS IS SOMETHING ONLY THOSE WHO HAVE HAD SEX CAN KNOW...
MRR
WELL EXCUSE ME FOR STILL BEING A VIRGIN.

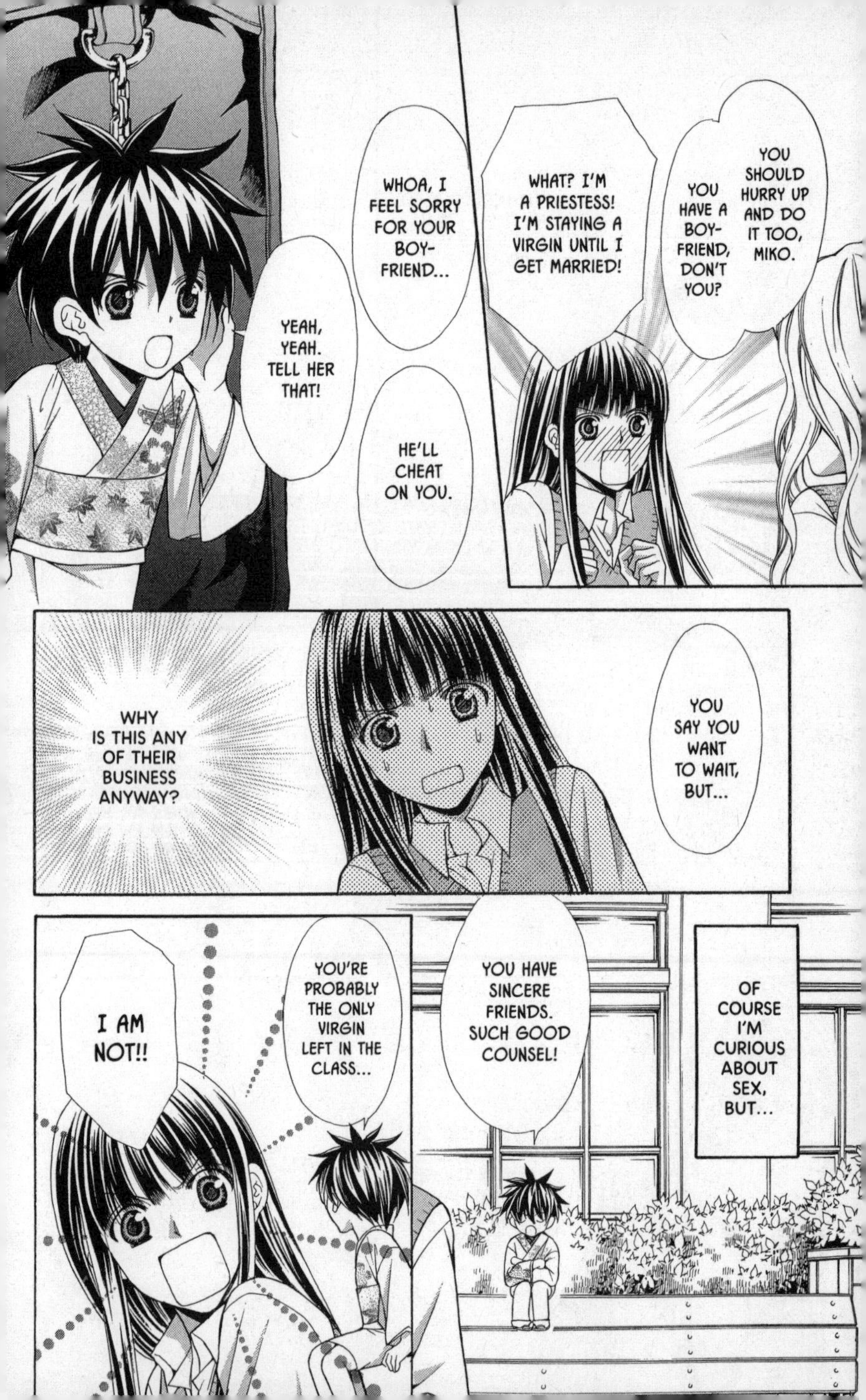
YOU SHOULD HURRY UP AND DO IT TOO, MIKO.
YOU HAVE A BOY-FRIEND, DON'T YOU?
WHAT? I'M A PRIESTESS! I'M STAYING A VIRGIN UNTIL I GET MARRIED!
WHOA, I FEEL SORRY FOR YOUR BOY-FRIEND...
HE'LL CHEAT ON YOU.
YEAH, YEAH. TELL HER THAT!
YOU SAY YOU WANT TO WAIT, BUT...
WHY IS THIS ANY OF THEIR BUSINESS ANYWAY?
OF COURSE I'M CURIOUS ABOUT SEX, BUT...
YOU HAVE SINCERE FRIENDS. SUCH GOOD COUNSEL!
YOU'RE PROBABLY THE ONLY VIRGIN LEFT IN THE CLASS...
I AM NOT!!

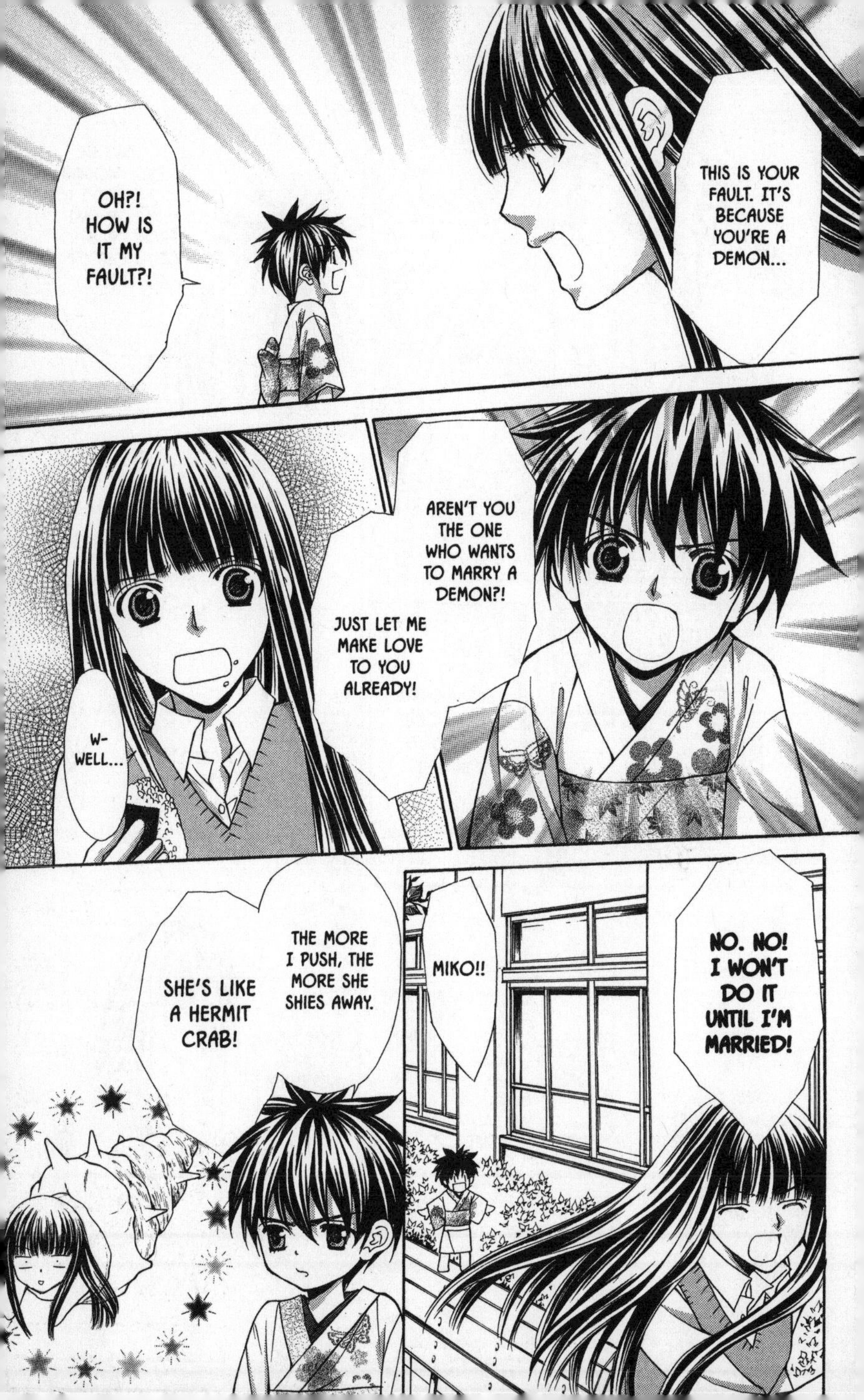
THIS IS YOUR FAULT. IT'S BECAUSE YOU'RE A DEMON...
OH?! HOW IS IT MY FAULT?!
AREN'T YOU THE ONE WHO WANTS TO MARRY A DEMON?!
JUST LET ME MAKE LOVE TO YOU ALREADY!
W-WELL...
NO. NO! I WON'T DO IT UNTIL I'M MARRIED!
MIKO!!
THE MORE I PUSH, THE MORE SHE SHIES AWAY.
SHE'S LIKE A HERMIT CRAB!

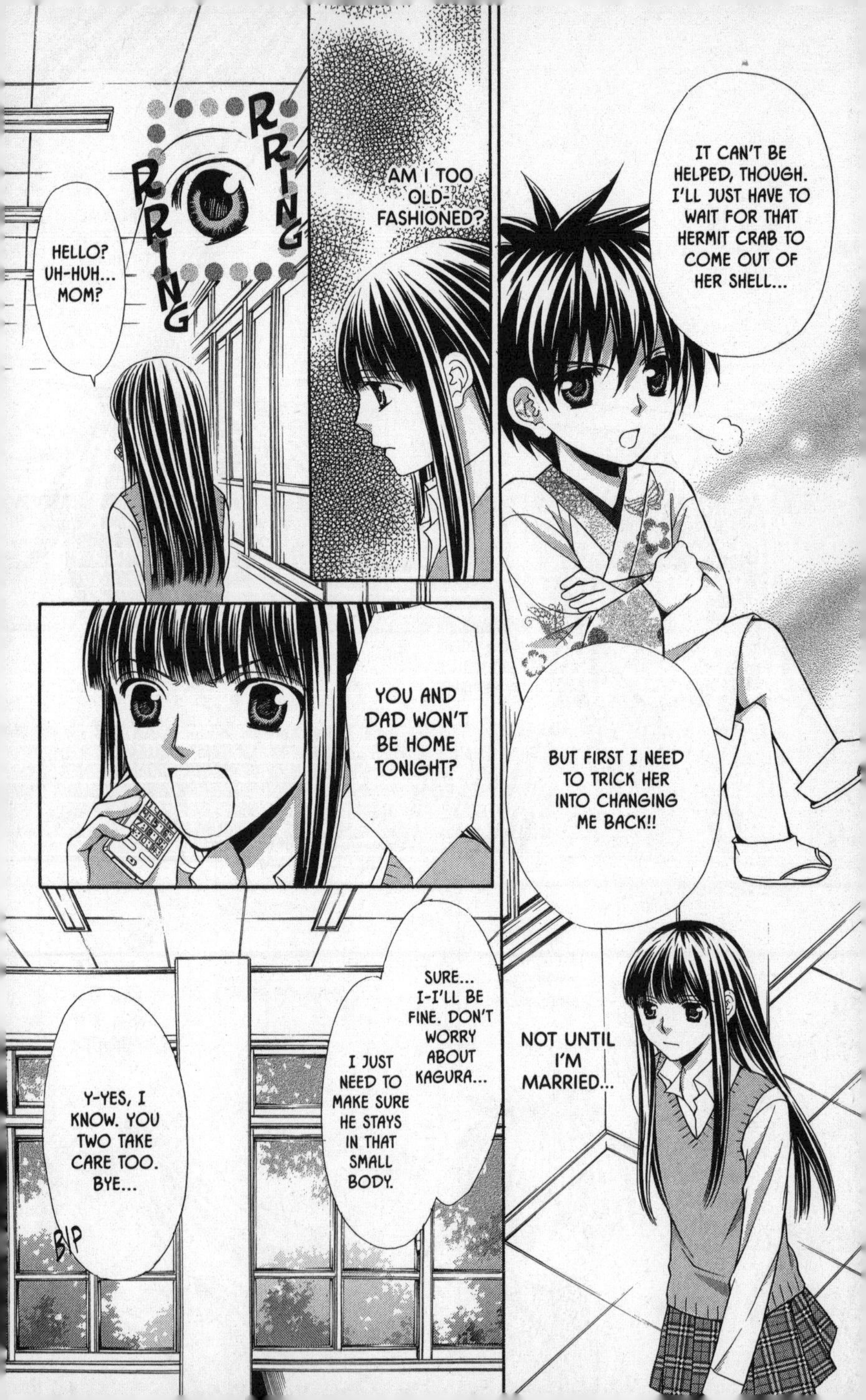
IT CAN'T BE HELPED, THOUGH. I'LL JUST HAVE TO WAIT FOR THAT HERMIT CRAB TO COME OUT OF HER SHELL...
BUT FIRST I NEED TO TRICK HER INTO CHANGING ME BACK!!
AM I TOO OLD-FASHIONED?
RRING RRING
HELLO? UH-HUH... MOM?
YOU AND DAD WON'T BE HOME TONIGHT?
NOT UNTIL I'M MARRIED...
SURE... I-I'LL BE FINE. DON'T WORRY ABOUT KAGURA...
I JUST NEED TO MAKE SURE HE STAYS IN THAT SMALL BODY.
Y-YES, I KNOW. YOU TWO TAKE CARE TOO. BYE...
BIP

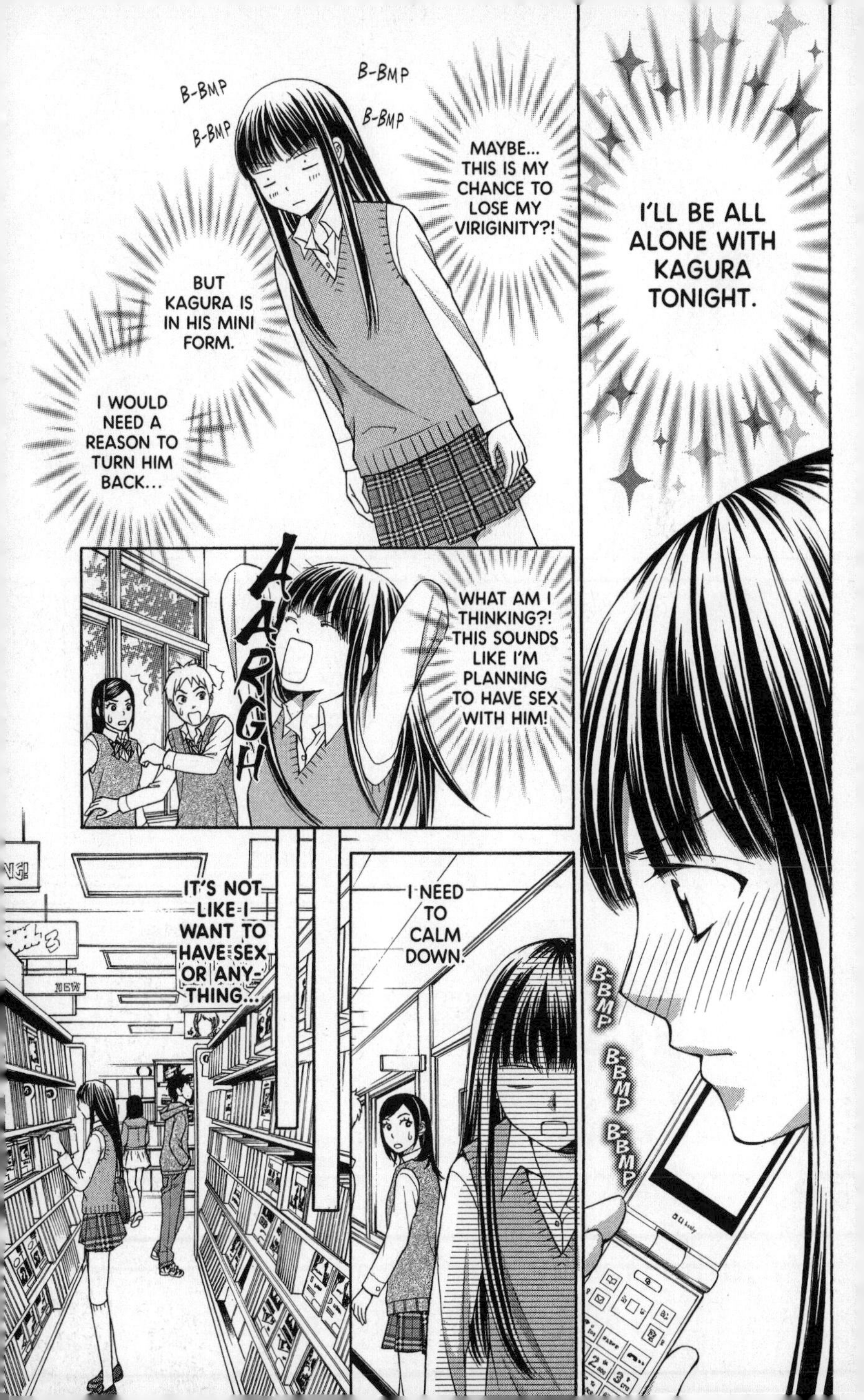
I'LL BE ALL ALONE WITH KAGURA TONIGHT.
B-BMP
B-BMP
B-BMP
B-BMP
B-BMP
B-BMP
B-BMP
MAYBE... THIS IS MY CHANCE TO LOSE MY VIRIGINITY?!
BUT KAGURA IS IN HIS MINI FORM.
I WOULD NEED A REASON TO TURN HIM BACK...
WHAT AM I THINKING?! THIS SOUNDS LIKE I'M PLANNING TO HAVE SEX WITH HIM!
AARGH
I NEED TO CALM DOWN.
IT'S NOT LIKE I WANT TO HAVE SEX OR ANYTHING...

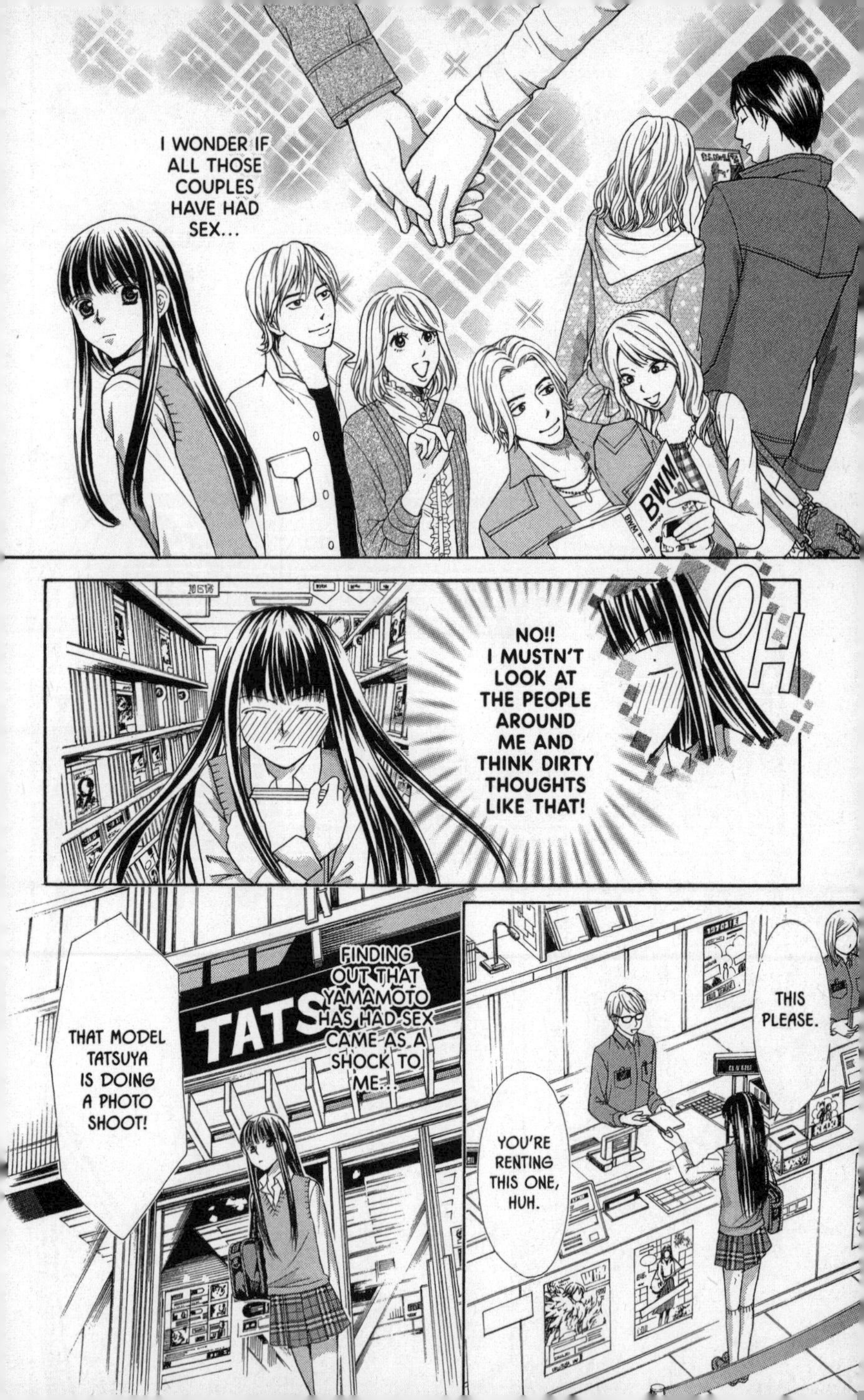

I WONDER IF ALL THOSE COUPLES HAVE HAD SEX...
BWM
OH
NO!! I MUSTN'T LOOK AT THE PEOPLE AROUND ME AND THINK DIRTY THOUGHTS LIKE THAT!
THIS PLEASE.
YOU'RE RENTING THIS ONE, HUH.
FINDING OUT THAT YAMAMOTO HAS HAD SEX CAME AS A SHOCK TO ME...
TATS
THAT MODEL TATSUYA IS DOING A PHOTO SHOOT!

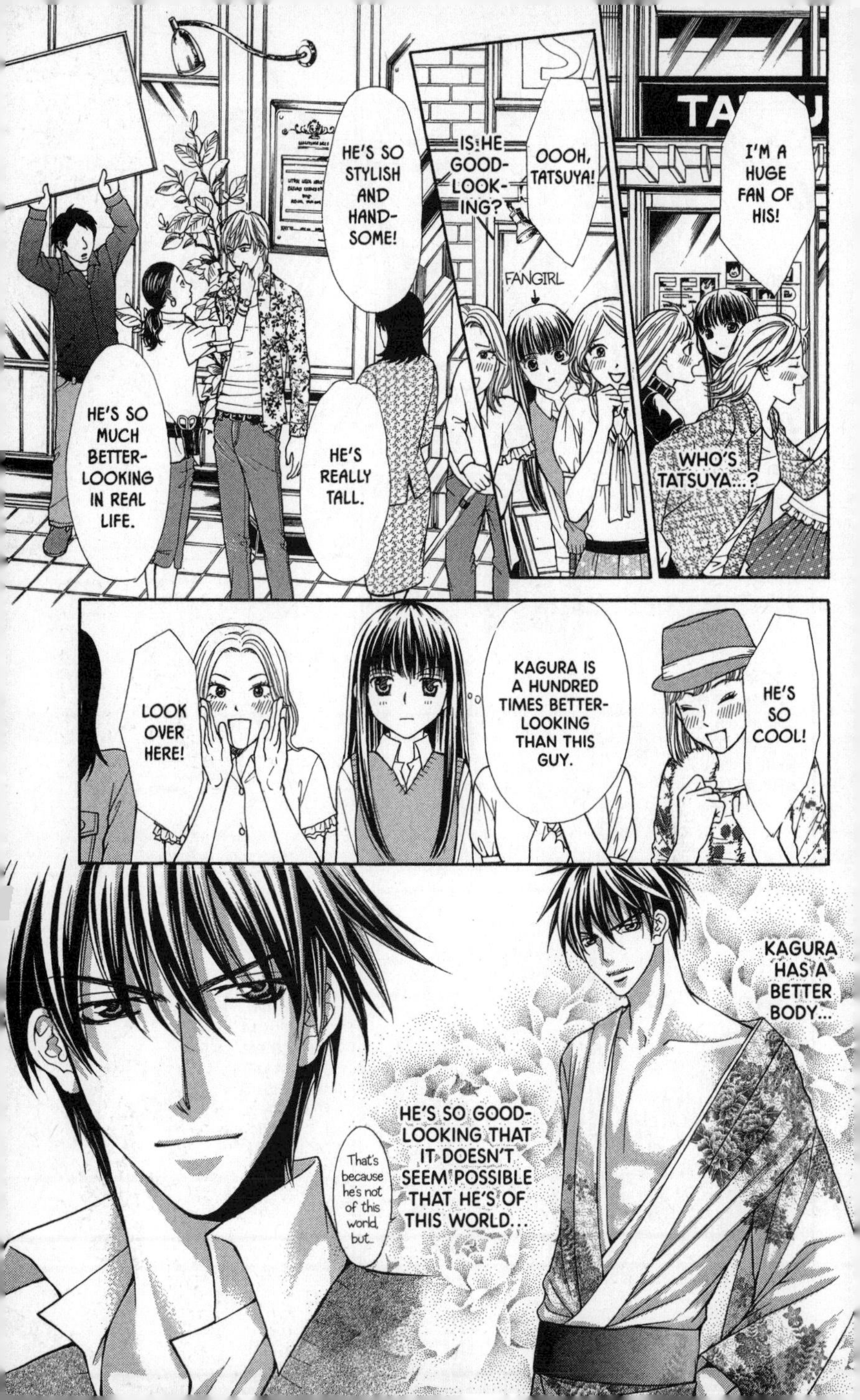

I'M A HUGE FAN OF HIS!
WHO'S TATSUYA...?
OOOH, TATSUYA!
IS HE GOOD-LOOKING?
FANGIRL
HE'S SO STYLISH AND HANDSOME!
HE'S REALLY TALL.
HE'S SO MUCH BETTER-LOOKING IN REAL LIFE.
HE'S SO COOL!
KAGURA IS A HUNDRED TIMES BETTER-LOOKING THAN THIS GUY.
LOOK OVER HERE!
KAGURA HAS A BETTER BODY...
HE'S SO GOOD-LOOKING THAT IT DOESN'T SEEM POSSIBLE THAT HE'S OF THIS WORLD...
That's because he's not of this world, but...

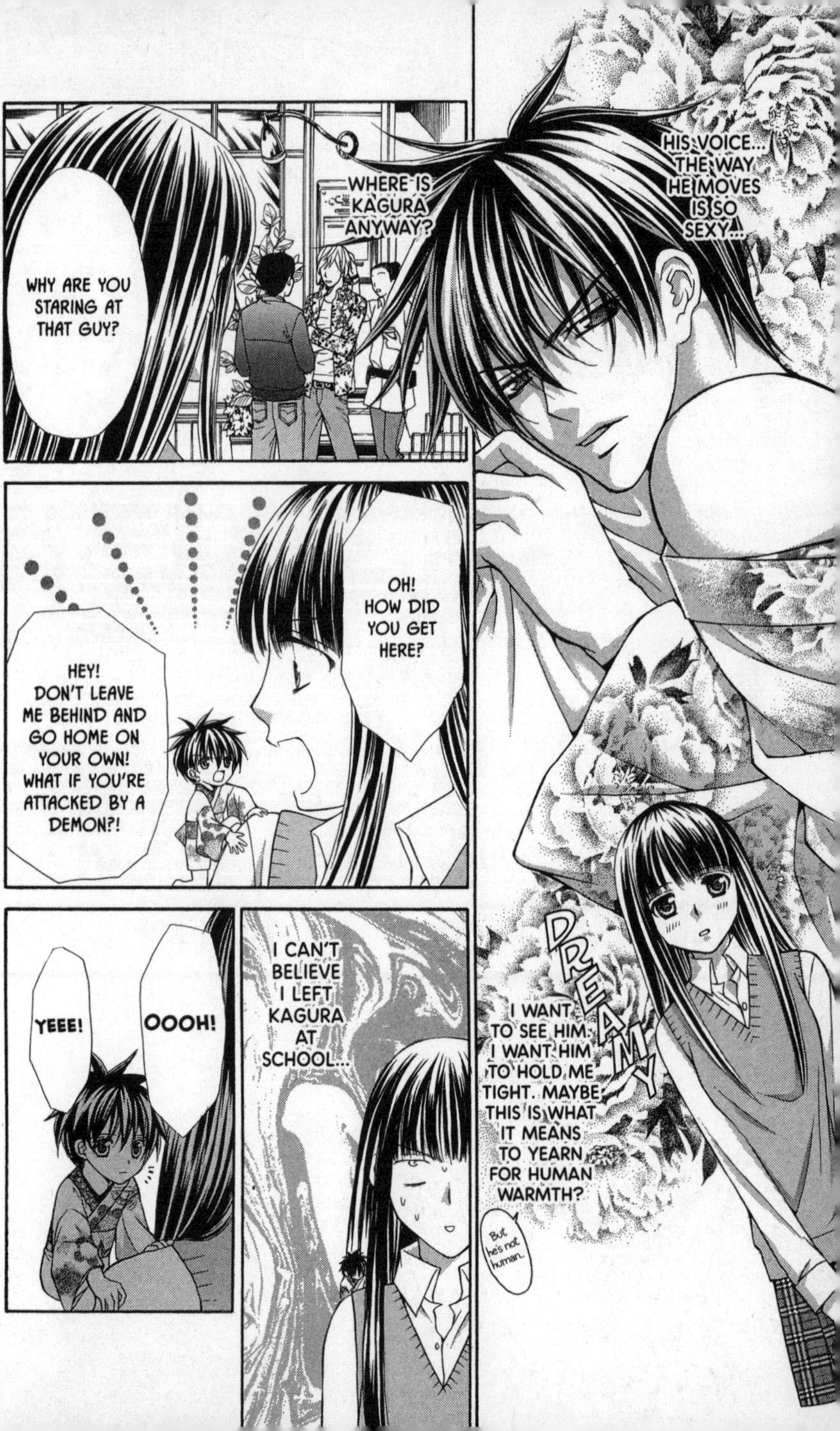
HIS VOICE... THE WAY HE MOVES IS SO SEXY...
DREAMY
I WANT TO SEE HIM. I WANT HIM TO HOLD ME TIGHT. MAYBE THIS IS WHAT IT MEANS TO YEARN FOR HUMAN WARMTH?
But he's not human..
WHERE IS KAGURA ANYWAY?
WHY ARE YOU STARING AT THAT GUY?
OH! HOW DID YOU GET HERE?
HEY! DON'T LEAVE ME BEHIND AND GO HOME ON YOUR OWN! WHAT IF YOU'RE ATTACKED BY A DEMON?!
I CAN'T BELIEVE I LEFT KAGURA AT SCHOOL...
OOOH!
YEEE!

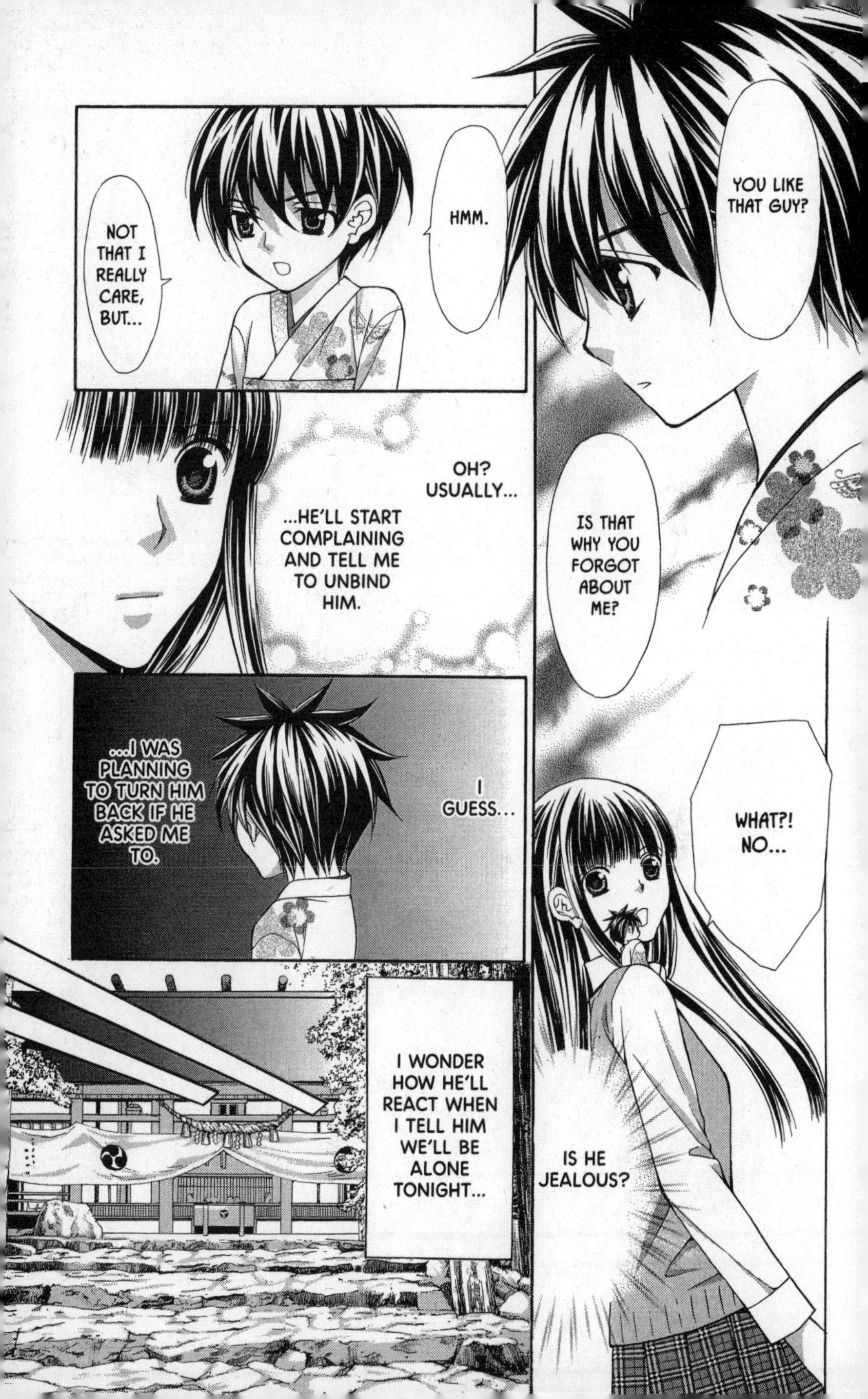
YOU LIKE THAT GUY?
IS THAT WHY YOU FORGOT ABOUT ME?
WHAT?! NO...
IS HE JEALOUS?
HMM.
NOT THAT I REALLY CARE, BUT...
OH? USUALLY...
...HE'LL START COMPLAINING AND TELL ME TO UNBIND HIM.
I GUESS...
...I WAS PLANNING TO TURN HIM BACK IF HE ASKED ME TO.
I WONDER HOW HE'LL REACT WHEN I TELL HIM WE'LL BE ALONE TONIGHT...

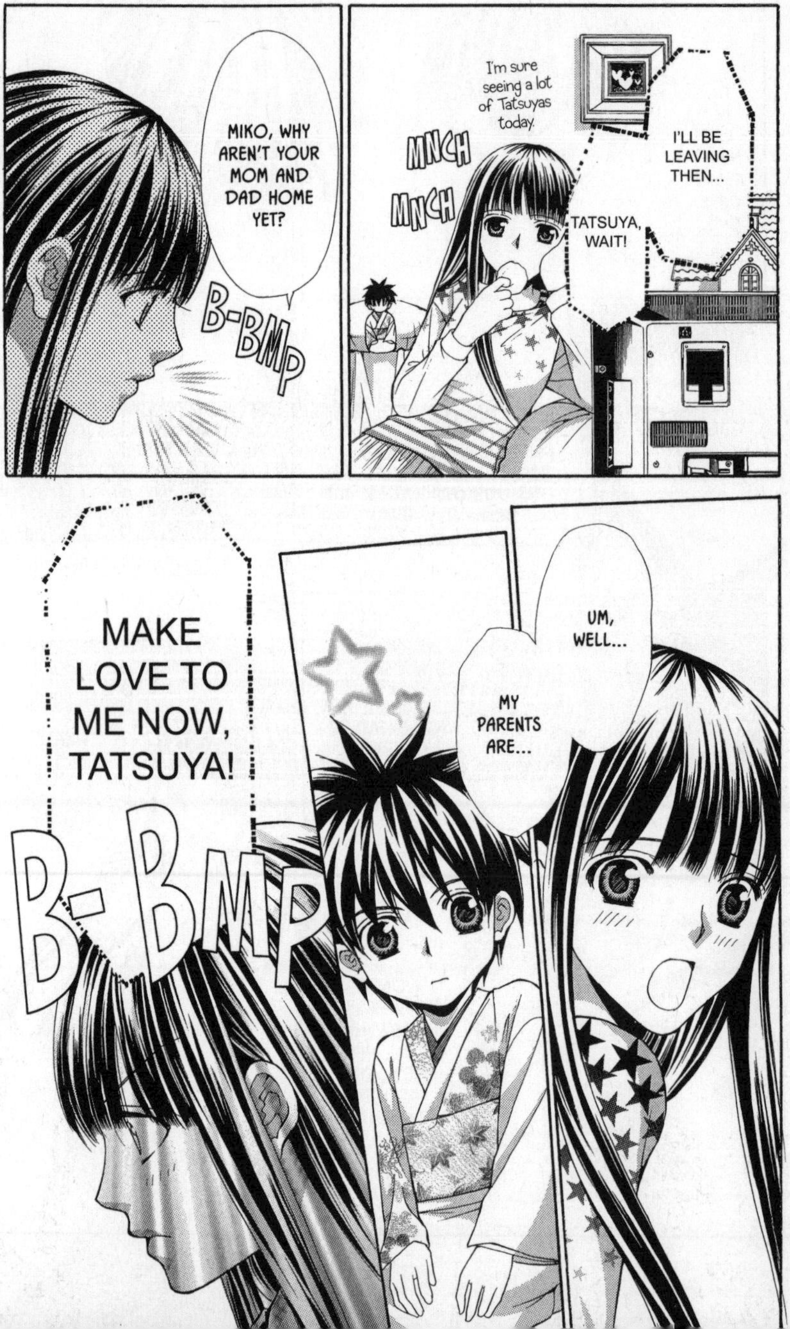
I'LL BE LEAVING THEN...
I'm sure seeing a lot of Tatsuyas today.
TATSUYA, WAIT!
MNCH
MNCH
MIKO, WHY AREN'T YOUR MOM AND DAD HOME YET?
B-BMP
UM, WELL...
MY PARENTS ARE...
MAKE LOVE TO ME NOW, TATSUYA!
B-BMP

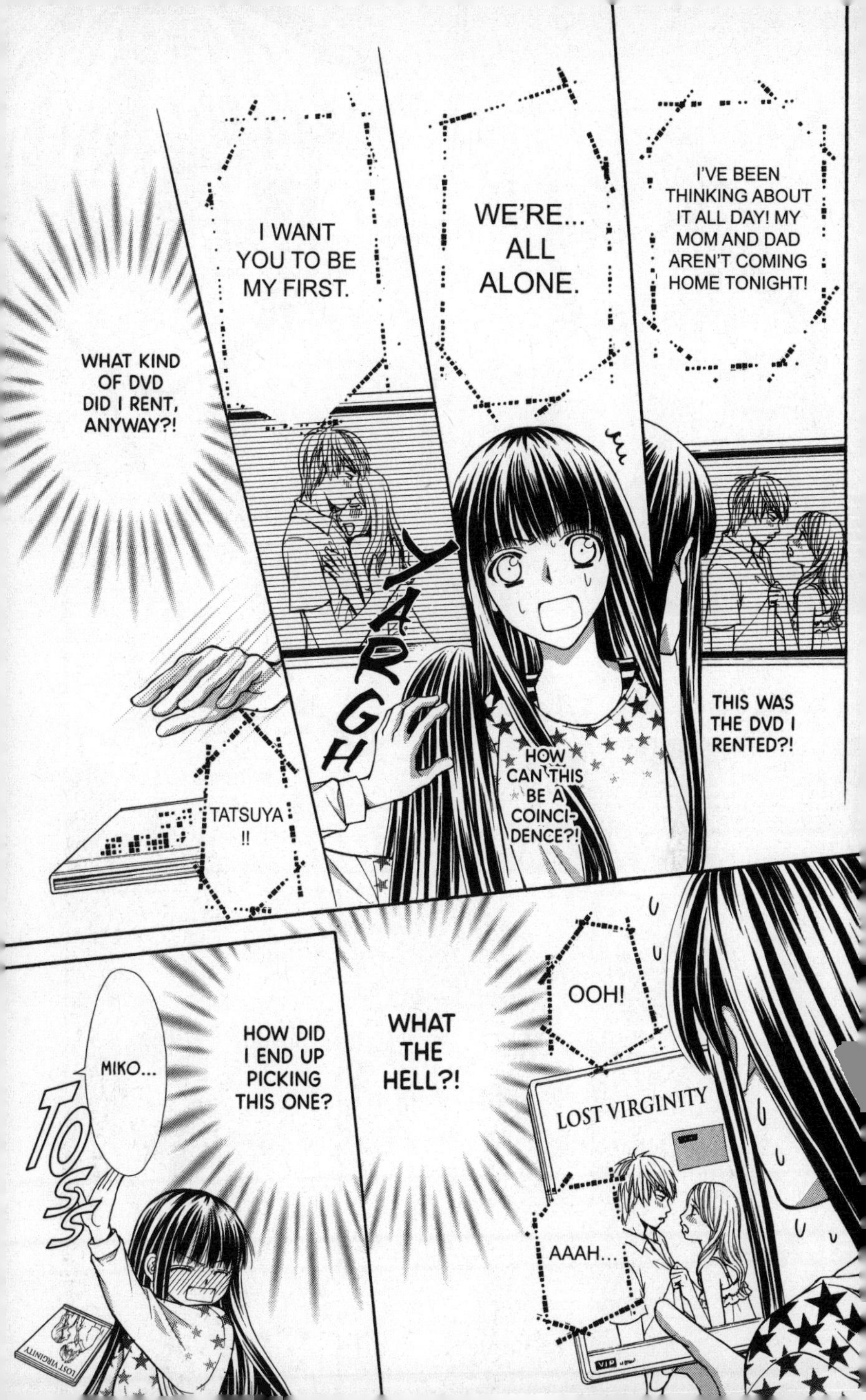
I'VE BEEN THINKING ABOUT IT ALL DAY! MY MOM AND DAD AREN'T COMING HOME TONIGHT!
WE'RE... ALL ALONE.
I WANT YOU TO BE MY FIRST.
THIS WAS THE DVD I RENTED?!
HOW CAN THIS BE A COINCIDENCE?!
YARGH
WHAT KIND OF DVD DID I RENT, ANYWAY?!
TATSUYA!!
OOH!
LOST VIRGINITY
AAAH...
WHAT THE HELL?!
HOW DID I END UP PICKING THIS ONE?
MIKO...
TOSS

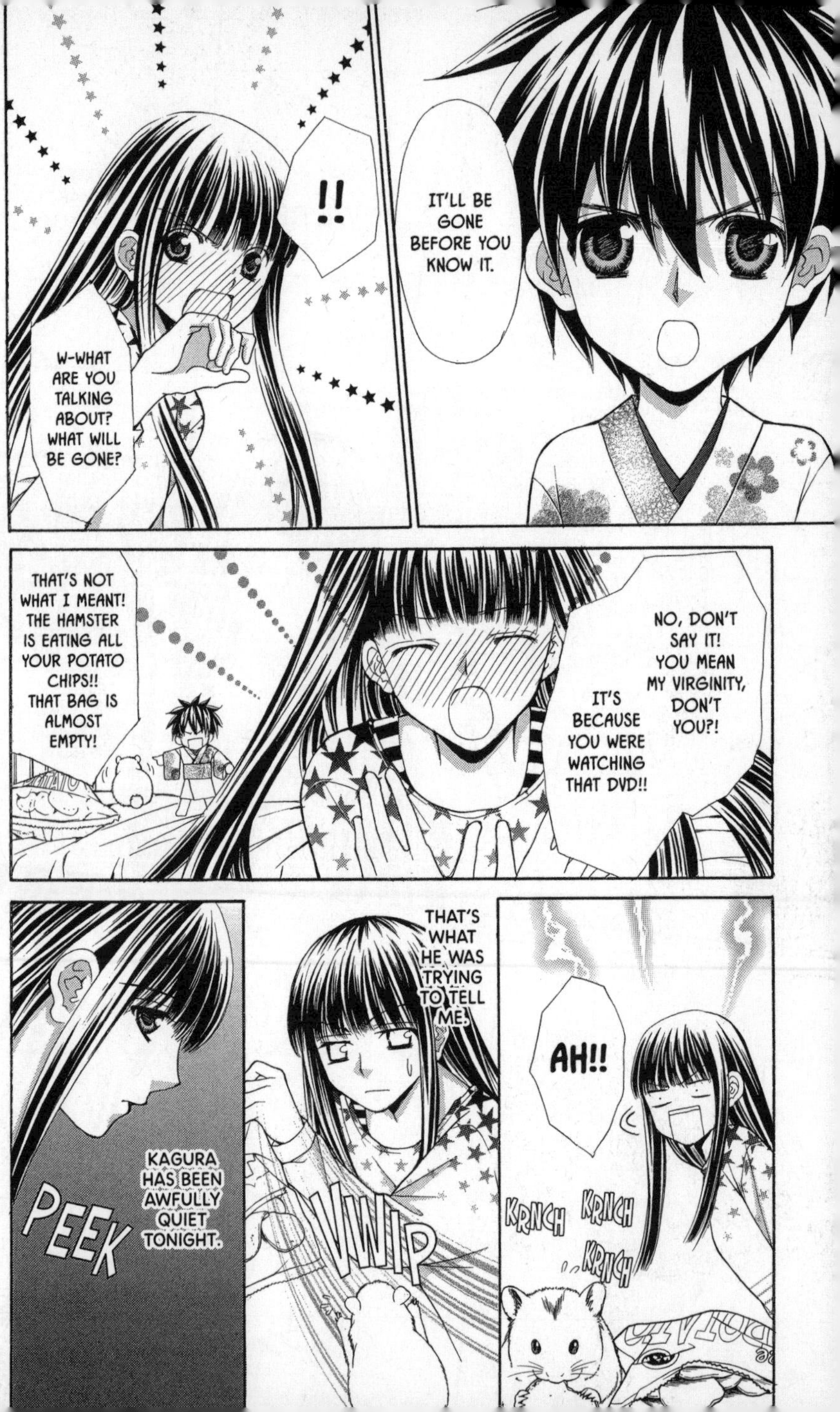
IT'LL BE GONE BEFORE YOU KNOW IT.
!!
W-WHAT ARE YOU TALKING ABOUT? WHAT WILL BE GONE?
NO, DON'T SAY IT! YOU MEAN MY VIRGINITY, DON'T YOU?!
IT'S BECAUSE YOU WERE WATCHING THAT DVD!!
THAT'S NOT WHAT I MEANT! THE HAMSTER IS EATING ALL YOUR POTATO CHIPS!! THAT BAG IS ALMOST EMPTY!
AH!!
KRNCH
KRNCH
KRNCH
THAT'S WHAT HE WAS TRYING TO TELL ME.
VWIP
KAGURA HAS BEEN AWFULLY QUIET TONIGHT.
PEEK

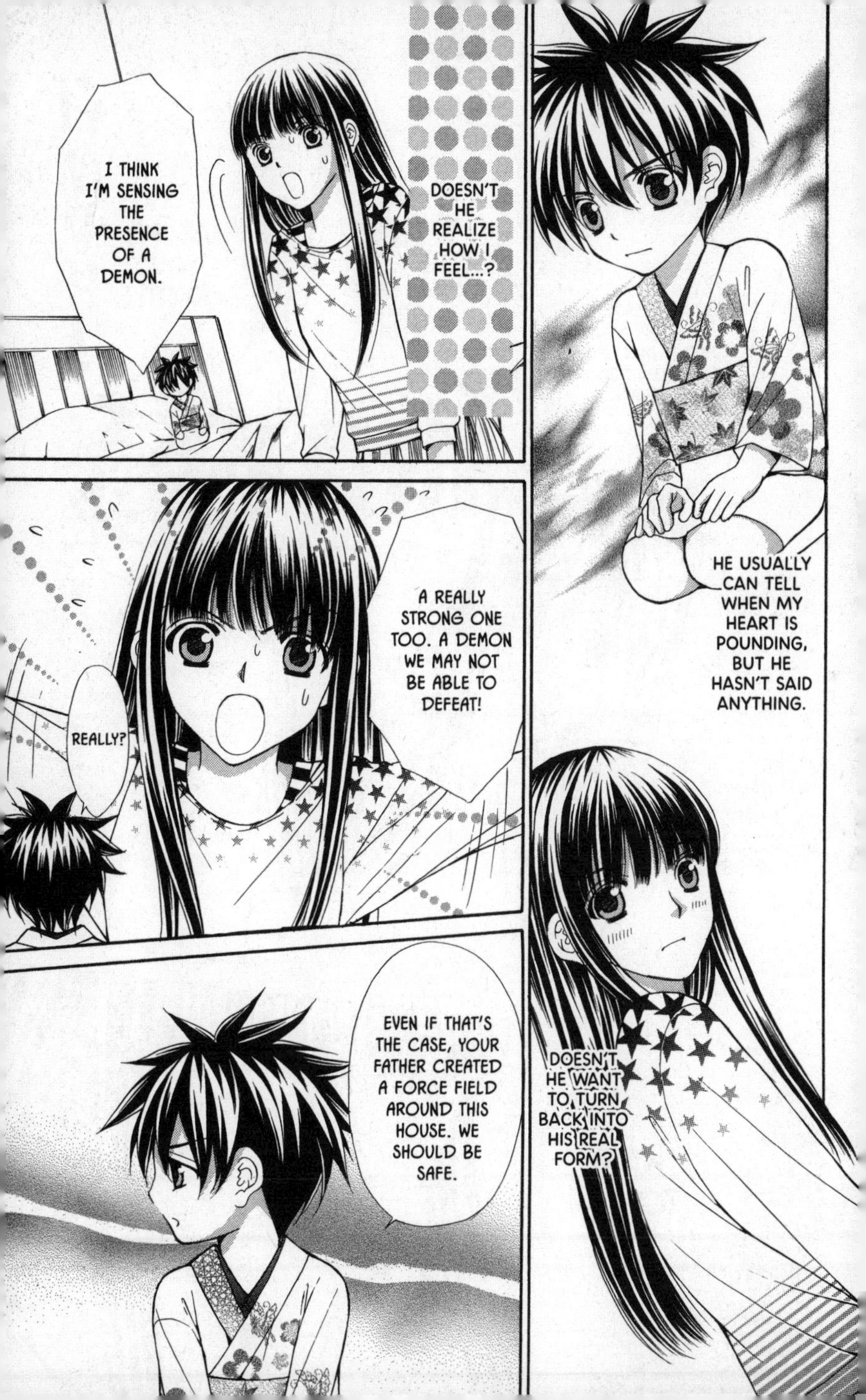
HE USUALLY CAN TELL WHEN MY HEART IS POUNDING, BUT HE HASN'T SAID ANYTHING.
DOESN'T HE WANT TO TURN BACK INTO HIS REAL FORM?
DOESN'T HE REALIZE HOW I FEEL...?
I THINK I'M SENSING THE PRESENCE OF A DEMON.
A REALLY STRONG ONE TOO. A DEMON WE MAY NOT BE ABLE TO DEFEAT!
REALLY?
EVEN IF THAT'S THE CASE, YOUR FATHER CREATED A FORCE FIELD AROUND THIS HOUSE. WE SHOULD BE SAFE.

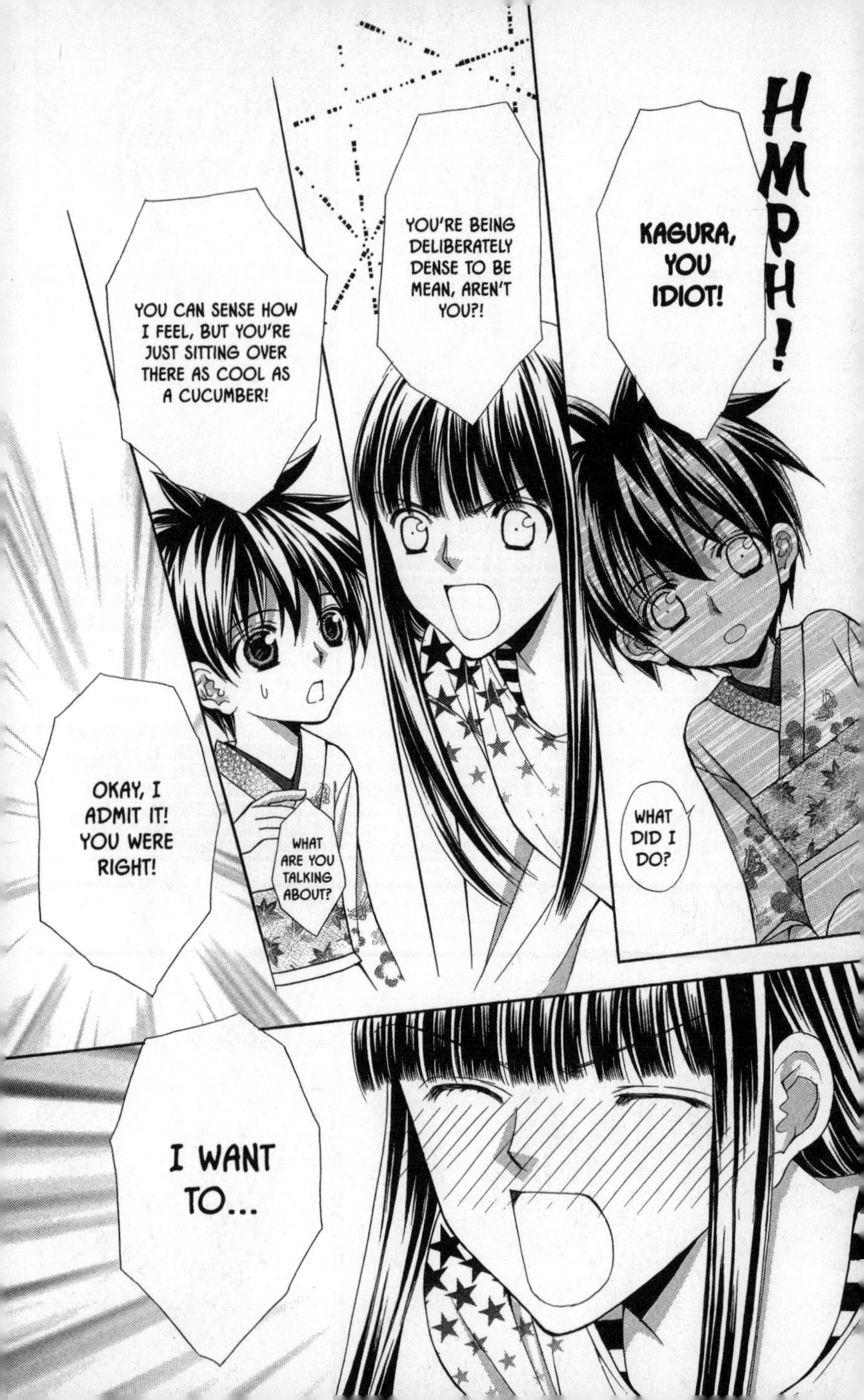
HMPH!
KAGURA, YOU IDIOT!
WHAT DID I DO?
YOU'RE BEING DELIBERATELY DENSE TO BE MEAN, AREN'T YOU?!
YOU CAN SENSE HOW I FEEL, BUT YOU'RE JUST SITTING OVER THERE AS COOL AS A CUCUMBER!
WHAT ARE YOU TALKING ABOUT?
OKAY, I ADMIT IT! YOU WERE RIGHT!
I WANT TO...

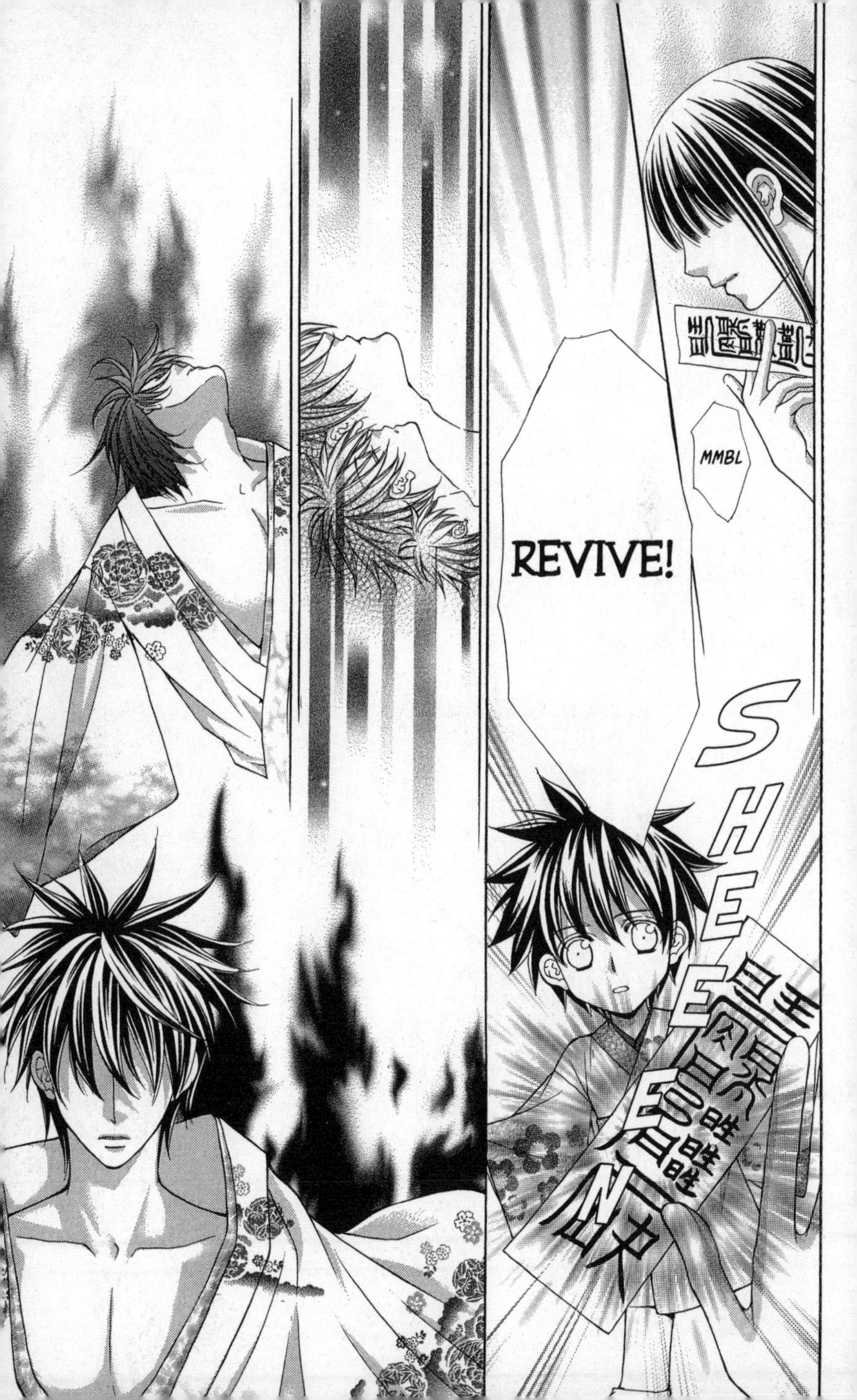
MMBL
REVIVE!
SHEEEEN

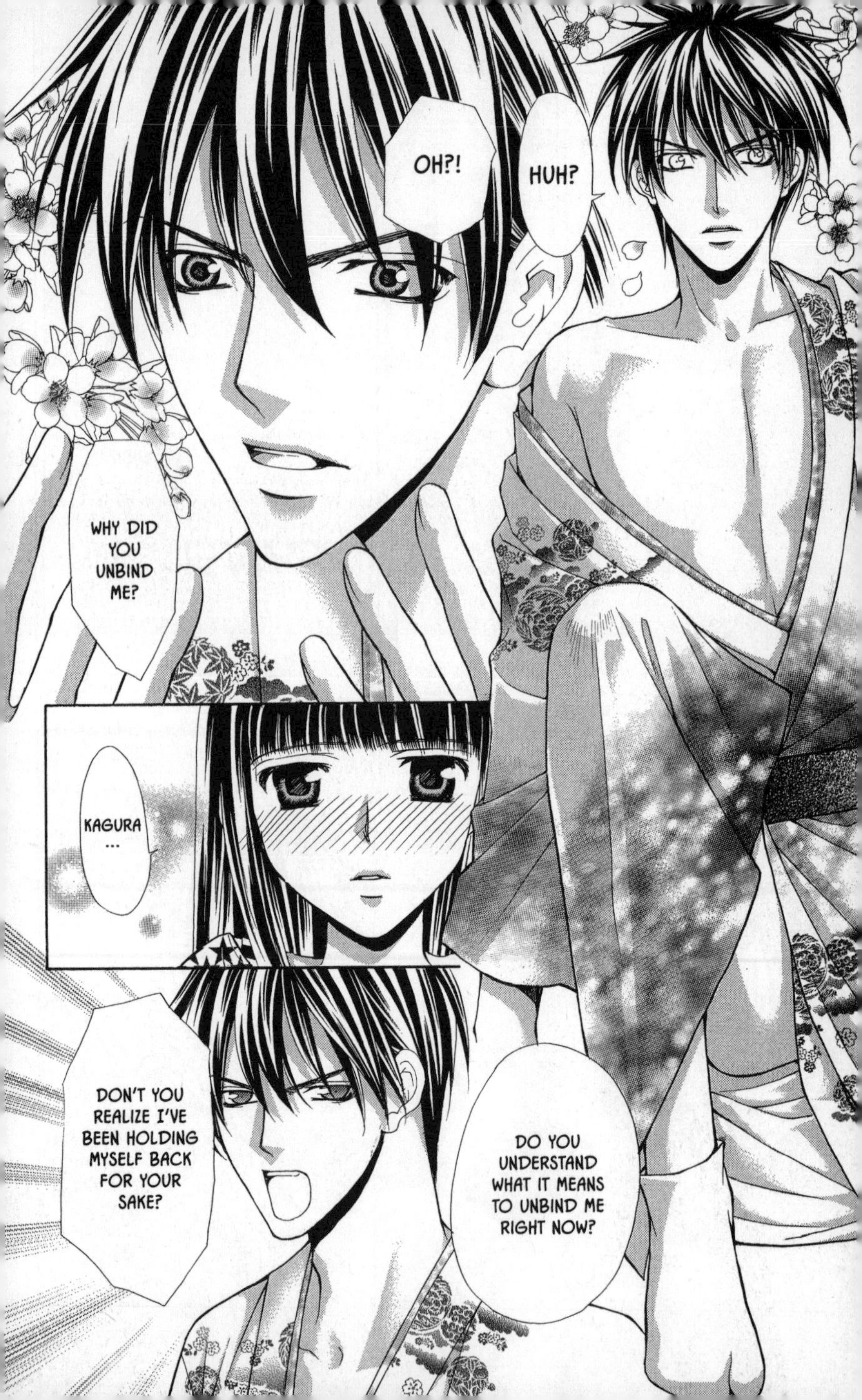
HUH?
OH?!
WHY DID YOU UNBIND ME?
KAGURA ...
DO YOU UNDERSTAND WHAT IT MEANS TO UNBIND ME RIGHT NOW?
DON'T YOU REALIZE I'VE BEEN HOLDING MYSELF BACK FOR YOUR SAKE?

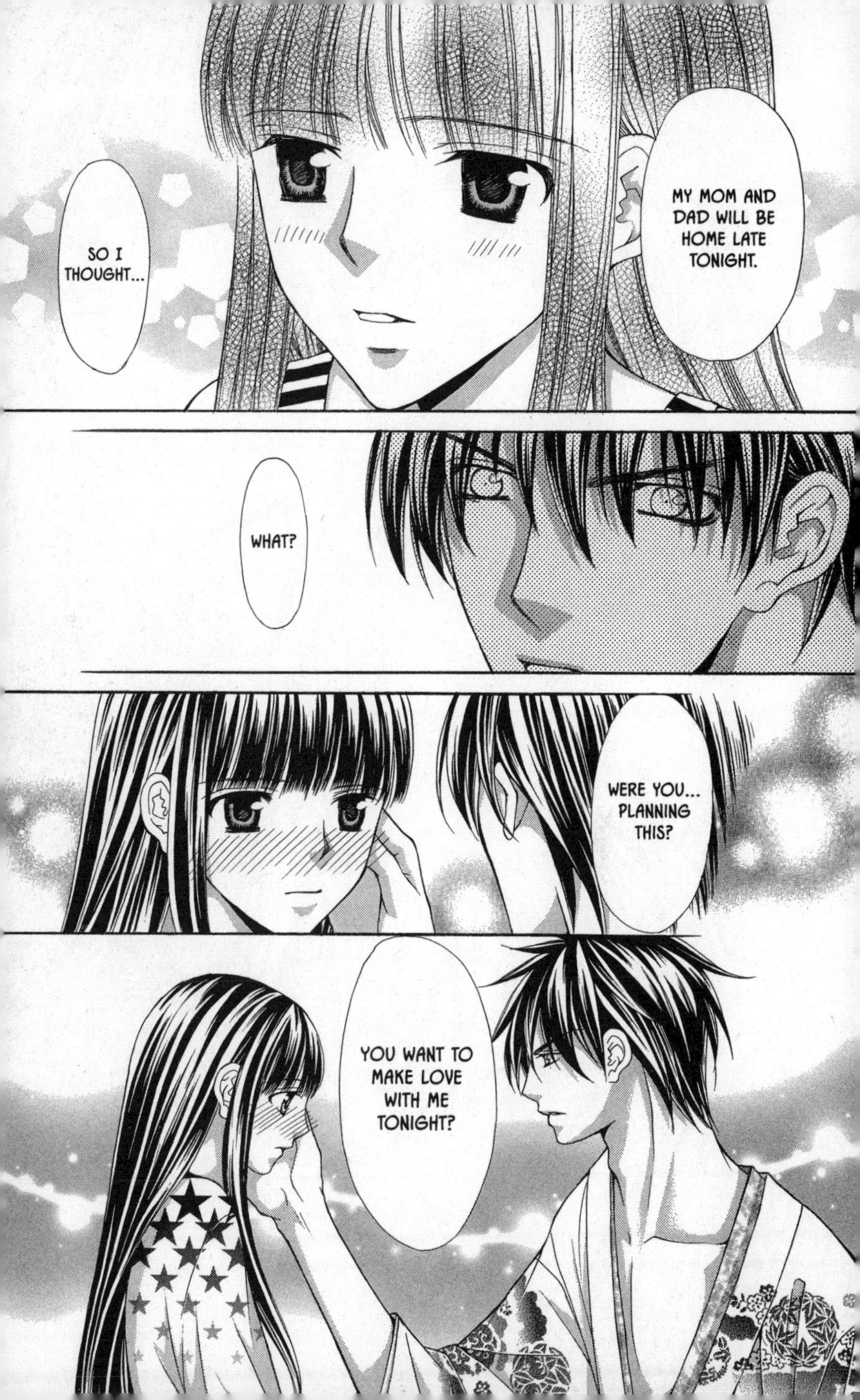
MY MOM AND DAD WILL BE HOME LATE TONIGHT.
SO I THOUGHT...
WHAT?
WERE YOU... PLANNING THIS?
YOU WANT TO MAKE LOVE WITH ME TONIGHT?

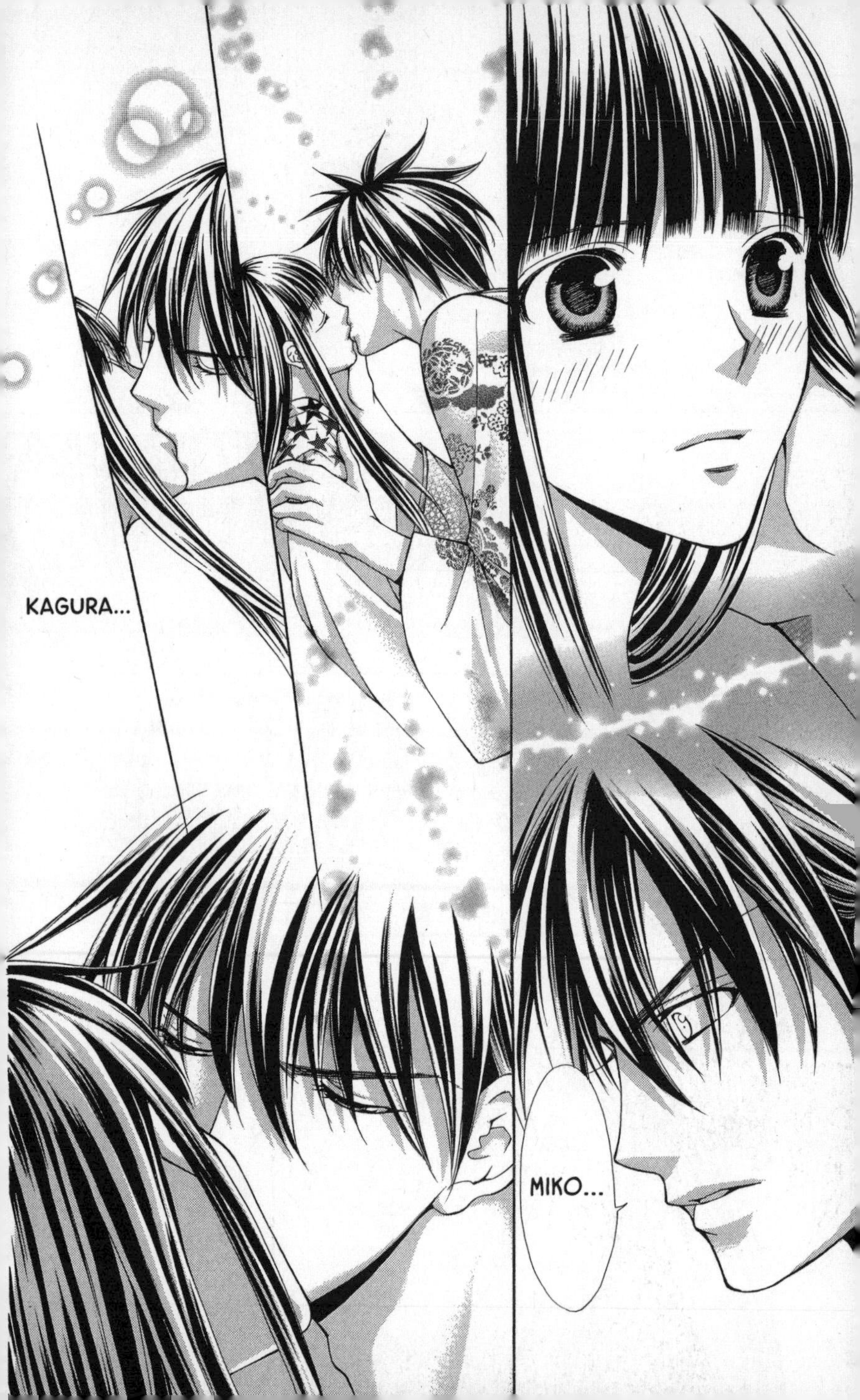
MIKO...
KAGURA...

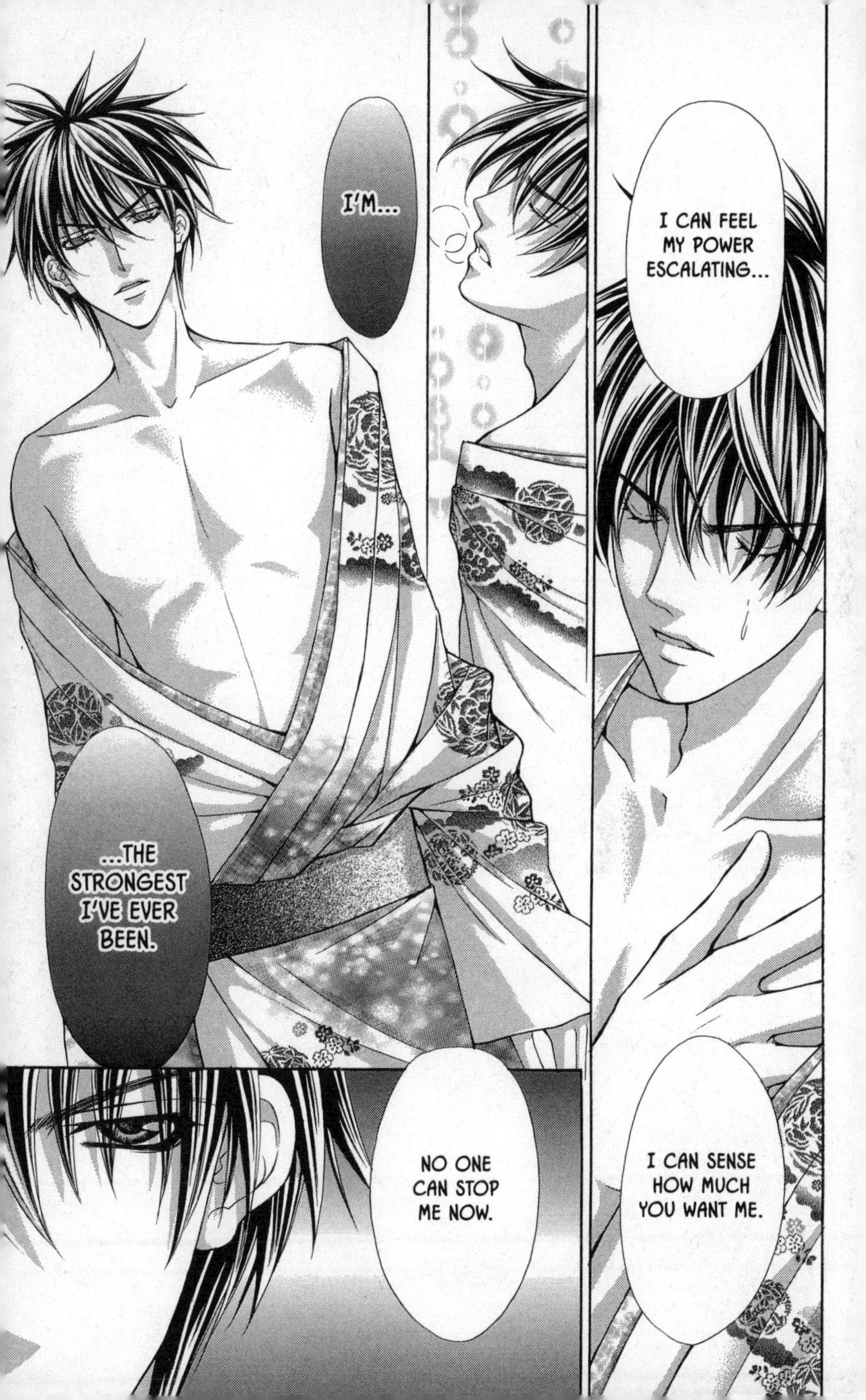
I CAN FEEL MY POWER ESCALATING...
I CAN SENSE HOW MUCH YOU WANT ME.
I'M...
...THE STRONGEST I'VE EVER BEEN.
NO ONE CAN STOP ME NOW.

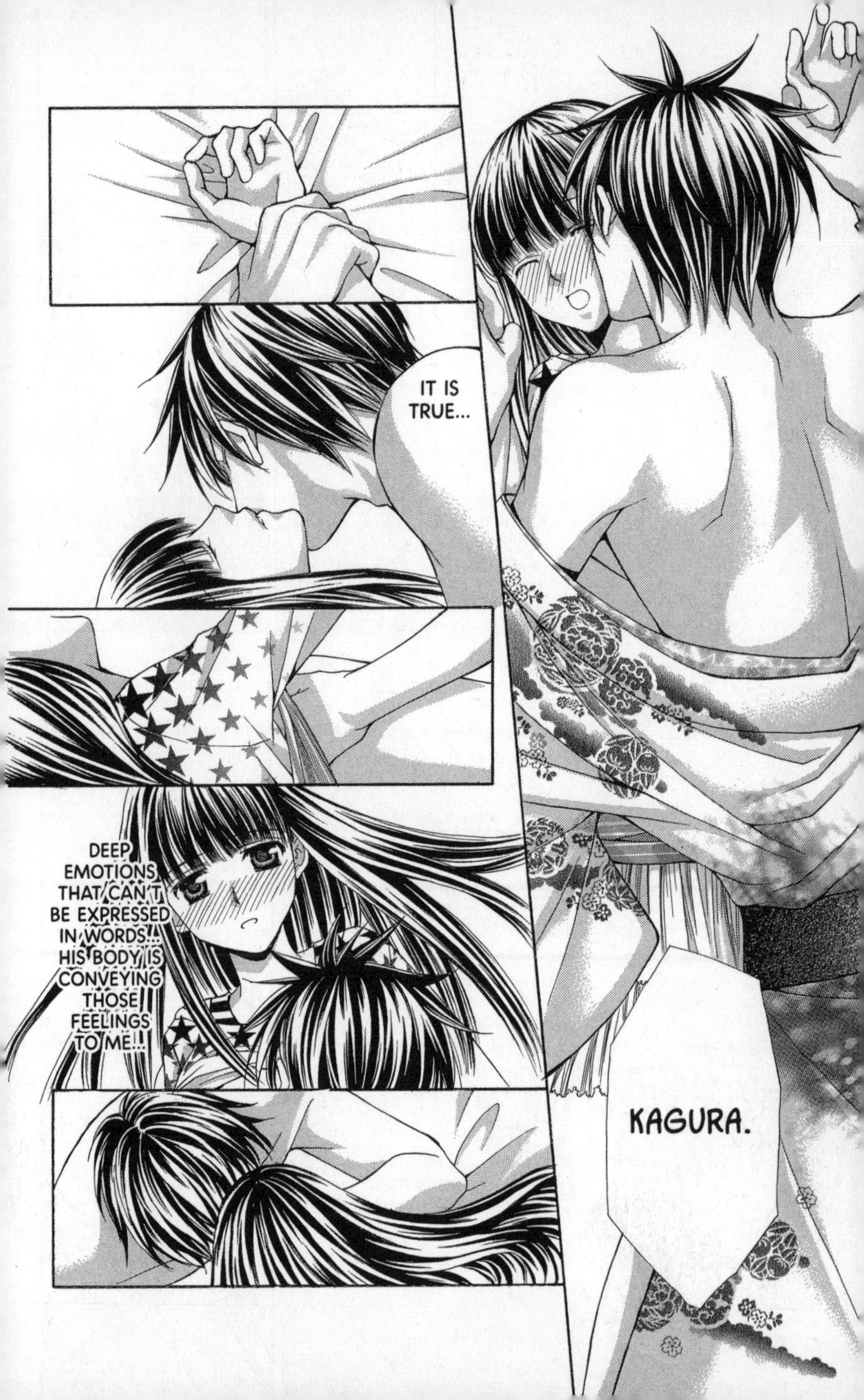
KAGURA.
IT IS TRUE...
DEEP EMOTIONS THAT CAN'T BE EXPRESSED IN WORDS... HIS BODY IS CONVEYING THOSE FEELINGS TO ME...

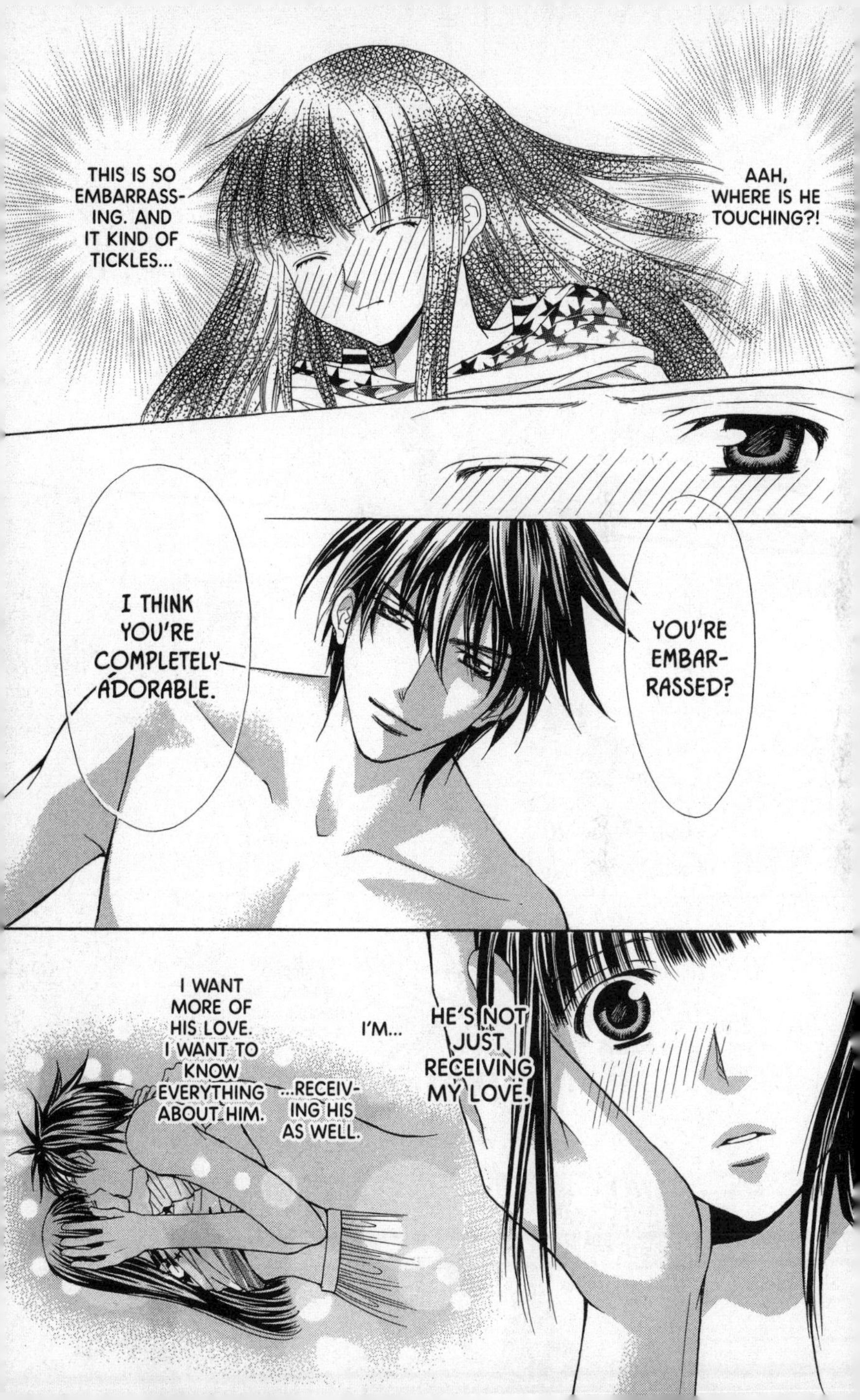
AAH, WHERE IS HE TOUCHING?!
THIS IS SO EMBARRASSING. AND IT KIND OF TICKLES...
YOU'RE EMBARRASSED?
I THINK YOU'RE COMPLETELY ADORABLE.
HE'S NOT JUST RECEIVING MY LOVE.
I'M...
...RECEIVING HIS AS WELL.
I WANT MORE OF HIS LOVE. I WANT TO KNOW EVERYTHING ABOUT HIM.

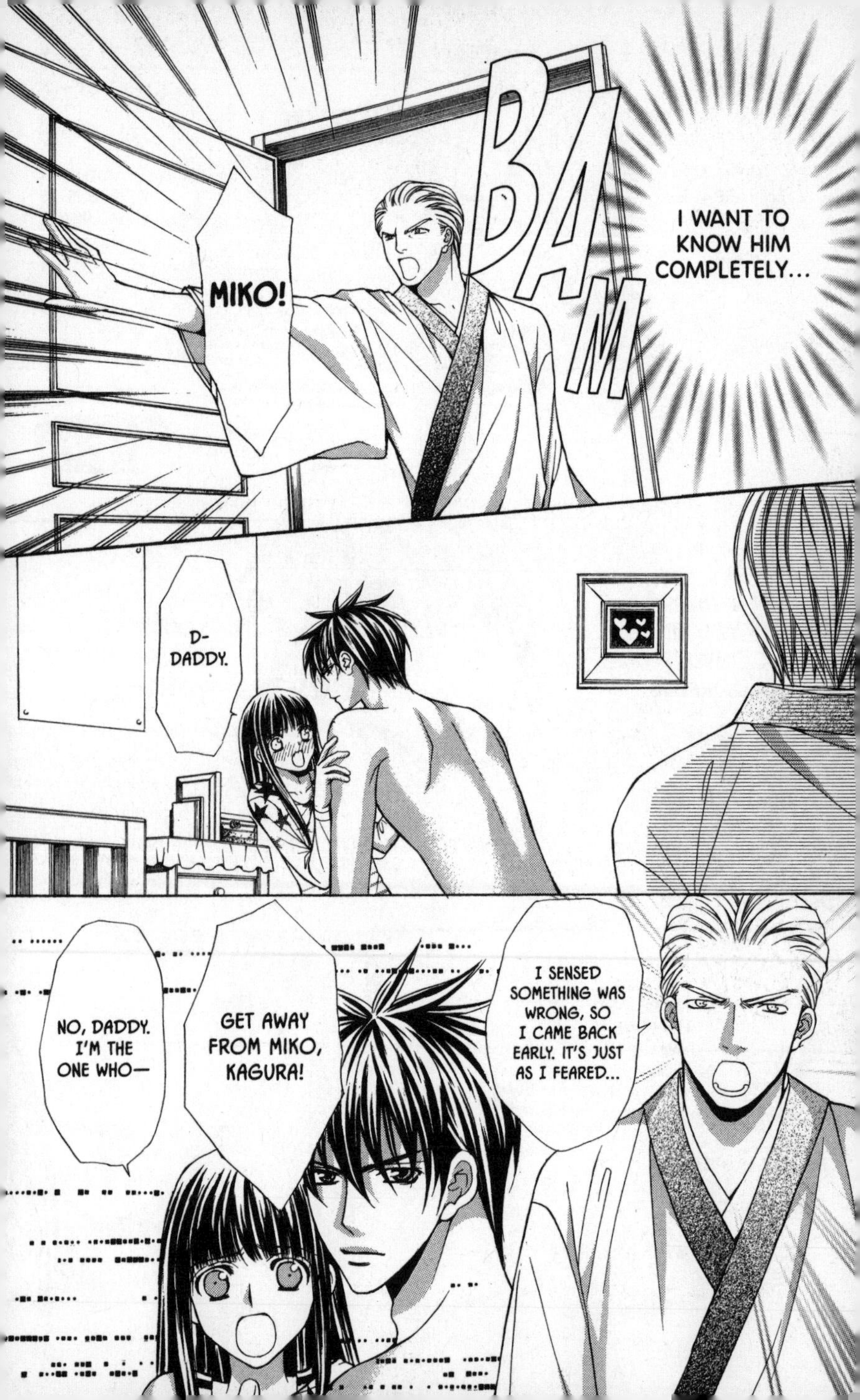
I WANT TO KNOW HIM COMPLETELY...
BAM
MIKO!
D-DADDY.
I SENSED SOMETHING WAS WRONG, SO I CAME BACK EARLY. IT'S JUST AS I FEARED...
GET AWAY FROM MIKO, KAGURA!
NO, DADDY. I'M THE ONE WHO—

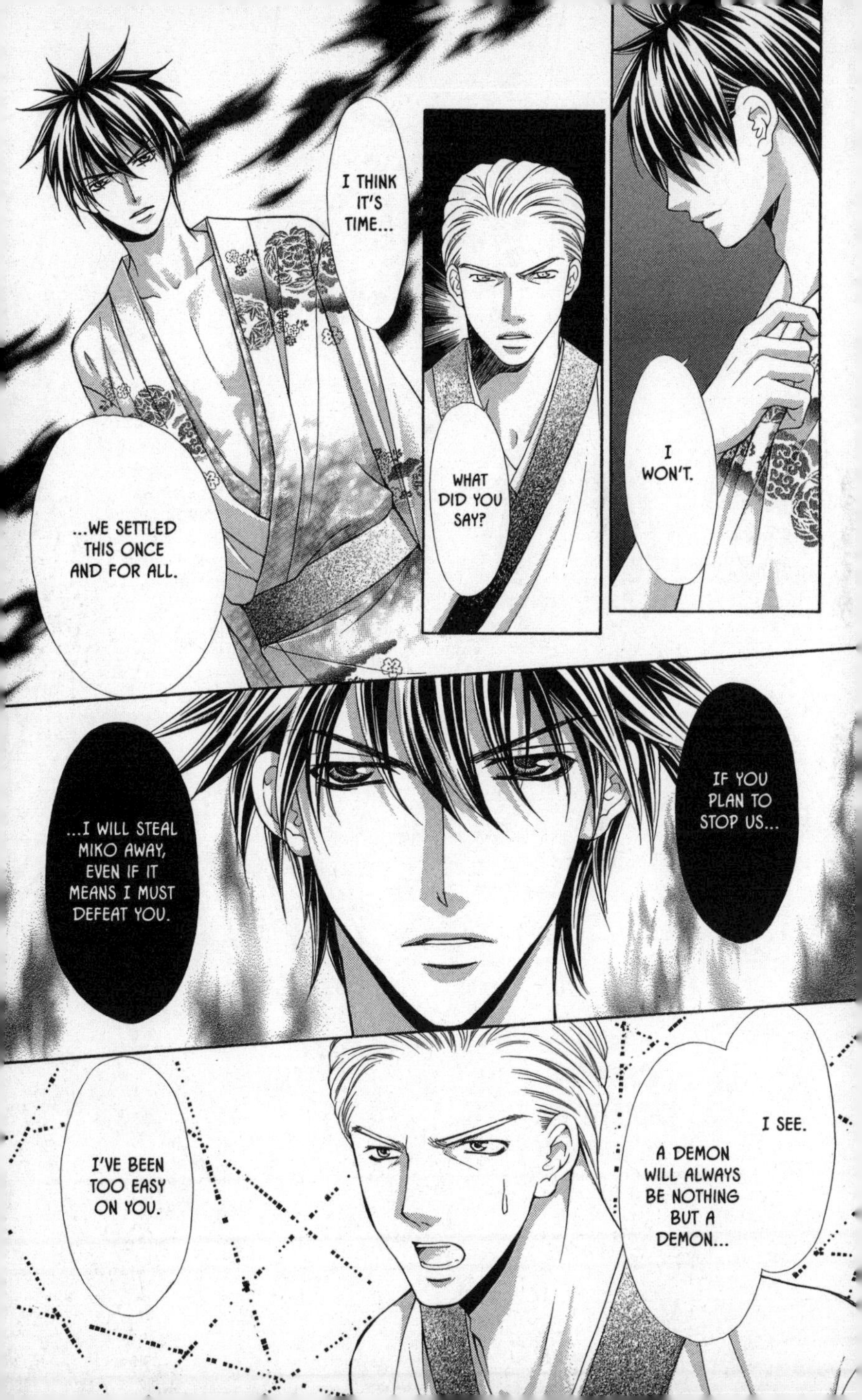
I WON'T.
WHAT DID YOU SAY?
I THINK IT'S TIME...
...WE SETTLED THIS ONCE AND FOR ALL.
IF YOU PLAN TO STOP US...
...I WILL STEAL MIKO AWAY, EVEN IF IT MEANS I MUST DEFEAT YOU.
I SEE.
A DEMON WILL ALWAYS BE NOTHING BUT A DEMON...
I'VE BEEN TOO EASY ON YOU.

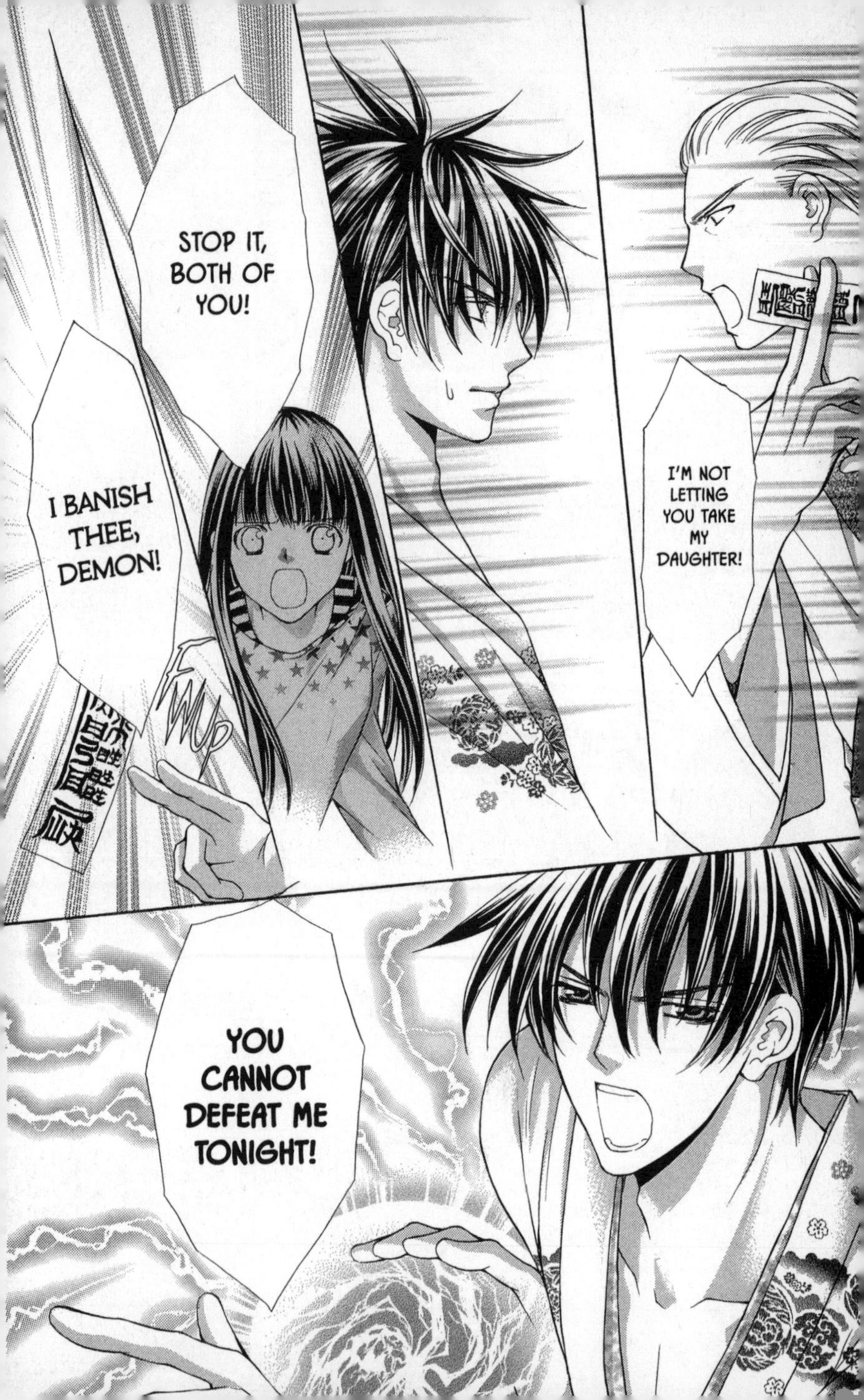
I'M NOT LETTING YOU TAKE MY DAUGHTER!
STOP IT, BOTH OF YOU!
I BANISH THEE, DEMON!
FWUP
YOU CANNOT DEFEAT ME TONIGHT!

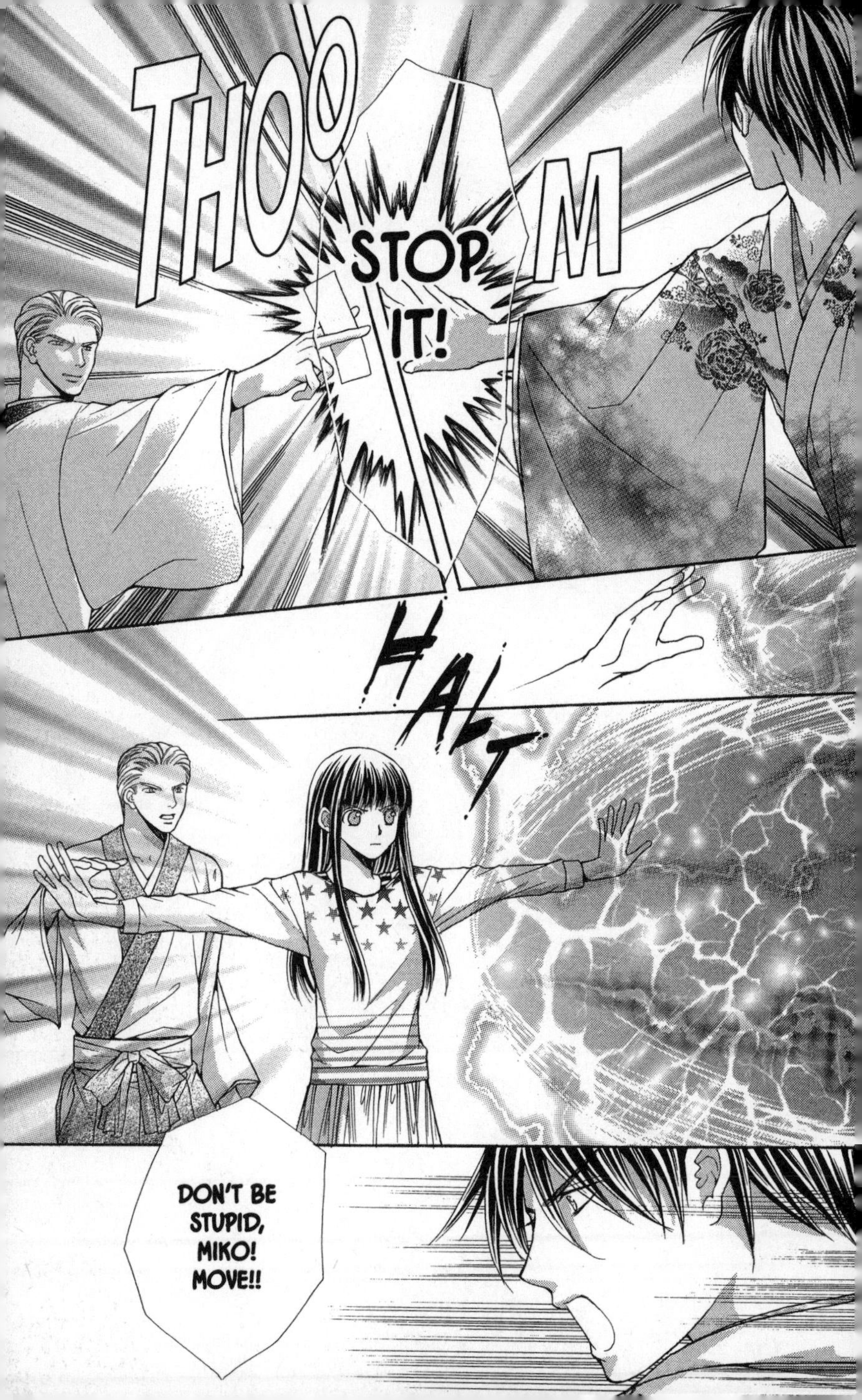
THOOOM
STOP IT!
HALT
DON'T BE STUPID, MIKO! MOVE!!

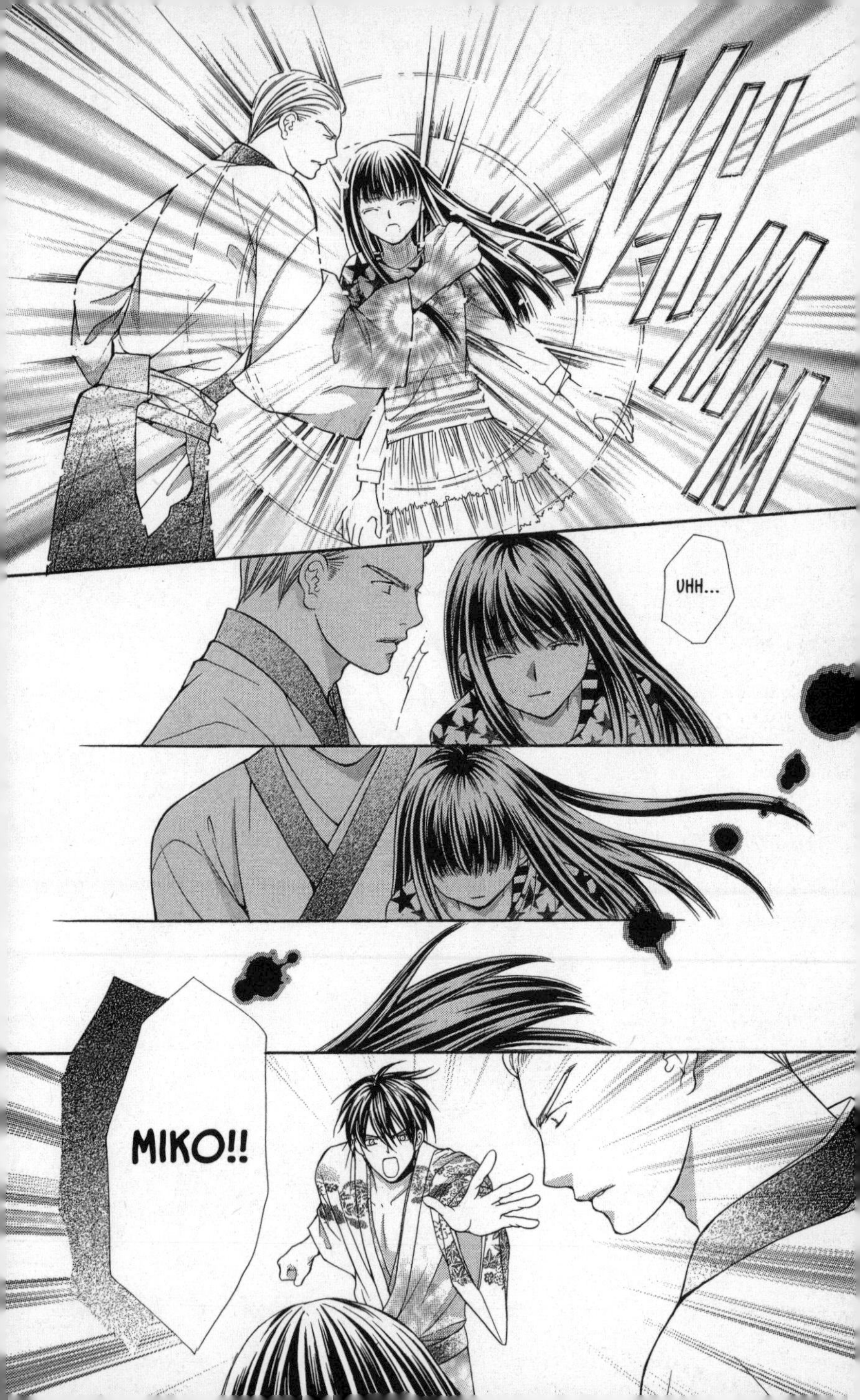
VWMMM
UHH...
MIKO!!

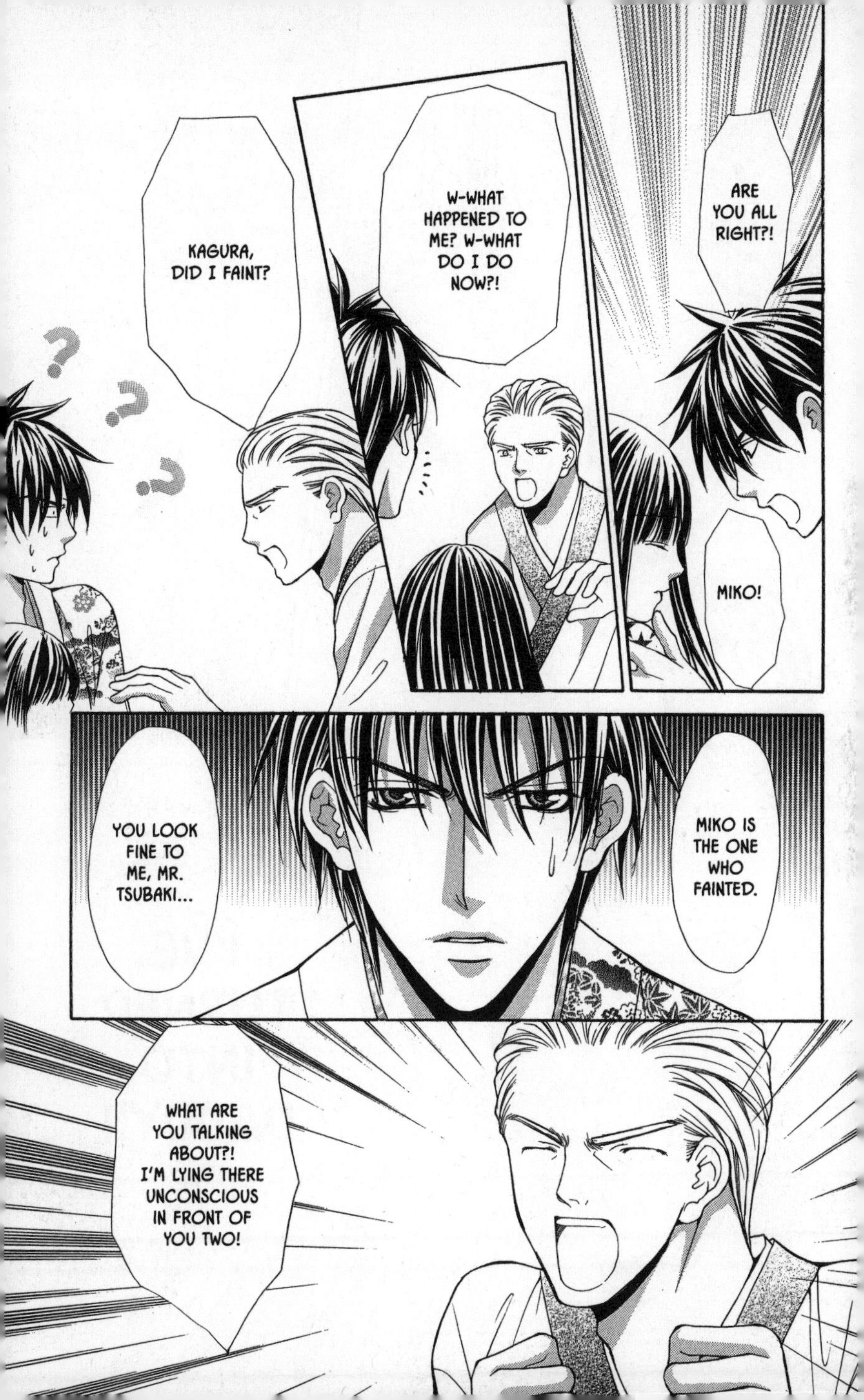
ARE YOU ALL RIGHT?!
MIKO!
W-WHAT HAPPENED TO ME? W-WHAT DO I DO NOW?!
KAGURA, DID I FAINT?
MIKO IS THE ONE WHO FAINTED.
YOU LOOK FINE TO ME, MR. TSUBAKI...
WHAT ARE YOU TALKING ABOUT?! I'M LYING THERE UNCONSCIOUS IN FRONT OF YOU TWO!

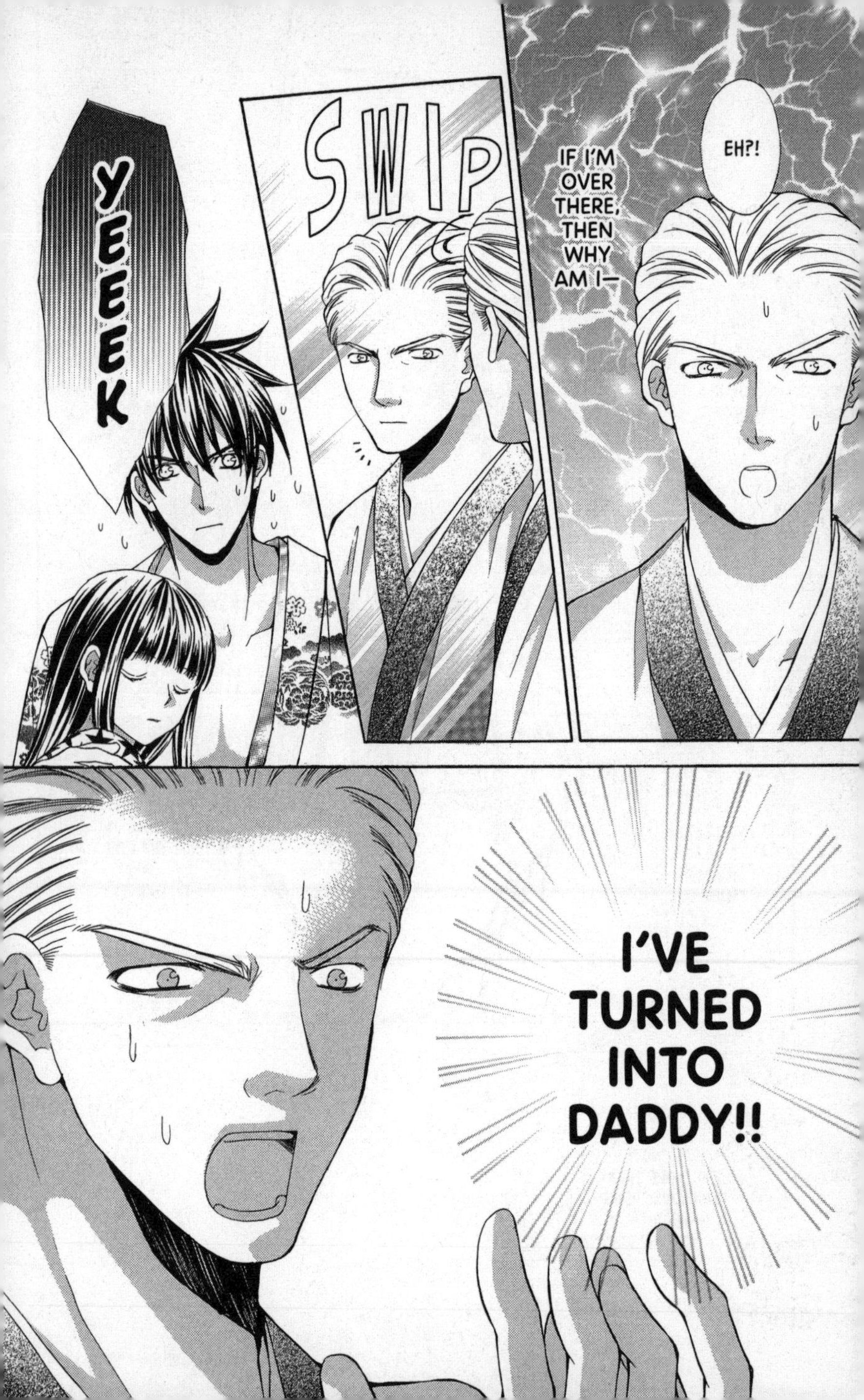
EH?!
IF I'M OVER THERE, THEN WHY AM I—
SWIP
YEEEK
I'VE TURNED INTO DADDY!!

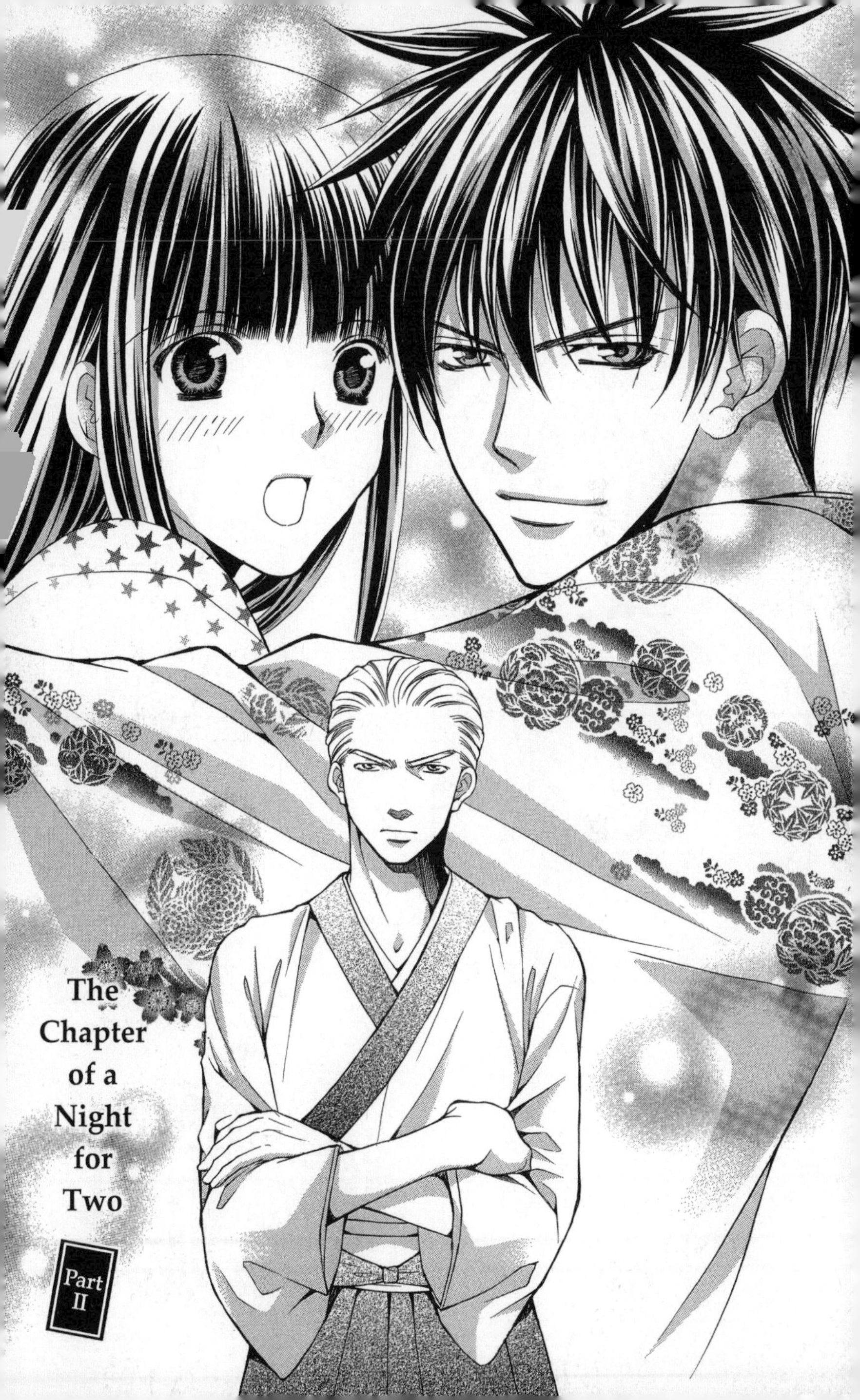
The Chapter of a Night for Two
Part II

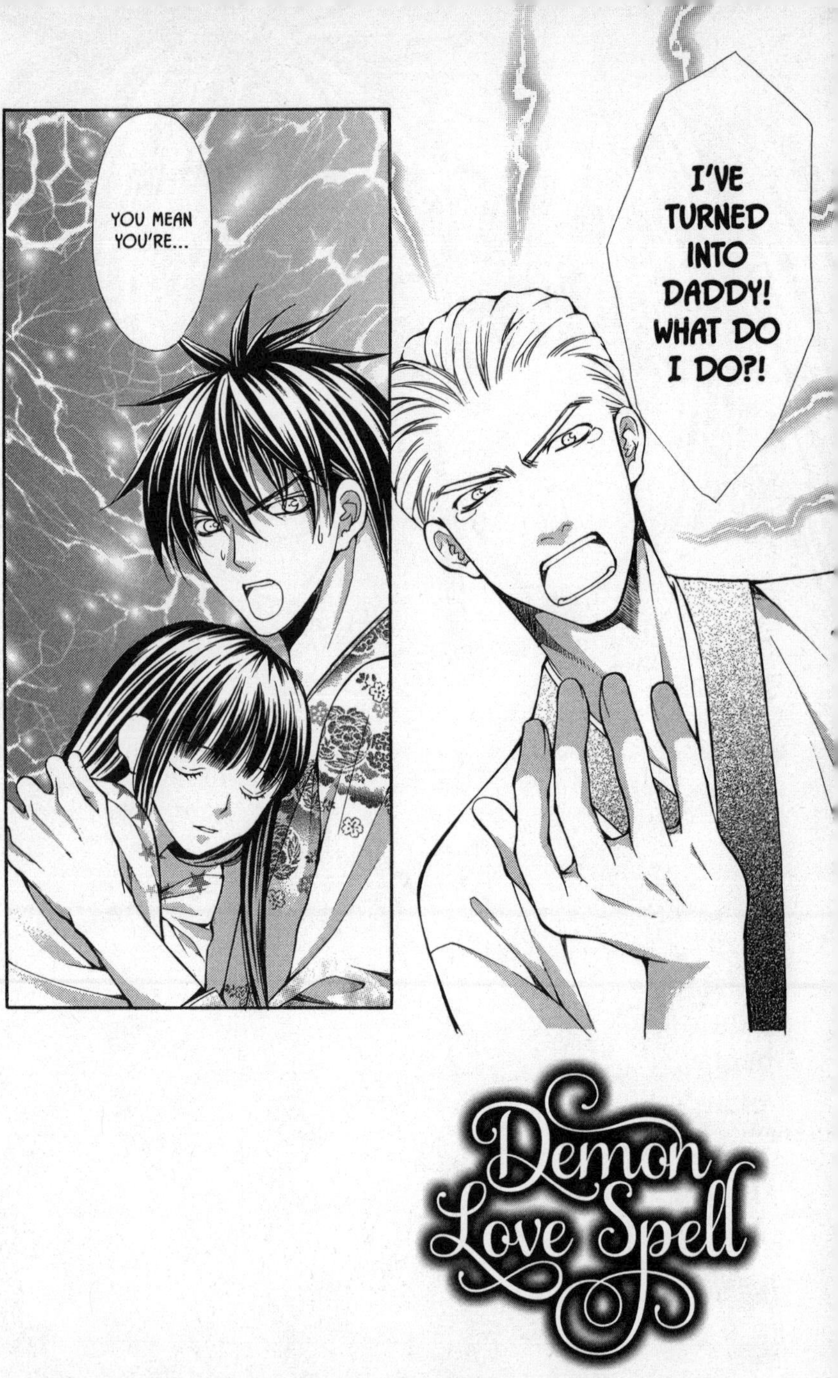
I'VE TURNED INTO DADDY! WHAT DO I DO?!
YOU MEAN YOU'RE...

Demon Love Spell

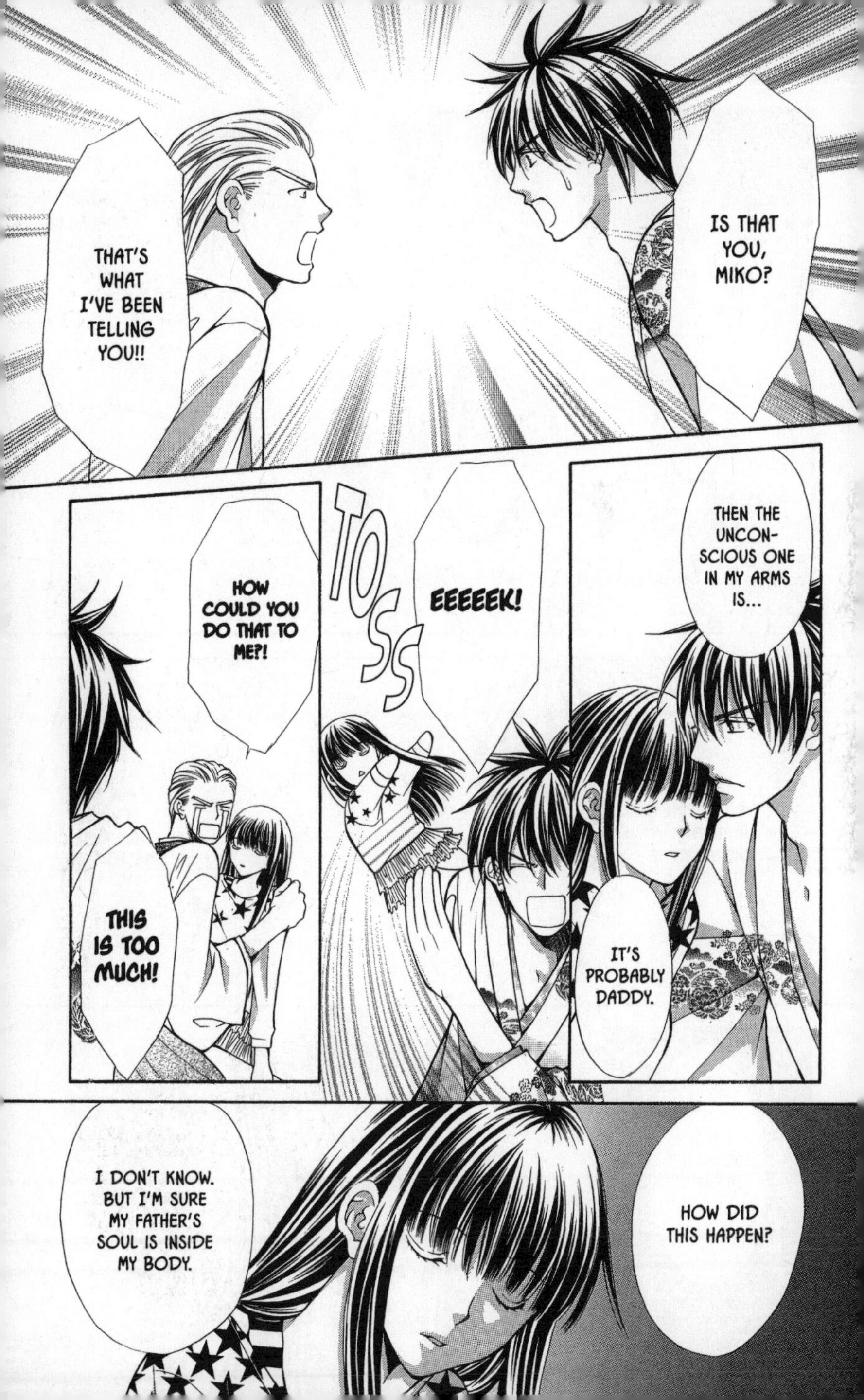
IS THAT YOU, MIKO?
THAT'S WHAT I'VE BEEN TELLING YOU!!
THEN THE UNCON-SCIOUS ONE IN MY ARMS IS...
IT'S PROBABLY DADDY.
EEEEEK!
TOSS
HOW COULD YOU DO THAT TO ME?!
THIS IS TOO MUCH!
HOW DID THIS HAPPEN?
I DON'T KNOW. BUT I'M SURE MY FATHER'S SOUL IS INSIDE MY BODY.

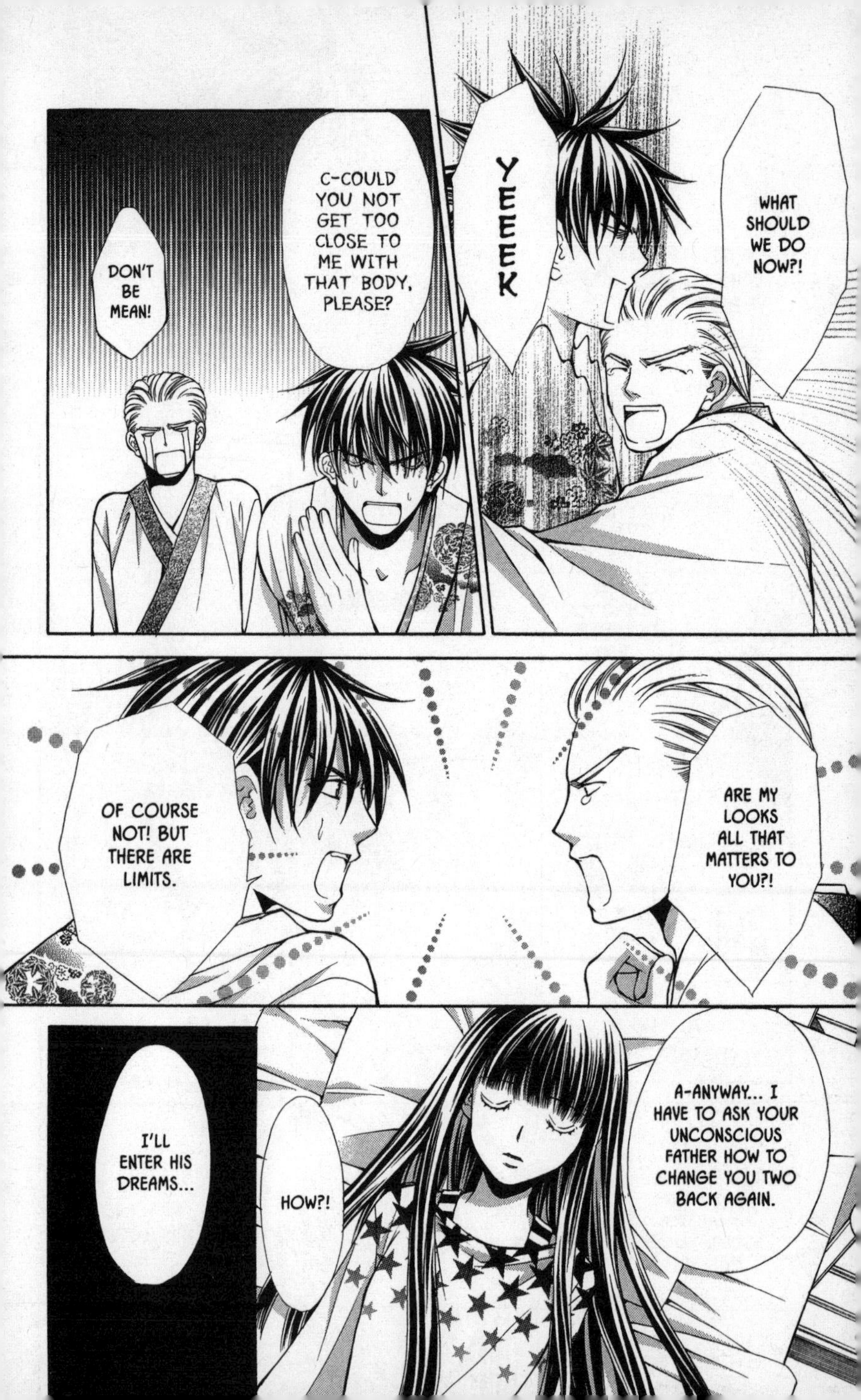
WHAT SHOULD WE DO NOW?!
YEEEK
C-COULD YOU NOT GET TOO CLOSE TO ME WITH THAT BODY, PLEASE?
DON'T BE MEAN!
ARE MY LOOKS ALL THAT MATTERS TO YOU?!
OF COURSE NOT! BUT THERE ARE LIMITS.
A-ANYWAY... I HAVE TO ASK YOUR UNCONSCIOUS FATHER HOW TO CHANGE YOU TWO BACK AGAIN.
HOW?!
I'LL ENTER HIS DREAMS...

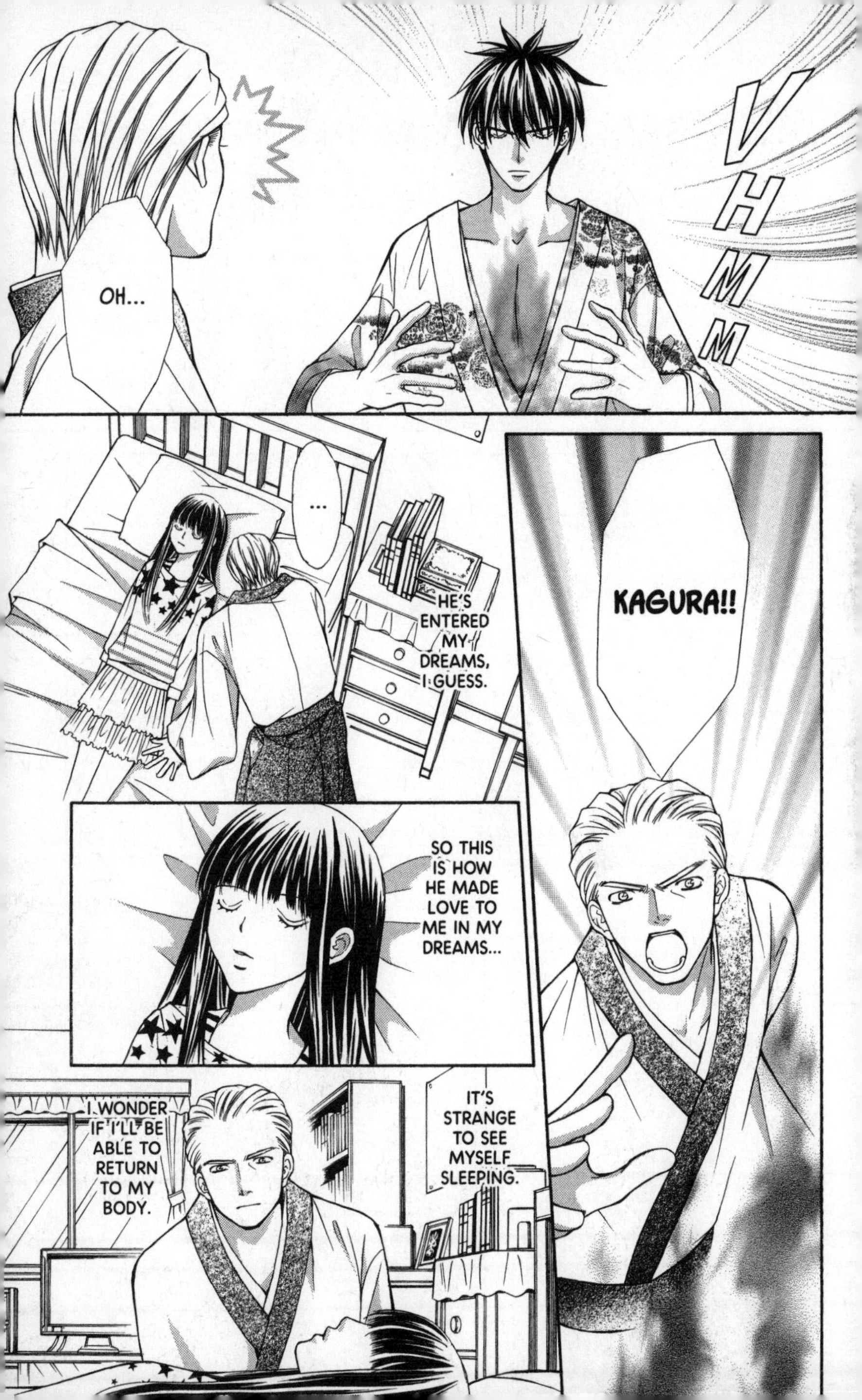
VHMM
OH...
KAGURA!!
...
HE'S ENTERED MY DREAMS, I GUESS.
SO THIS IS HOW HE MADE LOVE TO ME IN MY DREAMS...
IT'S STRANGE TO SEE MYSELF SLEEPING.
I WONDER IF I'LL BE ABLE TO RETURN TO MY BODY.

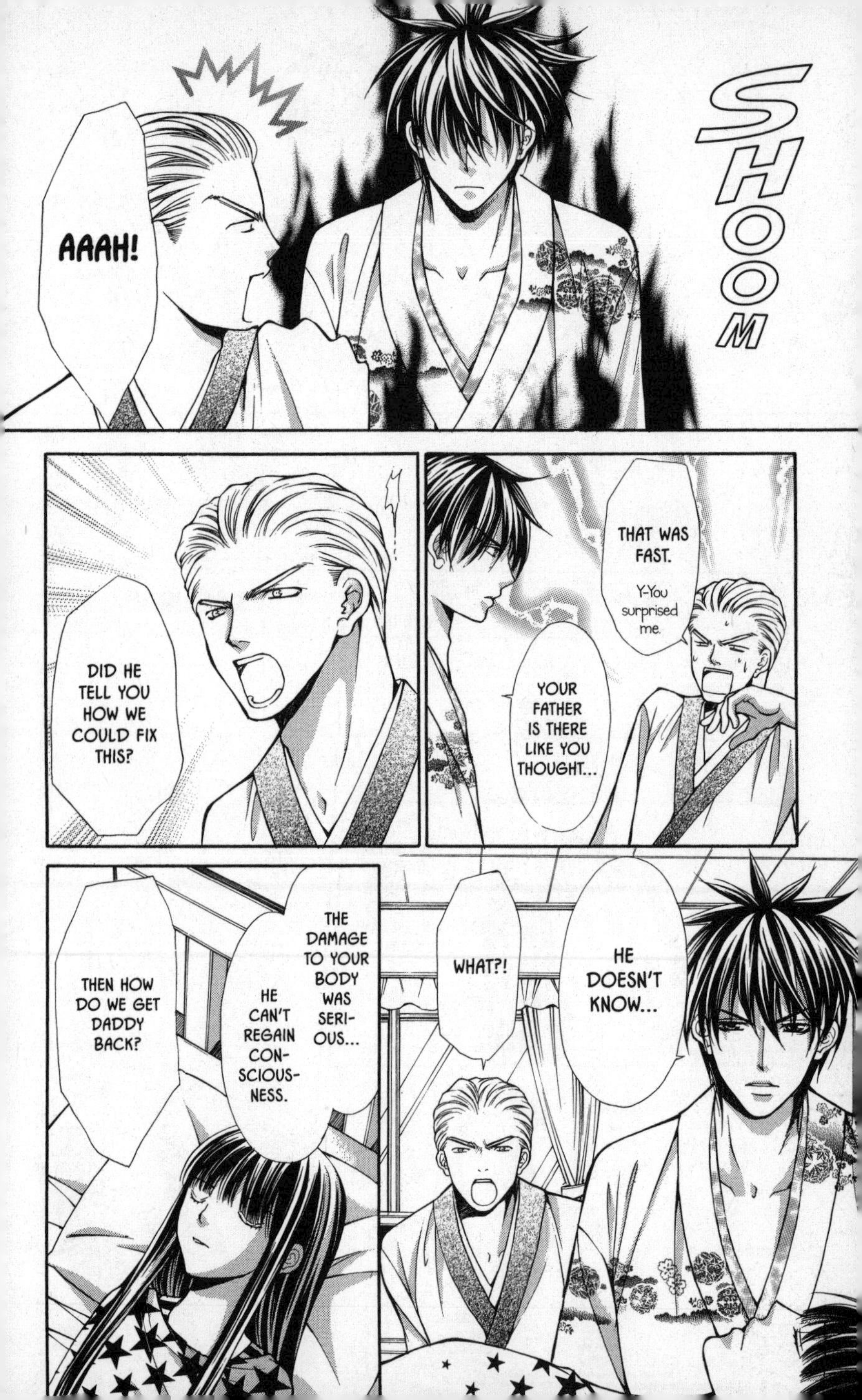
SHOOM
AAAH!
THAT WAS FAST.
Y-You surprised me.
YOUR FATHER IS THERE LIKE YOU THOUGHT...
DID HE TELL YOU HOW WE COULD FIX THIS?
HE DOESN'T KNOW...
WHAT?!
THE DAMAGE TO YOUR BODY WAS SERIOUS...
HE CAN'T REGAIN CONSCIOUSNESS.
THEN HOW DO WE GET DADDY BACK?

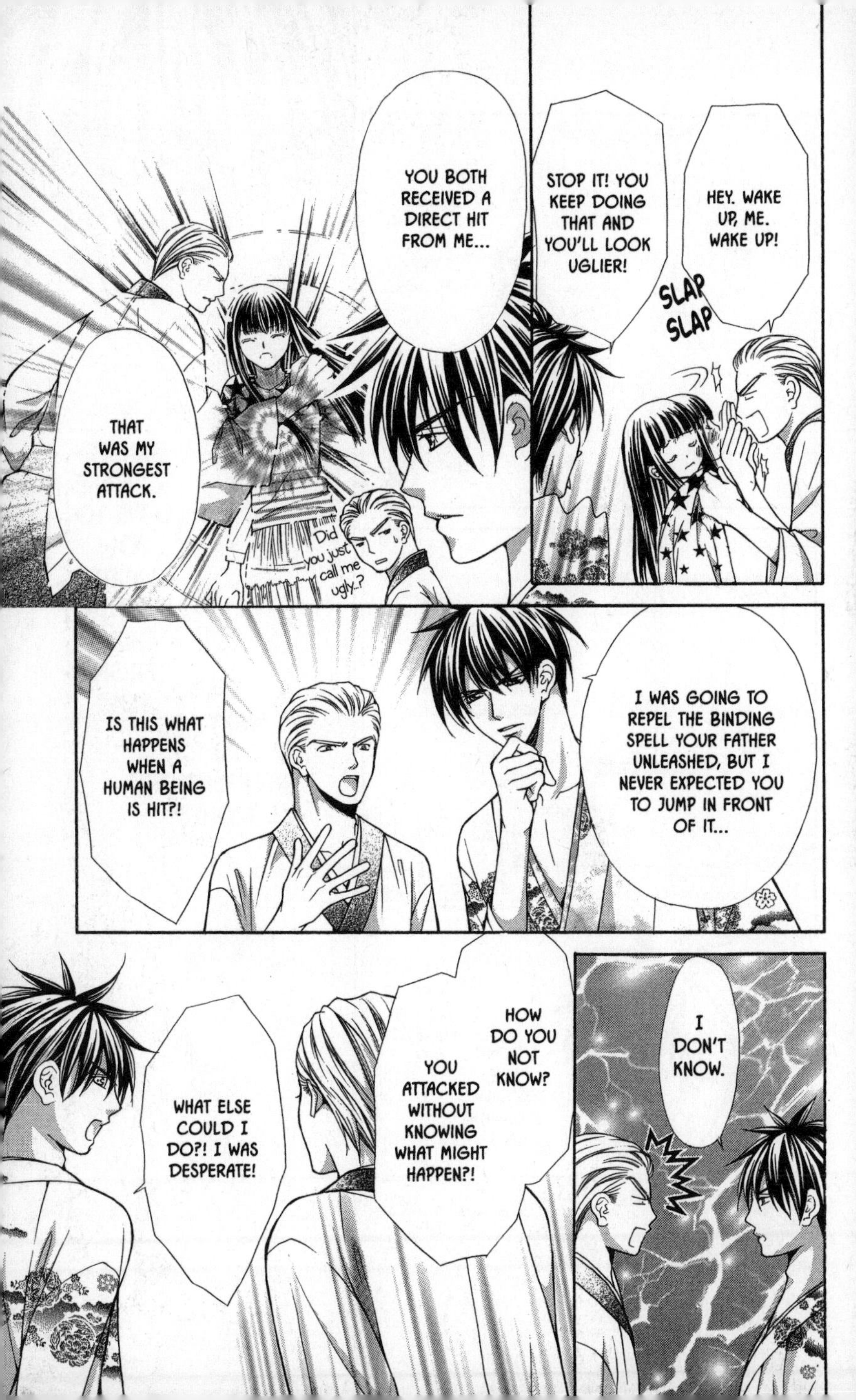
HEY. WAKE UP, ME. WAKE UP!
SLAP SLAP
STOP IT! YOU KEEP DOING THAT AND YOU'LL LOOK UGLIER!
YOU BOTH RECEIVED A DIRECT HIT FROM ME...
THAT WAS MY STRONGEST ATTACK.
Did you just call me ugly..?
I WAS GOING TO REPEL THE BINDING SPELL YOUR FATHER UNLEASHED, BUT I NEVER EXPECTED YOU TO JUMP IN FRONT OF IT...
IS THIS WHAT HAPPENS WHEN A HUMAN BEING IS HIT?!
I DON'T KNOW.
HOW DO YOU NOT KNOW?
YOU ATTACKED WITHOUT KNOWING WHAT MIGHT HAPPEN?!
WHAT ELSE COULD I DO?! I WAS DESPERATE!

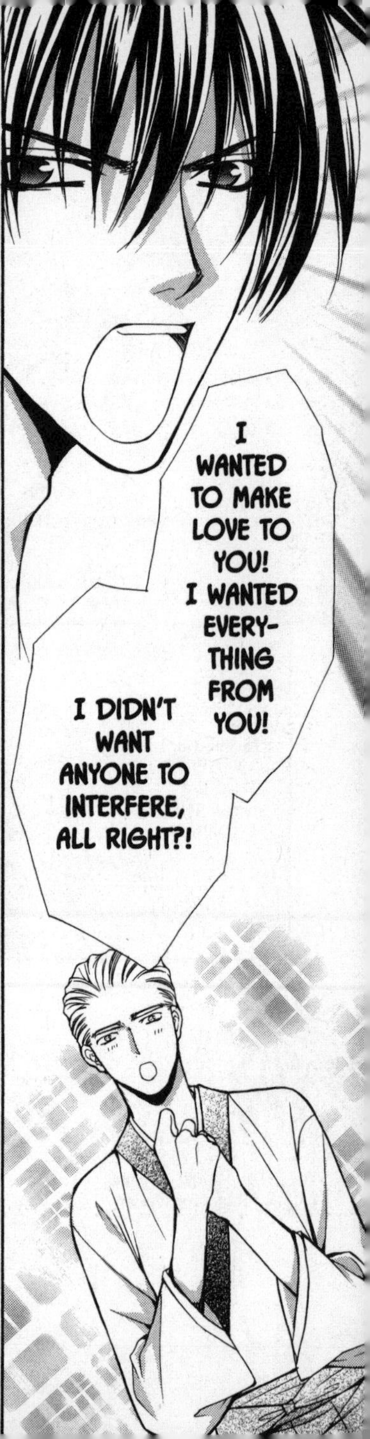
I WANTED TO MAKE LOVE TO YOU! I WANTED EVERY-THING FROM YOU!
I DIDN'T WANT ANYONE TO INTERFERE, ALL RIGHT?!
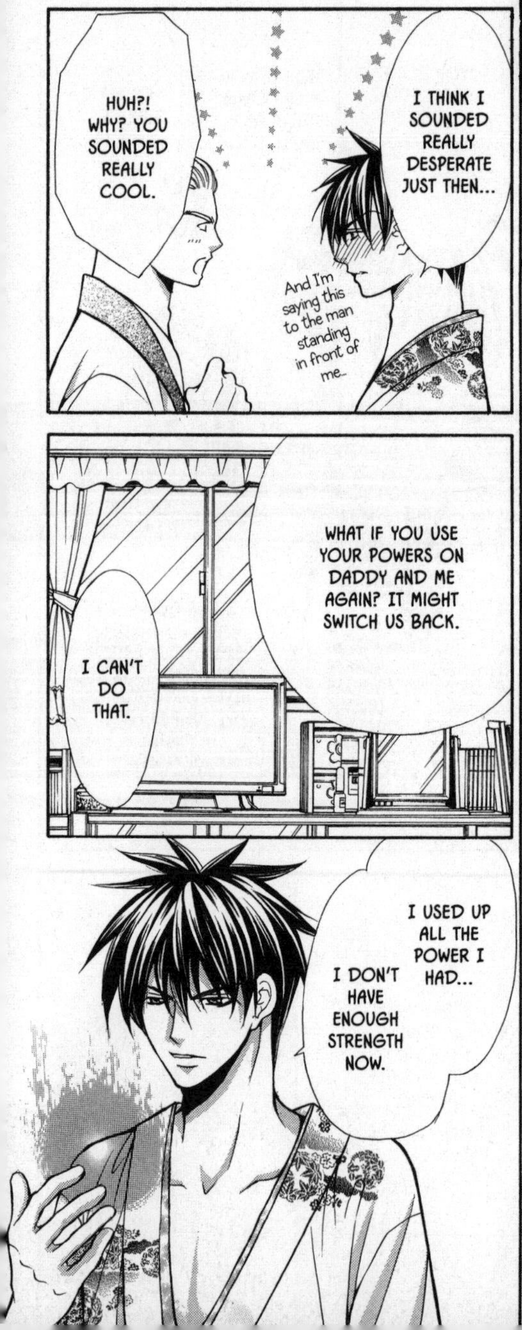
I THINK I SOUNDED REALLY DESPERATE JUST THEN...
And I'm saying this to the man standing in front of me..
HUH?! WHY? YOU SOUNDED REALLY COOL.
WHAT IF YOU USE YOUR POWERS ON DADDY AND ME AGAIN? IT MIGHT SWITCH US BACK.
I CAN'T DO THAT.
I USED UP ALL THE POWER I HAD...
I DON'T HAVE ENOUGH STRENGTH NOW.

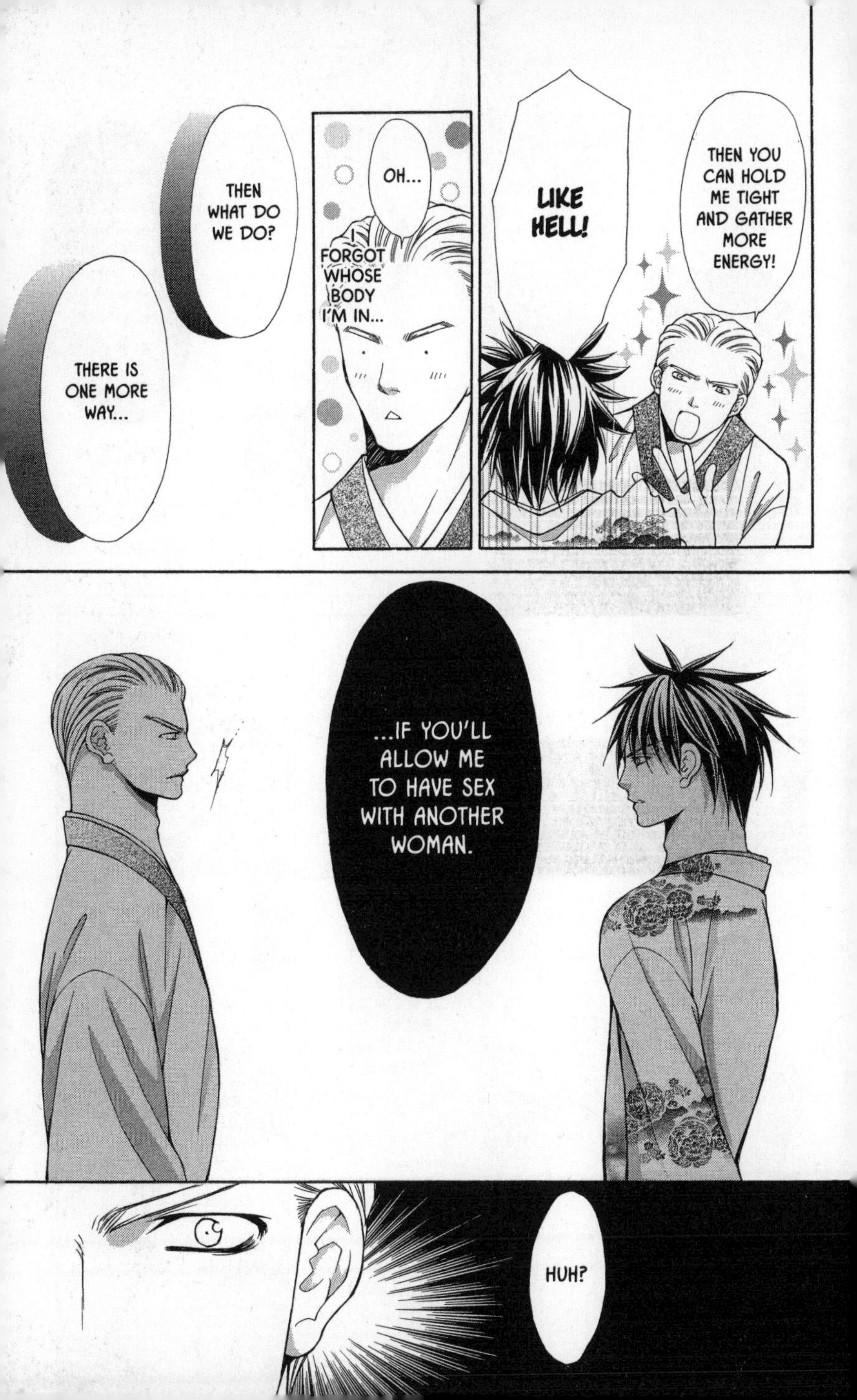
THEN YOU CAN HOLD ME TIGHT AND GATHER MORE ENERGY!
LIKE HELL!
OH...
I FORGOT WHOSE BODY I'M IN...
THEN WHAT DO WE DO?
THERE IS ONE MORE WAY...
...IF YOU'LL ALLOW ME TO HAVE SEX WITH ANOTHER WOMAN.
HUH?

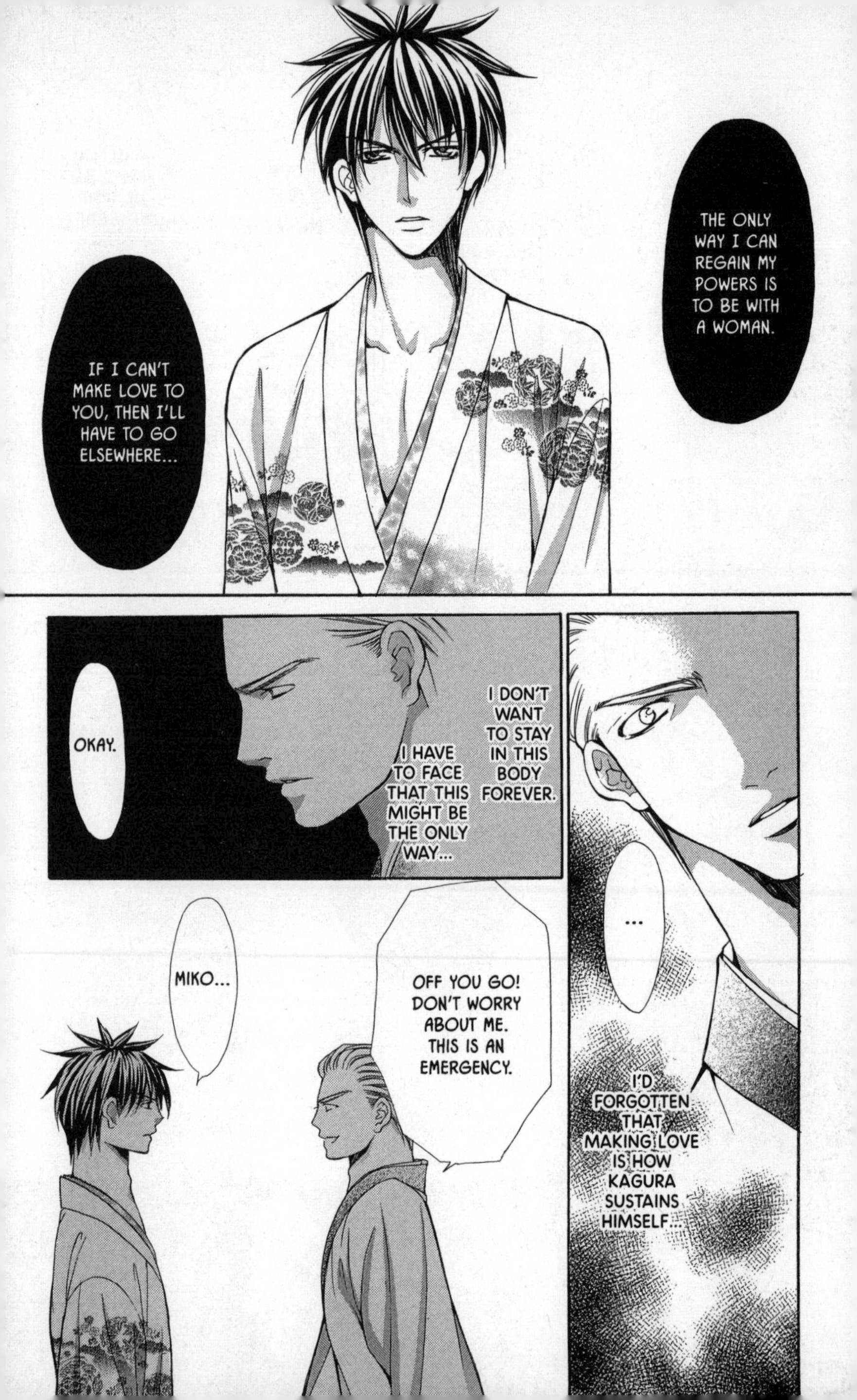
THE ONLY WAY I CAN REGAIN MY POWERS IS TO BE WITH A WOMAN.
IF I CAN'T MAKE LOVE TO YOU, THEN I'LL HAVE TO GO ELSEWHERE...
...
I'D FORGOTTEN THAT MAKING LOVE IS HOW KAGURA SUSTAINS HIMSELF...
I DON'T WANT TO STAY IN THIS BODY FOREVER.
I HAVE TO FACE THAT THIS MIGHT BE THE ONLY WAY...
OKAY.
OFF YOU GO! DON'T WORRY ABOUT ME. THIS IS AN EMERGENCY.
MIKO...

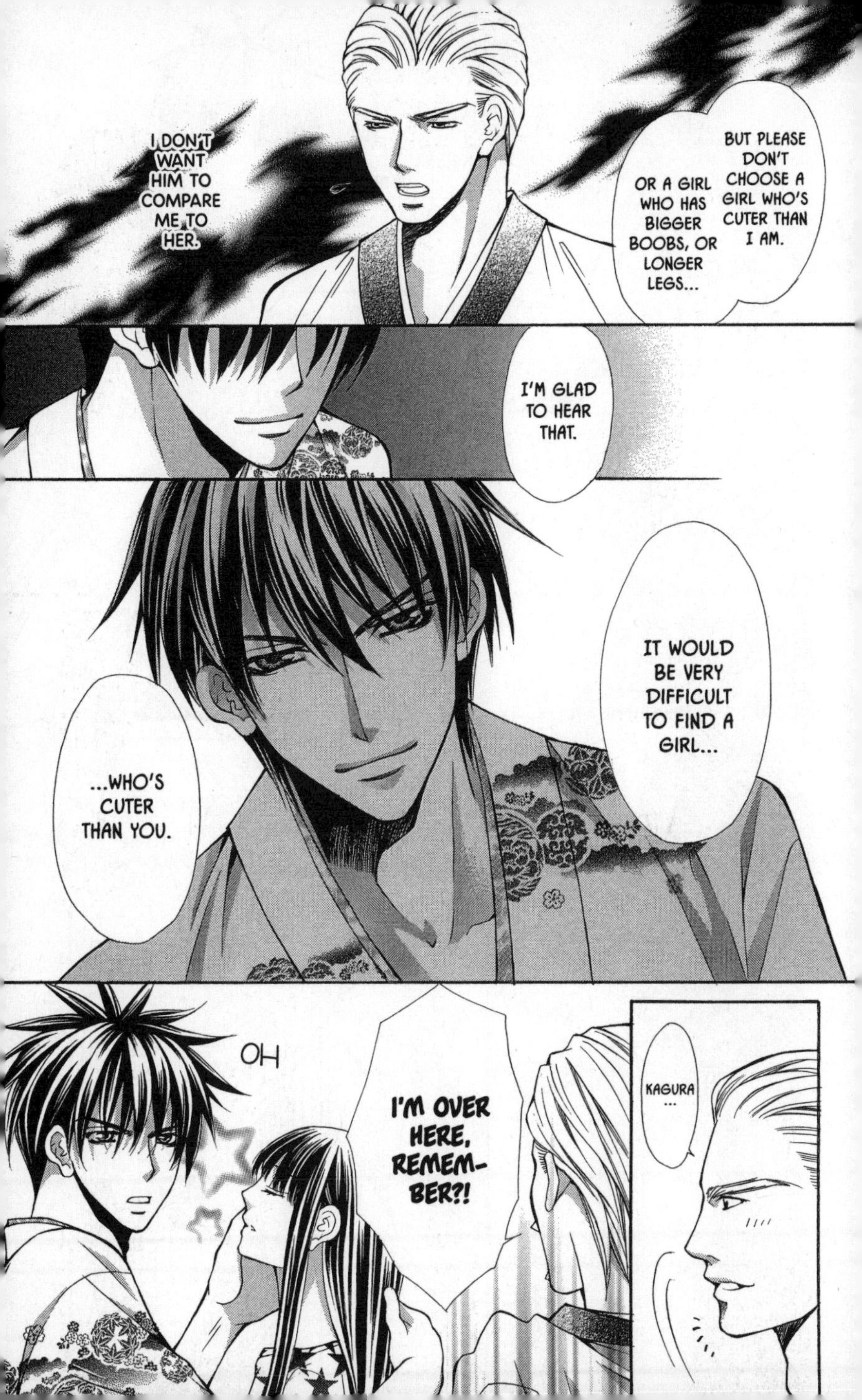
BUT PLEASE DON'T CHOOSE A GIRL WHO'S CUTER THAN I AM.
OR A GIRL WHO HAS BIGGER BOOBS, OR LONGER LEGS...
I DON'T WANT HIM TO COMPARE ME TO HER.
I'M GLAD TO HEAR THAT.
IT WOULD BE VERY DIFFICULT TO FIND A GIRL...
...WHO'S CUTER THAN YOU.
KAGURA ...
I'M OVER HERE, REMEMBER?!
OH

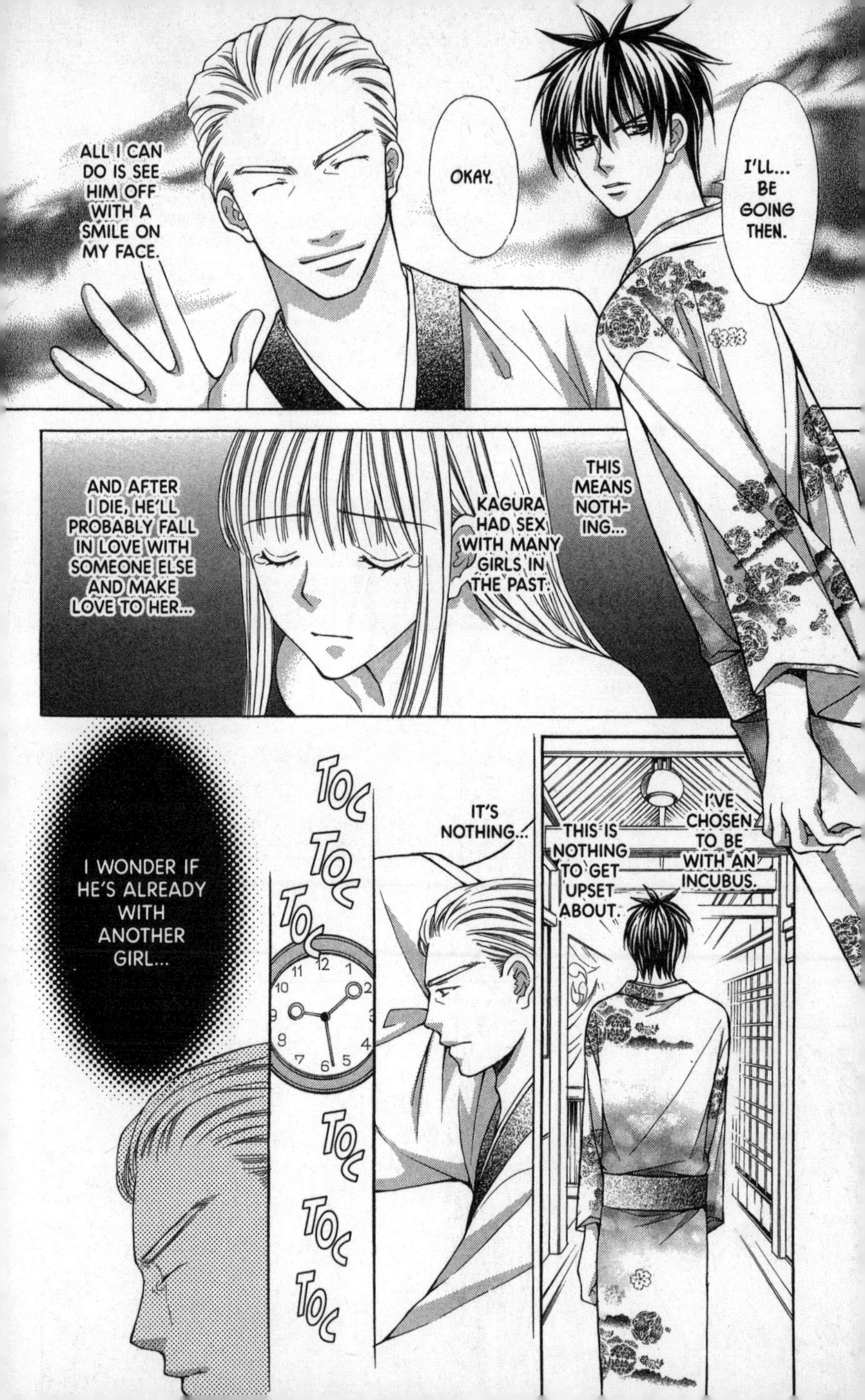
I'LL... BE GOING THEN.
OKAY.
ALL I CAN DO IS SEE HIM OFF WITH A SMILE ON MY FACE.
THIS MEANS NOTHING...
KAGURA HAD SEX WITH MANY GIRLS IN THE PAST.
AND AFTER I DIE, HE'LL PROBABLY FALL IN LOVE WITH SOMEONE ELSE AND MAKE LOVE TO HER...
I'VE CHOSEN TO BE WITH AN INCUBUS.
THIS IS NOTHING TO GET UPSET ABOUT.
IT'S NOTHING...
TOC TOC TOC
TOC TOC TOC
I WONDER IF HE'S ALREADY WITH ANOTHER GIRL...

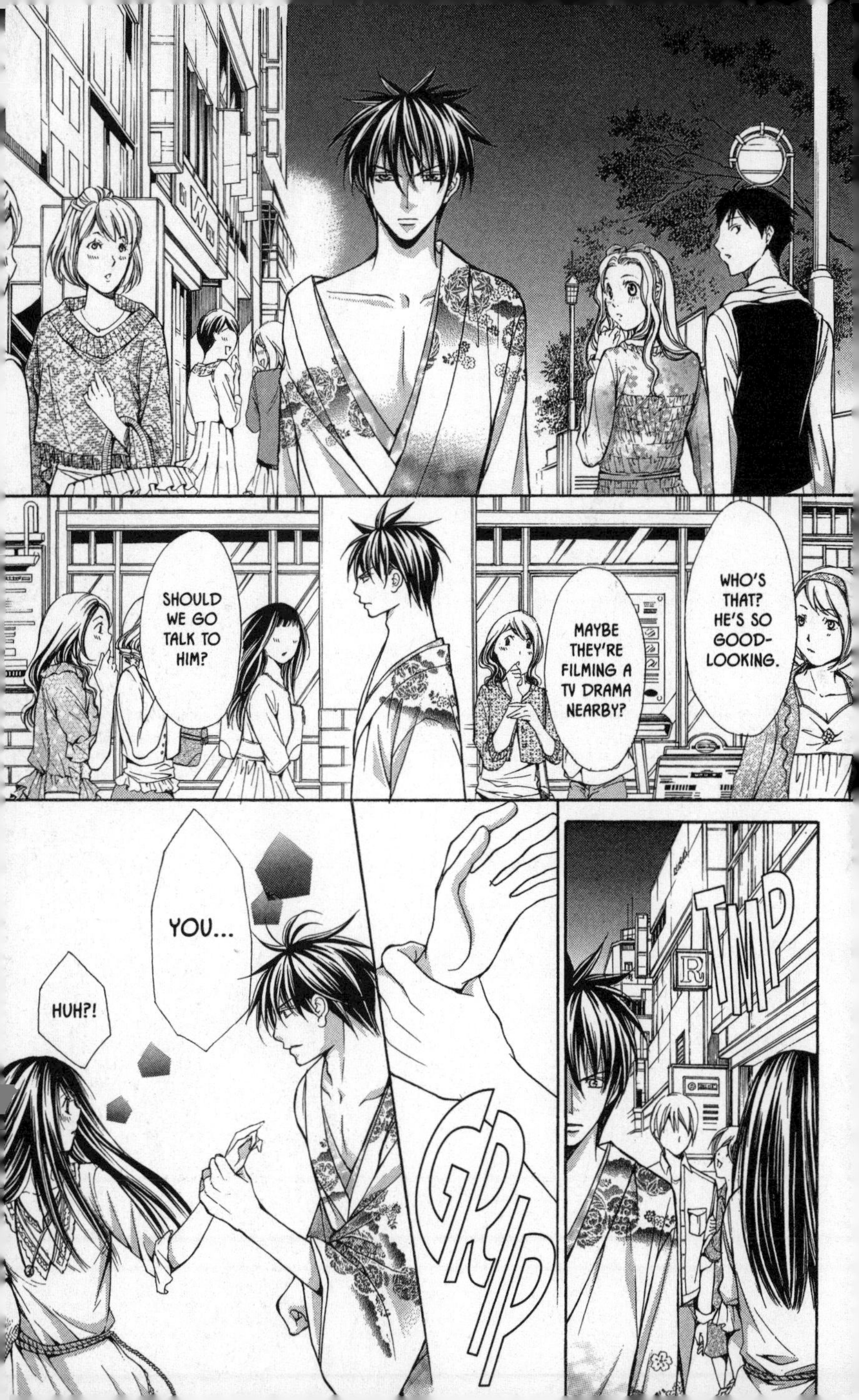
WHO'S THAT? HE'S SO GOOD-LOOKING.
MAYBE THEY'RE FILMING A TV DRAMA NEARBY?
SHOULD WE GO TALK TO HIM?
TMP
GRIP
YOU...
HUH?!

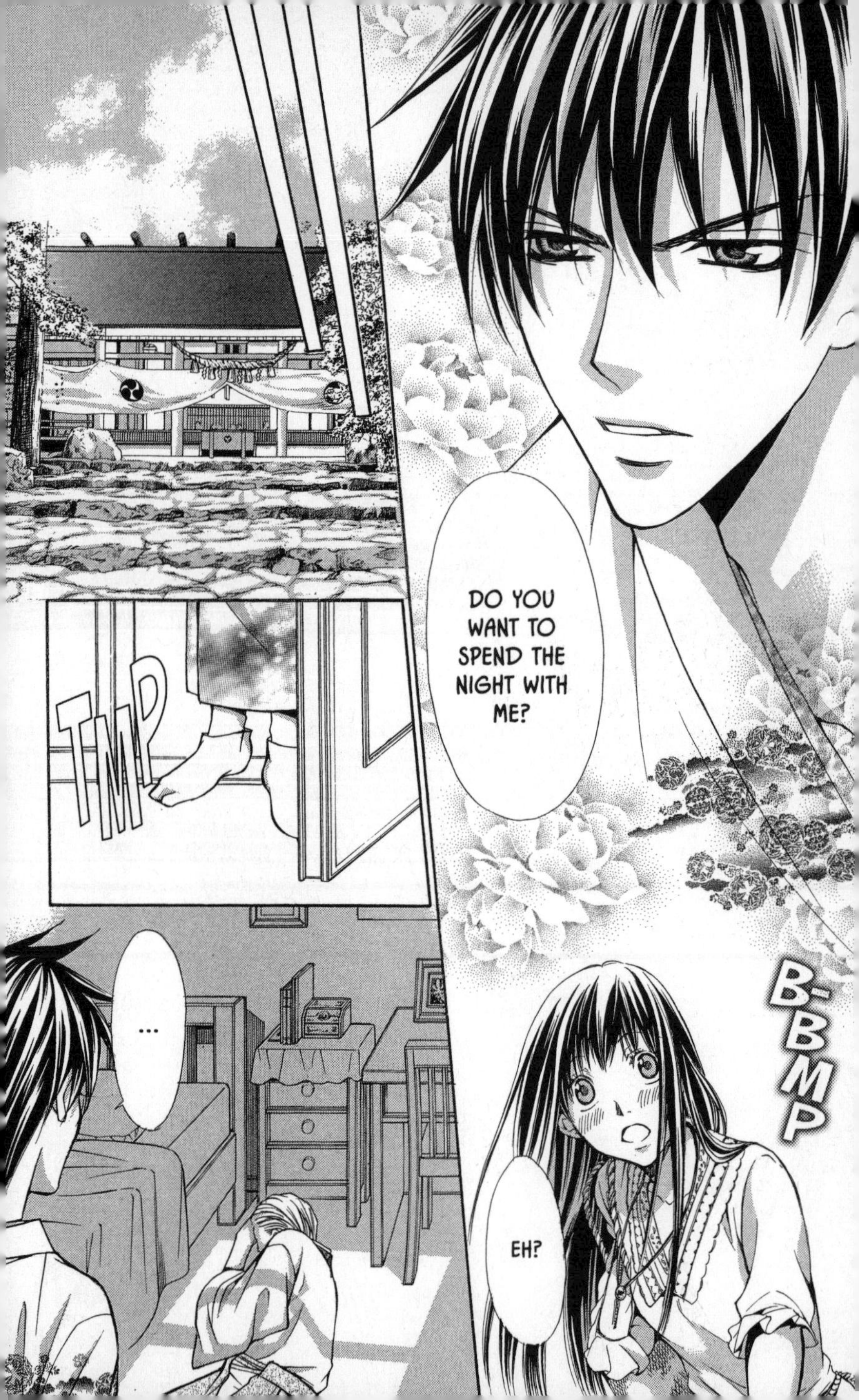
DO YOU WANT TO SPEND THE NIGHT WITH ME?
B-BMP
EH?
TMP
...

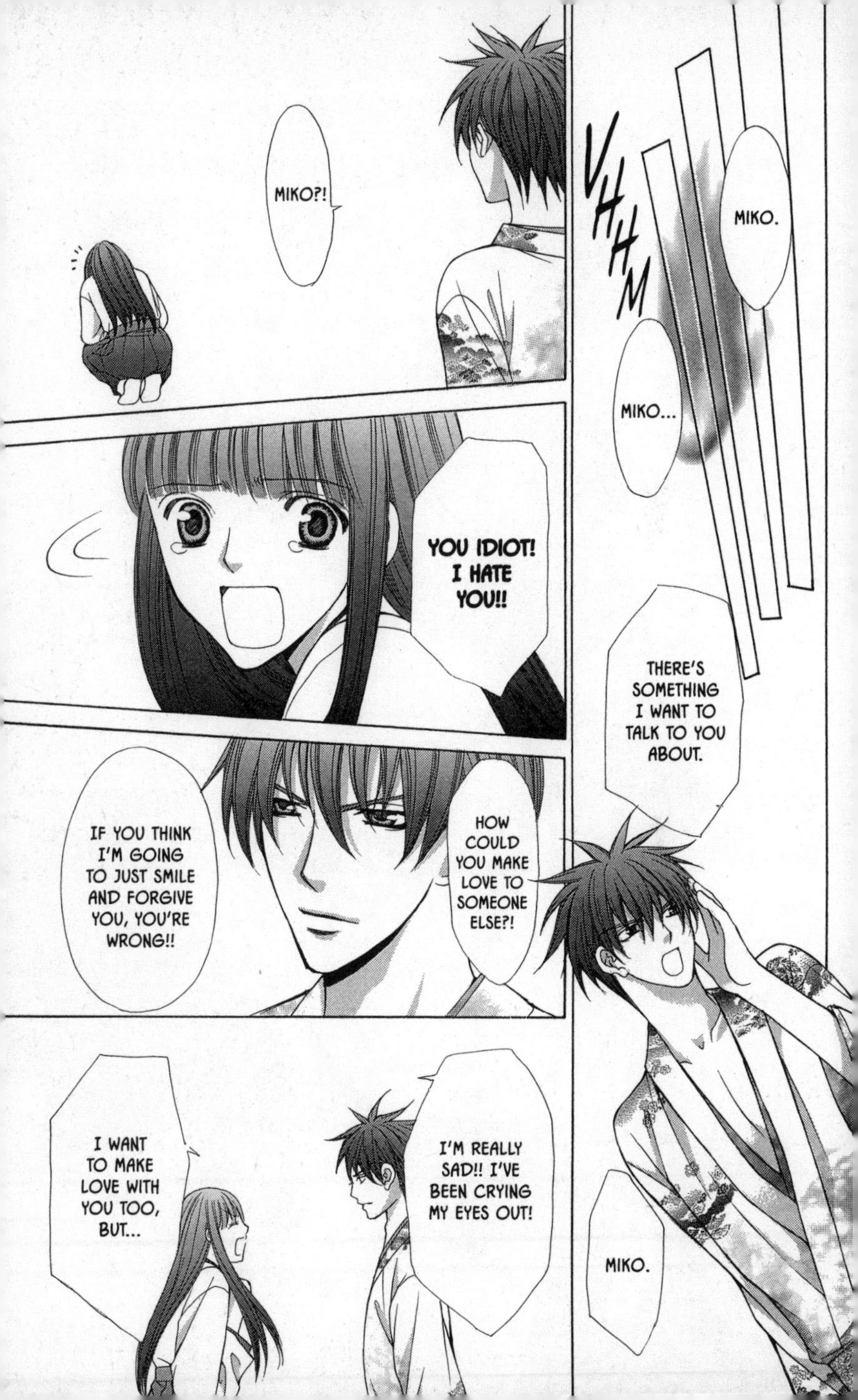
VHHM
MIKO.
MIKO...
THERE'S SOMETHING I WANT TO TALK TO YOU ABOUT.
MIKO.
MIKO?!
YOU IDIOT! I HATE YOU!!
HOW COULD YOU MAKE LOVE TO SOMEONE ELSE?!
IF YOU THINK I'M GOING TO JUST SMILE AND FORGIVE YOU, YOU'RE WRONG!!
I'M REALLY SAD!! I'VE BEEN CRYING MY EYES OUT!
I WANT TO MAKE LOVE WITH YOU TOO, BUT...

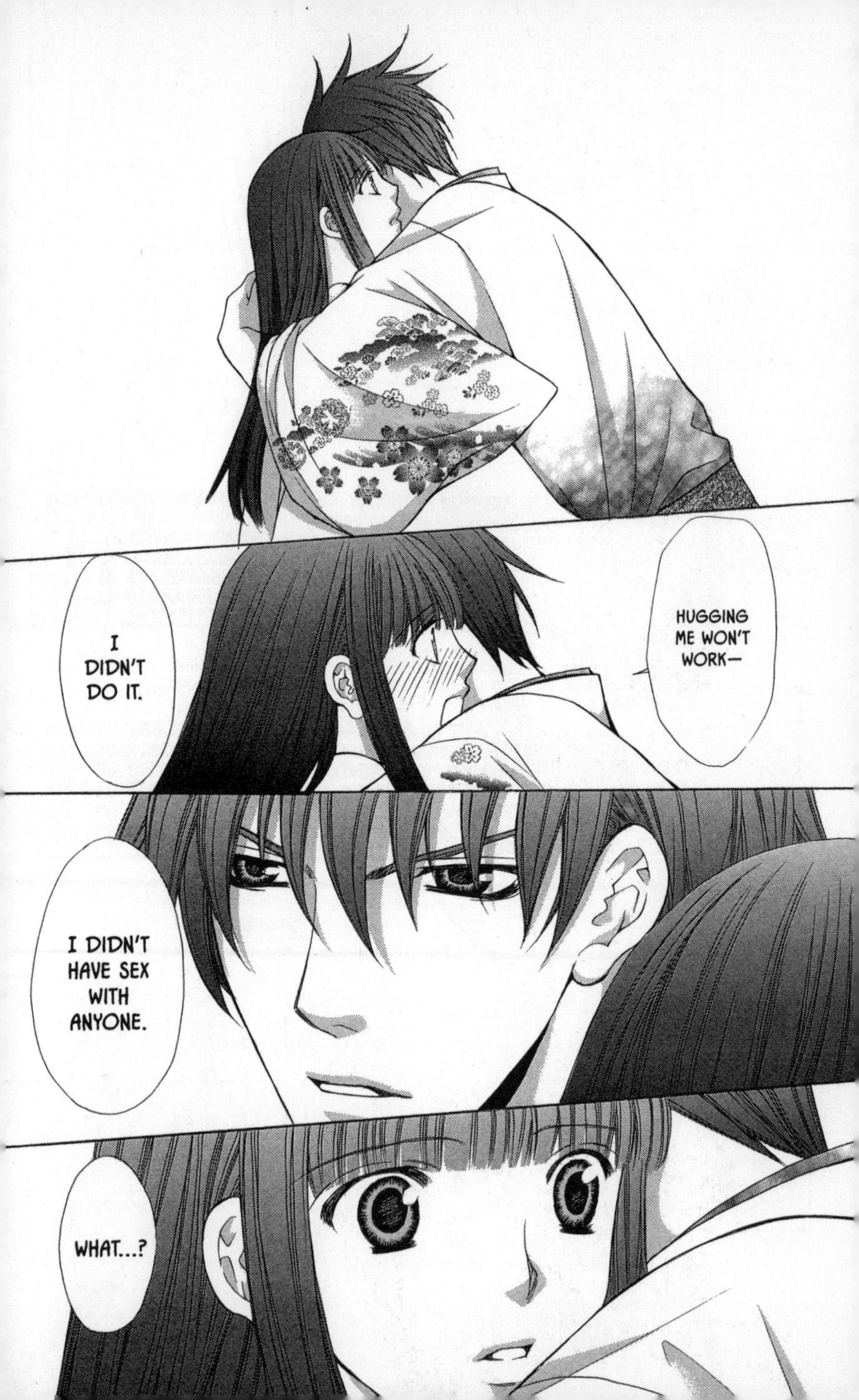
HUGGING ME WON'T WORK—
I DIDN'T DO IT.
I DIDN'T HAVE SEX WITH ANYONE.
WHAT...?

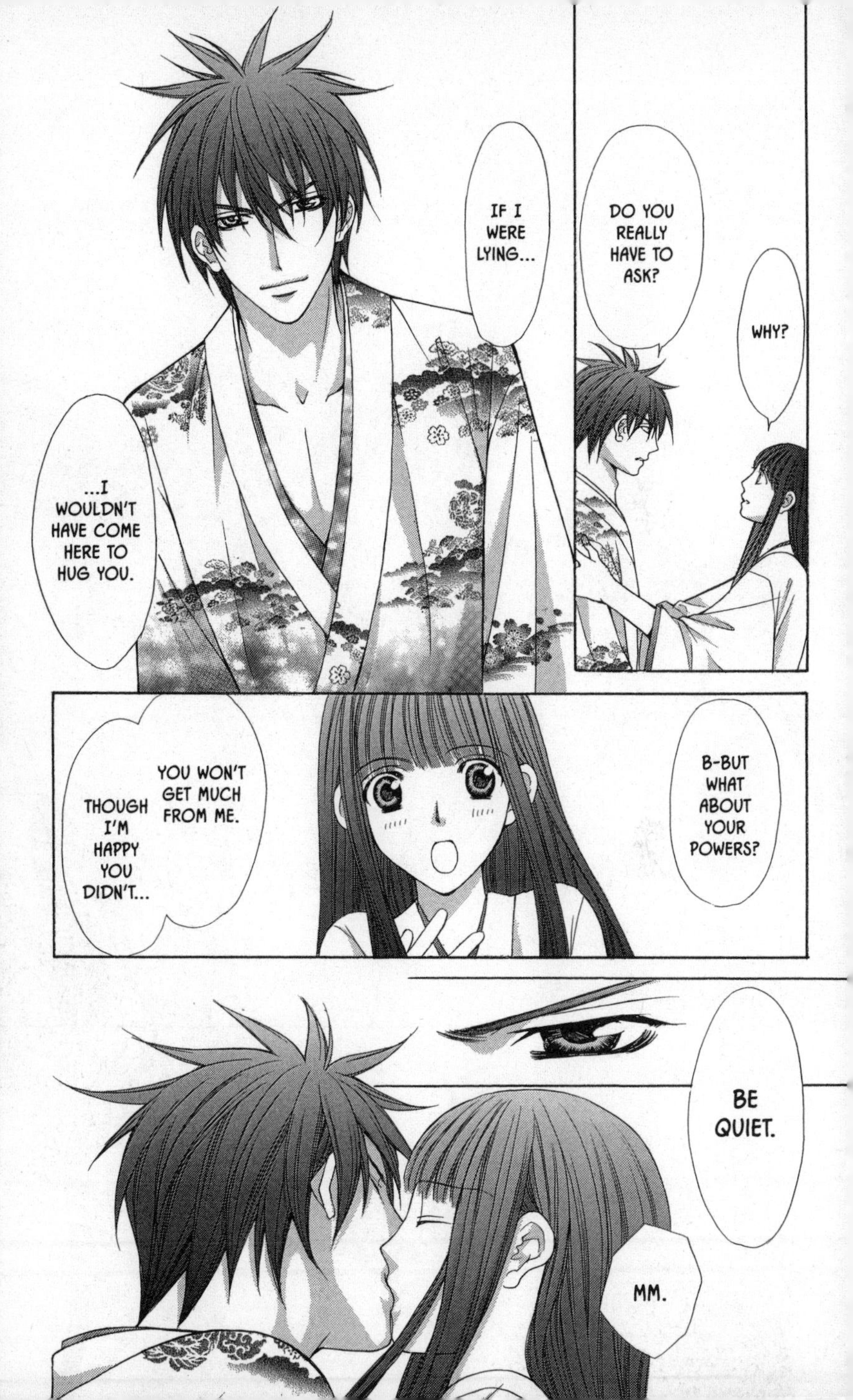
WHY?
DO YOU REALLY HAVE TO ASK?
IF I WERE LYING...
...I WOULDN'T HAVE COME HERE TO HUG YOU.
B-BUT WHAT ABOUT YOUR POWERS?
YOU WON'T GET MUCH FROM ME.
THOUGH I'M HAPPY YOU DIDN'T...
BE QUIET.
MM.

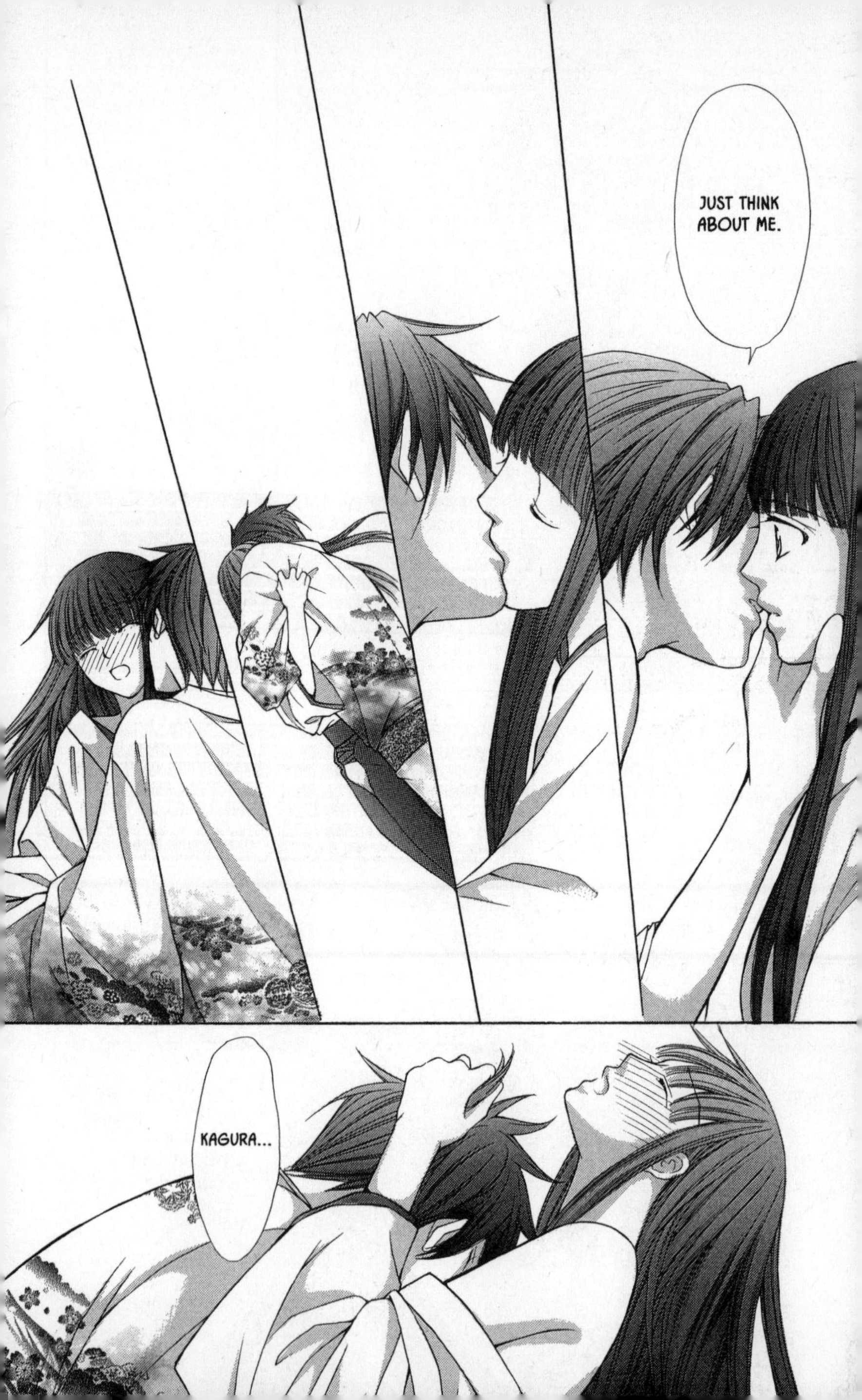
JUST THINK ABOUT ME.
KAGURA...

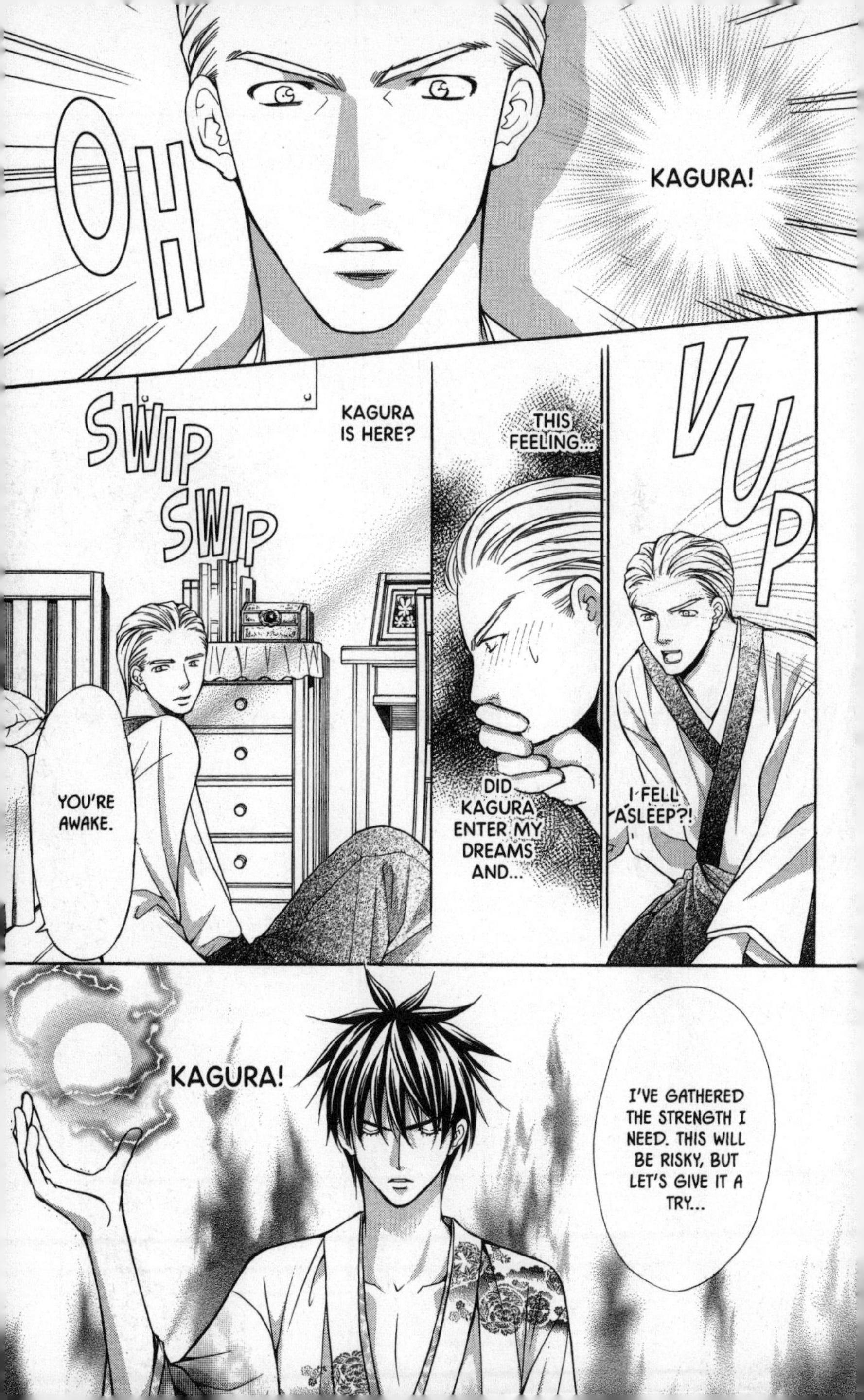
KAGURA!
OH
VUP
I FELL ASLEEP?!
THIS FEELING...
DID KAGURA ENTER MY DREAMS AND...
KAGURA IS HERE?
SWIP
SWIP
YOU'RE AWAKE.
I'VE GATHERED THE STRENGTH I NEED. THIS WILL BE RISKY, BUT LET'S GIVE IT A TRY...
KAGURA!

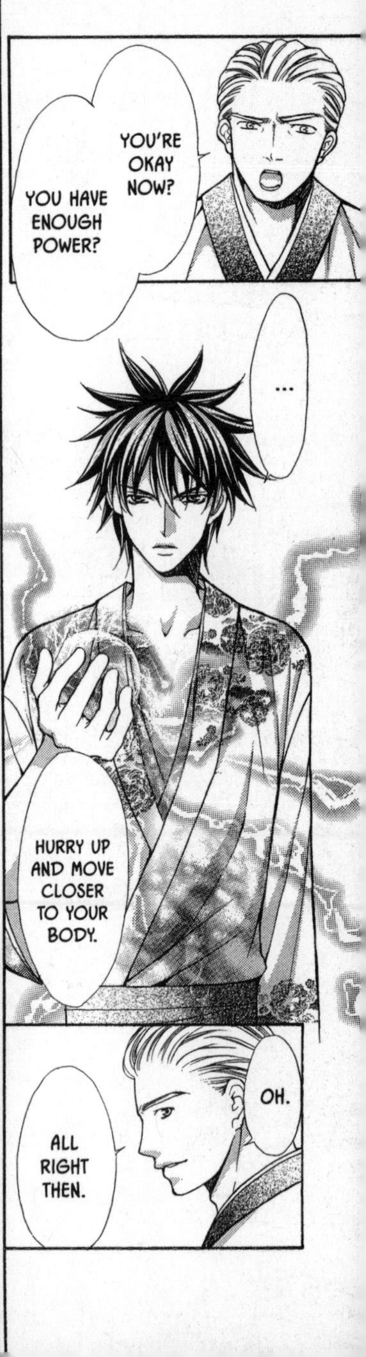
YOU'RE OKAY NOW?
YOU HAVE ENOUGH POWER?
...
HURRY UP AND MOVE CLOSER TO YOUR BODY.
OH.
ALL RIGHT THEN.

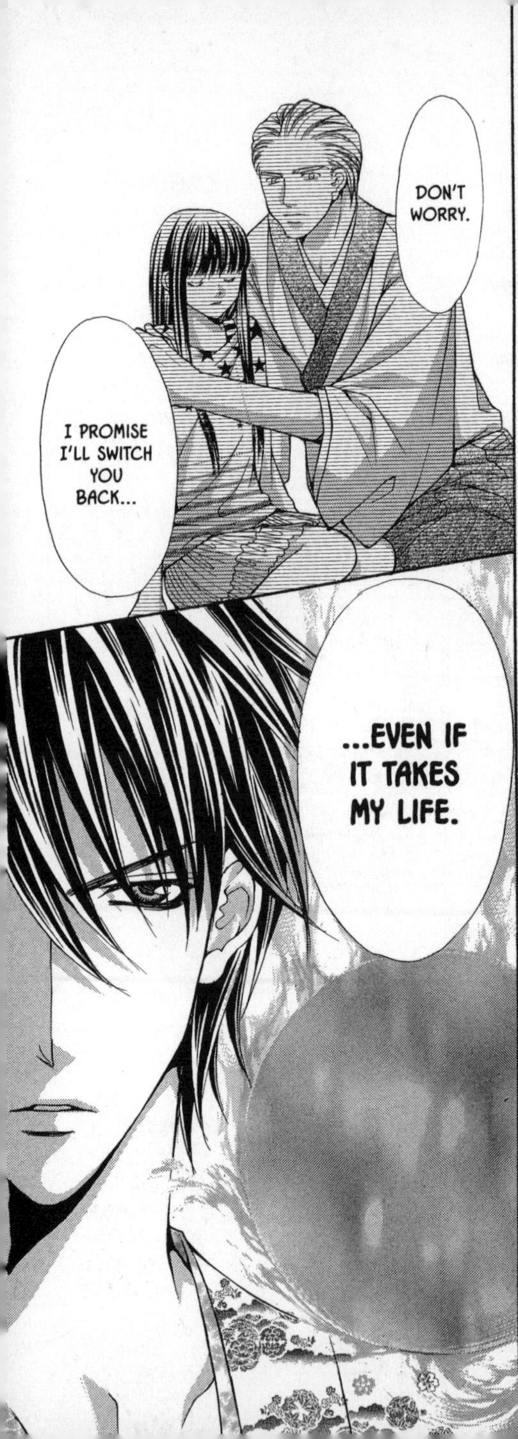
DON'T WORRY.
I PROMISE I'LL SWITCH YOU BACK...
...EVEN IF IT TAKES MY LIFE.

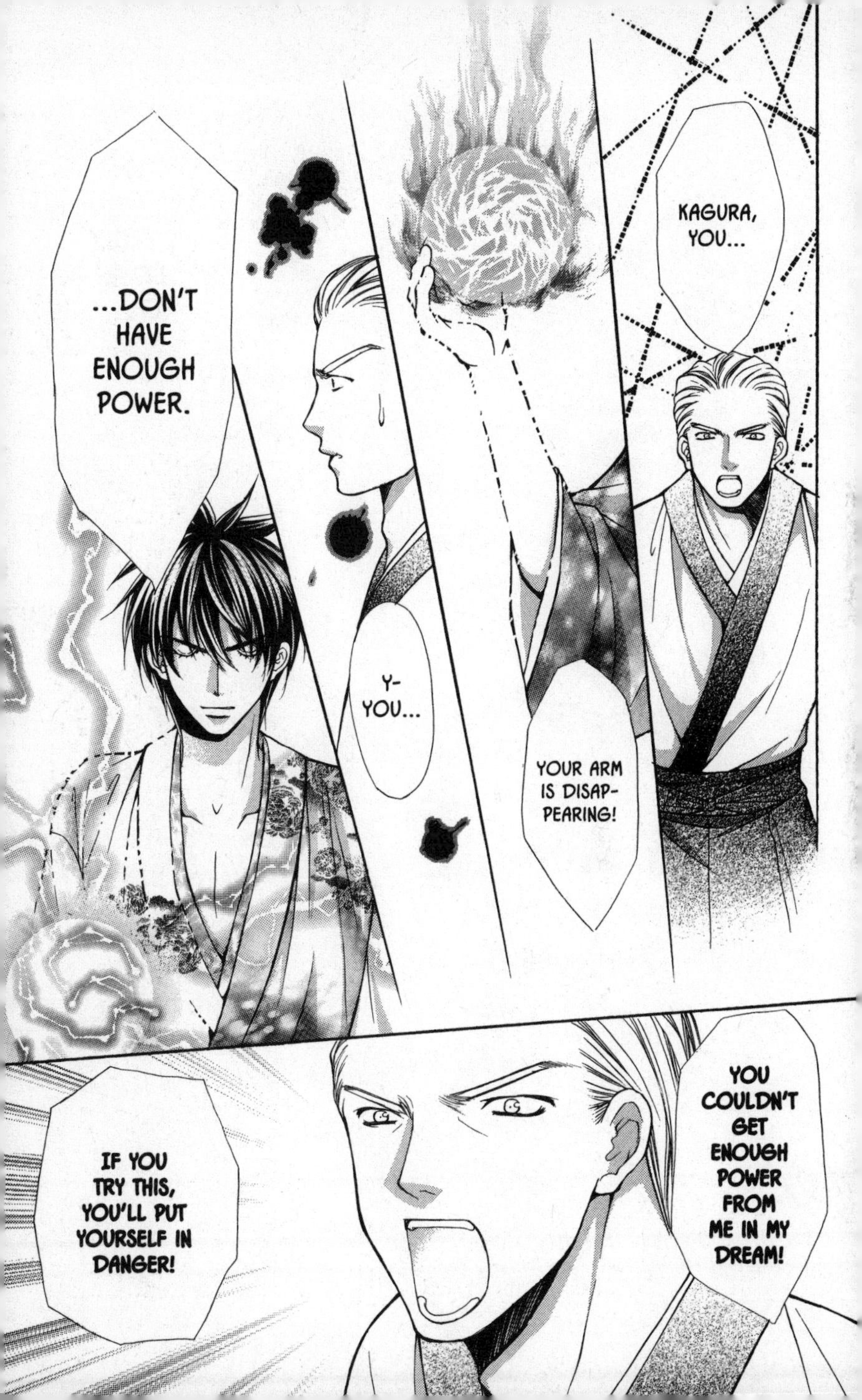
KAGURA, YOU...
YOUR ARM IS DISAPPEARING!
Y-YOU...
...DON'T HAVE ENOUGH POWER.
YOU COULDN'T GET ENOUGH POWER FROM ME IN MY DREAM!
IF YOU TRY THIS, YOU'LL PUT YOURSELF IN DANGER!

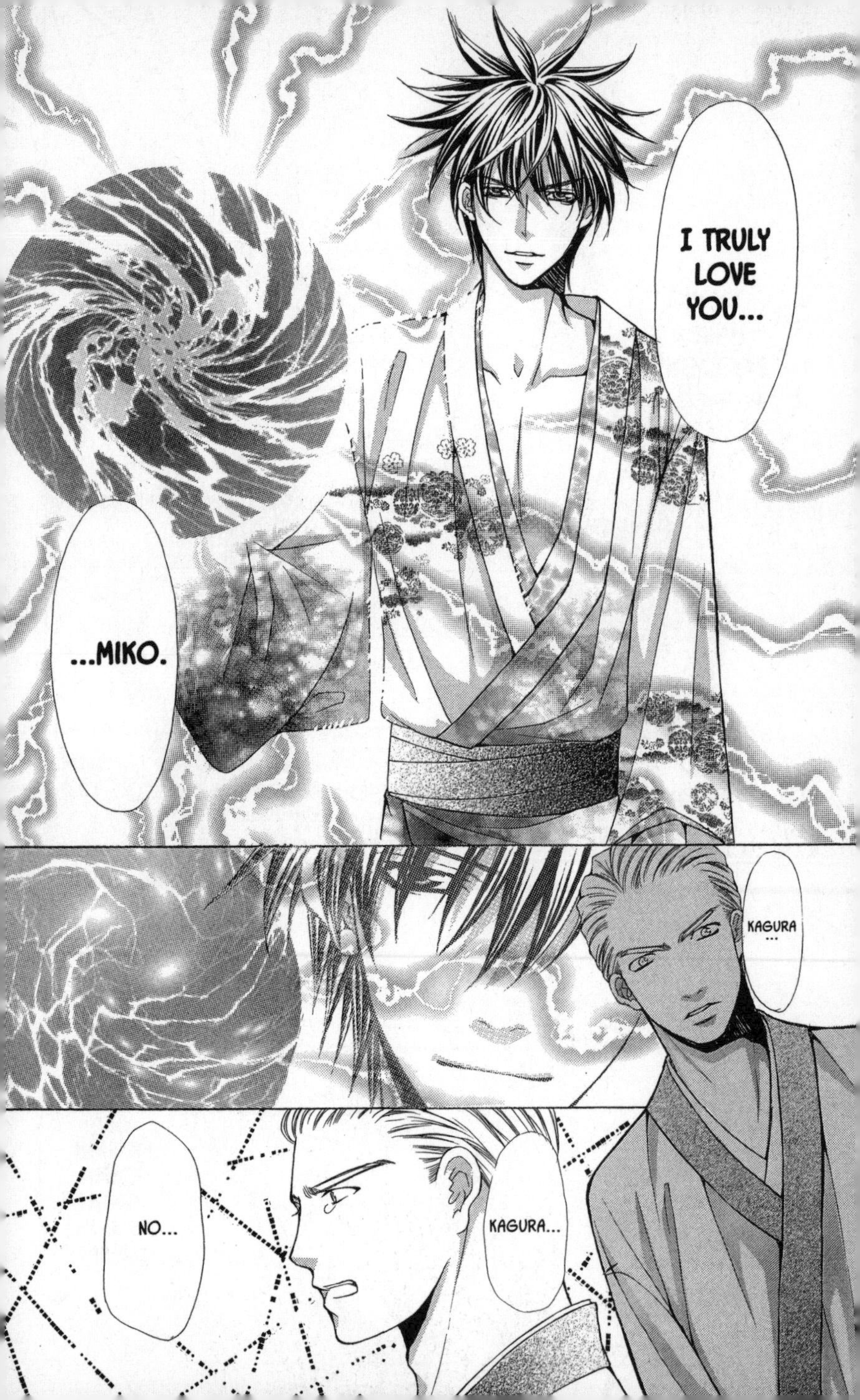
I TRULY LOVE YOU...
...MIKO.
KAGURA ...
KAGURA...
NO...

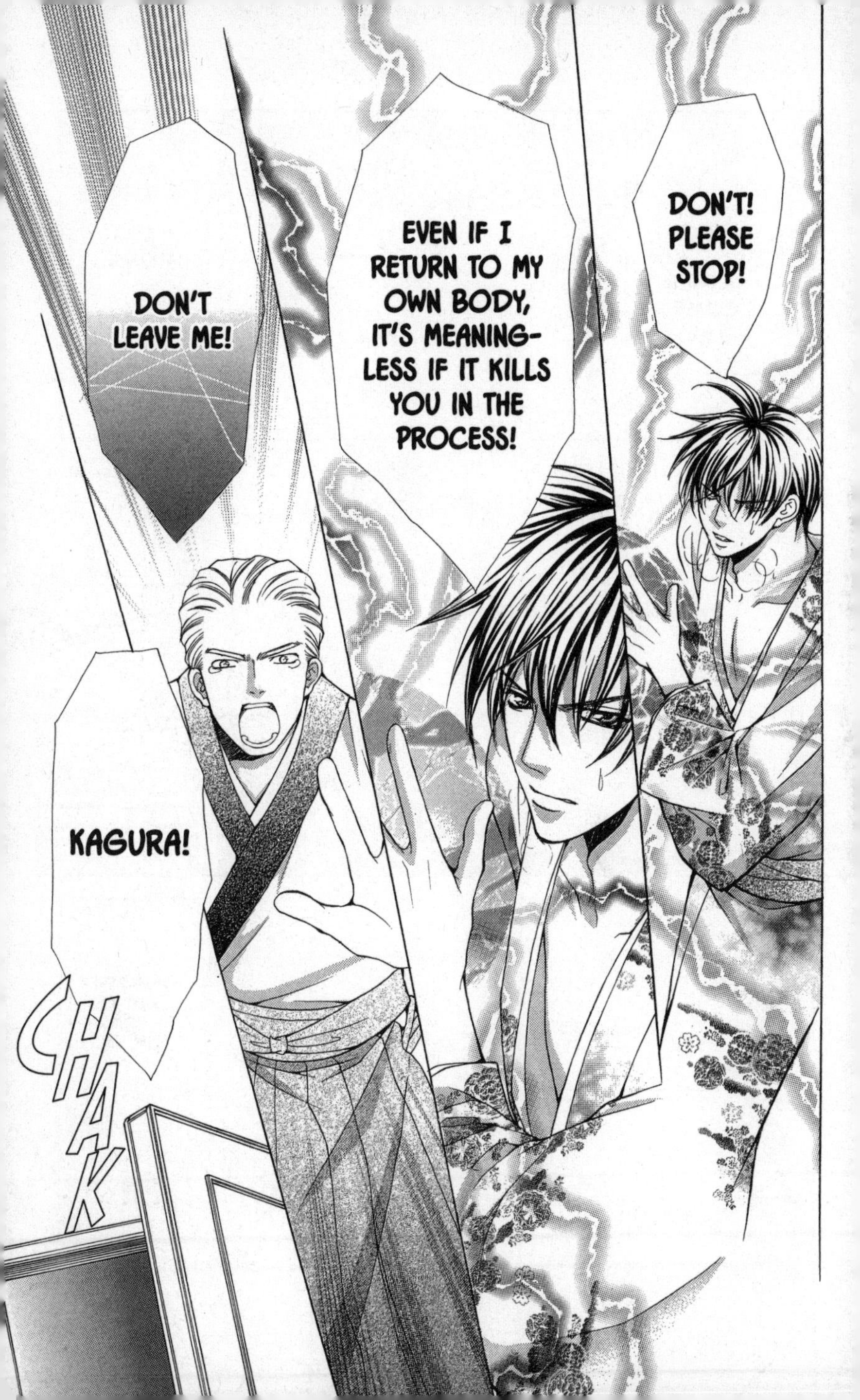
DON'T! PLEASE STOP!
EVEN IF I RETURN TO MY OWN BODY, IT'S MEANING-LESS IF IT KILLS YOU IN THE PROCESS!
DON'T LEAVE ME!
KAGURA!
CHAK

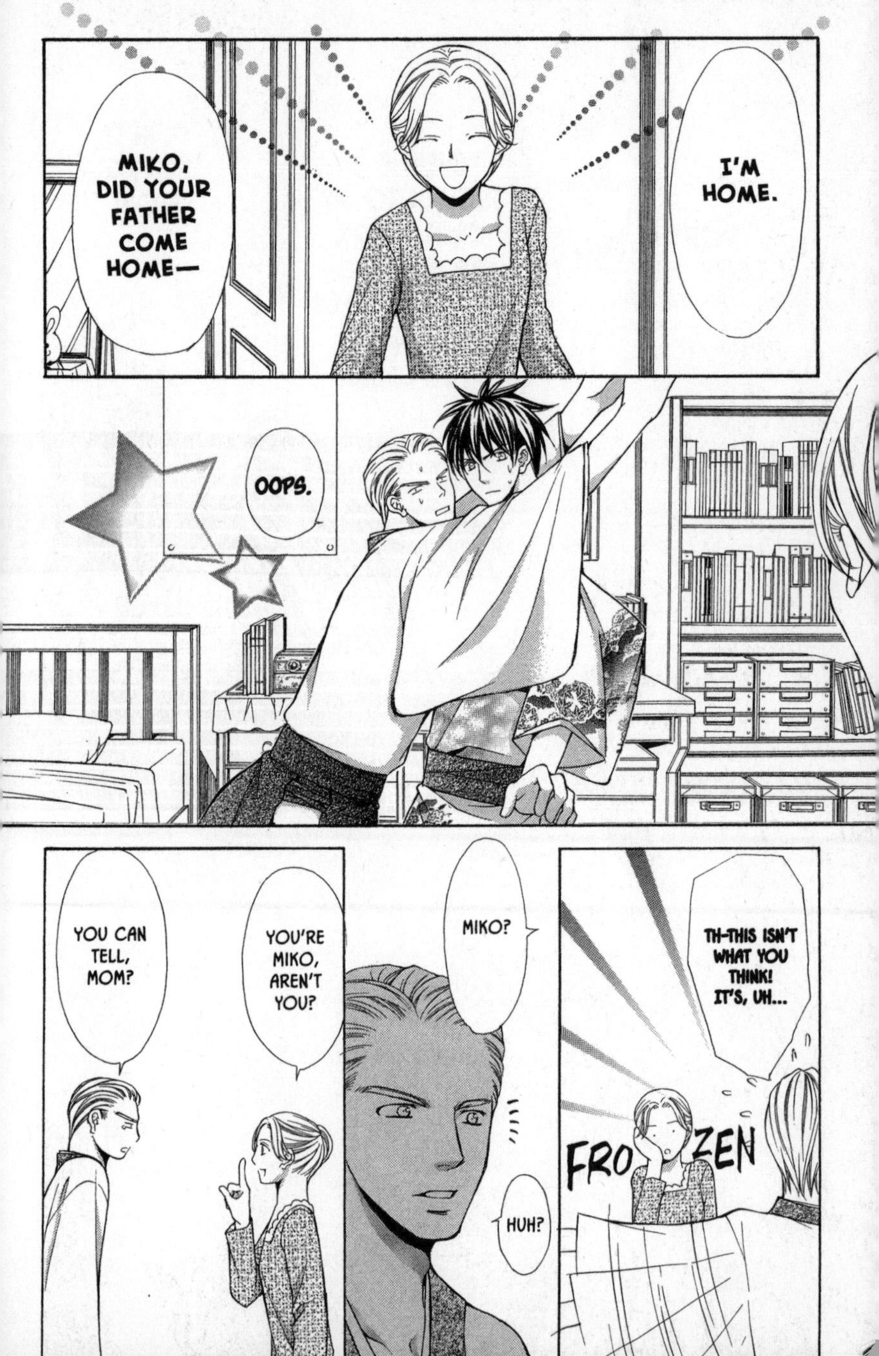
I'M HOME.
MIKO, DID YOUR FATHER COME HOME—
OOPS.
TH-THIS ISN'T WHAT YOU THINK! IT'S, UH...
FROZEN
MIKO?
HUH?
YOU'RE MIKO, AREN'T YOU?
YOU CAN TELL, MOM?

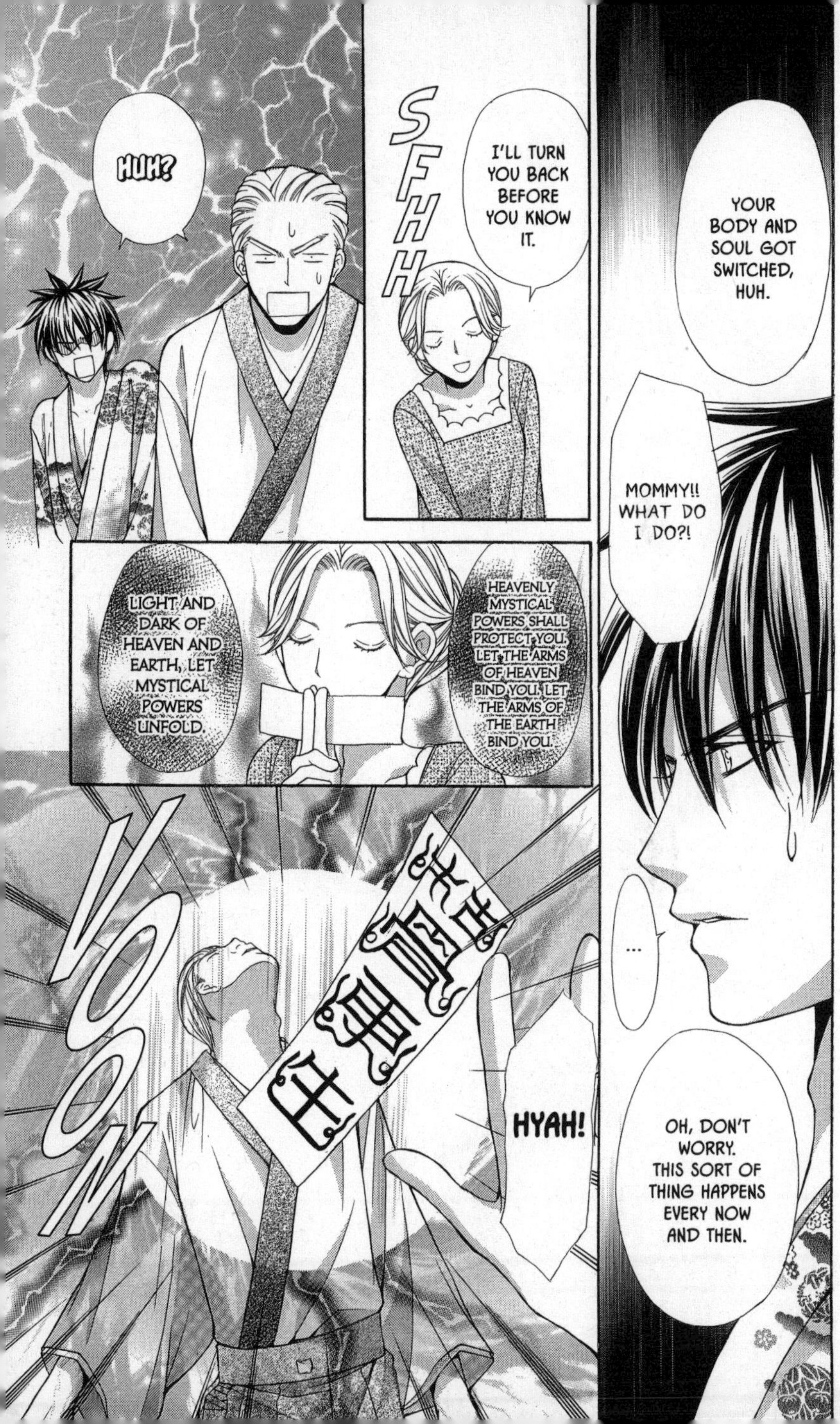
YOUR BODY AND SOUL GOT SWITCHED, HUH.
MOMMY!! WHAT DO I DO?!
...
OH, DON'T WORRY. THIS SORT OF THING HAPPENS EVERY NOW AND THEN.
SFHHH
I'LL TURN YOU BACK BEFORE YOU KNOW IT.
HUH?
HEAVENLY MYSTICAL POWERS SHALL PROTECT YOU. LET THE ARMS OF HEAVEN BIND YOU. LET THE ARMS OF THE EARTH BIND YOU.
LIGHT AND DARK OF HEAVEN AND EARTH, LET MYSTICAL POWERS UNFOLD.
HYAH!
VOOON

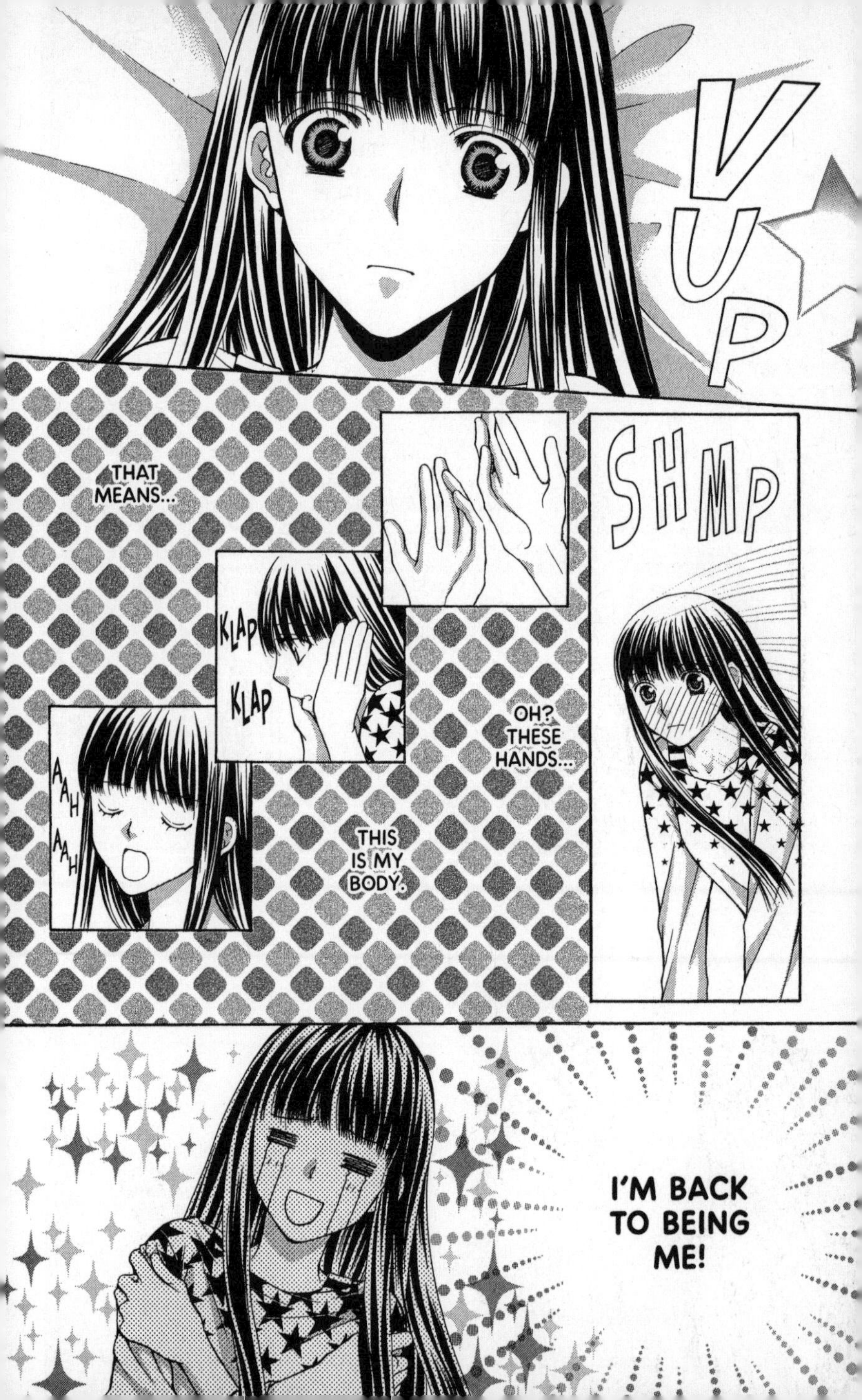
VUP
SHMP
OH? THESE HANDS...
KLAP
KLAP
THAT MEANS...
THIS IS MY BODY.
AAH
AAH
I'M BACK TO BEING ME!

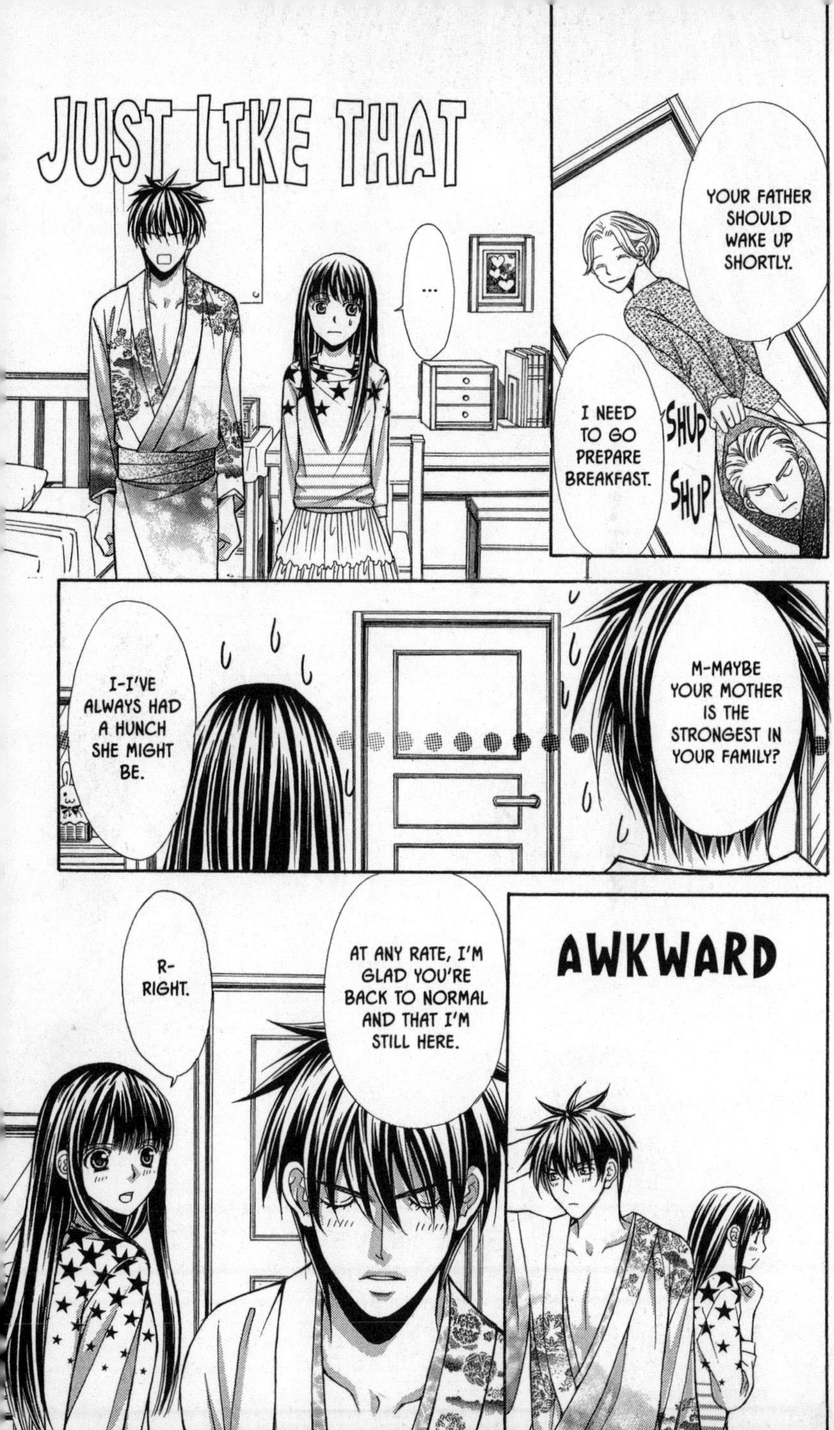
YOUR FATHER SHOULD WAKE UP SHORTLY.
I NEED TO GO PREPARE BREAKFAST.
SHUP
SHUP
JUST LIKE THAT
...
M-MAYBE YOUR MOTHER IS THE STRONGEST IN YOUR FAMILY?
I-I'VE ALWAYS HAD A HUNCH SHE MIGHT BE.
AWKWARD
AT ANY RATE, I'M GLAD YOU'RE BACK TO NORMAL AND THAT I'M STILL HERE.
R-RIGHT.

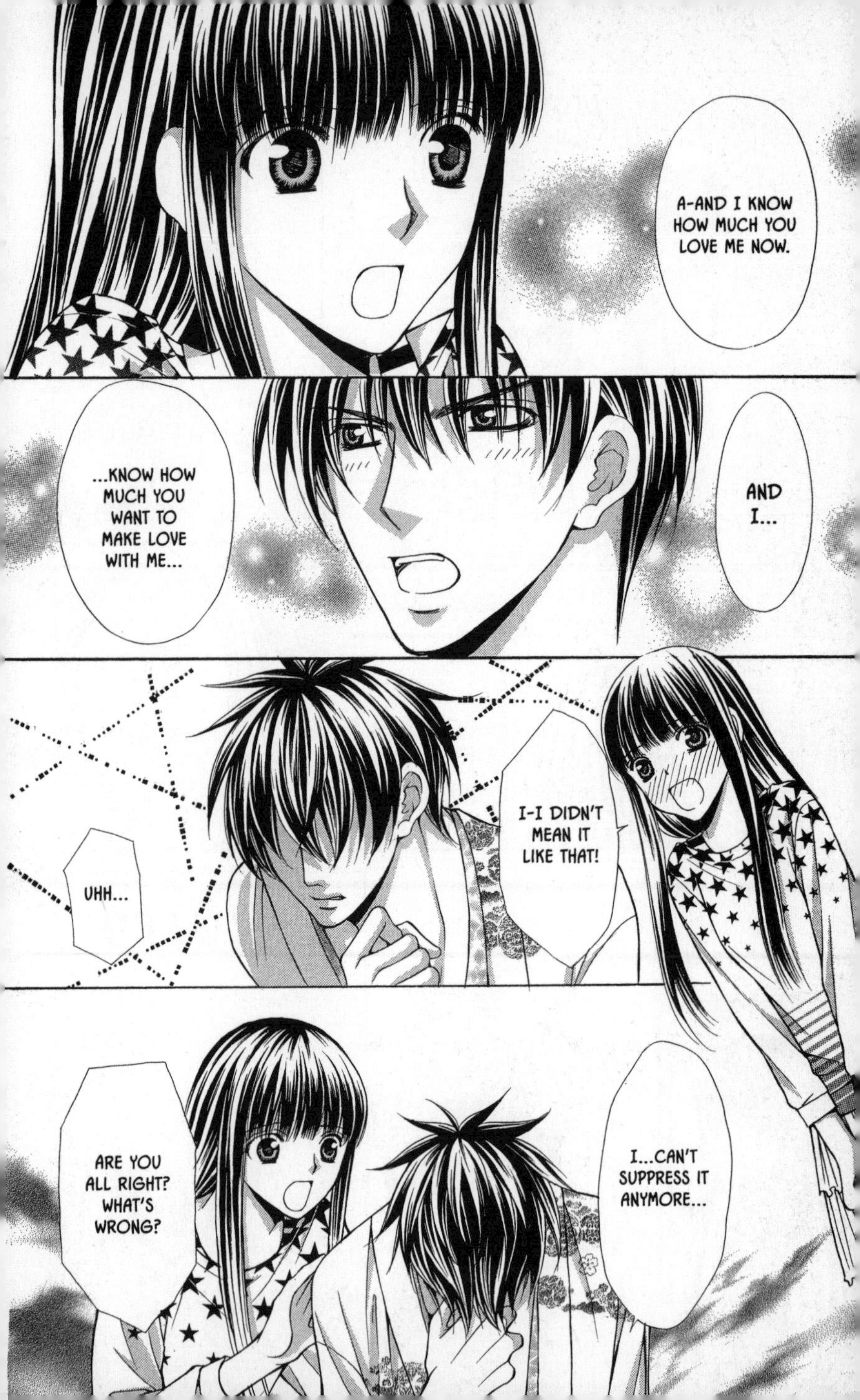
A-AND I KNOW HOW MUCH YOU LOVE ME NOW.
AND I...
...KNOW HOW MUCH YOU WANT TO MAKE LOVE WITH ME...
I-I DIDN'T MEAN IT LIKE THAT!
UHH...
I...CAN'T SUPPRESS IT ANYMORE...
ARE YOU ALL RIGHT? WHAT'S WRONG?

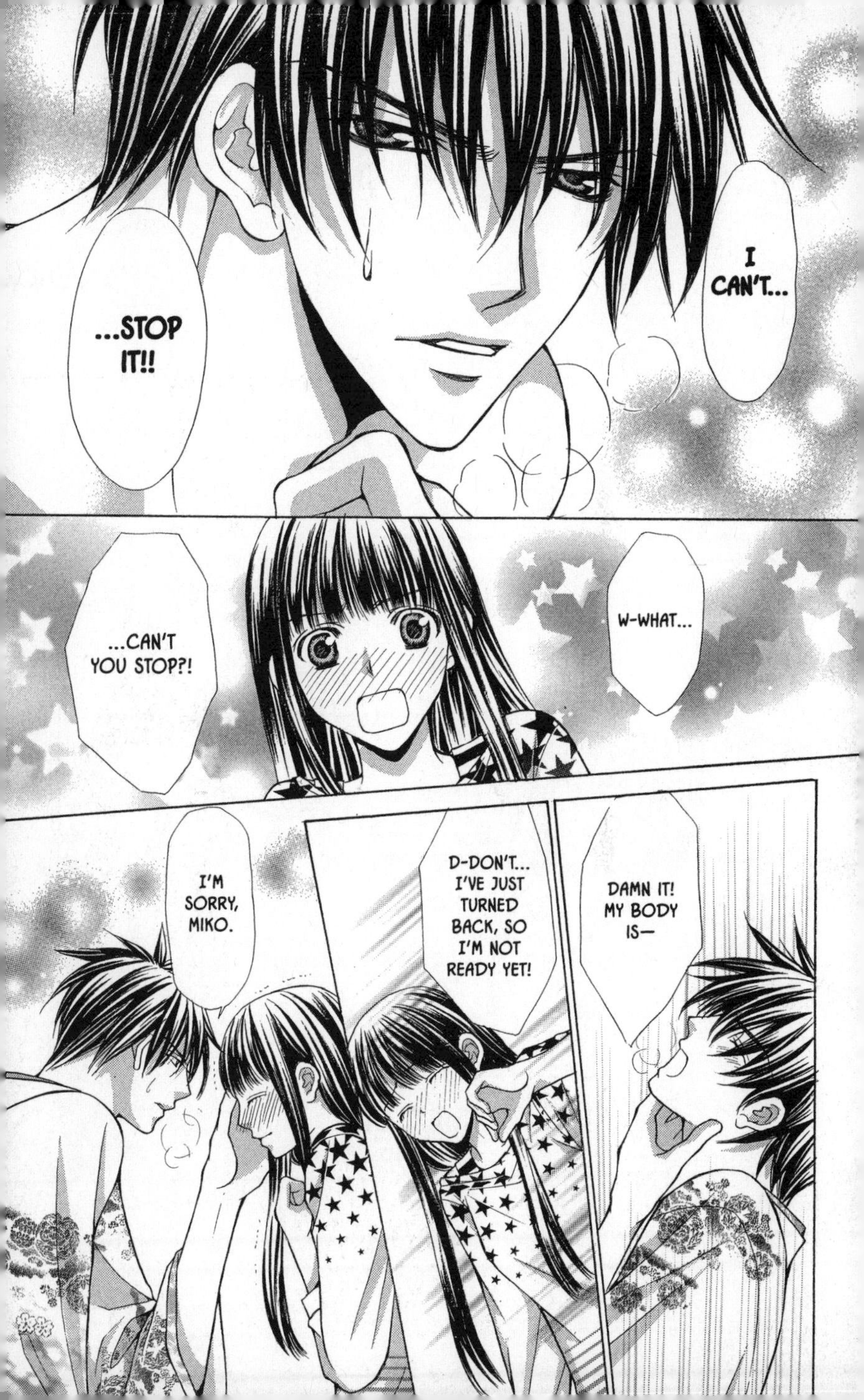
I CAN'T...
...STOP IT!!
W-WHAT...
...CAN'T YOU STOP?!
DAMN IT! MY BODY IS—
D-DON'T... I'VE JUST TURNED BACK, SO I'M NOT READY YET!
I'M SORRY, MIKO.

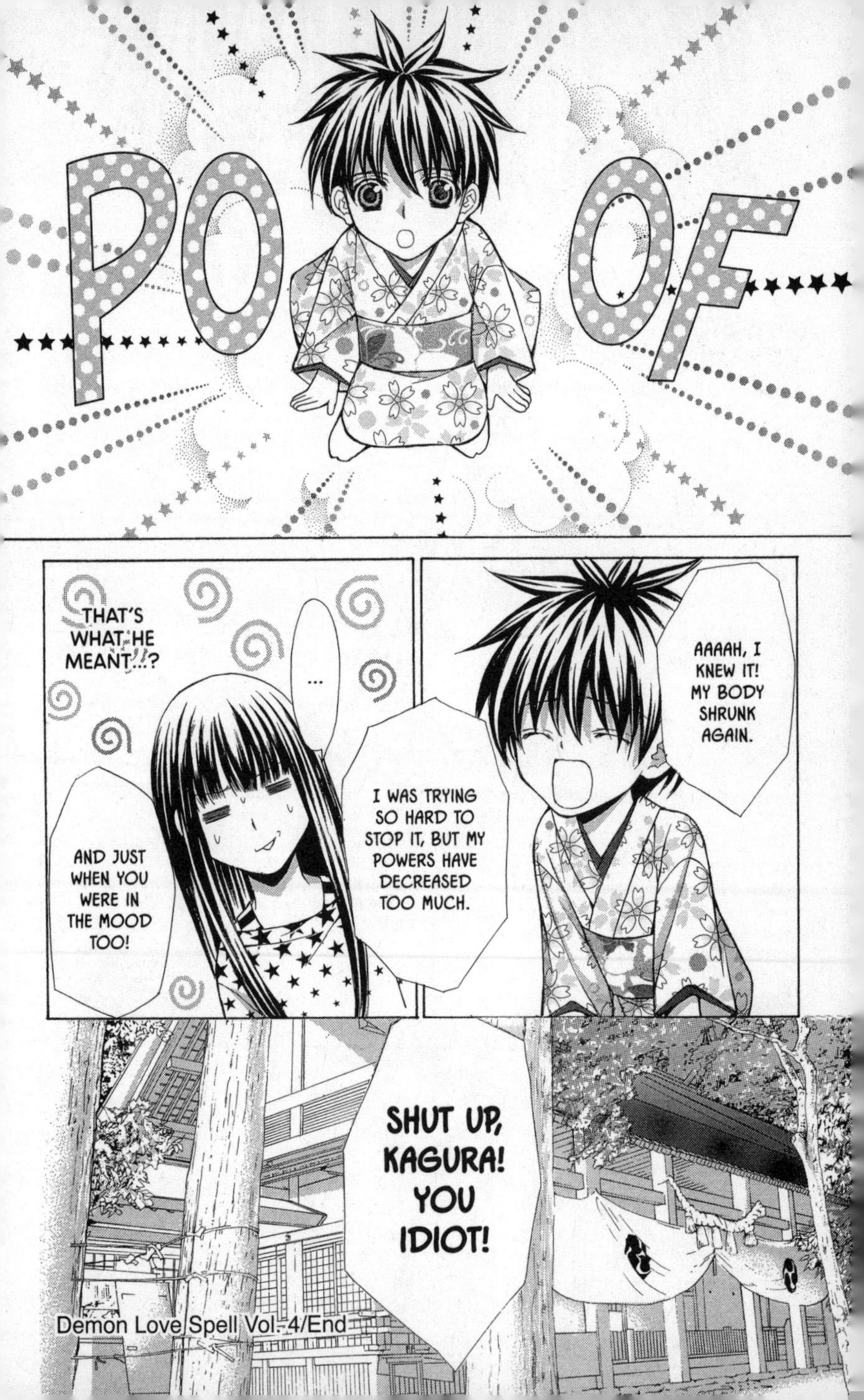
POOF
AAAAH, I KNEW IT! MY BODY SHRUNK AGAIN.
...
THAT'S WHAT HE MEANT!!?
I WAS TRYING SO HARD TO STOP IT, BUT MY POWERS HAVE DECREASED TOO MUCH.
AND JUST WHEN YOU WERE IN THE MOOD TOO!
SHUT UP, KAGURA! YOU IDIOT!
Demon Love Spell Vol. 4/End

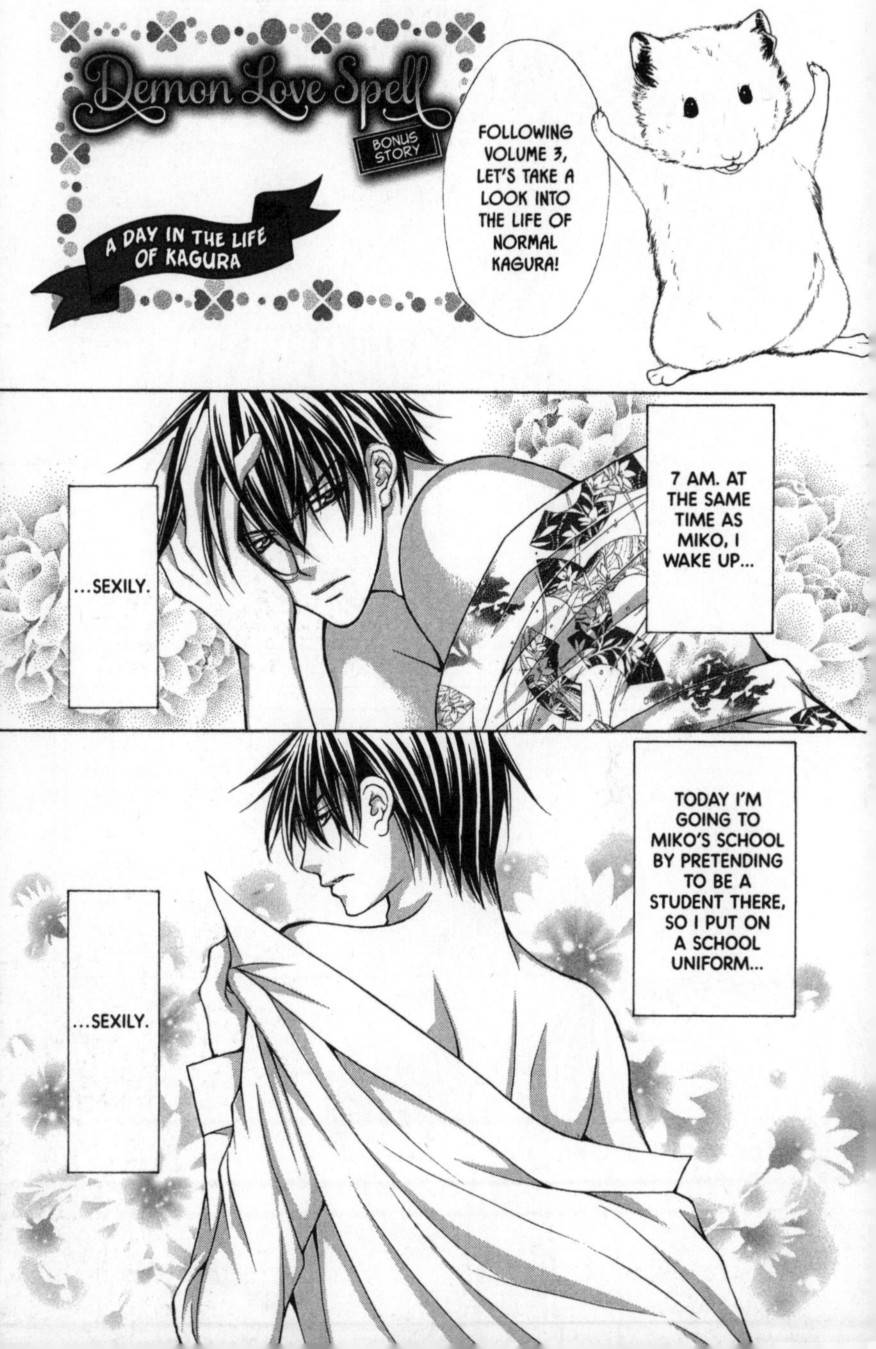
FOLLOWING VOLUME 3, LET'S TAKE A LOOK INTO THE LIFE OF NORMAL KAGURA!
Demon Love Spell
BONUS STORY
A DAY IN THE LIFE OF KAGURA
7 AM. AT THE SAME TIME AS MIKO, I WAKE UP...
...SEXILY.
TODAY I'M GOING TO MIKO'S SCHOOL BY PRETENDING TO BE A STUDENT THERE, SO I PUT ON A SCHOOL UNIFORM...
...SEXILY.

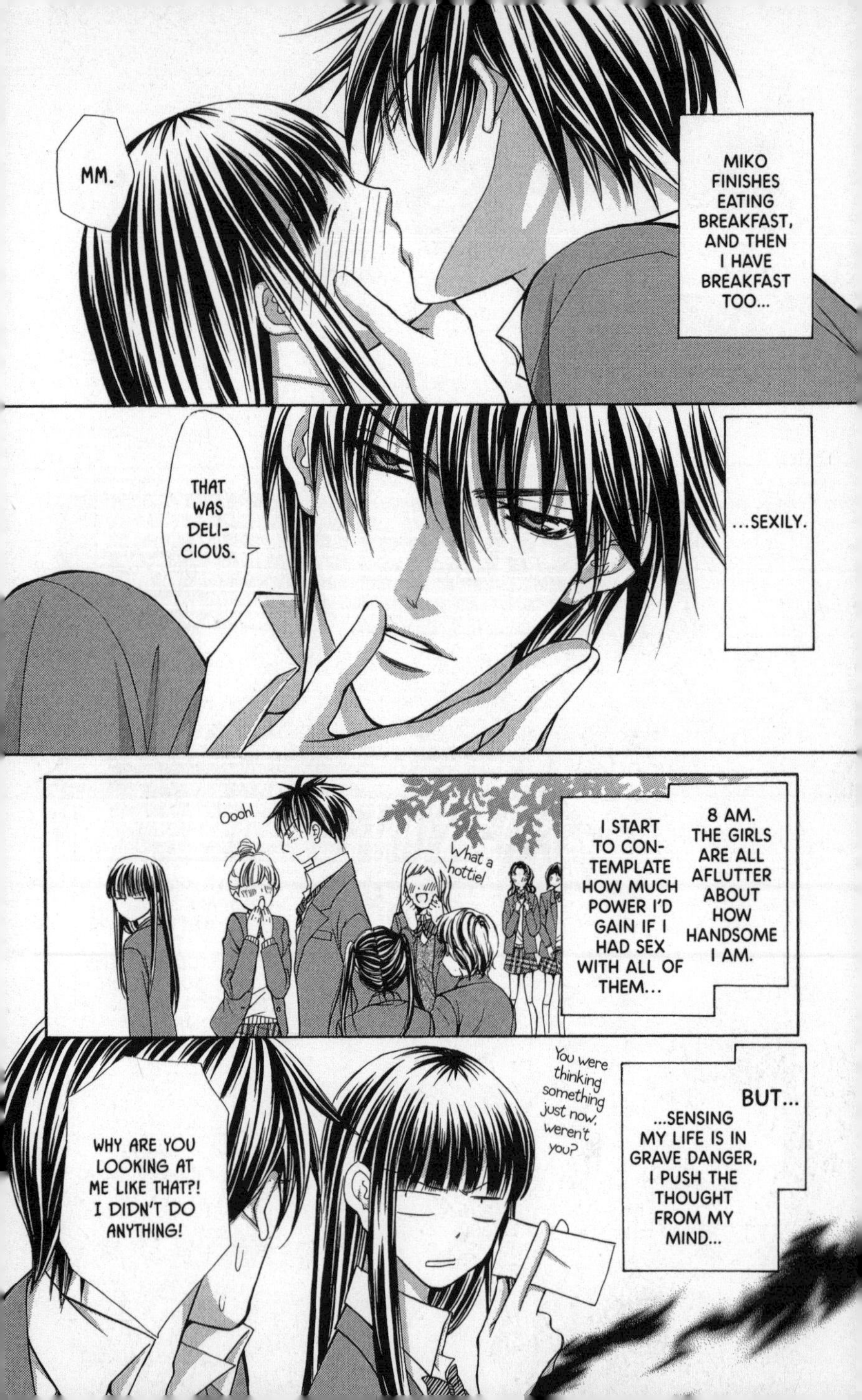

MIKO FINISHES EATING BREAKFAST, AND THEN I HAVE BREAKFAST TOO...
MM.
...SEXILY.
THAT WAS DELI-CIOUS.
8 AM. THE GIRLS ARE ALL AFLUTTER ABOUT HOW HANDSOME I AM.
I START TO CON-TEMPLATE HOW MUCH POWER I'D GAIN IF I HAD SEX WITH ALL OF THEM...
What a hottie!
Oooh!
BUT...
...SENSING MY LIFE IS IN GRAVE DANGER, I PUSH THE THOUGHT FROM MY MIND...
You were thinking something just now, weren't you?
WHY ARE YOU LOOKING AT ME LIKE THAT?! I DIDN'T DO ANYTHING!

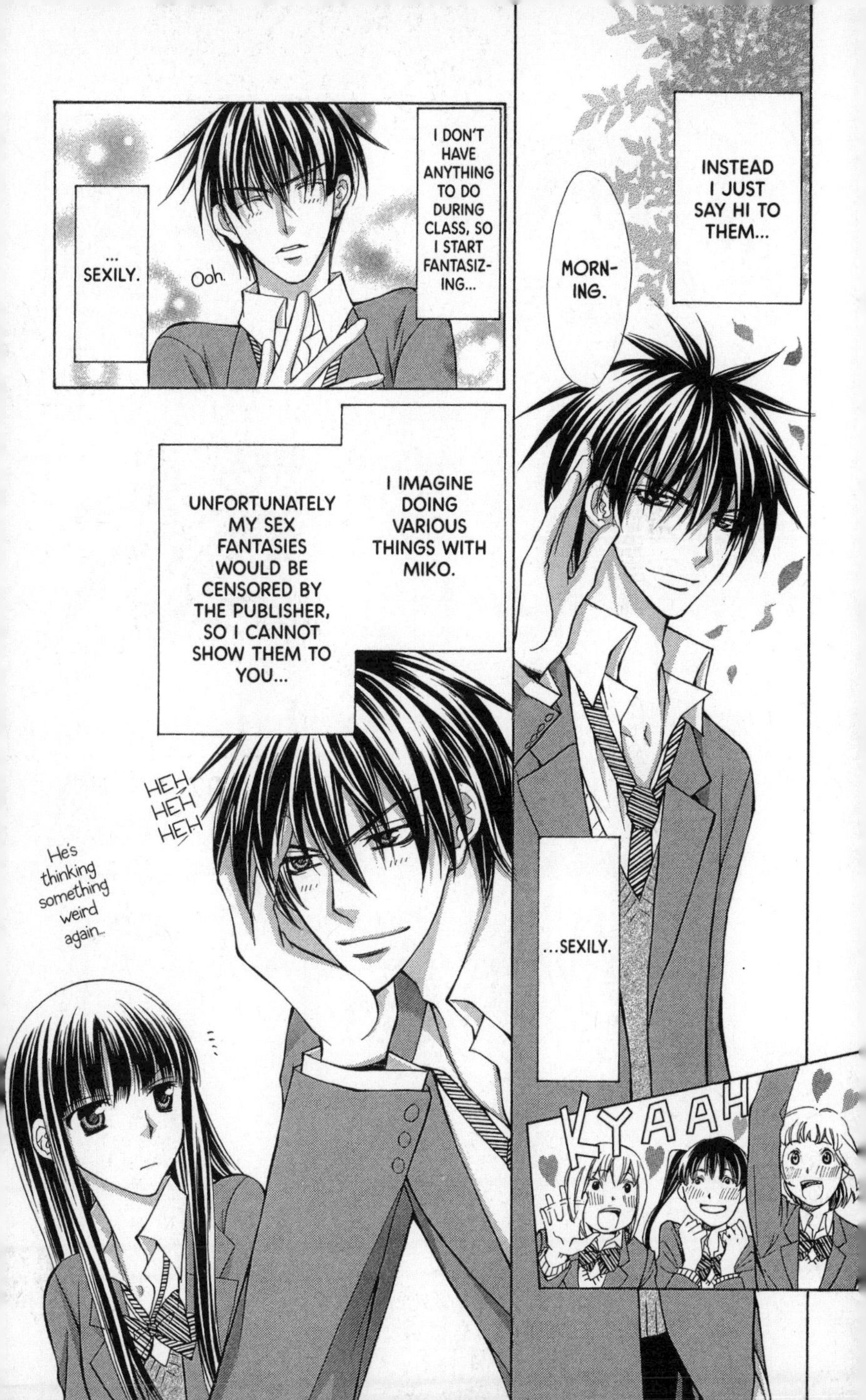
INSTEAD I JUST SAY HI TO THEM...
MORN-ING.
...SEXILY.
KYAAH
I DON'T HAVE ANYTHING TO DO DURING CLASS, SO I START FANTASIZ-ING...
Ooh.
...SEXILY.
I IMAGINE DOING VARIOUS THINGS WITH MIKO.
UNFORTUNATELY MY SEX FANTASIES WOULD BE CENSORED BY THE PUBLISHER, SO I CANNOT SHOW THEM TO YOU...
HEH HEH HEH
He's thinking something weird again...

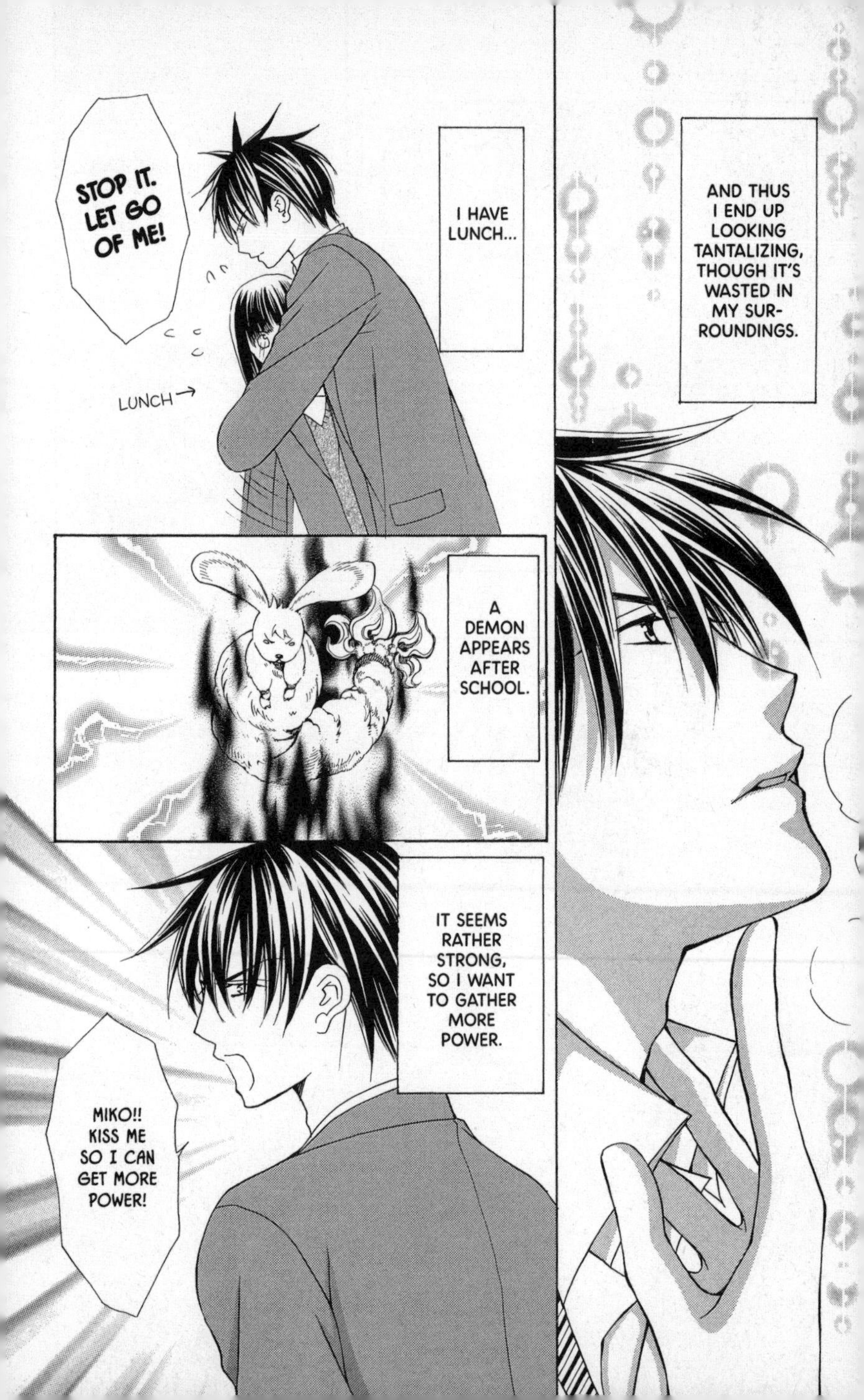
AND THUS I END UP LOOKING TANTALIZING, THOUGH IT'S WASTED IN MY SUR-ROUNDINGS.
I HAVE LUNCH...
STOP IT. LET GO OF ME!
LUNCH→
A DEMON APPEARS AFTER SCHOOL.
IT SEEMS RATHER STRONG, SO I WANT TO GATHER MORE POWER.
MIKO!! KISS ME SO I CAN GET MORE POWER!

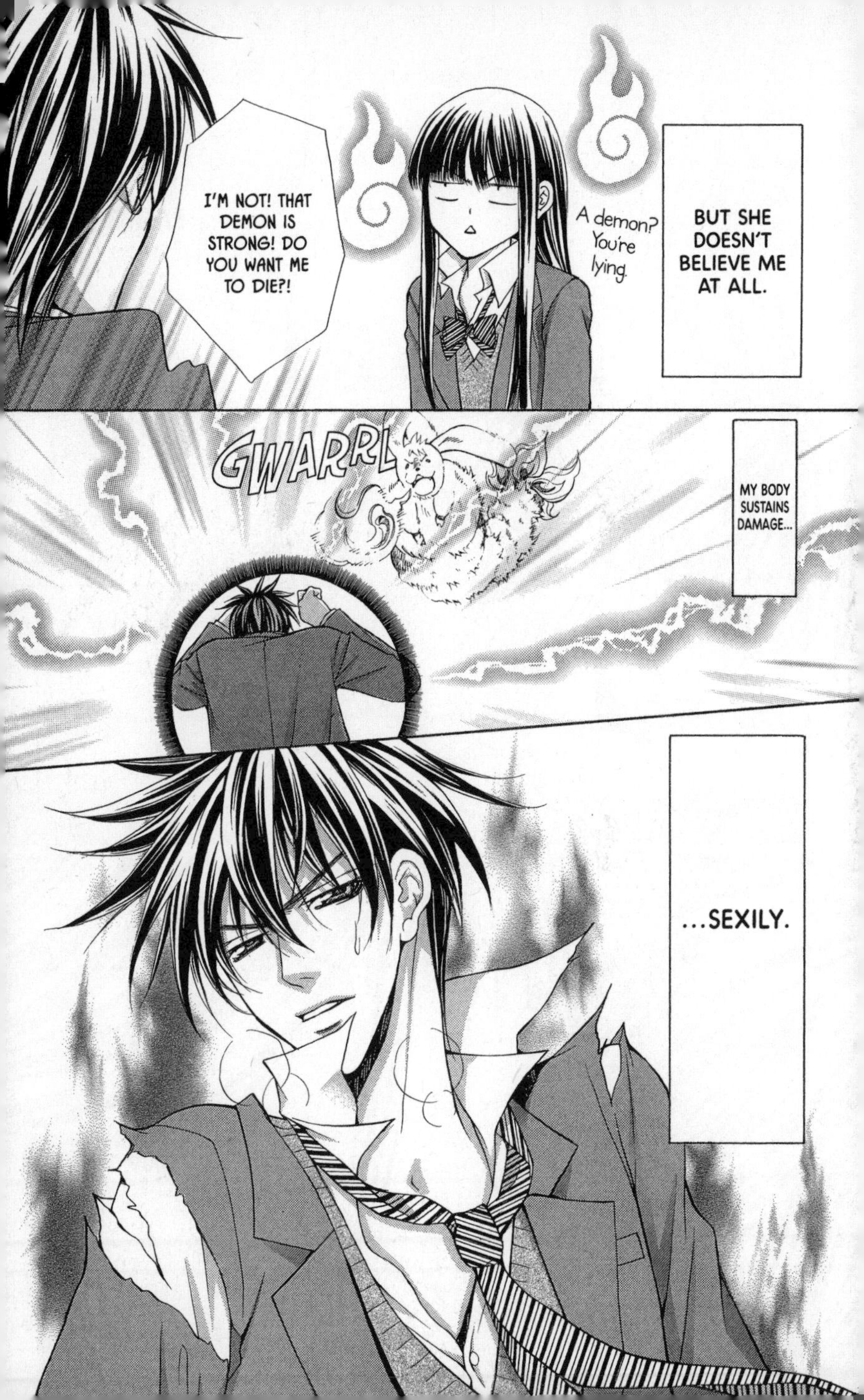
BUT SHE DOESN'T BELIEVE ME AT ALL.
A demon? You're lying.
I'M NOT! THAT DEMON IS STRONG! DO YOU WANT ME TO DIE?!
MY BODY SUSTAINS DAMAGE...
GWARRL
...SEXILY.

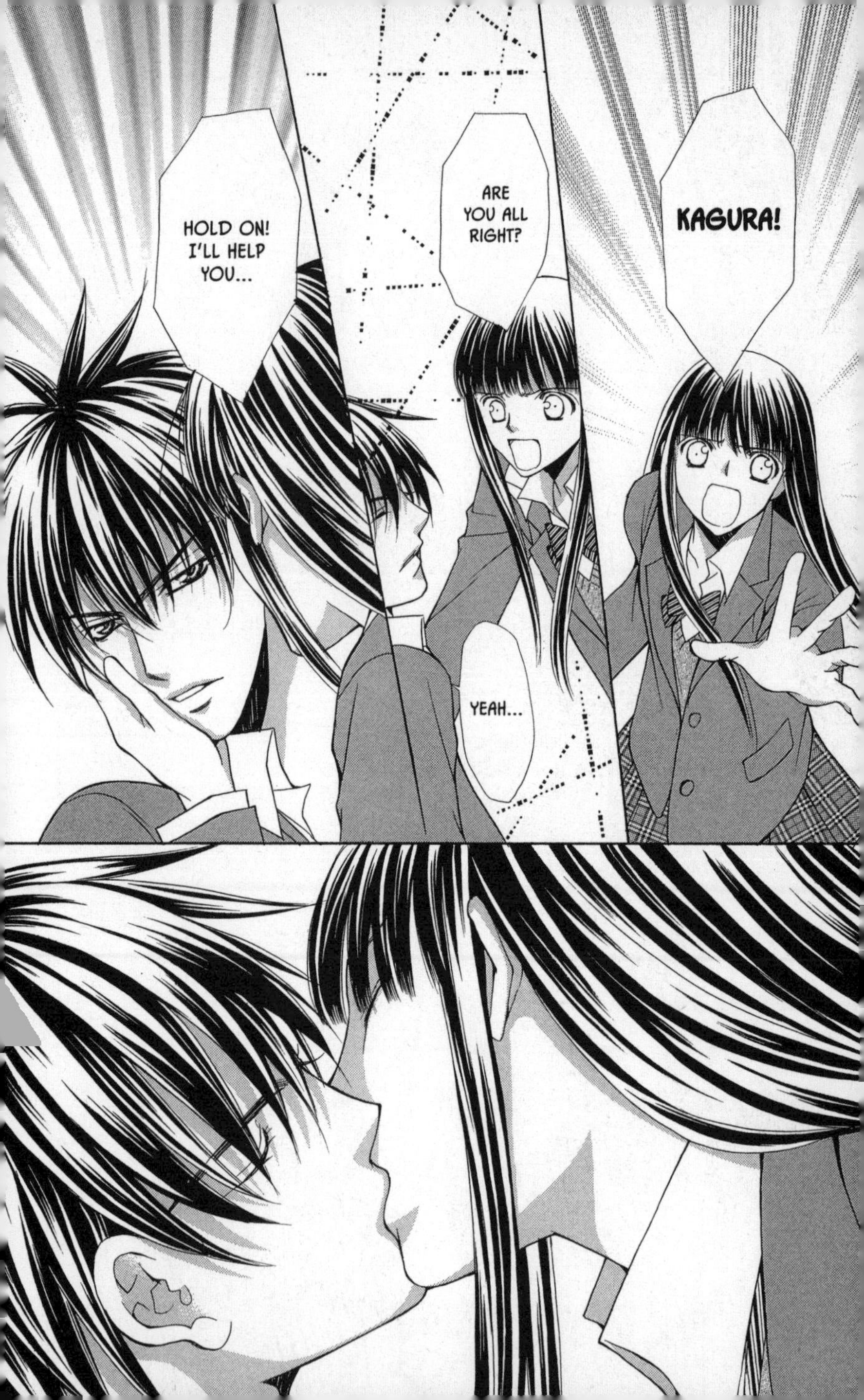
KAGURA!
ARE YOU ALL RIGHT?
YEAH...
HOLD ON! I'LL HELP YOU...

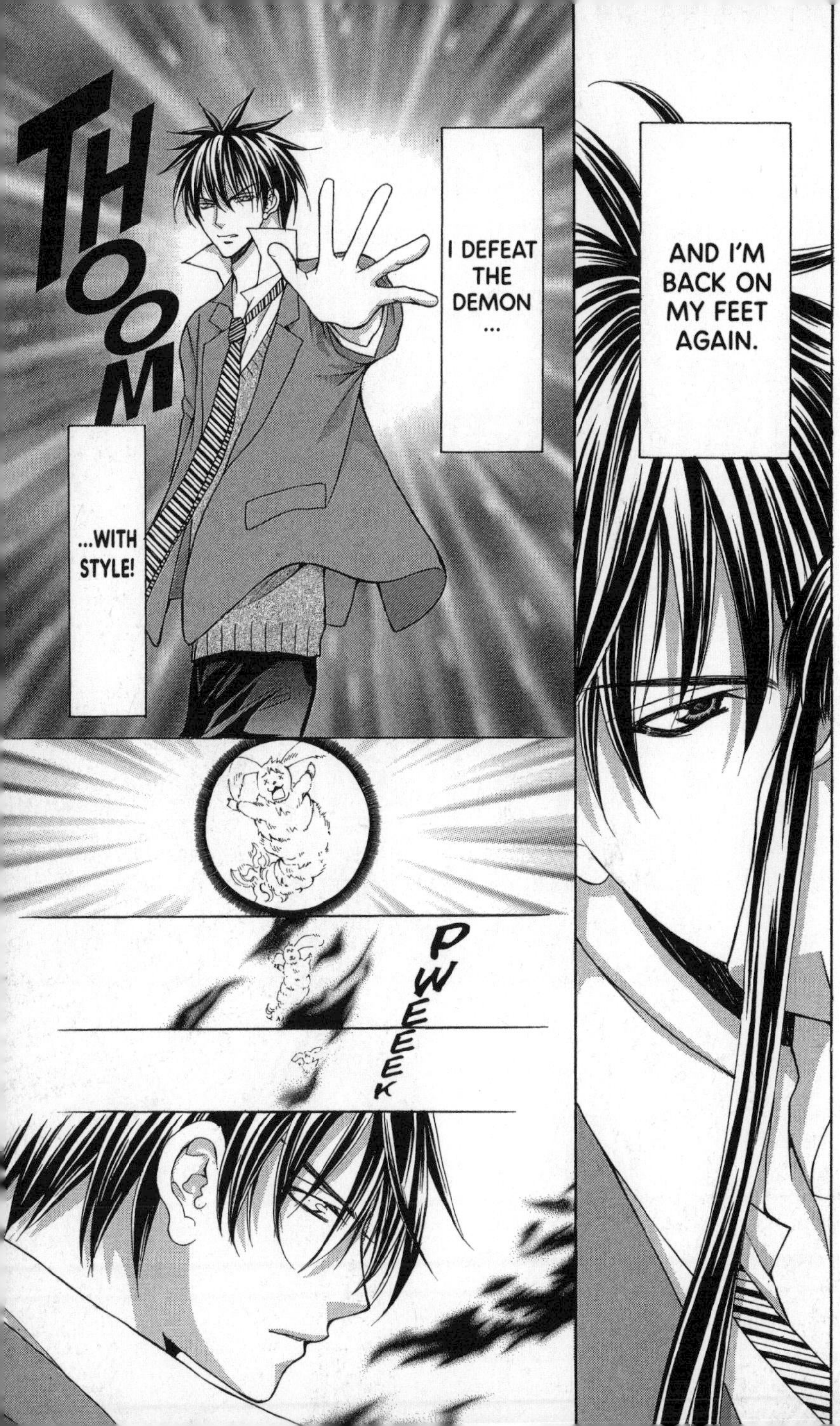
AND I'M BACK ON MY FEET AGAIN.
I DEFEAT THE DEMON ...
THOOM
...WITH STYLE!
PWEEEK

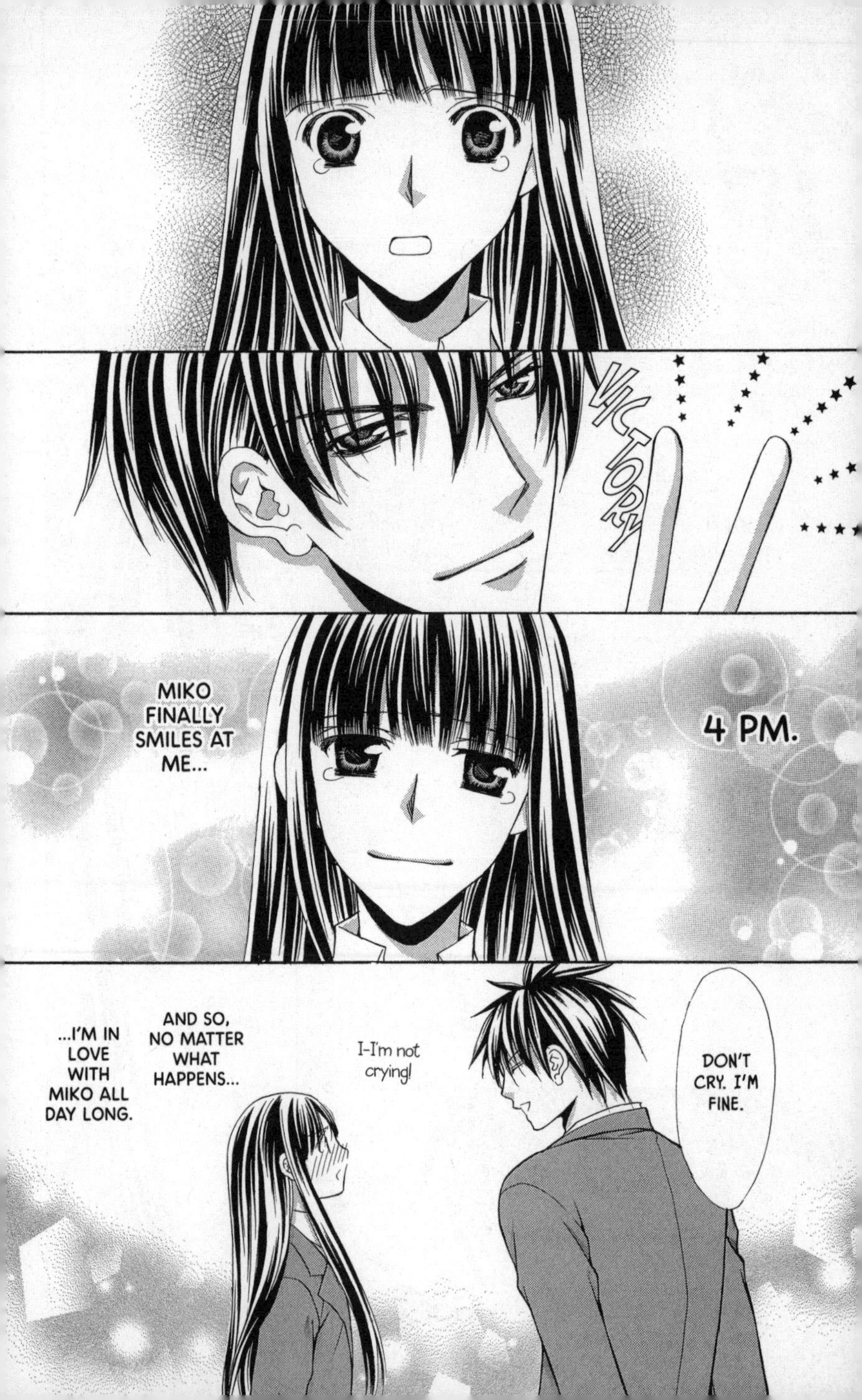
VICTORY
4 PM.
MIKO FINALLY SMILES AT ME...
DON'T CRY. I'M FINE.
I-I'm not crying!
AND SO, NO MATTER WHAT HAPPENS...
...I'M IN LOVE WITH MIKO ALL DAY LONG.

This manga is published in Japan at a pace of one volume per year, but we're already on volume 4. It doesn't come out often, so I'm glad there are people waiting to read this. Currently this is my only shojo manga series, and I would like to continue working on it as if it were my life's work.

–Mayu Shinjo

MAYU SHINJO was born on January 26. She is a prolific writer of shojo manga, including the series *Sensual Phrase* and *Ai Ore!* Her hobbies are cars, shopping and taking baths. Shinjo likes The Prodigy, Nirvana, U2 and Masaharu Fukuyama.

Demon Love Spell

Vol. 4
Shojo Beat Edition

STORY AND ART BY *Mayu Shinjo*

Translation
Tetsuichiro Miyaki

Touch-up Art & Lettering
Inori Fukuda Trant

Design
Fawn Lau

Editor
Nancy Thistlethwaite

AYAKASHI KOI EMAKI © 2008 by Mayu Shinjo.
All rights reserved.
First published in Japan in 2008 by SHUEISHA Inc., Tokyo.
English translation rights arranged by SHUEISHA Inc.

The stories, characters and incidents mentioned in
this publication are entirely fictional.

Printed in the U.S.A.

Published by VIZ Media, LLC
P.O. Box 77010
San Francisco, CA 94107

10 9 8 7 6 5 4 3 2
First printing, September 2013
Second printing, March 2015

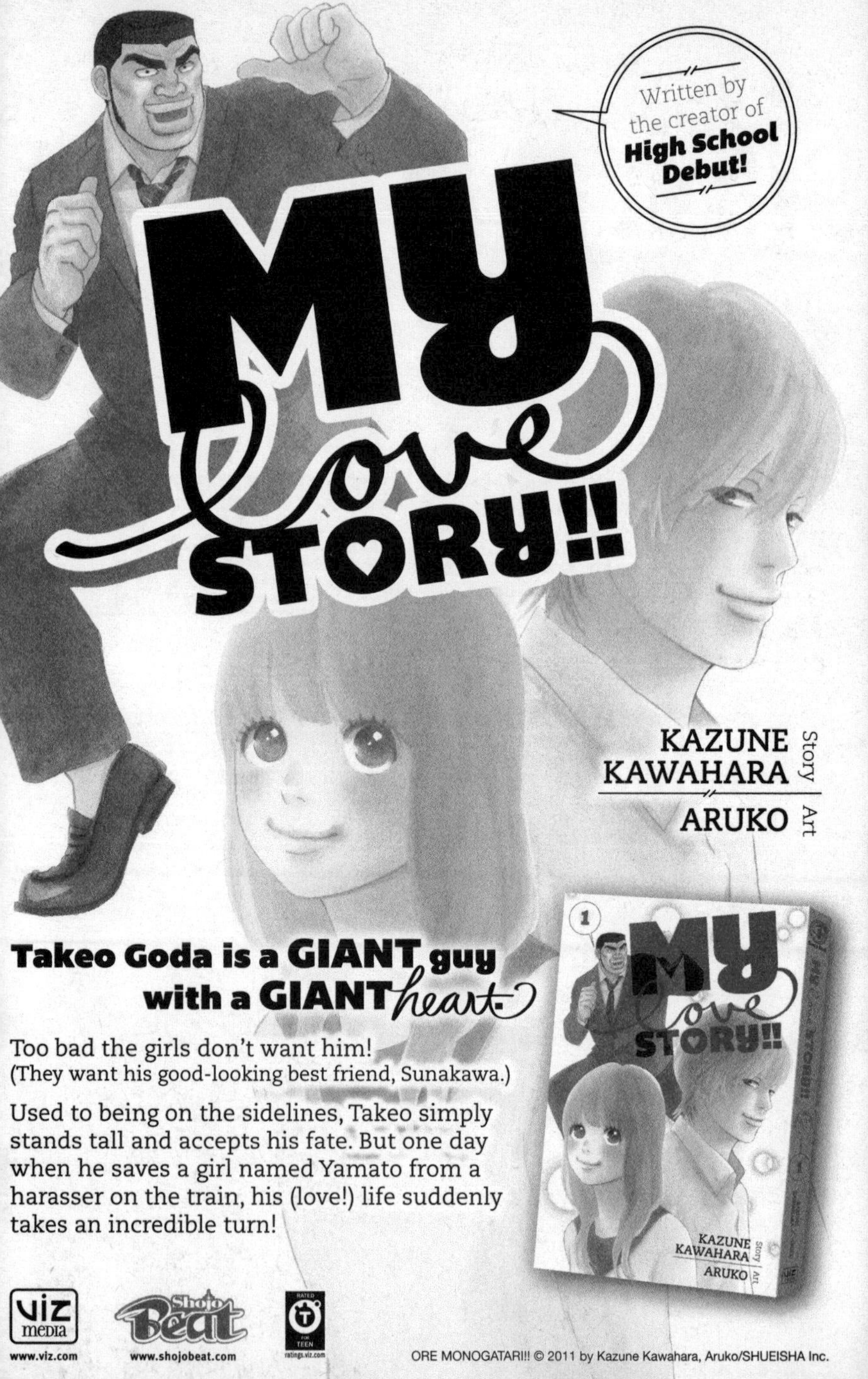
Written by the creator of High School Debut!
MY Love STORY!!
KAZUNE KAWAHARA Story
ARUKO Art
Takeo Goda is a GIANT guy with a GIANT heart.
Too bad the girls don't want him!
(They want his good-looking best friend, Sunakawa.)
Used to being on the sidelines, Takeo simply stands tall and accepts his fate. But one day when he saves a girl named Yamato from a harasser on the train, his (love!) life suddenly takes an incredible turn!
1
MY Love STORY!!
KAZUNE KAWAHARA Story
ARUKO Art
VIZ media
www.viz.com
Shojo Beat
www.shojobeat.com
RATED T FOR TEEN
ratings.viz.com
ORE MONOGATARI!! © 2011 by Kazune Kawahara, Aruko/SHUEISHA Inc.

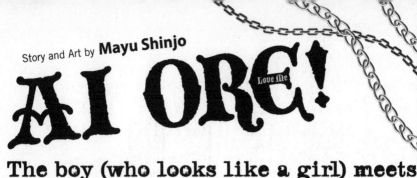

You may be reading the wrong way!

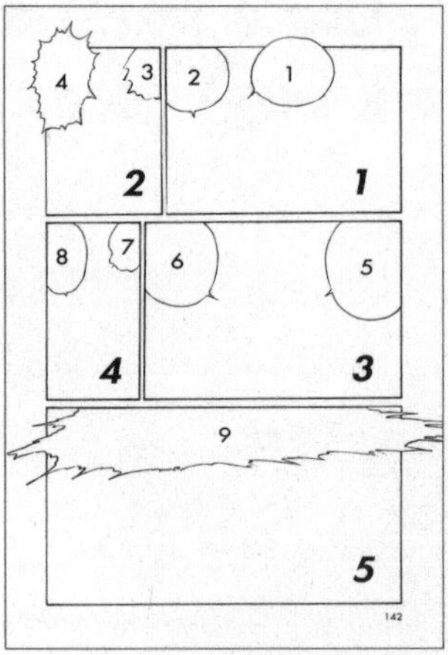

1
2
3
4
1
2
5
6
7
8
3
4
9
5
142

IT'S TRUE: In keeping with the original Japanese comic format, this book reads from right to left—so action, sound effects, and word balloons are completely reversed. This preserves the orientation of the original artwork—plus, it's fun! Check out the diagram shown here to get the hang of things, and then turn to the other side of the book to get started!

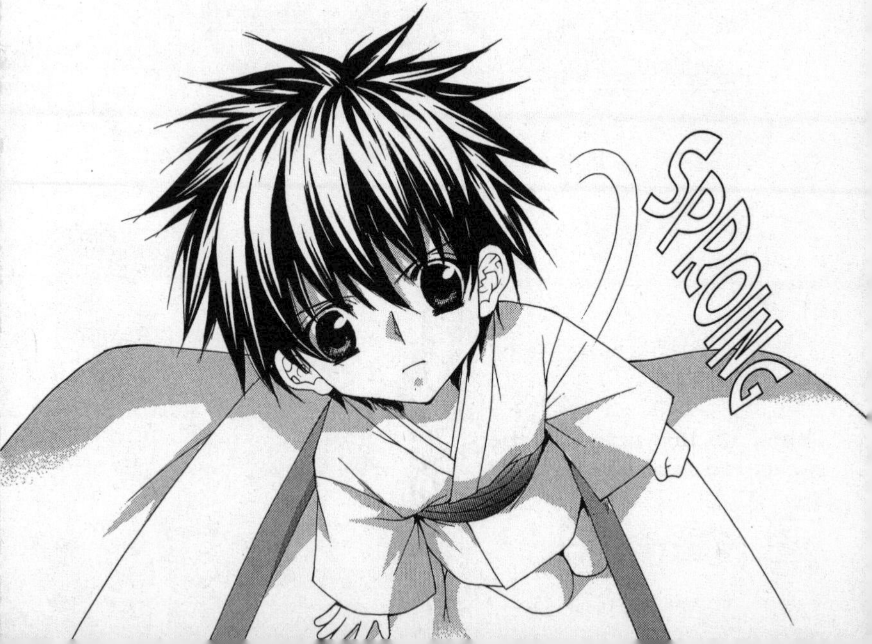

SPROING